Changing Organizations

McGRAW-HILL SERIES IN MANAGEMENT
Keith Davis, *Consulting Editor*

ALLEN: *Management and Organization*
ALLEN: *The Management Profession*
BENNIS: *Changing Organizations*
BERGEN AND HANEY: *Organizational Relations and Management Action*
BLOUGH: *International Business: Environment and Adaptation*
BOWMAN: *Management: Organization and Planning*
BROWN: *Judgment in Administration*
DAVIS: *Human Relations at Work*
DAVIS AND BLOMSTROM: *Business and Its Environment*
DAVIS AND SCOTT: *Readings in Human Relations*
FIEDLER: *A Theory of Leadership Effectiveness*
FLIPPO: *Principles of Personnel Management*
GOLEMBIEWSKI: *Men, Management, and Morality*
HARBISON AND MYERS: *Management in the Industrial World*
HICKS: *The Management of Organizations*
JOHNSON, KAST, AND ROSENZWEIG: *The Theory and Management of Systems*
KEITH AND GUBELLINI: *Business Management*
KOONTZ: *Toward a Unified Theory of Management*
KOONTZ AND O'DONNELL: *Principles of Management*
KOONTZ AND O'DONNELL: *Readings in Management*
MAIER: *Problem-solving Discussions and Conferences: Leadership Methods and Skills*
MAYER: *Production Management*
MC DONOUGH: *Information Economics and Management Systems*
MC NICHOLS: *Policy Making and Executive Action*
MINER: *The Management of Ineffective Performance*
MUNDEL: *A Conceptual Framework for the Management Sciences*
PETIT: *The Moral Crisis in Management*
PIGORS AND PIGORS: *Case Method in Human Relations*
READY: *The Administrator's Job*
SALTONSTALL: *Human Relations in Administration*
SARTAIN AND BAKER: *The Supervisor and His Job*
SCHRIEBER, JOHNSON, MEIER, FISCHER, AND NEWELL: *Cases in Manufacturing Management*
STEINER: *Managerial Long-range Planning*
SUTERMEISTER: *People and Productivity*
TANNENBAUM, WESCHLER, AND MASSARIK: *Leadership and Organization*
VANCE: *Industrial Administration*
VANCE: *Management Decision Simulation*

Changing Organizations

ESSAYS ON THE DEVELOPMENT AND EVOLUTION OF HUMAN ORGANIZATION

WARREN G. BENNIS

Provost, State University
of New York at Buffalo

McGRAW-HILL BOOK COMPANY

New York   St. Louis   San Francisco
Toronto   London   Sydney

CHANGING ORGANIZATIONS

Library of Congress Catalog Card Number 65-25915

04700

7 8 9 – M P – 9 8

To Clurie and Katie:
my living links with evolution

preface

It so happens that the world is undergoing a transformation to which no change that has yet occurred can be compared.

Charles de Gaulle

One thing that is new is the prevalence of new-ness, the changing scale and scope of change itself, so that the world alters as we walk on it, so that the years of man's life measure not some small growth or rearrangement or moderation of what he learned in childhood, but a great upheaval.

Robert Oppenheimer

"Everything nailed down is coming loose," a historian said recently, and it seems that no exaggeration, no hyperbole, no outrage can realistically describe the extent and pace of change which modernization involves. In fact, only the exaggerations appear to be true. And it is to our credit that the pseudo horror stories and futuristic fantasies about *increases* in the rate of change (rate of obsolescence of workers, growth of technology and science, and the number of "vanishing stories"—the vanishing salesman, the vanishing host, the vanishing adolescent, the vanishing village, etc.) fail to deter our compulsive desire to invent, to overthrow, to upset inherited patterns. As Ecclesiastes glumly observes, men persist in disordering their settled ways and beliefs by seeking out many inventions.

This book of essays approaches the problem of change from many different angles, all of which focus on the cause and consequences of change in *organizational* behavior. In a way, I suppose, these essays reveal my favorite intellectual preoccupations: (1) the problems of change, (2) how they affect human organizations, and (3) what the behavioral sciences can do about directing the rate, shape, and consequences of change. Man's fate today, as never before, is to understand this "prevalence of newness" so that we can welcome and even predict the force of change without a guarded frozenness or a heightened susceptibility. Justice Holmes's remark that "science has made major contributions to minor needs" no longer holds in my view. It seems to me that the behavioral sciences can contribute a good deal to an understanding of our contemporary crises.

The book is divided into two parts. Part 1 identifies some important evolutionary trends in organizational development. Part 2 focuses on the ways behavioral scientists can illuminate and direct processes of change. In other words, Part 1 discusses some developments and certain "natural" tendencies, for example, toward democracy and science. Part 2, on the other hand, shows how action based on knowledge and self-determination can change the nature of organizational life.

To use the language of child psychology, evolutionary tendencies are basic regularities of growth in certain directions, toward *maturation,* while planned change involves human or cultural interventions, toward *acculturation.* Of course, it is sometimes difficult or even meaningless to distinguish between the two. Illness, for example, can slow down the growth of long bones and delay the appearance of ossification centers, so that the natural process is retarded. At the same time, recent progress on bone and cartilage surgery has affected significantly the natural process of bone maturation. I would wager that as science progresses, the relationship between *evolutionary* and *directed* change will blur, just as so-called natural childbirth is damned unnatural for most.

In any case, while I forecast the structure and value coordinates for organizations of the future and contend that they are inevitable, it should not bar any of us from giving a little push here and there to that inevitability. And while the French moralist may be right when he says that there are no delightful marriages, just good ones, it is possible that if practitioners and students of organizations get their heads together, they will develop delightful organizations—just possibly.

If there is a strain of optimism in these essays, I hope it is not of the Pollyanna or ostrich kind. While I am by nature a "yea-sayer" (and this trait may become more pronounced as I work in India, where malaria has been wiped out in five years, where family planning is expected to curb the birthrate within five years and the absolute growth within twenty years, and where even the Himalayas are growing 2 inches a year), I do not think I am a "nature faker." Of course, I have tried to prophesy, and that is always risky. This reminds me of the story of the Polish visionary who claimed that he could see the synagogue burning to the ground in the town of Lwów (45 miles away). Late the next day, a visitor from Lwów appeared on the scene and discounted the whole story. The local villagers were still proud of their visionary: *so what* if he was wrong. Look how far he could see!

WARREN G. BENNIS

contents

part one

evolutionary trends in organizational development

Man is the animal that can direct and control his own evolution. Our species is probably a million years old. Homo sapiens emerged with twice the cortical capacity only 100,000 years ago. With cortical development came the ability to symbolize which enables us to transmit information from generation to generation. Agriculture was invented roughly 10,000 years ago and city-states about 5,000 years ago. Science, only recently institutionalized (say within the past 75 to 100 years), has accelerated the psycho-cultural evolution a thousand times faster than biological evolution has.

All the essays in Part One reflect a particular bias which is a belief that certain ideas, generated and maintained by institutions, are not only more appropriate for our times but irresistible to them. Henry Murray has coined the word "idene" to relate to social evolution as gene does to biological evolution. Some idenes accelerate evolution; others, like Nazism or apartheid or slavery, may be as dangerous as hemophilia.

The idenes revived in the following essays are inevitable, within plus or minus 50 years, and they are captivating as well. They have been enshrined, idolized, and monotonously enunciated at least since the American Revolution was exported via France. They are the values of (1) choice and freedom, (2) collaboration, and (3) science, i.e., an ethic of testing and predicting reality. Although these concepts are familiar, their radical and accelerating effects can probably

1

only be recognized in historical perspective. The first value is called by the political term "democracy" and is codified under certain constitutional guarantees of individual rights. The third dimly emerged about 300 years ago; ours is really the first and only "scientific age," and 90 per cent of the people who call themselves scientists are alive today. The second, collaboration, is the most recent value and the most ancient necessity, and it must surely preempt Darwin's emphasis on "competition." The price of competition, seen in Herman Kahn's Doomsday Machine and "Dr. Strangelove," is costly; we are committed to living together.

I see democracy, collaboration, and science as three broad streams moving steadily toward a confluence in the twentieth century. When I wrote Chapter 3 in 1961 I was convinced that democracy is a political twin of science and that their moral life is parallel. Collaboration is more implicit in science where there is an ethic of cooperation than in democracy which is fixated on independence rather than interdependence.

In any case, these essays suggest that when the true content of these three idenes surfaces and invades the institutional juglars we shall have not only coped with the tasks of our time but progressed further along the course of social evolution.

If these ideas sound ethnocentric and absolute, I must confess to a current revulsion from my collegiate belief in political and cultural relativism. I do believe that the values and moral imperatives of science and democracy are appropriate and necessary everywhere today. I do believe that they are the most civilized and advanced systems available. I do feel impatient with their visible alternatives: unskeptical and unquestioning faith in authority and totalitarianism.

Man, before Darwin, was elevated as the "darling of the gods." This Victorian fiction has been dissolved by too many wars, too much poverty, and too many diseased. But we remain a moral and ethical animal; our survival and security depend on the exploitation of moral and ethical systems.

1

the decline of bureaucracy and organizations of the future*

Most of us spend all of our working day and a great deal of our non-working day in a unique and extremely durable social arrangement called "bureaucracy." I use the term "bureaucracy" descriptively, not as an epithet about "those guys in Washington" or as a metaphor à la Kafka's *Castle*, which conjures up an image of red tape, faceless masses standing in endless lines, and despair. Bureaucracy, as I shall use the term here, is a social invention, perfected during the Industrial Revolution to organize and direct the activities of the firm. To paraphrase Churchill's ironic remark about democracy, we can say of bureaucracy that it is the worst possible theory of organization—apart from all the others that have so far been tried.

* Adapted from an Invited Address presented to the Division of Industrial and Business Psychology at the American Psychological Association meeting, Los Angeles, Calif., Sept. 5, 1964. Reprinted by permission from *Transaction*, where it was originally published in July, 1965.

The burden of this book rests upon the premise that this form of organization is becoming less and less effective, that it is hopelessly out of joint with contemporary realities, and that new shapes, patterns, and models—currently recessive—are emerging which promise drastic changes in the conduct of the corporation and in managerial practices in general. So within the next twenty-five to fifty years, we should all be witness to, and participate in, the end of bureaucracy and the rise of new social systems better able to cope with twentieth-century demands.*

The argument will be presented in the following sequence:

1 A quick look at bureaucracy: what it is and what its problems are;
2 A brief survey of how behavioral scientists and practitioners have attempted to modify and alter the bureaucratic mechanism so that it would respond more appropriately to changing times (in this section I shall show how these emergency remedies have been only stopgap measures and how more basic changes are required);
3 A general forecast of how most organizations of the future will operate.

BUREAUCRACY AND ITS DISCONTENTS

Corsica, according to Gibbon, is much easier to deplore than to describe. The same holds true for bureaucracy. Basically, though, it is simple: bureaucracy is a social invention which relies exclusively on the power to influence through reason and law. Max Weber, the German sociologist who conceptualized the idea of bureaucracy around the turn of the century, once likened the bureaucratic mechanism to a judge qua computer: "Bureaucracy is like a modern judge who is a vending machine into which the pleadings are inserted together with the fee and which then disgorges the judgment together with its reasons mechanically derived from the code."[1]

The bureaucratic "machine model" Weber outlined was devel-

* The number of years necessary for this transition is, of course estimated from forecasts for the prospects of industrialization. Sociological evolutionists are substantially agreed that within a twenty-five- to fifty-year period, most of the people in the world will be living in industrialized societies. And it is this type of society that concerns me here, not the so-called underadvanced, semiadvanced, or partially advanced societies.

oped as a reaction against the personal subjugation, nepotism, cruelty, emotional vicissitudes, and subjective judgment which passed for managerial practices in the early days of the Industrial Revolution. Man's true hope, it was thought, was his ability to rationalize and calculate—to use his head as well as his hands and heart. Thus, in this system roles are institutionalized and reinforced by legal tradition rather than by the "cult of personality"; rationality and predictability were sought for in order to eliminate chaos and unanticipated consequences; technical competence rather than arbitrary or "iron" whims was emphasized. These are oversimplifications, to be sure, but contemporary students of organizations would tend to agree with them. In fact, there is a general consensus that bureaucracy can be dimensionalized in the following way:

1   A division of labor based on functional specialization
2   A well-defined hierarchy of authority
3   A system of rules covering the rights and duties of employees
4   A system of procedures for dealing with work situations
5   Impersonality of interpersonal relations
6   Promotion and selection based on technical competence[2]

These six dimensions describe the basic underpinnings of bureaucracy, the pyramidal organization which dominates so much of our thinking and planning related to organizational behavior.

It does not take a great critical imagination to detect the flaws and problems in the bureaucratic model. We have all *experienced* them: bosses without technical competence and underlings with it; arbitrary and zany rules; an underworld (or informal) organization which subverts or even replaces the formal apparatus; confusion and conflict among roles; and cruel treatment of subordinates, based not upon rational or legal grounds, but upon inhumane grounds. Unanticipated consequences abound and provide a mine of material for those comics, like Chaplin or Tati, who can capture with a smile or a shrug the absurdity of authority systems based on pseudologic and inappropriate rules.

Almost everybody, including many students of organizational behavior, approaches bureaucracy with a chip on his shoulder. It has been criticized for its theoretical confusion and contradictions, for moral and ethical reasons, on practical grounds such as its inefficiency, for its methodological weaknesses, and for containing too many implicit values or for containing too few. I have recently cataloged the criticisms of bureaucracy, and they outnumber and outdo the Ninety-five Theses tacked on the church door at Wittenberg in attacking another bureaucracy.[3] For example:

1 Bureaucracy does not adequately allow for personal growth and the development of mature personalities.
2 It develops conformity and "group-think."
3 It does not take into account the "informal organization" and the emergent and unanticipated problems.
4 Its systems of control and authority are hopelessly outdated.
5 It has no adequate juridical process.
6 It does not possess adequate means for resolving differences and conflicts among ranks and, most particularly, among functional groups.
7 Communication (and innovative ideas) are thwarted or distorted because of hierarchical divisions.
8 The full human resources of bureaucracy are not being utilized because of mistrust, fear of reprisals, etc.
9 It cannot assimilate the influx of new technology or scientists entering the organization.
10 It will modify the personality structure such that man will become and reflect the dull, gray, conditioned "organization man."

Max Weber himself, the developer of the theory of bureaucracy, came around to condemning the apparatus he helped immortalize. While he felt that bureaucracy was inescapable, he also thought it might strangle the spirit of capitalism or the enterprenuerial attitude, a theme which Schumpeter later on developed. And in a debate on bureaucracy he once said, more in sorrow than in anger:

> It is horrible to think that the world could one day be filled with nothing but those little cogs, little men clinging to little jobs and striving towards bigger ones—a state of affairs which is to be seen once more, as in the Egyptian records, playing an ever-increasing part in the spirit of our present administrative system, and especially of its offspring, the students. This passion for bureaucracy . . . is enough to drive one to despair. It is as if in politics . . . we were deliberately to become men who need "order" and nothing but order, who become nervous and cowardly if for one moment this order wavers, and helpless if they are torn away from their total incorporation in it. That the world should know no men but these: it is such an evolution

that we are already caught up in, and the great question is therefore not how we can promote and hasten it, but what can we oppose to this machinery in order to keep a portion of mankind free from this parcelling-out of the soul from this supreme mastery of the bureaucratic way of life.[4]

I think it would be fair to say that a good deal of the work on organizational behavior over the past two decades has been a footnote to the bureaucratic "backlash" which aroused Weber's passion: saving mankind's soul "from the supreme mastery of the bureaucratic way of life." At least, very few of us have been indifferent to the fact that the bureaucratic mechanism is a social instrument in the service of repression; that it treats man's ego and social needs as a constant, or as nonexistent or inert; that these confined and constricted needs insinuate themselves into the social processes of organizations in strange, unintended ways; and that those very matters which Weber claimed escaped calculation—love, power, hate—not only are calculable and powerful in their effects but must be reckoned with.

MODIFICATIONS OF BUREAUCRACY

In what ways has the system of bureaucracy been modified in order that it may cope more successfully with the problems that beset it? Before answering that, we have to say something about the nature of organizations, *all* organizations, from mass-production leviathans all the way to service industries such as the university or hospital. Organizations are primarily complex goal-seeking units. In order to survive, they must also accomplish the secondary tasks of (1) maintaining the internal system and coordinating the "human side of enterprise" —a process of mutual compliance here called "reciprocity"—and (2) adapting to and shaping the external environment—here called "adaptability." These two organizational dilemmas can help us organize the pivotal ways the bureaucratic mechanism has been altered—and found wanting.

Resolutions of the Reciprocity Dilemma

Reciprocity has to do primarily with the processes which can mediate conflict between the goals of management and the individual goals of the workers. Over the past several decades, a number of interesting theoretical and practical resolutions have been made which truly allow for conflict and mediation of interest. They revise, if not transform, the very nature of the bureaucratic mechanism by explicit recognition of the inescapable tension between individual and organizational goals. These theories can be called, variously, "exchange," "group," "value," "structural," or "situational," depending on what variable of the situation one wishes to modify.

The exchange theories postulate that wages, incomes, and services are given to the individual for an equal payment to the organization in work. If the inducements are not adequate, the individual may withdraw and work elsewhere.[5] This concept may be elaborated by increasing the payments to include motivational units. That is to say, the organization provides a psychological anchor in times of rapid social change and a hedge against personal loss, as well as position, growth and mastery, success experience, and so forth, in exchange for energy, work, and commitment.[6]

I shall discuss this idea of payment in motivational units further, as it is a rather recent one to gain acceptance. Management tends to interpret motivation by economic theory. Man is logical; man acts in the manner which serves his self-interest; man is competitive. Elton Mayo and his associates were among the first to see human affiliation as a motivating force, to consider industrial organization a social system as well as an economic-technical system. They judge a manager in terms of his ability to sustain cooperation.[7] In fact, once a cohesive, primary work group is seen as a motivating force, a managerial elite may become obsolete, and the work group itself become the decision maker. This allows decisions to be made at the most relevant point of the organizational social space, where the data are most available.[8]

Before this is possible, some believe that the impersonal value system of bureaucracy must be modified.[9] In this case the manager plays an important role as the instrument of change, as an interpersonal specialist. He must instill values which permit and reinforce expression of feeling, experimentalism and norms of individuality, trust, and concern. Management, according to Blake,[10] is successful as it maximizes "concern for people"—along with "concern for production."

Others[11,12] believe that a new conception of the structure of bureaucracy will create more relevant attitudes toward the function of management than formal role specifications do. If the systems are seen as organic rather than mechanistic, as adapting spontaneously to the needs of the system, then decisions will be made at the critical point, and roles and jobs will devolve to the "natural" incumbent. The shift would probably be from the individual to cooperative group effort, from delegated to shared responsibility, from centralized to decentralized authority, from obedience to confidence, and from antagonistic arbitration to problem solving.[13] Management which is centered around problem solving, which assumes or relaxes authority according to task demands, has most concerned some theorists. They are as concerned with organizational success and productivity as with the social system.[14,15,16,17]

However, on all sides we find a growing belief that the effectiveness of bureaucracy should be evaluated on human as well as economic criteria. Social satisfaction and personal growth of employees must be considered, as well as the productivity and profit of the organization.

The criticisms and revisions of the *status quo* tend to concentrate on the internal system and its human components. But although it appears on the surface that the case against bureaucracy has to do with its ethical-moral posture and the social fabric, the real *coup de grâce* has come from the environment. While various proponents of "good human relations" have been fighting bureaucracy on humanistic grounds and for Christian values, bureaucracy seems most likely to founder on its inability to adapt to rapid change in the environment.

The Problem of Adaptability

Bureaucracy thrives in a highly competitive, undifferentiated, and stable environment, such as the climate of its youth, the Industrial Revolution. A pyramidal structure of authority, with power concentrated in the hands of few with the knowledge and resources to control an entire enterprise was, and is, an eminently suitable social arrangement for routinized tasks.

However, the environment has changed in just those ways which make the mechanism most problematical. Stability has vanished. As Ellis Johnson said: ". . . the once-reliable constants have now become 'galloping' variables. . . ."[18] One factor accelerating change is the growth of science, research and development activities, and intellectual technology. Another is the increase of transactions with social institutions and the importance of the latter in conducting the enterprise—including government, distributors and consumers, shareholders, competitors, raw-material and power suppliers, sources of employees (particularly managers), trade unions, and groups within the firms.[19] There is, as well, more interdependence between the economic and other facets of society, resulting in complications of legislation and public regulation. Thirdly, and significantly, competition between firms diminishes as their fates intertwine and become positively correlated.[20]

My argument so far, to summarize quickly, is that the first assault on bureaucracy arose from its incapacity to manage the tension between individual and management goals. However, this conflict is somewhat mediated by the growth of an ethic of productivity which includes personal growth and/or satisfaction. The second and more major shock to bureaucracy has been caused by the scientific and technological revolution. It is the requirement of adaptability to the environment which leads to the predicted demise of bureaucracy and to the collapse of management as we know it now.

A Forecast for the Future

A forecast falls somewhere between a prediction and a prophecy. It lacks the divine guidance of the latter and the empirical foundation of the former. On thin empirical ice, I want to set forth some of the conditions that will dictate organizational life in the next twenty-five to fifty years.

1 *The environment* Those factors already mentioned will continue in force and will increase. That is, rapid technological change and diversification will lead to interpenetration of the government and legal and economic policies in business. Partnerships between industry and government (like Telstar) will be typical, and because of the immensity and expense of the projects, there will be fewer identical units competing for the same buyers and sellers. Or, in reverse, imperfect competition leads to an oligopolistic and government-business-controlled economy. The three main features of the environment will be interdependence rather than competition, turbulence rather than stability, and large rather than small enterprises.

2 *Aggregate population characteristics* We are living in what Peter Drucker calls the "educated society," and I think this is the most distinctive characteristic of our times. Within fifteen years, two-thirds of our population (living in metropolitan areas) will attend

college. Adult education programs, especially the management development courses of such universities as M.I.T., Harvard, and Stanford, are expanding and adding intellectual breadth. All this, of course, is not just "nice," but necessary. As Secretary of Labor Wirtz recently pointed out, computers can do the work of most high school graduates—more cheaply and effectively. Fifty years ago, education was called "nonwork," and intellectuals on the payroll (and many staff) were considered "overhead." Today, the survival of the firm depends, more than ever before, on the proper exploitation of brainpower.

One other characteristic of the population which will aid our understanding of organizations of the future is increasing job mobility. The lowered expense and ease of transportation, coupled with the real needs of a dynamic environment, will change drastically the idea of "owning" a job— and of "having roots," for that matter. Participants will be shifted from job to job even from employer to employer with much less fuss than we are accustomed to.

3 *Work-relevant values* The increased level of education and mobility will change the values we hold vis-à-vis work. People will be more intellectually committed to their jobs and will probably require more involvement, participation, and autonomy in their work. [This turn of events is due to a composite of the following factors: (1) There is a positive correlation between education and need for autonomy; (2) job mobility places workers in a position of greater influence in the system; and (3) job requirements call for more responsibility and discretion.]

Also, people will tend to be more "other-directed" in their dealings with others. McClelland's data suggest that as industrialization increases, other-directedness increases;[21] so we will tend to rely more heavily than we do even now on temporary social arrangements, on our immediate and constantly changing colleagues.

4 *Tasks and goals of the firm* The tasks of the firm will be more technical, complicated, and unprogrammed. They will rely more on intellect than on muscles. And they will be too complicated for one person to handle or for individual supervision. Essentially, they will call for the collaboration of specialists in a project form of organization.

Similarly there will be a complication of goals. "Increased profits" and "raised productivity" will sound like oversimplifications and clichés. Business will concern itself with its adaptive or innovative-creative capacity. In addition, *meta*-goals will have to be articulated and developed; that is, supra-goals which shape and provide the foundation for the goal structure. For example, one *meta*-goal might be a system for detecting new and changing goals; another could be a system for deciding priorities among goals.

Finally, there will be more conflict, more contradiction among effectiveness criteria, just as in hospitals and universities today there is conflict between teaching and research. The reason for this is the number of professionals involved, who tend to identify as much with the supra-goals of their profession as with those of their immediate employer. University professors are a case in point. More and more of their income comes from outside sources, such as private or public foundations and consultant work. They tend not to make good "company men" because they are divided in their loyalty to professional values and organizational demands. Role conflict and ambiguity are both causes and consequences of goal conflict.

5 *Organizational structure* The social structure in organizations of the future will have some unique characteristics. The key word will be "temporary"; there will be adaptive, rapidly changing *temporary systems*.[22] These will be organized around *problems-to-be-solved*. The problems will be solved by groups of relative *strangers* who represent a set of diverse professional skills. The groups will be conducted on *organic* rather than mechanical models; they will evolve in response to the problem rather than programmed role expectations. The function of the "executive" thus becomes *coordinator*, or "linking pin" between various project groups. He must be a man who can speak the diverse languages of research and who can relay information and mediate among the groups. *People will be differentiated not vertically according to rank and role but flexibly according to skill and professional training.*

Adaptive, temporary systems of diverse specialists, solving problems, linked together by coordinating and task-evaluative specialists, in organic flux, will gradually replace bureaucracy as we know it. As no catchy phrase comes to mind, let us call this an "organic-adaptive" structure.

As an aside, what will happen to the rest of society, to the manual laborers, to the less educated, to those who desire to work in conditions of high authority, and so forth? Many such jobs will disappear; automatic jobs will be automated. However, there will be a corresponding growth in the service-type of occupation, such as the "War on Poverty" and the Peace Corps programs. In times of change, where there is a discrepancy between cultures, industrialization, and especially urbanization, society becomes the client for skill in human interaction. Let us hypothesize that approximately 40 per cent of the population would be involved in jobs of this nature and 40 per cent in technological jobs, making an *organic-adaptive* majority, with, say, a 20 per cent bureaucratic minority.

6 *Motivation in organic-adaptive structures* The section of this chapter on reciprocity stated the shortcomings of bureaucracy in maximizing employee effectiveness. The organic-adaptive structure should increase motivation and thereby effectiveness because of the satisfactions intrinsic to the task. There is a congruence between the educated individual's need for meaningful, satisfactory, and creative tasks and flexible structure or autonomy.

Of course, where the reciprocity issue is ameliorated, there are corresponding stresses between professional identification and high task involvement. Professionals are notoriously disloyal to organizational demands. For example, during the Oppenheimer hearing, Boris Pash of the FBI reported: "It is believed that the only undivided loyalty that he [Oppenheimer] can give is to science and it is strongly felt that if in his position the Soviet government could offer more for the advancement of scientific cause he would select that government as the one to which he would express his loyalty."[23]

There will be, as well, reduced commitment to work groups. These groups, as I have already mentioned, will be transient and changing. While skills in human interaction will become more important because of the necessity of collaboration in complex tasks, there will be a concomitant reduction in group cohesiveness. I would predict that in the organic-adaptive system, people will have to learn to develop quick and intense relationships on the job and to endure their loss.

In general I do not agree with the emphasis of Kerr et al.[24] on the "new bohemianism," whereby leisure—not work—becomes the emotional-creative sphere of life, or with Leavitt,[25] who holds similar views. They assume a technological slowdown and leveling off and a stabilizing of social mobility. This may be a society of the future, but long before then we will have the challenge of creating that push-button society and a corresponding need for service-type organizations with the organic-adaptive structure.

Jobs in the next century should become *more*, rather than less, involving; man is a problem-solving animal, and the tasks of the future guarantee a full agenda of problems. In addition, the adaptive process itself may become captivating to many. At the same time, I think the future I describe is far from a utopian or a necessarily "happy" one. Coping with rapid change, living in temporary systems, and setting up (in quickstep time) meaningful relations—and then breaking them—all augur strains and tensions. Learning how to live with ambiguity and to be self-directing will be the task of education and the goal of maturity.

NEW STRUCTURES OF FREEDOM

In these new organizations, participants will be called on to use their minds more than at any other time in history. Fantasy and imagination will be legitimized in ways that today seem strange. Social structures will no longer be instruments of repression (see Marcuse,[26] who says that the necessity of repression and the suffering derived from it decreases with the maturity of the civilization) but will exist to promote play and freedom on behalf of curiosity and thought.

Not only will the problem of adaptability be overcome through the organic-adaptive structure, but the problem we started with, reciprocity, will be resolved. Bureaucracy, with its "surplus repression," was a monumental discovery for harnessing muscle power via guilt and instinctual renunciation. In today's world, it is a prosthetic device, no longer useful. For we now require organic-adaptive systems as structures of freedom to permit the expression of play and imagination and to exploit the new pleasure of work.

NOTES

1. Bendix, R., *Max Weber: An Intellectual Portrait*, Doubleday & Company, Inc., Garden City, N.Y., 1960, p. 421.
2. Hall, R. H., "The Concept of Bureaucracy: An Empirical Assessment," *The American Journal of Sociology*, vol. 69, p. 33, 1963.
3. Bennis, W. G., "Theory and Method in Applying Behavioral Science to Planned Organizational Change," MIT Paper presented at the International Operational Research Conference, Cambridge University, Cambridge, Sept. 14, 1964.
4. Bendix, *op. cit.*, pp. 455–456.
5. March, J. G., and H. A. Simon, *Organizations*, John Wiley & Sons, Inc., New York, 1958.

6. Levinson, H., "Reciprocation: The Relationship between Man and Organization," Invited Address presented to the Division of Industrial and Business Psychology, Washington, D.C., Sept. 3, 1963.

7. Mayo, E., *The Social Problems of an Industrial Civilization*, Harvard University Press, Cambridge, Mass., 1945, p. 122.

8. Likert, R., *New Patterns of Management*, McGraw-Hill Book Company, New York, 1961.

9. Argyris, C., *Interpersonal Competence and Organizational Effectiveness*, Dorsey Press, Homewood, Ill., 1962.

10. Blake, R. R., and J. S. Mouton, *The Managerial Grid*, Gulf Publishing Company, Houston, 1964.

11. Shepard, H. A., "Changing Interpersonal and Intergroup Relationships in Organizations," in J. March (ed.), *Handbook of Organization*, Rand McNally & Company, Chicago, 1965.

12. Burns, T., and G. M. Stalker, *The Management of Innovation*, Quadrangle, Chicago, 1961.

13. Shepard, *op. cit.*

14. McGregor, D., *The Human Side of Enterprise*, McGraw-Hill Book Company, New York, 1960.

15. Leavitt, H. J., "Unhuman Organizations," in H. J. Leavitt and L. Pondy (eds.), *Readings in Managerial Psychology*, The University of Chicago Press, Chicago, 1964, pp. 542–556.

16. Leavitt, H. J., and T. L. Whisler, "Management in the 1980's," in Leavitt and Pondy, *ibid.*

17. Thompson, J. D., and A. Tuden, "Strategies, and Processes of Organizational Decision," in J. D. Thompson, P. B. Hammond, R. W. Hawkes, B. H. Junker, and A. Tuden (eds.), *Comparative Studies in Administration*, The University of Pittsburgh Press, Pittsburgh, Pa., 1959, pp. 195–216.

18. Johnson, E. A., "Introduction," in McClosky and Trefethen (eds.), *Operations Research for Management*, The Johns Hopkins Press, Baltimore, 1954, p. xii.

19. Wilson, A. T. M., "The Manager and His World," *Industrial Management Review*, Fall, 1961.

20. Emery, F. E., and E. L. Trist, "The Causal Texture of Organizational Environments," Paper read at the International Congress of Psychology, Washington, September, 1963.

21. McClelland, D., *The Achieving Society*, D. Van Nostrand Company, Inc., Princeton, N.J., 1961.

22. Miles, M. B., "On Temporary Systems," in M. B. Miles (ed.), *Innovation in Education*, Bureau of Publications, Teachers College, Columbia University, New York, 1964, pp. 437–490.

23. Jungk, R., *Brighter than a Thousand Suns*, Grove Press, Inc., New York, 1958, p. 147.

24. Kerr, C., J. T. Dunlop, F. Harbison, and C. Myers, *Industrialism and Industrial Man*, Harvard University Press, Cambridge, Mass., 1960.

25. Leavitt, *op. cit.*

26. Marcuse, H., *Eros and Civilization*, Beacon Press, Boston, 1955.

2

*democracy is inevitable**

Cynical observers have always been fond of pointing out that business leaders who extol the virtues of democracy on ceremonial occasions would be the last to think of applying them to their own organizations. To the extent that this is true, however, it reflects a state of mind which by no means is peculiar to businessmen but which characterizes all Americans, if not perhaps all citizens of democracies.

This attitude, briefly, is that democracy is a nice way of life for nice people, despite its manifold inconveniences—a kind of expensive and inefficient luxury, like owning a large medieval castle. Feelings about it are for the most part affectionate, even respectful, but a little impatient. There are probably few men of affairs in America who have not at some time nourished in their hearts the blasphemous

* Reprinted by permission of the coauthor and the publisher from *Harvard Business Review*, pp. 51–59, March–April, 1964. Written in collaboration with Philip E. Slater, of Brandeis University.

16

thought that life would go much more smoothly if democracy could be relegated to some kind of Sunday morning devotion.

The bluff practicality of the "nice-but-inefficient" stereotype masks a hidden idealism, however, for it implies that institutions can survive in a competitive environment through the sheer good-heartedness of those who maintain them. We would like to challenge this notion and suggest that even if all those benign sentiments were eradicated today, we would awaken tomorrow to find democracy still firmly entrenched, buttressed by a set of economic, social, and political forces as practical as they are uncontrollable.

We shall argue that democracy has been so widely embraced not because of some vague yearning for human rights but because *under certain conditions* it is a more "efficient" form of social organization. (Our concept of efficiency includes the ability to survive and prosper.) We do not regard it as accidental that those nations of the world which have endured longest under conditions of relative wealth and stability are democratic, while authoritarian regimes have, with few exceptions, either crumbled or eked out a precarious and backward existence.

Despite this evidence, even so acute a statesman as Adlai Stevenson argued in a *New York Times* article on November 4, 1962, that the goals of the Communists are different from ours. "They are interested in power," he said, "we in community. With such fundamentally different aims, how is it possible to compare communism and democracy in terms of efficiency? You might as well ask whether a locomotive is more efficient than a symphony orchestra."

Is this not simply the speech of an articulate man who believes that democracy is inefficient but who does not like to say so? Actually, we are concerned with locomotives and symphony orchestras, with power and community. The challenges of communism and democracy are, in fact, identical: to compete successfully for the world's resources and imagination.

Our position is, in brief, that democracy (whether capitalistic or socialistic is not at issue here) is the only system which can successfully cope with the changing demands of contemporary civilization. We are not necessarily endorsing democracy as such; one might reasonably argue that industrial civilization is pernicious and should be abolished. We suggest merely that given a desire to survive in this civilization, democracy is the most effective means to achieve this end.

DEMOCRACY TAKES OVER

There are signs, in fact, that our business community is becoming aware of this law. Several of the newest and most rapidly blooming companies in the United States boast unusually democratic organizations. Even more surprising is the fact that some of the largest of the established corporations have been moving steadily, if accidentally, toward democratization. Frequently they began by feeling that administrative vitality and creativity were lacking in the older systems of organization. In increasing numbers, therefore, they enlisted the support of social scientists and of outside programs, the net *effect* of which has been to democratize their organizations. Executives and even entire management staffs have been sent to participate in human relations and organizational laboratories to learn skills and attitudes which ten years ago would have been denounced as anarchic and revolutionary. At these meetings, status prerogatives and traditional concepts of authority are severely challenged.

Many social scientists have played an important role in this development toward humanizing and democratizing large-scale bureaucracies. The contemporary theories of McGregor, Likert, Argyris, and Blake have paved the way to a new social architecture. Research and training centers at the National Training Laboratories, Tavistock Institute, Massachusetts Institute of Technology, Harvard Business School, Boston University, the University of California at Los Angeles, Case Institute of Technology, and others have pioneered in the application of social science knowledge to the improvement of organizational effectiveness. So far, the data are not all in; conclusive evidence is missing, but the forecast seems to hold genuine promise: that it is possible to bring about greater organizational effectiveness through the utilization of valid social knowledge.*

System of Values

What we have in mind when we use the term "democracy" is not permissiveness or laissez faire, but a system of values—a "climate

---

* For a complete review of this work, see W. G. Bennis, "Effecting Organizational Change: A New Role for the Behavioral Scientist," *Administrative Science Quarterly*, September, 1963. See also C. Argyris, "T-groups for Organizational Effectiveness," *Harvard Business Review*, March–April, 1964.

of beliefs" governing behavior—which people are internally compelled to affirm by deeds as well as words. These values include:

1 Full and free communication, regardless of rank and power
2 A reliance on consensus, rather than on the more customary forms of coercion or compromise, to manage conflict
3 The idea that influence is based on technical competence and knowledge rather than on the vagaries of personal whims or prerogatives of power
4 An atmosphere that permits and even encourages emotional expression as well as task-oriented acts
5 A basically human bias, one which accepts the inevitability of conflict between the organization and the individual but which is willing to cope with and mediate this conflict on rational grounds

Changes along these dimensions are being promoted widely in American industry. Most important, for our analysis, is what we believe to be the reason for these changes: *Democracy becomes a functional necessity whenever a social system is competing for survival under conditions of chronic change.*

Adaptability to Change

The most familiar variety of such change to the inhabitants of the modern world is technological innovation. This has been characterized most dramatically by J. Robert Oppenheimer: "One thing that is new is the prevalence of newness, the changing scale and scope of change itself, so that the world alters as we walk on it, so that the years of a man's life measure not some small growth or rearrangement or moderation of what he learned in childhood but a great upheaval."[1]

But if change has now become a permanent and accelerating factor in American life, then adaptability to change becomes increasingly the most important single determinant of survival. The profit, the saving, the efficiency, and the morale of the moment become secondary to keeping the door open for rapid readjustment to changing conditions.

Organization and communications research at the Massachusetts Institute of Technology reveals quite dramatically what type of organization is best suited for which kind of environment. Specifically, for simple tasks under static conditions, an autocratic centralized structure, such as has characterized most industrial organizations in the past, is quicker, neater, and more efficient. But for adaptability to changing conditions, for "rapid acceptance of a new idea," for "flexibility in dealing with novel problems, generally high morale and loyalty . . . the more egalitarian or decentralized type seems to work better." One of the reasons for this is that the centralized decision maker is "apt to discard an idea on the grounds that he is too busy or the idea too impractical."[2]

Our argument for democracy rests on an additional factor, one that is fairly complicated but profoundly important in shaping our ideas. First of all, it is interesting to note that modern industrial organization has been based roughly on the antiquated system of the military. Relics of the military system of thought can still be found in the clumsy terminology used, such as "line and staff," "standard operating procedure," "table of organization," and so on. Other remnants can be seen in the emotional and mental assumptions regarding work and motivation held today by some managers and industrial consultants. By and large these conceptions are changing, and even the military is moving away from the oversimplified and questionable assumptions on which its organization was originally based. Even more striking, as we have mentioned, are developments taking place in industry, no less profound than a fundamental change away from the autocratic and arbitrary vagaries of the past and toward democratic decision making.

This change has been coming about because of the palpable inadequacy of the military-bureaucratic model, particularly its response to rapid change, and also because the institution of science is now emerging as a more suitable model.

Scientific Attitude

But why is science gaining acceptance as a model? Most certainly not because we teach and conduct research within research-oriented universities. Curiously enough, universities have been stubbornly resistant to democratization, far more so than most other institutions.

We believe that science is winning out because the challenges facing modern enterprises are, at base, *knowledge*-gathering, *truth*-requiring dilemmas. Managers are not scientists, nor do we expect them to be. But the processes of problem solving, conflict resolution, and recognition of dilemmas have great kinship with the academic pursuit of truth. The institution of science is the only institution based on, and geared for, change. It is built not only to adapt to change but to overthrow and create change. So it is—and will be—with modern industrial enterprises.

And here we come to the point. In order for the "spirit of inquiry," the foundation of science, to grow and flourish, there is a necessity for a democratic environment. Science encourages a political view which is egalitarian, pluralistic, and liberal. It accentuates freedom of opinion and dissent. It is against all forms of totalitarianism, dogma, mechanization, and blind obedience. As a prominent social psychologist has pointed out: "Men have asked for freedom, justice and respect precisely as science has spread among them."* In short, we believe that the only way in which organizations can ensure a scientific *attitude* is by providing conditions where it can flourish. Very simply, this means democratic social conditions.

In other words, democracy in industry is not an idealistic conception but a hard necessity in those areas in which change is ever present and in which creative scientific enterprise must be nourished. For democracy is the only system of organization which is compatible with perpetual change.

RETARDING FACTORS

It might be objected here that we have been living in an era of rapid technological change for 100 years, without any noticeable change in the nature of the average industrial firm. True, there are many restrictions on the power of the executive over his subordinates now compared with those prevailing at the end of the nineteenth century. But this hardly constitutes industrial democracy; the decision-making function is still an exclusive and jealously guarded prerogative of the top echelons. If democracy is an inevitable consequence of perpetual change, why then have we not seen more dramatic changes in the structure of industrial organizations? The answer is twofold.

Obsolete Individuals

First, the rate of technological change is rapidly accelerating. Take advance in scientific knowledge as one criterion: it shows a

* N. Sanford, "Social Science and Social Reform," Presidential Address presented to the Society for the Psychological Study of Social Issues at the annual meeting of the American Psychological Association, Washington, Aug. 28, 1958

doubling every ten years. Casamir calculated that if the *Physical Review* continued to grow as rapidly as it did between 1945 and 1960, it would weigh more than the earth during the next century.[3] Prior to World War I, a businessman might live a productive and successful life and find himself outmoded at the end of it. By the end of World War II, a similar man could find that his training, skills, outlook, and ways of thinking were obsolescent in the middle of his career. James R. Killian, Jr., chairman of the Corporation of Massachusetts Institute of Technology, estimates that already several hundred thousand engineers are obsolete.[4] This is undoubtedly matched by an equal number of managers.

We are now beginning an era when a man's knowledge and approach can become obsolete before he has even begun the career for which he was trained. The value of what one learns is always slipping away, like the value of money in a runaway inflation. We are living in an era which could be characterized as a runaway inflation of knowledge and skill, and it is this which is perhaps responsible for the feelings of futility, alienation, and lack of individual worth which are said to characterize our time.

Under such conditions, the individual is of relatively little significance. No matter how imaginative, energetic, and brilliant he may be, time will soon catch up with him to the point where he can be profitably replaced by someone who is equally imaginative, energetic, and brilliant but who has a more up-to-date viewpoint and fewer obsolete preconceptions. As Martin Gardner says, with regard to the difficulty some physicists have in grasping Einstein's theory of relativity: "If you are young, you have a great advantage over these scientists. Your mind has not yet developed those deep furrows along which thoughts so often are forced to travel."[5] This situation is just beginning to be felt as an immediate reality in American industry, and it is this kind of uncontrollably rapid change which generates democratization.

Powers of Resistance

The second reason is that the mere existence of a dysfunctional tendency, such as the relatively slow adaptability of authoritarian structures, does not automatically bring about its disappearance. This drawback must first either be recognized for what it is or become so severe as to destroy the structures in which it is embedded. Both these conditions are only now beginning to make themselves felt, primarily through the peculiar nature of modern technological competition.

The crucial change has been that the threat of technological defeat no longer comes necessarily from rivals within the industry, who usually can be imitated quickly without too great a loss, but often from outside—from new industries using new materials in new ways. One can therefore make no intelligent prediction about "what the next likely development in our industry will be." The blow may come from anywhere. Correspondingly, a viable corporation cannot merely develop and advance in the usual ways. In order to survive and grow, it must be prepared to go anywhere—to develop new products or techniques even if they are irrelevant to the present activities of the organizations.* It is perhaps for this reason that the beginnings of democratization have appeared most often in industries (such as electronics) which depend heavily on invention. It is undoubtedly for this reason that more and more sprawling behemoths are planning consequential changes in their organizational structures and climates toward releasing democratic potentiality.

FAREWELL TO "GREAT MEN"

The passing of years has also given the *coup de grâce* to another force that retarded democratization—the "great man," who with brilliance and farsightedness could preside with dictatorial powers at the head of a growing organization and keep it at the vanguard of American business. In the past he was usually a man with a single idea, or a constellation of related ideas, which he developed brilliantly. This is no longer enough.

Today, just as he begins to reap the harvest of his imagination, he finds that someone else (perhaps even one of his stodgier competitors, aroused by desperation) has suddenly carried the innovation a step further or found an entirely new and superior approach to it, and he is suddenly outmoded. How easily can he abandon his idea, which contains all his hopes, his ambitions, his very heart? His aggressiveness now begins to turn in on his own organization, and the absolutism of his position begins to be a liability, a dead hand, an

* For a fuller discussion of this trend, see Theodore Levitt, "Marketing Myopia," *Harvard Business Review*, p. 45, July–August, 1960.

iron shackle upon the flexibility and growth of the company. But he cannot be removed—in the short run the firm would even be hurt by his loss, since its prestige derives to such an extent from his reputation. And by the time he has left, the organization will have receded into a secondary position within the industry. It may even decay further when his personal touch is lost.

The cult of personality still exists, of course, but it is rapidly fading. More and more large corporations (General Motors, for one) predicate their growth not on "heroes" but on solid management teams.

"Organization Men"

Taking the place of the great man, we are often told, is the organization man. A good many tears have been shed over this transition by liberals and conservatives alike. The liberals, of course, have in mind, as the "individual," some sort of creative deviant—an intellectual, artist, or radical politician. The conservatives are thinking of the old captains of industry and perhaps of some great generals. (In the Soviet Union they think of Stalin.)

Neither is at all unhappy to lose the individuals mourned by the other, dismissing them contemptuously as Communists and rabble-rousers, on the one hand, and as criminals and Fascists, on the other. What is particularly confusing in terms of the present issue is a tendency to equate conformity with autocracy—to see the new industrial organization as one in which all individualism is lost except in the case of a few villainous individualistic manipulators at the top.

But this, of course, is absurd in the long run. The trend toward the organization man is also a trend toward a looser and more flexible organization in which the roles are to some extent interchangeable and in which no one is indispensable. To many people this trend is a monstrous nightmare, but one should at least not confuse it with the nightmares of the past. It may mean anonymity and homogeneity, but it does not and cannot mean authoritarianism in the long run, despite the bizarre anomalies and hybrids that may arise in a period of transition.

The reason it cannot is that it arises out of a need for flexibility and adaptability. Democracy and the dubious trend toward the organization man alike (for this trend is a part of democratization, whether we like this aspect of democracy or not) arise from the need to maximize the availability of appropriate knowledge, skill, and insight under conditions of great variability.

Rise of the Professional

While the organization-man idea has titillated the imagination of the American public, it has masked a far more fundamental change now taking place: the rise of the "professional man." Professional specialists, holding advanced degrees in such abstruse sciences as cryogenics or computer logic as well as the more mundane business disciplines, are entering all types of organizations at a higher rate than any other sector of the labor market.

And these men can hardly be called "organization men." They seemingly derive their rewards from inward standards of excellence, from their professional societies, and from the intrinsic satisfaction of their task. In fact, they are committed to the task, not the job; to their standards, not their boss. And because they have degrees, they travel. They are not good "company men"; they are uncommitted except to the challenging environments where they can "play with problems."

These new professional men are remarkably compatible with our conception of a democratic system. For like these new men, democracy seeks no new stability, no end point; it is purposeless, save that it purports to ensure perpetual transition, constant alteration, and ceaseless instability. It attempts to upset nothing, but only to facilitate the potential upset of anything. Democracy and our new professional men identify primarily with the adaptive process, not the "establishment."

Yet it must also be remembered that all democratic systems are not entirely so—there are always limits to the degree of fluidity which can be borne. Thus, it is not a contradiction to the theory of democracy to find that a particular democratic society or organization may be more "conservative" than some autocratic one. Indeed, the most dramatic, violent, and drastic changes have always taken place under autocratic regimes, for such changes usually require prolonged self-denial, while democracy rarely lends itself to such voluntary asceticism. But these changes have been viewed as finite and temporary, aimed at a specific set of reforms, and moving toward a new state of nonchange. It is only when the society reaches a level of technological development in which survival is dependent on the institutionalization of perpetual change that democracy becomes necessary.

REINFORCING FACTORS

The Soviet Union is rapidly approaching this level and is beginning to show the effects, as we shall see. The United States has already reached it. Yet democratic institutions existed in the United States when it was still an agrarian nation. Indeed, democracy has existed in many places and at many times, long before the advent of modern technology. How can we account for these facts?

Expanding Conditions

In the first place, it must be remembered that modern technology is not the only factor which could give rise to conditions of necessary perpetual change. Any situation involving rapid and unplanned expansion, sustained over a sufficient period of time, will tend to produce great pressure for democratization. Second, when we speak of democracy, we are referring not only or even primarily to a particular political format. Indeed, American egalitarianism has perhaps its most important manifestation not in the Constitution but in the family.

Historians are fond of pointing out that Americans have always lived under expanding conditions—first the frontier, then the successive waves of immigration, and now a runaway technology. The social effects of these kinds of expansion are, of course, profoundly different in many ways, but they share one impact in common: all have made it impossible for an authoritarian family system to develop on a large scale. Every foreign observer of American mores since the seventeenth century has commented that American children "have no respect for their parents," and every generation of Americans since 1650 has produced forgetful native moralists who complain about the decline in filial obedience and deference.

Descriptions of family life in colonial times make it quite clear that American parents were as easygoing, permissive, and child-oriented then as they are now and that the children were as independent and "disrespectful." This "lack of respect" is, of course, not for the "parents" as individuals but for the concept of parental authority as such.

The basis for this loss of respect has been outlined quite

dramatically by historian Oscar Handlin, who points out that in each generation of early settlers, the children were more at home in their new environment than their parents—they had less fear of the wilderness and fewer inhibiting European preconceptions and habits.[6] Furthermore, their parents were heavily dependent on them physically and economically. This was less true of the older families after the East became settled. But as one moved nearer to the frontier, the conditions for familial democracy became again strikingly marked, so that the cultural norm was ever protected from serious decay.

Further reinforcement came later from new immigrants, who similarly found their children better adapted to the world than themselves because of their better command of the language, better knowledge of the culture, better occupational opportunities, and so forth. It was the children who were expected to improve the social position of the family and who, through their exposure to peer groups and the school system, could act as intermediaries between their parents and the New World. It was not so much "American ways" that shook up the old family patterns, but the demands and requirements of a new situation. How could the young look to the old as the ultimate fount of wisdom and knowledge when, in fact, that knowledge was irrelevant—when, indeed, the children had a better practical grasp of the realities of American life than their elders?

The New Generation

These sources of reinforcement have now disappeared. But a third has only begun. Rapid technological change again means that the wisdom of elders is largely obsolete and that the young are better adapted to their culture than their parents. How many of the latter can keep up with their children in knowledge of the sciences, for example? Santayana put it beautifully when he said: "No specific hope about distant issues is ever likely to be realized. The ground shifts, the will of mankind deviates, and what the father dreamt of the children neither fulfill nor desire."[7]

It is this fact that reveals the basis for the association between democracy and change. The old, the learned, the powerful, the wealthy, those in authority—these are the ones who are committed. They have learned a pattern and have succeeded in it. But when change comes, it is often the uncommitted who can best realize it, take advantage of it. This is why primogeniture has always lent itself so easily to social change in general and to industrialization in particular. The uncommitted younger sons, barred from success in the older system, are always ready to exploit new opportunities. In Japan, these younger sons were treated more indulgently by the parents and were given more freedom to choose an occupation, since ". . . in Japanese folk wisdom, it is the younger sons who are the innovators."[8]

Democracy is a superior technique for making more available to the uncommitted. The price it extracts is the price of uninvolvement, alienation, and skepticism. The benefits that it gives are flexibility and the joy of confronting new dilemmas.

DOUBTS AND FEARS

Indeed, we may even in this way account for the poor opinion which democracy has of itself. We underrate the strength of democracy because it creates a general attitude of doubt, of skepticism, and of modesty. It is only among the authoritarian that we find the dogmatic confidence, the self-righteousness, the intolerance, and the cruelty that permit one never to doubt oneself and one's beliefs. The looseness, the sloppiness, and the untidiness of democratic structures express the feeling that what has been arrived at today is probably only a partial solution and may well have to be changed tomorrow.

In other words, one cannot believe that change is in itself a good thing and still believe implicitly in the rightness of the present. Judging from the report of history, democracy has always underrated itself—one cannot find a democracy anywhere without also discovering (side by side with expressions of outrageous chauvinism) an endless pile of contemptuous and exasperated denunciations of it. (One of the key issues in our national politics today, as in the presidential campaign in 1960, is our "national prestige.") And perhaps this is only appropriate. For when a democracy ceases finding fault with itself, it has probably ceased to be a democracy.

Overestimating Autocracy

But feeling doubt about our own social system need not lead us to overestimate the virtues and efficiency of others. We can find this kind of overestimation in the exaggerated fear of the "Red menace"—mere exposure to which is seen as leading to automatic con-

version. Few authoritarians can conceive of the possibility that an individual could encounter an authoritarian ideology and not be swept
away by it.

Of a similar nature, but more widespread, is the "better dead
than Red" mode of thinking. Here again we find an underlying assumption that communism is socially, economically, and ideologically
inevitable—that once the military struggle is lost, all is lost. It is interesting that in all our gloomy war speculations, there is never any
mention of an American underground movement. It is everywhere assumed that if a war were fought in which anyone survived and the
Soviet Union won, then:

1   All Americans would immediately become Communists.
2   The Soviet Union would set up an exact replica of itself in this
    country.
3   It would work.
4   The Soviet system would remain unchanged.
5   The Soviets in America would be uninfluenced by what they found
    here.

Not only are these assumptions patently ridiculous, but they also
reveal a profound misconception about the nature of social systems.
The structure of a society is not determined merely by a belief. It
cannot be maintained if it does not work—that is, if no one, not even
those in power, is benefiting from it. How many times in history have
less civilized nations conquered more civilized ones only to be entirely
transformed by the cultural influence of their victims? Do we then
feel ourselves to be less civilized than the Soviet Union? Is our system
so brittle and theirs so enduring?

Actually, quite the contrary seems to be the case. For while
democracy seems to be on a fairly sturdy basis in the United States
(despite the efforts of self-appointed vigilantes to subvert it), there
is considerable evidence that autocracy is beginning to decay in the
Soviet Union.

SOVIET DRIFT

Most Americans have great difficulty in evaluating the facts when
they are confronted with evidence of decentralization in the Soviet
Union, of relaxation of repressive controls, or of greater tolerance for

criticism. We seem bewildered. And we do not seem to sense the contradiction when we say that these changes were made in response to public discontent. For have we not also believed deeply that an authoritarian regime, if efficiently run, can get away with ignoring the public's clamor?

There is a secret belief among us that Khrushchev must have been mad to relax his grip in this way, or a contradictory suspicion that it is all part of a secret plot to throw the West off guard: a plot which is too clever for naïve Americans to fathom. It is seldom suggested that "de-Stalinization" took place because the rigid, repressive authoritarianism of the Stalin era was inefficient and that many additional relaxations will be forced upon the Soviet Union by the necessity of remaining amenable to technological innovation.

But the inevitable Soviet drift toward a more democratic structure is not dependent on the realism of leaders. Leaders come from communities and families, and their patterns of thought are shaped by their experiences with authority in early life as well as by their sense of what the traffic will bear. We saw that the roots of American democracy were to be found in the nature of the American family. What does the Russian family tell us in this respect?

Pessimism regarding the ultimate destiny of Soviet political life has always been based on the seemingly fathomless capacity of the Russian people for authoritarian submission. Their tolerance for autocratic rulers was matched only by their autocratic family system, which was equal to that of Germany, China, or many Latin countries in its demand for filial obedience. On this early experience in the family the acceptance of authoritarian rule was based.

Role of the Family

But modern revolutionary movements, both Fascist and Communist, have tended to regard the family with some suspicion, as the preserver of old ways and as a possible refuge from the state. Fascist dictators have extolled its conservatism but tended at times to set up competitive loyalties for the young. Communist revolutionaries, on the other hand, have more unambivalently attacked family loyalty as reactionary and have deliberately undermined familiar allegiances, partly to increase loyalty to the state and partly to facilitate industrialization and modernization by discrediting traditional mores.

Such destruction of authoritarian family patterns is a two-edged sword, which eventually cuts away political autocracy as well as the familial variety. The state may attempt to teach submission in its own youth organizations, but so long as the family remains as an institution, this earlier and more enduring experience will outweigh all others. And if the family has been forced by the state to be less authoritarian, the result is obvious.

In creating a youth which has a knowledge, a familiarity, and a set of attitudes more appropriate for successful living in the changing culture than those of its parents, the autocratic state has created a Frankenstein monster which will eventually sweep away the authoritarianism in which it is founded. Russian attempts during the late 1930s to reverse their stand on the family perhaps reflect some realization of this fact. Khrushchev's denunciations of certain Soviet artists and intellectuals also reflect fear of a process going beyond what was originally intended.

A similar ambivalence has appeared in Communist China, where the slogan "all for the children" recently produced the unforeseen consequence of a rash of articles stressing filial obligations. As Goode points out: ". . . the propaganda campaign against the power of the elders may lead to misunderstanding on the part of the young, who may at times abandon their filial responsibilities to the State."[9]

Further, what the derogation of parental wisdom and authority has begun, the fierce drive for technological modernization will finish. Each generation of youth will be better adapted to the changing society than its parents. And each generation of parents will feel increasingly modest and doubtful about overvaluing its wisdom and superiority as it recognizes the brevity of its usefulness.*

CONCLUSION

We cannot, of course, predict what forms democratization might take in any nation of the world, nor should we become unduly optimistic about its impact on international relations. Although our thesis predicts the ultimate democratization of the entire globe, this is a view

---

* See, for example, O. Handlin, *The Uprooted,* Little, Brown and Company, Boston, 1951, pp. 252–253; and Kent Geiger, "Changing Political Attitudes in Totalitarian Society: A Case Study of the Role of the Family," *World Politics,* pp. 187–205, January, 1956.

so long-range as to be academic. There are infinite opportunities for global extermination before any such stage of development can be achieved.

We should expect that, in the earlier stages of industrialization, dictatorial regimes will prevail in all the less developed nations, and as we well know, autocracy is still highly compatible with a lethal if short-run military efficiency. We may expect many political grotesques, some of them dangerous in the extreme, to emerge during this long period of transition, as one society after another attempts to crowd the most momentous social changes into a generation or two, working from the most varied structural base lines.

But barring some sudden decline in the rate of technological change, and on the (outrageous) assumption that war will somehow be eliminated during the next half century, it is possible to predict that after this time democracy will be universal. Each revolutionary autocracy, as it reshuffles the family structure and pushes toward industrialization, will sow the seeds of its own destruction, and democratization will gradually engulf it. Lord Acton once remarked about Christianity that it is not that people have tried it and found it wanting; it is that they have been afraid to try it and found it impossible. The same comment may have once applied to democracy, but the outlook has changed to the point where people may *have* to try it.

We may, of course, rue the day. A world of mass democracies may well prove homogenized and ugly. It is perhaps beyond human social capacity to maximize both equality and understanding, on the one hand, and diversity, on the other. Faced with this dilemma, however, many people are willing to sacrifice quaintness to social justice, and we might conclude by remarking that just as Marx, in proclaiming the inevitability of communism, did not hesitate to give some assistance to the wheels of fate, so our thesis that democracy represents the social system of the electronic era should not bar these persons from giving a little push here and there to the inevitable.

NOTES

1. Oppenheimer, J. Robert, "Prospects in the Arts and Sciences," *Perspectives USA*, pp. 10–11, Spring, 1955.
2. Bennis, W. G., "Towards a 'Truly' Scientific Management: The Concept of Organization Health," *General Systems Yearbook*, p. 273, December, 1962. A similar version of this article appears as Chap. 3 of this book.

3. Oppenheimer, J. Robert, "On Science and Culture," *Encounter*, p. 5, October, 1962.

4. Killian, J. R., Jr., "The Crisis in Research," *The Atlantic Monthly*, p. 71, March, 1963.

5. Gardner, M., *Relativity for the Million*, The Macmillan Company, New York 1962, p. 11.

6. Handlin, O., *The Uprooted*, Little, Brown and Company, Boston, 1951.

7. Edman, I. (ed.), *The Philosophy of Santayana*, Modern Library, Inc., New York, 1936.

8. Goode, W. J., *World Revolution and Family Patterns*, The Free Press of Glencoe, New York, 1963, p. 355.

9. *Ibid.*, pp. 313–315.

3

toward a "truly" scientific management: the concept of organization health*

MUGGERIDGE: Now, Charles, you, because you're a scientist . . . you have this idea, as I understand from your writings, that one of the failings of our sort of society, is that the people who exercise authority, we'll say Parliament and so on, are singularly unversed in scientific matters.

SNOW: Yes, I think this is a terrible weakness of the whole of Western society, and one that we're not going to get out of without immense trouble and pain.

MUGGERIDGE: Do you mean by that, for instance, an M.P. would be a better M.P. if he knew a bit about science?

SNOW: I think some M.P.'s ought to know a bit about science. They'd be better M.P.'s in the area where scientific insight becomes important. And there are quite a number of such areas.[1]

* A similar version of this paper appears in *General Systems Yearbook*, p. 273, December, 1962.

Extolling science has become something of a national and international pastime which typically stops short of the truly radical reforms in social organization that scientific revolution implies. Knowing "a bit about science" is a familiar and increasingly popular example of that which C. P. Snow treats in his *Two Cultures and the Scientific Revolution*.[2] But if culture is anything it is a way of life, the way real people live and grow, the way ideals and moral imperatives are transmitted and infused. Culture is more *value* than knowledge. Dr. Bronowski, who shares with Snow the view that "humanists" tend to be ignorant of and removed from science, understands better than Snow seems to that a fundamental unification of cultural outlook is what is required.[3] The connective tissue required, then, is cultural, social, and institutional, not grafted-on evening courses in science.

In this connection, and closer to some of the general aims of this paper, Nevitt Sanford has said:

> The ethical systems of other professions, such as business or the military, have become models for whole societies. Why should not the practice of science become such a model? After we have shown, as we can, that joy and beauty have their places in this system? At any rate, anyone who takes it upon himself to be a scientist, and succeeds in living up to its requirements, may be willing for his behavior to become a universal norm.[4]

This foreshadows the general theme of this chapter: the recognition that the *institution* of science can and should provide a viable model for other institutions not solely concerned with developing knowledge. To demonstrate this proposition, this chapter first discusses the criterion problem in relation to organizations.* An attempt is made to show that the usual criteria for evaluating organizational effectiveness, "enhancement of satisfaction on the part of industry's participants and improvement of effectiveness of performance,"[5] are inadequate, incorrect, or both, as valid indicators of organizational "health." (For the moment let us use the term "health" in the same vague way as "effectiveness." Organizational health is defined later in the chapter.) Next it is suggested that an alternative set of criteria, extracted from the normative and value processes of science, provides

---

* For the purposes of this discussion, organization is defined as any institution from which one receives cash for services rendered. This chapter deals with all such supra-individual entities, although reference is made mostly to industrial organizations.

a more realistic basis for evaluating organizational performance. These criteria are related to those of positive mental health, for it will be argued that there is a profound kinship between the mores of science and the criteria of health for an individual. From this confluence is fashioned a set of psychologically based criteria for examining organizational health. Finally, a discussion is presented of some of the consequences of these effectiveness criteria for organizational theory and practice.

THE SEARCH FOR EFFECTIVENESS CRITERIA

There is hardly a term in current psychological thought as vague, elusive and ambiguous as the term "mental health." That it means many things to many people is bad enough. That many people use it without even attempting to specify the idiosyncratic meaning the term has for them makes the situation worse . . . for those who wish to introduce concern with mental health into systematic psychological theory and research.[6]

No one can say with any degree of certainty by what standards an executive ought to appraise the performance of his organization. And it is questionable whether the time will ever arrive when there will be any pattern answers to such a question—so much does the setting of an organization and its own goal orientation affect the whole process of appraisal.[7]

Raising the problem of criteria, the standards for judging the "goodness" of an organization seldom fail to generate controversy and despair. Establishing criteria for an organization (or, for that matter, for education, marriage, psychotherapy, etc.) accentuates questions of value, choice, and normality and all the hidden assumptions that are used to form judgments of operations. Often, as Jahoda has said in relation to mental-health criteria, the problem ". . . seems so difficult that one is almost tempted to claim the privilege of ignorance."[8]

However, as tempting as ignorance can be, researchers on organizations—particularly industrial organizations—have struggled heroically to identify and measure a number of dimensions associated with organizational effectiveness.[9] Generally, these dimensions have been of two kinds: those dealing with some index of organizational performance, such as profit, cost, rates of productivity, or individual output, and those associated with the human resources, such as morale, motivation, mental health, job commitment, cohesiveness, or

TABLE 1   Major variables employed in the study of organizational behavior

		Criteria Variables	
		Organizational efficiency	*Satisfaction or health*
Independent Variables	*Technology (rationalized procedures)*	Management science: systems research, operations research, decision processes, etc.	Human engineering
	Human factors	Personnel psychology, training, and other personnel functions	Industrial social psychology and sociology

attitudes toward employer or company. In short, as Katzell pointed out in his 1957 review of industrial psychology, investigations in this area typically employ measures of *performance* and *satisfaction*.[10] In fact, it is possible to construct a simple table that adequately accounts for most of the research on organizations that has been undertaken to date, as shown in Table 1. On one axis are located the criteria variables: organizational efficiency (the ethic of work performance) and member satisfaction (the ethic of "health"). On the other axis are located the two main independent variables employed: human factors and rationalized procedures. In other words, it is possible to summarize most of the research literature in the organizational area by locating the major independent variables (technological and human) on one axis and the dependent variables (efficiency and health) on the other.

This classification is necessarily crude and perhaps a little puzzling, principally because research on organizations lacks sufficient information concerning the empirical correlation between the two dependent variables, organizational efficiency and health factors. For a time it seemed (or was hoped) that personal satisfaction and efficiency were positively related, that as satisfaction increased so did performance. This alleged correlation allowed the "human relations" school and the industrial engineers (Taylorism being one example)*

* For a recent historical review, see Aitken.[11]

to proceed coterminously without necessarily recognizing the tension between "happy workers" and "high performance."

As Likert put it: "It is not sufficient merely to measure morale and the attitudes of employees toward the organization, their supervision, and their work. Favorable attitudes and excellent morale do not necessarily assure high motivation, high performance, and an effective human organization. A good deal of research indicates that this relationship is much too simple."[12]

Indeed, today we are not clear about the relation of performance to satisfaction, or even whether there is any interdependence between them. Likert and his associates have found organizations with all the logical possibilities—high morale with low productivity, low productivity with low morale, etc. Argyris's work,[13,14] with a popular assist from William H. Whyte, Jr.,[15] clouds the picture even further by postulating the inevitability of conflict between human need-satisfaction and organizational performance (as formal organizations are presently conceived). This creates, as Mason Haire has recognized,[16] a calculus of values: How much satisfaction or health is to be yielded for how many units of performance?

Generally speaking, this is the state of affairs: two criteria, crudely measured, ambiguous in meaning, questionable in utility, and fraught with value connotations.[17] In view of these difficulties, a number of other, more promising approaches have been suggested. The most notable of these are the criterion of multiple goals, the criterion of the situation, and the criterion of system characteristics.

The Criterion of Multiple Goals

This approach rests on the assumption that ". . . organizations have more than a single goal and that the interaction of goals will produce a different value framework in different organizations."[18] Likert, who is a proponent of the multiple-criteria approach, claims that very few organizations, if any, obtain measurements that clearly reflect the quality and capacity of their human resources. This situation is due primarily to (1) the shadow of traditional theory, which tends to overlook the human and motivational variables, and (2) the relatively new developments in social science that only now permit measurements of this type. Likert goes on to enumerate twelve criteria, covering such dimensions as loyalty and identification with the institution and its objectives, degree of confidence and trust, adequacy and efficiency of communication, amount and quality of teamwork, etc.[19] By and large, Likert's criteria are psychologically based, and they substantially enrich the impoverished state of effectiveness criteria.*

The Criterion of the Situation

This approach is based on the reasoning that organizations differ with respect to goals and that they can be analytically distinguished in terms of goal orientation. As Parsons pointed out: "As a formal analytical point of reference, *primacy of orientation to the attainment of a specific goal is used as the defining characteristic of an organization* which distinguishes it from other types of social systems."[21]

In an earlier paper by Bennis,[22] a framework was presented for characterizing four different types of organizations based on a specific criterion variable. These "pure" types are rarely observed empirically, but they serve to sharpen the differences among formally organized activities. Table 2 represents an example of developing effectiveness variables on the basis of organizational parameters.

The Criterion of System Characteristics

This approach, most cogently advanced by sociologists, is based on a "structural-functional" analysis. Selznick, one of its chief proponents, characterizes the approach in the following way: "Structural-functional analysis relates contemporary and variable behavior to a presumptively stable system of needs and mechanisms. This means that a given empirical system is deemed to have basic needs, essentially related to self-maintenance; the system develops repetitive means of self-defense, and day-to-day activity is interpreted in terms of the function served by that activity for the maintenance and defense of the system."[23]

Derivable from this system model are basic needs or institutional imperatives that have to be met if the organism is to survive and "grow." Selznick, for example, lists five: (1) the security of the organization as a whole in relation to social forces in its environment, (2) the stability of the lines of authority and communication, (3) the stability of informal relations within the organization, (4) the continuity

---

* See also Kahn et al.[20] for other suggestions for criteria.

TABLE 2 Typology of organization*

Type of organization	Major function	Examples	Effectiveness criterion
Habit	Replicating standard and uniform products	Highly mechanized factories, etc.	Number of products
Problem-solving	Creating new ideas	Research organizations, design and engineering divisions, consulting organizations, etc.	Number of ideas
Indoctrination	Changing people's habits, attitudes, intellect, behavior (physical and mental)	Universities, prisons, hospitals, etc.	Number of "clients" leaving
Service	Distributing services either directly to consumer or to above types	Military, government, advertising, taxi companies, etc.	Extent of services performed

* From W. G. Bennis, "Leadership Theory and Administrative Behavior: The Problem of Authority," *Administrative Science Quarterly*, vol. 4, no. 3, p. 299, December, 1959.

of policy and of the sources of its determination, and (5) a homogeneity of outlook with respect to the meaning and role of the organization.[24]

Caplow, starting from the fundamental postulate that organizations tend to maintain themselves in continuous operation, identifies three criteria of organizational success: (1) the performance of objective functions, (2) the minimization of spontaneous conflict, and (3) the maximization of satisfaction for individuals.[25] Obviously, with the exception of the second criterion, these resemble the old favorites, performance and satisfaction.

The preceding summaries do not do full justice to the nuances of these three approaches or the enormous creative effort that went into their development, nor do they include the ideas of many thoughtful practitioners.* Despite these limitations, the discussion of multiple criteria, situational parameters, and system characteristics represents the main attempts to solve the criterion problem.†

INADEQUACY OF CRITERION VARIABLES
FOR THE MODERN ORGANIZATION

> The history of other animal species shows that the most successful in the struggle for survival have been those which were most adaptable to change in their world.[28]

The present ways of thinking about and measuring organizational effectiveness are seriously inadequate and often misleading. These criteria are insensitive to the important needs of the organization and are out of joint with the emerging view of contemporary organization that is held by many organizational theorists and practitioners. The present techniques of evaluation provide static indicators of certain output characteristics (i.e., performance and satisfaction) without illuminating the processes by which the organization searches for, adapts to, and solves its changing goals.[29] However, it is these dynamic processes of problem solving that provide the critical dimensions of organizational health, and without knowledge of them, output measurements are woefully inadequate.‡

This rather severe charge is based upon the belief that the main challenge confronting the modern organization (and society) is that of coping with external stress and change. This point hardly needs elaboration or defense. The recent work in the field of organizational behavior reflects this need and interest; it is virtually a catalog of the problems of organizational change.§ In a 1961 monograph on managing major change in organizations, Mann and Neff stated the

* See, for example, Urwick.[26]

† Another approach, advocated by A. L. Comrey, is the deliberate (and often wise) avoidance of a definition of effectiveness or health by obtaining judgments of knowledgeable observers. "This method of defining 'effectiveness' seems to be the only feasible course of action in view of the tremendous number of meanings involved in a conceptual definition of this term and the obvious impossibility of providing a criterion which would reflect all or most of those meanings."[27]

‡ See Ridgway[30] for other criticisms of the use of performance measurements.

§ See, for example, March and Simon;[31] Argyris;[32] Shepard[33]; Gibb and Lippitt;[34] Lippitt et al.;[35] Bennis et al.;[36] and Walker.[37]

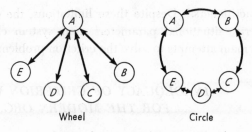

Wheel   Circle

FIG. 1   Two types of communication networks for problem solving by a
group of five persons

issue this way: "Among the most conspicuous values in American culture of the twentieth century are progress, efficiency, science and rationality, achievement and success. These values have helped to produce a highly dynamic society—a society in which the predominant
characteristic is *change*."[38] Kahn, Mann, and Seashore, when
discussing a criterion variable, the "ability of the organization to
change appropriately in response to some objective requirement for
change," remarked: "Although we are convinced of the theoretical importance of this criterion, which we have called organizational flexibility, we have thus far been unable to solve the operational problems
involved in its use."[39]

The basic flaw in the present effectiveness criteria is their inattention to the problem of adapting to change. To illuminate some of
the consequences of this omission, let us turn to one rather simple example. The example is drawn from an area of research, started at
the Massachusetts Institute of Technology about 1949, on the effects
of certain organizational patterns (communication networks) on problem solving by groups.[40] Two of these networks, the Wheel and the
Circle, are shown in Fig. 1.

The results of these experiments showed that an organization with
a structure like the Wheel can solve simple tasks (e.g., identification
of the color of a marble that is common to all five group members)
more rapidly, more clearly, and more efficiently than an organization
with a structure like the Circle. Thus the Wheel arrangement is plainly
superior in terms of the usual criteria employed to evaluate effectiveness. However, if we consider two other criteria of organizational
effectiveness that are relevant to the concern with change flexibility
and creativity, we discover two interesting phenomena. First, the
rapid acceptance of a new idea is more likely in the Circle than in

the Wheel. The man in the middle of the Wheel is apt to discard an idea on the grounds that he is too busy or the idea is impractical. Second, when the task is changed, for example, by going from "pure-color" marbles to unusually colored marbles (such as ginger-ale color or blue-green), the Circle organization is better able to adapt to this change by developing a new code.[41]

As Leavitt pointed out:

> By certain industrial engineering-type (speed, clarity of organization and job descriptions, parsimonious use of paper, etc.), the highly structured, highly routinized, non-involving centralized net seems to work best. But if our criteria of effectiveness are more ephemeral, more general (like acceptance of creativity, flexibility in dealing with novel problems, general high morale and loyalty), then the moral egalitarian or decentralized type net seems to work better.[42]

If we view organizations as adaptive, problem-solving, organic structures, then inferences about effectiveness have to be made, not from static measures of output, though these may be helpful, but on the basis of the processes through which the organization approaches problems. In other words, no single measurement of organizational efficiency or satisfaction—no single time-slice of organizational performance—can provide valid indicators of organizational health. An organization may be essentially healthy despite measurements that reveal that its performance and satisfaction measurements are lower than last month's; it can be unhealthy even if its performance and efficiency figures are higher than last month's—unhealthy or healthy, that is, in relation to the ability to cope with change, with the future. Discussing the neurotic processes, Kubie makes the same point:

> There is not a single thing which a human being can do or feel, or think, whether it is eating or sleeping or drinking or fighting or killing or hating or loving or grieving or exulting or working or playing or painting or inventing, which cannot be either sick or well. . . . The measure of health is flexibility, the freedom to learn through experience, the freedom to change with changing internal and external circumstances, to be influenced by reasonable argument, admonitions, exhortations, and the appeal to emotions; the freedom to respond appropriately to the stimulus of reward and punishment, and especially the freedom to cease when sated. The essence of normality is flexibility in all of these vital ways.[43]

Any moment of behavior is unhealthy if the processes that set it in motion predetermine its automatic repetition, regardless of the environmental stimuli or consequences of the act. For example, it is plausible that lowering efficiency in order to adjust to some product change may be quite appropriate when market demands are considered. It is equally plausible that morale, or whatever measure is used to gauge the human factor, may also plummet during this period. In fact, maintaining the same level of efficiency and morale under new circumstances may be dysfunctional for the health of the organization.

Let me review the argument thus far. The main challenge confronting today's organization, whether it is a hospital or a business enterprise, is that of responding to changing conditions and adapting to external stress. The salience of change is forced on organizations because of the growing interdependence between their changing boundary conditions and society (a point that will be elaborated later) and the increasing reliance on scientific knowledge. The traditional ways that are employed to measure organizational effectiveness do not adequately reflect the true determinants of organizational health and success. Rather, these criteria yield static time-slices of performance and satisfaction, which may be irrelevant or misleading. These static, discrete measurements do not provide viable measures of health, for they tell us nothing about the processes by which the organization copes with its problems. Therefore, different effectiveness criteria have to be identified, criteria that reveal the processes of problem solving. This point is corroborated by some recent works on organizational theory. Consider, for example, these remarks by Wilfred Brown, chairman and managing director of the Glacier Metal Company:

> Effective organization is a function of the work to be done and the resources and techniques available to do it. The changes in methods of production bring about changes in the number of work roles, in the distribution of work between roles and in their relationship to one another. Failure to make explicit acknowledgement of this relationship between work and organization gives rise to non-valid assumptions (e.g., that optimum organization is a function of the personalities involved, that it is a matter connected with the personal style and arbitrary decision of the chief executive, that there are choices between centralized and decentralized types of organization, etc.). Our observations lead us to accept that optimum organization must be derived from an analysis of the work to be done and the techniques and resources available[44]

The work of Emery and Trist, which has influenced the thinking of Brown, stressed the "socio-technical system," based on Bertalanffy's "open system" theorizing.[45] They conclude that ". . . the primary task of managing an enterprise as a whole is to relate the total system to its environment, and not internal regulation per se."[46] They further conclude that:

> If management is to control internal growth and development it must in the first instance control the "boundary conditions"—the forms of exchange between the enterprise and the environment. . . . The strategic objective should be to place the enterprise in a position in its environment where it has some assured conditions for growth—unlike war the best position is not necessarily that of unchallenged monopoly. Achieving this position would be the primary task or overriding mission of the enterprise.[47]

In reference to management development, A. T. M. Wilson, former director of Tavistock Institute, pointed out:

> One general point of high relevance can be seen in these discussions of the firm as an institution. The tasks of the higher level managers center on problems in which there is a continuously high level of uncertainity; complex value decisions are inevitably involved; and this has a direct bearing on the requirements of personality for top level management. . . .[48]

And H. J. Leavitt said on the same subject:

> Management development programs need, I submit, to be oriented much more toward the future, toward change, toward differences from current forms of practice and behavior. . . . We ought to allocate more of the effort of our programs to making our student a more competent analyst. We ought, in other words, to try to teach them to think a little more like scientists, and indeed to know a good deal more about the culture and methods of scientists.[49]

What relevance have these quotations* to the main theme of this chapter? Note, first of all, that these theorists all view the organization (or institution) as an adaptive structure actively encountering many different environments, both internal and external, in its productive efforts. Note also the key terms: "change," "uncertainty," "future," "task," "mission," "work to be done," "available resources," "exchange between the enterprise and environment." There is no dialogue here on the relation between productivity and satisfaction, no fruitless

---

* Although not quoted here, a book by Selznick[50] is also directly relevant.

arguments between the "human relationists" and scientific-management advocates. Indeed, it seems that it is no longer adequate to perceive organization as an analog to the machine as Max Weber indicated: ". . . [bureaucracy is like] a modern judge who is a vending machine into which the pleadings are inserted together with the fee and which then disgorges the judgment together with its reasons mechanically derived from the code."[51] Nor is it reasonable to view the organization solely in terms of the socio-psychological characteristics of the persons involved at work, a viewpoint that has been so fashionable of late.* Rather, the approach that should be taken is that of these quoted writers: organizations are to be viewed as "open systems" defined by their primary task or mission and encountering boundary conditions that are rapidly changing their characteristics.† Given this rough definition, we must locate some effectiveness criteria and the institutional prerequisities that provide the conditions for the attainment of these criteria.

THE SPIRIT OF INQUIRY AS A
MODEL FOR ORGANIZATION

Findings are science's short-range benefits, but the method of inquiry is its long-range value. I have said that the invention of organization was Man's first most important achievement; I now add that the development of inquiry will be his second. Both of these inventions change the species and are necessary for its survival. But both must become a part of the nature of Man himself, not just given house room in certain groups. Organization is by now a part of every man, but inquiry is not. The significant product of science and education will be the incorporation within the human animal of the capability and habit of inquiry.[54]

Whether our work is art or science or the daily work of society, it is only the form in which we explore our experience which is different; the need to explore remains the same. This is why, at bottom, the society of scientists is more important than their discoveries. What

* See Bennis[52] for elaboration of this point.
† Wilson lists six "areas of social activity; each of which contains a number of significant social institutions and social groups. These areas may be rather summarily labelled as: (i) Government, (ii) Consumers, (iii) Shareholders, (iv) Competitors, (v) Raw material and power suppliers, and (vi) Groups within the firm."[53] These represent some of the boundary conditions for the manager.

science has to teach us here is not its techniques but its spirit; the irresistible need to explore.[55]

It has been asserted throughout this chapter that organizations must be viewed as adaptive, problem-solving systems operating and embedded in complicated and rapidly changing environments. If this view is valid, then it is fair to postulate that the methodological rules by which the organization approaches its task and "exchanges with its environments" are the critical determinants of organizational effectiveness. These methodological rules or operating procedures bear a close resemblance to the rules of inquiry or scientific investigation. Therefore, the rules and norms of science may provide a valuable, possibly necessary, model for organizational behavior.

First, it should be stated what is meant and what is not meant by "science" in this context. I do not mean the findings of science, the vast array of data that scientists produce. Nor do I mean barren operationalism—what some people refer to as "scientism"—or the gadgetry utilized for routine laboratory work. Rather, what is meant may be called the scientific "temper" or "spirit." It is this "spirit of inquiry," which stems from the value position of science and which such authors as Dewey, Bronowski, Geiger, and Sanford have emphasized, that must be considered if our world is to survive. This position says essentially that the roles of scientist and citizen cannot be sharply separated. As Waddington put it:

> The true influence of science is an attitude of mind, a general method of thinking about and investigating problems. It can, and I think it will, spread gradually throughout the social consciousness without any very sharp break with the attitudes of the past. But the problems for which it is wanted face us already; and the sooner the scientific method of handling them becomes more generally understood and adopted, the better it will be.[56]

Now it is necessary to look a bit more closely at what is meant by this "scientific attitude." This complex includes many elements, only two of which are considered here. The first may be called the "hypothetical spirit," the feeling for tentativeness and caution, the respect for probable error. As Geiger says: ". . . the hypothetical spirit is the unique contribution scientific method can offer to human culture; it certainly is the only prophylactic against the authoritarian mystique so symptomatic of modern nerve failure."[57]

The second ingredient is experimentalism, the willingness to expose ideas to empirical testing, to procedures, to action. The hypothetical stance without experimentalism would soon develop into a rather arid scholasticism. Experimentalism without the corrective of the hypothetical imagination would bring about a radical, "dust-bowl" empiricism lacking significant insight and underlying structures capable of generalization. These two features, plus the corrective of criticism, are what is meant by the methodological rules of science; it is the *spirit of inquiry*, a love of truth relentlessly pursued, that ultimately creates the objectivity and intelligent action associated with science.

But the scientific attitude of which I speak can most easily flourish under specific conditions usually associated with the social organization of the scientific enterprise. A number of social scientists, inspired by the work of Parsons[58,59] and Merton,[60] have examined the society of scientific enterprise.[61,62,63,64] What they have said is important for the argument presented here. Only when the social conditions of science are realized, can the scientific attitude exist. As Sanford pointed out:

> Science flourishes under that type of democracy that accents freedom of opinion and dissent, and respect for the individual. It is against all forms of totalitarianism, of mechanization and regimentation. . . . In the historical development of the ends that are treasured in Western societies there is reason to believe that science has had a determining role. Bronowski again: Men have asked for freedom, justice, and respect precisely as science has spread among them.[65]

Or as Parsons states:

> Science is intimately integrated with the whole social structure and cultural tradition. They mutually support one another—only in certain types of society can science flourish and conversely without a continuous and healthy development and application of science such a society cannot function properly.[66]

What are the conditions that constitute the ethos of science? Barber identifies five that are appropriate to this discussion: rationality, universalism, individualism, communality, and disinterestedness.[67] A brief word about each of these is in order. The goal of science is understanding, understanding in as abstract and general a fashion as possible. "Universalism," as the term is used here, means that all men have morally equal claims to discover and to understand. Individualism, according to Barber, expresses itself in science as antiauthoritarianism; no authority but the authority of science need be accepted or trusted. Communality is close to the utopian Communist slogan: "From each according to his abilities, to each according to his needs." This simply means that all scientific peers have the right to share in existing knowledge; withholding knowledge and secrecy are cardinal sins. The last element, disinterestedness, is to be contrasted with the self-interest usually associated with organizational and economic life. Disinterestedness in science requires that role incumbents serve others and gain gratification from the pursuit of truth itself. These five conditions constitute the moral imperatives of the social organization of science. They are, of course, derived from an "ideal type" of system, an empirically imaginable possibility but a rare phenomenon. Nevertheless, insofar as they are imperatives, they do in fact determine significantly the behavior of scientific organization.

There are two points to be made in connection with this model of organization. The first was made earlier but may require reiteration: The spirit of inquiry can flourish only in an environment where there is a commitment toward the five institutional imperatives. The second point is that what is now called the "human relations school"* has been preoccupied primarily with the study of those factors which this chapter has identified as the institutional imperatives of the science of organization. In fact, only if we look at the human relationists' approach with this perspective do we obtain a valid view of their work. For example, a great deal of work in human relations has focused on "communication," [69] "participation,"[70] and "decision making." Overgeneralizing a bit, we can say that most of the studies have been (from a *moral* point of view) predicated on, and lean toward, the social organization of science as has been outlined here. Note, for instance, that many studies have shown that increased participation, better communication (keeping the worker "informed"), more "self-control," and decreased authoritarianism are desirable ends. Because of their emphasis on these factors, the researchers and theoreticians associated with human relations research have sometimes been perceived as "softheaded," unrealistic, too academic, and even utopian. In some cases, the social scientists themselves have invited these criticisms by being mainly interested in demonstrating that these participative beliefs would lead to heightened morale and, on occasion,

* See Bennis.[68]

to increased efficiency. So they have been accused by many writers of being advocates of "happiness" or a moo-cow psychology.*

These are invalid criticisms, mainly because the issue is being fought on the wrong grounds. One of the troubles is that the social scientists have not foreseen the full implications of their studies. Rather than debating the viability of socio-psychological variables in terms of the traditional effectiveness variables, which at this point is highly problematical, they should be saying that the only way in which organizations can develop a scientific attitude is by providing conditions where it can flourish. In short, the norms of science are both compatible and remarkably homogeneous with those of a liberal democracy. We argue, then, that the way in which organizations can master their dilemmas and solve their problems is by developing a spirit of inquiry. This can flourish only under the social conditions associated with the scientific enterprise (i.e., democratic ideals). Thus it is *necessary* to emphasize the "human side of enterprise," that is, institutional conditions of science, if organizations are expected to maintain mastery over their environment.†

Now, assuming that the social conditions of science have been met, let us return to the designated task of identifying those organizational criteria that are associated with the scientific attitude.

THE CRITERIA OF SCIENCE AND MENTAL HEALTH APPLIED TO ORGANIZATIONS

Perhaps no other area of human functioning has more frequently been selected as a criterion for mental health than the individual's reality orientation and his efforts at mastering the environment.[73]

I now propose that we gather the various kinds of behavior just mentioned, all of which have to do with effective interaction with the environment, under the general heading of competence.[74]

All aspects of the enterprise must be subordinated to . . . *its primary task*. It is not only industrial enterprises, however, which must remain loyal to their primary tasks. This is so of all human groups, for these are all compelled, in order to maintain themselves in existence, to

---

* See Baritz.[71]

† Shepard notes the irony that as research organizations expand their operations, they become more like the classical, ideal type of bureaucracy. See Shepard [72] for another approach to the social conditions of science.

undertake some form of appropriate action in relation to their environment. . . . An organism, whether individual or social, must do work in order to keep itself related to its external environment, that is, to meet reality.[75]

These quotations provide the framework for the following analysis. They express what has been the major concern throughout this chapter: that, when organizations are considered as "open systems," adaptive structures coping with various environments, the most significant characteristic for understanding effectiveness is competence, mastery, or (the term that has been used in this chapter) problem solving. It has been shown that competence can be gained only through certain adaptations of science: its attitude and social conditions. It is now possible to go a step further by underlining what the above quotations reveal, that the criteria of science bear a close kinship to the characteristics of what mental-health specialists and psychiatrists call "health."

There is an interesting historical parallel between the development of criteria for the evaluation of mental health and the evolution of standards for evaluating organizational health. The terms "mastery," "competence," and "adaptive, problem-solving abilities" are relatively new to both fields. In the area of organizational behavior, they are replacing the old terms "satisfaction" and "work competence." Similarly, an important change has taken place in the mental-health field, which has had some of the same problems in determining adequate criteria. Rather than viewing health exclusively in terms of some highly inferential intrapsychic reconstitutions, these specialists are stressing "adaptive mechanisms" and "conflict-free," relatively autonomous ego-functioning, independent of id energies. The studies of White,[76] Rapaport,[77] Erikson,[78] Hartmann,[79] and other so-called ego psychologists all point in this direction.

The main reason for the confluence of organizational behavior and mental health is basically quite simple. Both the norms of science and the methodology of psychotherapeutic work have the same goal and methodology: to perceive reality, both internal and external, and to examine unflinchingly the positions of these realities in order to act intelligently. It is the belief here that what a patient takes away and can employ *after* treatment is the methodology of science, the ability to look facts in the face and to use the hypothetical and experimental methods—the spirit of inquiry—in understanding experience.

Sanford has said in this connection:

> . . . most notably in Freud's psychoanalytic method of investigation and treatment. (This method is in my view, Freud's greatest, and it will be his most lasting contribution.) By the method I mean the whole contractual arrangement according to which both the therapist and patient become investigators, and both objects of careful observation and study; in which the therapist can ask the patient to face the truth because he, the therapist, is willing to try to face it in himself; in which investigation and treatment are inseparable aspects of the same humanistic enterprise.[80]

And in Freud's words: "Finally, we must not forget that the relationship between analyst and patient is based on a love of truth, that is, on the acknowledgement of reality, and that it precludes any kind of sham or deception."[81]

It is now possible to postulate the criteria for organizational health. These are based on a definition by Marie Jahoda, according to which a healthy personality " . . . actively masters his environment, shows a certain unit of personality, and is able to perceive the world and himself correctly."[82] Let us take each of these elements and extrapolate it into organizational criteria.

1 *"Actively masters his environment": adaptability* In terms of this chapter, this characteristic coincides with problem-solving ability, which in turn depends upon the organization's flexibility. Earlier it was pointed out that flexibility is the freedom to learn through experience, to change with changing internal and external circumstances. Another way of putting it, in terms of organizational functioning, is to say that it is "learning how to learn." This is equivalent to Bateson's notion of "deutero-learning," the progressive change in rate of simple learning.[83]

2 *"Certain unit of personality": the problem of identity* In order for an organization to develop adaptabilty, it needs to know who it is and what it is to do; that is, it has to have some clearly defined identity.* The problem of identity, which is central to much of the contemporary literature in the mental-health field, can in organizations be examined in at least two ways: (1) by determining to what extent the organizational goals are understood and accepted by the personnel and (2) by ascertaining to what extent the organization is perceived veridically by the personnel.

* See Selznick[84] for similar emphasis.

As to the problem of goals, Selznick pointed out:

> The aims of large organizations are often very broad. A certain vagueness must be accepted because it is difficult to foresee whether more specific goals will be realistic or wise. This situation presents the leader with one of his most difficult but indispensable tasks. *He must specify and recast the general aims of his organization so as to adapt them, without serious corruption, to the requirements of institutional survival.* This is what we mean by the definition of institutional mission and role.[85]

The same point is made by Simon, Smithburg, and Thompson: "No knowledge of administrative techniques, then, can relieve the administrator from the task of moral choice—choice as to organizational goals and methods and choice as to his treatment of the other human beings in his organization."[86]

In addition to the clear definition of mission, which it is the responsibility of the leader to communicate, there also has to be a working consensus on the organization of work. Wilfred Brown's work is extremely useful in this connection. He enumerates four concepts of organization: (1) the *manifest* organization, or the one which is seen on the "organization chart" and which is formally displayed; (2) the *assumed* organization, or the one that individuals perceive as the organization (were they asked to draw their phenomenological view of the way that things work); (3) the *extant* organization, or the situation as revealed through systematic investigation, say, by a student of organizations; and (4) the *requisite* organization, or the situation as it would be if it were "in accord with the real properties of the field in which it exists."

"The ideal situation," Brown goes on to say, "is that in which the manifest, the assumed, the extant, and the requisite are as closely as possible in line with each other."[87] Wherever these four organizational concepts are in contradiction, we find a case of what Erikson calls "identity diffusion."[88] Certainly this phenomenon is a familiar one to students and executives of organizations. Indeed, the great attention paid to the "informal group" and its discrepancy with the formal (the difference between the manifest and the assumed organizations or between the manifest and the extant) testifies to this.

Another useful analogy to the mental-health field shows up in this discussion. Many psychotherapeutic schools base their notions of health on the degree to which the individual brings into harmony the various "selves" that make up his personality. According to Fromm-Reichmann: ". . . the successfully treated mental patient, as he then knows himself, will be much the same person as he is known to others."[89]

Virtually the same criterion is used here for organizational health, i.e., the degree to which the organization maintains harmony—and knowledge—about and among the manifest, assumed, extant, and requisite situations. This point should be clarified. It is not necessary to organizational health that all four concepts of organization be identical. Rather, all four types should be recognized and allowance made for all the tensions attendant upon their imbalance. It is doubtful that there will always be total congruence in organizations. The important factor is recognition; the executive function is to strive toward congruence insofar as it is possible.

3 *"Is able to perceive the world and himself correctly": reality-testing* If the conditions requisite for an organization are to be met, the organization must develop adequate techniques for determining the "real properties" of the field in which it exists. The field contains two main boundaries, the internal organization and the boundaries relevant to the organization. March and Simon, in their cognitive view of organization, place great emphasis on adequate "search behavior." Ineffective search behavior—cycling and stereotypy—are regarded as "neurotic."[90]

However, it is preferable here to think about inadequate search behavior in terms of perception that is free from need-distortion.[91] Abraham Maslow places this in perspective: "Recently Money-Kyrle, an English psychoanalyst, has indicated that he believes it possible to call a neurotic person not only *relatively* inefficient, simply because he does not perceive the real world as accurately or as efficiently as does the healthy person. The neurotic is not only emotionally sick—he is cognitively *wrong!*[92] The requisite organization requires reality-testing, within the limits of rationality, for successful mastery over the relevant environments.*

In summary, then, I am saying that the basic features of organization rely on adequate methods for solving problems. These methods stem from the elements of what has been called the "scientific attitude." From these ingredients have been fashioned three criteria of

---

* See March and Simon[93] for a formal model of search behavior and an excellent discussion of organizational reality-testing.

organizational mechanisms, which fulfill the prerequisites of health. These criteria are in accord with what mental-health specialists call "health" in the individual.

Undeniably, some qualifications have to be made. The mensuration problem has not been faced, nor have the concrete details for organizational practice been fully developed. Nonetheless, it has been asserted that the processes of problem solving—of adaptability—stand out as the single most important determinant of organizational health and that this adaptability depends on a valid identity and valid reality-testing.*

SOME IMPLICATIONS OF THE SCIENCE MODEL FOR ORGANIZATIONAL BEHAVIOR

There is one human characteristic which today can find a mode of expression in nationalism and war, and which, it may seem would have to be completely denied in a scientific society. That is the tendency to find some dogma to which can be attached complete belief, forthright and unquestioning. That men do experience a need for certainty of such a kind can scarcely be doubted. . . . Is science, for all its logical consistency, in a position to satisfy this primary need of man?[94]

We are not yet emotionally an adaptive society, though we try systematically to develop forces that tend to make us one. We encourage the search for new inventions; we keep the mind stimulated, bright, and free to seek out fresh means of transport, communication, and energy; yet we remain, in part, appalled by the consequences of our ingenuity and, too frequently, try to find security through the shoring up of ancient and irrelevant conventions, the extension of purely physical safeguards, or the delivery of decisions we ourselves should make into the keeping of superior authority like the state. These solutions are not necessarily unnatural or wrong, but historically they have not been enough and I suspect they will never be enough to give us the serenity and competence we seek. . . . We may find at least part of our salvation in identifying ourselves with the adaptive process and thus share . . . some of the joy, exuberance, satisfaction and security . . . to meet the changing time.[95]

* Dr. M. B. Miles has suggested that an important omission in this approach is organization "memory" or storage of information. Organizations modeled along the lines suggested here require a "theory" based on an *accumulated* storage of information. This is implied, I believe, in the criterion of adaptability.

The use of the model of science as a form for the modern organization implies some profound reforms in current practice, reforms that may appear to some as too adventurous or utopian. This criticism is difficult to deny, particularly since not all the consequences can be clearly seen at this time. However, let us examine a few consequences that do stand out rather sharply.

1 *The problem of commitment and loyalty* Although the viewpoint does have its critics, such as William H. Whyte, Jr., most administrators desire to develop high commitment and loyalty to the organization. Can the scientific attitude, with its ascetic simplicity and acceptance of risk and uncertainty, substitute for loyalty to the organization and its purpose? Can science, as Waddington wonders, provide the belief in an illusion that organizational loyalty is thought to provide? The answer to this is a tentative "yes and no." Substituting the scientific attitude for loyalty would be difficult for those people to whom the commitment to truth, to the pursuit of knowledge, is both far too abstract and far too threatening. For some, the "escape from freedom" is a necessity, and the uncertain nature of the scientific attitude would be difficult to accept. However, it is likely that even these individuals would be influenced by the adoption of the science model by the organization. Loyalty to the organization per se would be transformed into loyalty and commitment directed to the spirit of inquiry. What effect would this have on commitment?

Gouldner, in another context, has supplied an important clue. He pointed to a difference between individuals in terms of two organizational roles, "locals" and "cosmopolitans."[96] The cosmopolitan derives his rewards from inward standards of excellence, internalized and reinforced through professional (usually scientific) identification. On the other hand, the local (what Marvick calls the "bureaucratic orientation"[97]) derives his rewards from manipulating power within the hierarchy. The locals are considered to be better organization men than the cosmopolitans. Loyalty within the scientific organizational conditions specified here would be directed not to particular ends or products or to work groups but to identification with the adaptive process of the organization.

2 *Recruitment and training for the spirit of inquiry* There are some indications that the problems of recruitment and training for the social organization of science are not as difficult as has been expected. For one thing, as Bruner has shown,[98] today's schoolchildren

are getting more and better science teaching. It is to be hoped that they will learn as much about the attitude of science as they will about its glamour and techniques. In addition, more and more research-trained individuals are entering organizations.* As McGregor points out: "Creative intellectual effort by a wide range of professional specialists will be as essential to tomorrow's manager as instruments and an elaborate air traffic control system are to today's jet pilot."[100] Individuals trained in scientific methodology can easily adapt to, in fact will probably demand, more and more freedom for intellectual inquiry. If McGregor's and Leavitt and Whisler's[101] prognostications are correct, as they presently seem to be, then there is practically no choice but to prepare a social milieu in which the adaptive, problem-solving processes can flourish.

As to training, only a brief word needs to be said. The training program of the National Training Laboratories[102] and the work of Blake,[103] Blansfied,[104] and Shepard[105] are based rather specifically on developing better diagnosticians of human behavior. It is apparent from such training studies that the organization of tomorrow, heavily influenced by the growth of science and technology and manned by an increasing number of professionals, will be based on inquiry.

3 Intergroup competition Blake and Mouton, guided partly by the work of the Sherifs,[106] have disclosed for examination one of organization's most troublesome problems, intergroup conflict and collaboration. These chronic conflicts probably dissipate more energy and money than any other single organizational disease. Intergroup conflict, with its "win-lose" orientation, its dysfunctional loyalty (to the group or product, not to the truth), its cognitive distortions of the outsider (the "enemy"), and its inability to reach what has been called "creative synthesis," effectively disrupts the commitment to truth. By means of a laboratory approach, Blake and Mouton have managed to break

> . . . the mental assumptions underlying win-lose conflict. Factually based mutual problem identification, fluidity in initial stages of solution, proposing rather than fixed position taking, free and frequent interchange between representatives and their constituent groups and focussing on communalities as well as differences as the basis for achieving agreement and so on, are but a few of the ways which have been experimentally demonstrated to increase the likelihood of

* See Harbison[99] on this point.

arriving at mutually acceptable solutions under conditions of collaboration between groups.[107]

What the authors do not explicitly say but only imply is that the structure of their experimental laboratory approach is based on the methods of inquiry that have been advocated in this chapter. Theirs is an action-research model, in which the subjects are the inquirers who learn to collect, use, and generalize from data in order to understand organizational conflict. Rational problem solving is the only means presently known by which organizations may be rid of persistent intergroup conflict.

Loyalty, recruitment and training, and intergroup hostility are by no means all the organizational consequences that this chapter suggests. The distribution of power, the problems of group cohesiveness,* the required organizational fluidity for arranging task groups on a rational basis, and the change in organizational roles and status all have to be considered. More time and energy than are now available are needed before these problems can be met squarely.

However, one thing is certain: whatever energy, competence, and time are required, it will be necessary to think generally along the lines outlined here. Truth is a cruel master, and the reforms that have been mentioned or implied may not be altogether pleasant to behold. The light of truth has a corrosive effect on vested interests, outmoded technologies, and rigid, stereotyped patterns of behavior. Moreover, if this scientific ethos is ever realized, the remnants of what are now known as "morale" and "efficiency" may be buried. For the spirit of inquiry implies a confrontation of truth that may not be "satisfying" and a deferral of gratification that may not, in the short run, be "efficient." However, this is the challenge that must be met if organizations are to cope more successfully within their increasingly complicated environments.

NOTES

1. "Muggeridge and Snow," *Encounter*, vol. 27, p. 90, February, 1962.
2. Snow, C. P., *The Two Cultures and the Scientific Revolution*, Mentor Books, New American Library of World Literature, Inc., New York, 1962.

* It is suspected that group cohesiveness will decrease as the scientific attitude infuses organizational functioning. With the depersonalization of science, the rapid turnover, and some expected individualism, cohesiveness may not be functional or even possible.

3. Bronowski, J., *Science and Human Values*, Harper & Row, Publishers, Incorporated, New York, 1959.

4. Sanford, N., "Social Science and Social Reform," Presidential address for SPSSI at the Annual Meeting of the American Psychological Association, Washington, Aug. 28, 1958.

5. Katzell, R. A., "Industrial Psychology," in P. R. Farnsworth (ed.), *Annual Review of Psychology*, Annual Reviews, Inc., Palo Alto, Calif., 1957, pp. 237–268.

6. Jahoda, M., *Current Concepts of Positive Mental Health*, Basic Books, Inc., Publishers, New York, 1958.

7. Pfiffner, J. M., and F. P. Sherwood, *Administrative Organization*, Prentice-Hall, Inc., Englewood Cliffs, N.J., 1960.

8. Jahoda, *op. cit.*

9. Wasserman, P., *Measurement and Evaluation of Organizational Performance*, McKinsey Foundation Annotated Bibliography, Graduate School of Business and Public Administration, Cornell University, Ithaca, N.Y., 1959.

10. Katzell, *op. cit.*

11. Aitken, H. G. J., *Taylorism at Watertown Arsenal: Scientific Management in Action, 1908–1915*, Harvard University Press, Cambridge, Mass., 1960.

12. Likert, R., "Measuring Organizational Performance," *Harvard Business Review*, vol. 36, pp. 41–50, March-April, 1958.

13. Argyris, C., "The Integration of the Individual and the Organization," Paper presented at the University of Wisconsin, Madison, Wis., May, 1961.

14. Argyris, C., *Personality and Organization*, Harper & Row, Publishers, Incorporated, New York, 1957.

15. Whyte, W. H., Jr., *The Organization Man*, Simon and Schuster, Inc., New York, 1956.

16. Haire, M., "What Price Value?" *Contemporary Psychology*, vol. 4, pp. 180–182, June, 1959.

17. Kahn, R., F. C. Mann, and S. Seashore, "Human Relations Research in Large Organizations. II," *Journal of Social Issues*, vol. 12, no. 2, p. 4, 1956.

18. Pfiffner and Sherwood, *op. cit.*

19. Likert, *op. cit.*

20. Kahn et al., *op. cit.*, introduction.

21. Parsons, T., "Suggestions for a Sociological Approach to the Theory of Organizations. I," *Administrative Science Quarterly*, vol. 1, pp. 63–85. 1956.

22. Bennis, W. G., "Leadership Theory and Administrative Behavior: The Problem of Authority," *Administrative Science Quarterly*, vol. 4, no. 3, pp. 259–301, December, 1959.

23. Selznick, P., "Foundations of the Theory of Organizations," *American Sociological Review*, vol. 13, pp. 25–35, 1948.

24. Selznick, *op. cit.*

25. Caplow, T., "The Criteria of Organizational Success," in K. Davis and W. G. Scott (eds.), *Readings in Human Relations*, McGraw-Hill Book Company, New York, 1959, p. 96.

26. Urwick, L. F., "The Purpose of a Business," in K. Davis and W. G. Scott (eds.), *Readings in Human Relations*, McGraw-Hill Book Company, New York, 1959, pp. 85–91.

27. Comrey, A. L., "A Research Plan for the Study of Organizational Effectiveness," in A. H. Rubenstein and C. J. Haberstroh (eds.), *Some Theories of Organization*, Dorsey-Irwin Press, Homewood, Ill., 1960, p. 362.

28. Bronowski, J., *The Common Sense of Science*, Modern Library, Inc., New York, no date.

29. Paul, B., "Social Science in Public Health," *American Journal of Public Health*, vol. 46, pp. 1390–1393, November, 1956.

30. Ridgway, V. F., "Dysfunctional Consequences of Performance Measurements," in A. H. Rubenstein and C. J. Haberstroh (eds.), *Some Theories of Organization*, Dorsey-Irwin Press, Homewood, Ill., 1960, pp. 371–377.

31. March, J., and H. Simon, *Organizations*, John Wiley & Sons, Inc., New York, 1958, chap. 7.

32. Argyris, C., *Organizational Development: An Inquiry into the Esso Approach*, Yale University Press, New Haven, Conn., July, 1960.

33. Shepard, H., "Three Management Programs and the Theories behind Them," in *An Action Research Program for Organization Improvement*, Foundation for Research on Human Behavior, Ann Arbor, Mich., 1960.

34. Gibb, J. R., and R. Lippitt (eds.), "Consulting with Groups and Organizations," *Journal of Social Issues*, vol. 15, no. 2, pp. 1–74, 1959.

35. Lippitt, R., J. Watson, and B. Westley, *The Dynamics of Planned Change*, Harcourt, Brace & World, Inc., New York, 1958.

36. Bennis, W. G., K. Benne, and R. Chin, *The Planning of Change*, Holt, Rinehart and Winston, Inc., New York, 1961.

37. Walker, C. R. (ed.), *Modern Technology and Civilization*, McGraw-Hill Book Company, New York, 1961.

38. Mann, F. C., and F. W. Neff, *Managing Major Change in Organizations*, Foundation for Research on Human Behavior, Ann Arbor, Mich., 1961.

39. Kahn et al., *op. cit.*

40. Leavitt, H. J., "Effects of Certain Communication Patterns on Group Performance," *Journal of Abnormal and Social Psychology*, vol. 46, pp. 38–50, 1951.

41. Smith, S., "Communication Pattern and the Adaptability of Task-oriented Groups: An Experimental Study," unpublished paper, Massachusetts Institute of Technology, Cambridge, Mass., 1950.

42. Leavitt, H. J., "Unhuman Organizations," Address presented at the Centennial Symposium on Executive Development, School of Industrial Management, Massachusetts Institute of Technology, Cambridge, Mass., Apr. 27, 1961.

43. Kubie, L. S., *Neurotic Distortions of the Creative Process*, Porter Lectures, Series 22, University of Kansas Press, Lawrence, Kans., 1958.

44. Brown, W., *Exploration in Management*, John Wiley & Sons, Inc., New York, 1960.

45. Bertalanffy, L. V., "The Theory of Open Systems in Physics and Biology," *Science,* vol. 111, pp. 23–29, 1950.

46. Emery, F. E., and E. L. Trist, "Socio-technical Systems," Paper presented at the 6th Annual International Meeting of the Institute of Management Sciences, Paris, September, 1959.

47. *Ibid.*

48. Wilson, A. T. M., "The Manager and His World," Paper presented at the Centennial Symposium on Executive Development, School of Industrial Management, Massachusetts Institute of Technology, Cambridge, Mass., Apr. 27, 1961.

49. Leavitt, "Unhuman Organizations."

50. Selznick, P., *Leadership in Administration,* Row, Peterson & Company, Evanston, Ill., 1957.

51. Bendix, R., *Max Weber: An Intellectual Portrait,* Doubleday & Company, Inc., Garden City, N.Y., 1960.

52. Bennis, *op. cit.*

53. Wilson, *op. cit.,* p. 3.

54. Thelen, H., *Education and the Human Quest,* Harper & Row, Publishers, Incorporated, New York, 1960.

55. Bronowski, *Science and Human Values.*

56. Waddington, C. H., *The Scientific Attitude,* Penguin Books, Inc., Baltimore, 1941.

57. Geiger, G., "Values and Social Science," *The Journal of Social Issues,* vol. 6, no. 4, pp. 8–16, 1950.

58. Parsons, T., *The Social System,* The Free Press of Glencoe, New York, 1951, chap. 8.

59. Parsons, T., "The Professions and Social Structure," in *Essays in Sociological Theory,* The Free Press of Glencoe, New York, 1949, chap. 8.

60. Merton, R., "The Sociology of Knowledge" and "Science and Democratic Social Structure," in *Social Theory and Social Structure,* The Free Press of Glencoe, New York, 1949, chaps. 8 and 12.

61. Barber, B., *Science and the Social Order,* The Free Press of Glencoe, New York, 1952.

62. Bush, G. P., and D. H. Hattery, *Teamwork in Research,* American University Press, Washington, D.C., 1953.

63. Marcson, S., *The Scientist in American Industry,* Industrial Relations Section, Princeton University, Princeton, N.J., 1960.

64. Rubenstein, A. H., and H. A. Shepard, *Annotated Bibliography on Human Relations in Research Laboratories,* School of Industrial Management, Massachusetts Institute of Technology, Cambridge, Mass., February, 1956.

65. Sanford, *op. cit.*

66. Barber, *op. cit.*

67. *Ibid.*

68. Bennis, *op. cit.*

69. Berkowitz, N., and W. Bennis, "Interaction in Formal Service-oriented Organizations," *Administrative Science Quarterly*, vol. 6, no. 1, pp. 25–50, June, 1961.

70. McGregor, D., *The Human Side of Enterprise*, McGraw-Hill Book Company, New York, 1960.

71. Baritz, L., *The Servants of Power*, Wesleyan University Press, Middletown, Conn., 1960.

72. Shepard, H., "Superiors and Subordinates in Research," *Journal of Business*, vol. 29, pp. 261–267, October, 1956.

73. Jahoda, *op. cit.*

74. White, R. W., "Motivation Reconsidered: The Concept of Competence," *Psychological Review*, vol. 66, no. 5, pp. 297–333, September, 1959.

75. E. L. Trist in Brown, *op. cit.*

76. White, *op. cit.*

77. Rapaport, D., "The Theory of Ego Autonomy: A Generalization," *Bulletin of the Menninger Clinic*, vol. 22, no. 2, pp. 13–35, January, 1958. (See also "The Structure of Psychoanalytic Theory," *Psychological Issues*, vol. 2, no. 2, monograph 6, 1960.)

78. Erikson, E., "Identity and the Life Cycle," *Psychological Issues*, vol. 1, no. 1, monograph 1, 1959.

79. Hartmann, H., *Ego Psychology and the Problem of Adaption*, International Universities Press, Inc., New York, 1958.

80. Sanford, *op. cit.*

81. Freud, S., "Analysis Terminable and Interminable," in E. Jones (ed.), *Collected Papers*, vol. 5, Basic Books, Inc., Publishers, New York, 1959.

82. Jahoda, *op. cit.*

83. Bateson, G., "Social Planning and the Concept of Deutero-learning," in T. M. Newcomb and E. L. Hartley (eds.), *Readings in Social Psychology*, 1st ed., Holt, Rinehart and Winston, Inc., New York, 1947, pp. 121–128.

84. Selznick, *Leadership in Administration*, chap. 3.

85. *Ibid.*

86. Simon, H. A., D. W. Smithburg, and V. A. Thompson, *Public Administration*, Alfred A. Knopf, Inc., New York, 1950.

87. Brown, *op. cit.*

88. Erikson, *op. cit.*

89. Fromm-Reichmann, F., *Principles of Intensive Psychotherapy*, The University of Chicago Press, Chicago, 1950.

90. March and Simon, *op. cit.*

91. Katzell, *op. cit.*

92. Jahoda, *op. cit.*

93. March and Simon, *op. cit.*, p. 50 and chap. 6.

94. Waddington, *op. cit.*

95. Morison, E., "A Case Study of Innovation," *Engineering Science Monthly*, vol. 13, pp. 5–11, April, 1950.

96. Gouldner, A., "Locals and Cosmopolitans: Towards an Analysis of Latent Social Roles. I," *Administrative Science Quarterly*, vol. 2, pp. 281–306, 1957.

97. Marvick, D., *Career Perspectives in a Bureaucratic Setting,* University of Michigan Government Study 27, University of Michigan Press, Ann Arbor, Mich., 1954.

98. Bruner, J., *The Process of Education,* Harvard University Press, Cambridge, Mass., 1961.

99. Harbison, F. H., "Management and Scientific Manpower," Paper presented at the Centennial Symposium on Executive Development, School of Industrial Management, Massachusetts Institute of Technology, Cambridge, Mass., Apr. 27, 1961.

100. McGregor, D., "New Concepts of Management," *Technology Review,* vol. 63, no. 4, pp. 25–27, February, 1961.

101. Leavitt, H. J., and T. L. Whisler, "Management in the 1980's," *Harvard Business Review,* vol. 36, pp. 41–48, November-December, 1958.

102. Bradford, L. P., J. R. Gibb, and K. D. Benne (eds.), *T-group Theory and Laboratory Method,* John Wiley & Sons, Inc., New York, 1964.

103. Blake, R. R., and J. S. Mouton, "Developing and Maintaining Corporate Health through Organic Management Training," unpublished paper, University of Texas, Austin, Tex., 1961.

104. Blansfield, M. G., and W. F. Robinson, "Variations in Training Laboratory Design: A Case Study in Sensitivity Training," *Personnel Administration,* vol. 24, no. 2, pp. 17–22, 49, March-April, 1961.

105. Shepard, "Three Management Programs and the Theories behind Them."

106. Sherif, M., and C. Sherif, *Groups in Harmony and Tension,* Harper & Row, Publishers, Incorporated, New York, 1953.

107. Blake, R. R., and J. S. Mouton, "Industrial Warfare to Collaboration: A Behavioral Science Approach," Korzybski Memorial Address, Apr. 20, 1961.

4

*changing patterns of leadership**

The problem is to find a form of association which will defend and protect with the whole common force the person and good of each associate, and in which each, while uniting himself with all, may still obey himself alone, and remain as free as before. This is the fundamental problem[1]

How is it possible to create an organization in which the individuals may obtain optimum expression and, simultaneously, in which the organization itself may obtain optimum satisfaction of its demands?[2]

We have not learned enough about the utilization of talent, about the creation of an organizational climate conductive to human growth. The blunt fact is that we are a long way from realizing the potential represented by the human resources we now recruit into industry.[3]

Santayana once remarked that history has a curious way of repeating itself unless it is understood. The three quotations above seem to lend some support to this apothegm, for the first dates from 1762, while the latter two are taken from recent works on organizational

* First published in *Harvard Business Review* as "Revisionist Theory of Leadership," pp. 26–36, 146–150, January-February, 1961.

theory. All three are concerned with the same pivotal problem, quite possibly the essential problem of the Western tradition: the relationship of the individual and his fulfillment to the demands and constraints of some supra-individual entity.* History has presented us with this explosive legacy, transformed and ossified through many stages and forms, but ultimately reducible to the age-old puzzle of the uneasy balance between individual and organizational needs, between freedom and authority.

On the surface, the conflict seems inevitable. To make matters worse, it probably is deepened by the dominant emphasis in American ideology, which tends to understress principles of authority in favor of exalting the rights of the individual.† Perhaps the best recent demonstration of this riddle is reflected in the past presidential campaign. Both candidates seemed to be promising to create greater national purpose and a strong executive office and also to preserve the eternal verities of freedom and individuality.‡

Organizational and group theories are similarly honeycombed with this duality. For Chester I. Barnard, satisfying the requirements of efficiency (personnel relations) and effectiveness (productivity) is the prime task of the effective manager.[4] Harold J. Leavitt refers to "pyramids and people";[5] Argyris, to the essential conflict between the restricted nature of the formal organization and the individual "self-actualization"; and McGregor, to "theory X" and "theory Y" stressing either the organization's or the individual's goals.

How these seemingly incompatible demands can be fulfilled simultaneously presents today's managers with their most formidable

---

* For a concise, popularly written account from the history-of-ideas point of view, see J. Bronowski and Bruce Mazlish, *The Western Intellectual Tradition: From Leonardo to Hegel,* Harper & Row, Publishers, Incorporated, New York, 1960. Whereas earlier writings deal with the relationship of man to the state, the church, and the nation, our present-day concern appears to be mainly with man and organization. Witness the popularity of the recent polemic of William H. Whyte, Jr., *The Organization Man,* Simon and Schuster, Inc., New York, 1956.

† The best single book on the social and philosophical undertones of this issue is Kenneth D. Benne's *A Conception of Authority,* Bureau of Publications, Teachers College, Columbia University, New York, 1943. My debt to this book is shown throughout.

‡ This was written about the 1960 election. The conflict was as real in 1964, however, with one protagonist advocating "individualism" and the other calling for the "Great Society."

challenge. It is my contention that *effective leadership depends primarily on mediating between the individual and the organization in such a way that both can obtain maximum satisfaction.* But aside from the practical considerations, this conflict and its resolution provide a sharp analytical tool with which we can analyze the tortuous twists and turns, the zigzag fads, and the massive reversals-of-emphasis in leadership theory.

Before we consider some recent books on leadership in organization, we must review recent history and map out, rather arbitrarily, some landmarks which provide the building blocks of contemporary thought.* The two major pillars upon which current theory stands I shall refer to here as "scientific management" and the "human relations" approach.

SCIENTIFIC MANAGEMENT

The first approach, really scientific management *and* bureaucracy, describes a body of theory (prevalent from 1910 to 1935) which tended to view organizations as if they existed without people. Max Weber, the German sociologist, contributed the first fully developed theory of bureaucracy.[6] For Weber, bureaucracy was a descriptive term for characterizing what we now call "formal, large-scale organizations."

Two main influences on Weber probably contributed to his later theory: (1) He was deeply impressed by the growth of industrial organizations in his native country and by his military experience in the German army, and (2) he was concerned with human frailty and the general unreliability of human judgment and passion.

His answer was to develop an apparatus of abstract depersonalization, a system that would rationally dispense solutions without the friction of subjective coloring and human error.

Writing about the same time as Weber (1910) was an American engineer, Frederick W. Taylor, who more than any other individual advanced the professionalization of management.[7] Taylor, the "father of scientific management," attempted to rely on a "third force" that would mediate between man and the organization. Whereas Weber

---

* A more detailed explanation of these factors, and of a great many other points only touched on here, can be found in my article, "Leadership Theory and Administrative Behavior: The Problem of Authority," *Administrative Science Quarterly*, December, 1959.

emphasized the legal domination of "role" or position in a status hierarchy, Taylor stressed the impersonal rationality of measurement.

Loosely speaking, the classical organizational theory developed from these roots. But possibly even more important than those structures which took shape from the theories were the assumptions, both hidden and explicit, which the classical theorists made about "human nature." They created organizations which could be construed as predesignated, omniscient machines, and any deviation from prediction was probably occasioned by the fact that man is regrettably unpredictable and unstable or by outright engineering inadequacies. Henry Ford, the prophet of this earlier age, put it neatly when he said: "All we ask of the men is that they do the work which is set before them." Man was viewed as a passive, inert instrument, performing the tasks assigned to him.

In classical theory, then, the conflict between the man and the organization was neatly settled in favor of the organization. The only road to efficiency and productivity was to surrender man's needs to the service of the bloodless machine.

HUMAN RELATIONS

The second group of theories (thriving from 1938 to 1950) represents what is appropriately called the "human relations" approach. Here people are regarded essentially as if they existed without organizations. It is often jokingly said that the Ford Motor Company has grown so much that if "old Henry" were alive today, there would be no place for him in the organization. What happened to create this change, this shift away from the mechanical resolution typified by Weber and Taylor and characterized by Henry Ford?

What precipitated the change was the formulation of the human relations model, crystallized in the early 1930s by Fritz Roethlisberger and W. J. Dickson in *Management and the Worker*.[8] Now, the dominant focus of organization was transformed from a rational model, free from the friction of man's emotions, to a model which appears less determined (or mechanistic) and hence more unfathomable. That is, the new look in organizational theory took cognizance of unanticipated consequences of organizations—workers' feelings, attitudes, beliefs, perceptions, ideas, sentiments (exactly those elements of passion Weber believed escaped calculation).

Management—partly through the seminal work of several social scientists—began to take seriously not only the formal organizational chart but also the informal and interpersonal contexts. The major assumption of the human relations model was that man could be motivated to work more productively on the basis of fulfilling certain social and psychological needs. This "new look" of organizations was no less "rational" than the earlier machine model, except that man's motivation was a trickier and more elusive concept than the concept of the machine.

The men primarily associated with this pioneering work are Elton Mayo, with his emphasis on the significance of the human group and *affiliation* as the strongest human need; Kurt Lewin, who stressed the promise of democratic and group decision making as well as the importance of *participation* in motivating people; J. L. Moreno, with his emphasis on *positive feelings* and liking as fundamentals in effective group action; and Carl Rogers, the founder of "nondirective therapy," who underscored the need for understanding, *empathy,* and self-realization. These men and their associates, spanning the range of the behavioral sciences, forged the conceptual framework of the human relations approach.

Let us now return to our original focus, the conflict between man and the organization. For the human relations model, there is no essential conflict; satisfying the workers' social and psychological needs is entirely congruent with the organization's goals of effectiveness and productivity. Thus there is no need for an authority to govern between these forces.

The leader is seen as a facilitator in this context, as an agent who helps smooth the pathway toward goal achievement. This model assumes that there is no essential conflict between individual satisfaction and organizational satisfaction, that the former (whether described as "morale," "job satisfaction," or whatever) will lead to greater efficiency, and that authority, insofar as it exists, attempts to facilitate forces which will increase personal satisfaction.

If the reader feels that in my description of the classical and human relations models of organization I have been guilty of exaggeration and of building straw men, he is right. I have not meant to imply that Weber et al. were proposing a "brave new world" where all man's impulses are controlled and dictated wholly by the organization. Nor do I really believe that the human relations proponents were postulating a world of "Huck Finns" actualizing themselves.

I have tried, however, to dramatize in fairly stark terms the key differences between the two models. And when the contrast is made between the broad outlines of the theories, it is clear that the earlier vision elevated the apparatus, the structure, and took man as a given, while the more recent focus on human relations has worked the other side of the street.

Undoubtedly, the building of knowledge goes on in this way. Otto Neurath, the mathematician, once compared the development of science to a man repairing a leaky boat. As he patches up one side while standing on the other, dry side, the latter starts leaking, so he shifts over to the new dry side, and so on and so forth. If such jerky rhythm and patchwork characterize most knowledge building, then in any reversal of emphasis, such as that evoked by the human relations movement, exaggeration of an inattention to some factors inevitably occurs. After any revolution in thought, the debris in terms of fads, unsubstantiated theories, and overstatements has to be put in perspective and incorporated into more formal theory.

THE REVISIONISTS

Accordingly, since 1950 a number of authors have attempted to reconcile and integrate classical and modern organizational theory. I shall refer to these theorists as the "revisionists." In general, they share a common concern for revising the native, unsubstantiated, and unrealistic aspects of the human relations approach without sacrificing its radical departure from traditional theory. These revisionists, only three of whom will be discussed here,* have modified their view for any number of reasons, but the chief ones are probably related to new research findings and some "reality" considerations.

As to research findings, the idea that productivity is strongly correlated with morale turns out to be more a wish than reality. As Rensis Likert put it: "On the basis of a study I did in 1937, I believed that morale and productivity were positively related; that the higher the morale, the higher the production. Substantial research findings since then have shown that this relationship is much too simple."[9]

The fact of the matter is that we are not at all clear today about the relationship of morale to productivity, nor, indeed, are we sure

* Other writers such as Philip Selznick, Mason Haire, William F. Whyte, Rensis Likert, Herbert Shepard, Alvin W. Gouldner, Herbert A. Simon, Abraham Zaleznik, and many others deserve to be mentioned.

that there *is* any interdependence between them; Likert and his associates have found organizations with all the logical possibilities—high morale with low productivity, low productivity with low morale, etc.

Other research findings, as well, have challenged some of the basic assumptions of the human relations model, for example, whether attention to group process factors leads to greater efficiency of group operations, whether the leader who attempts to get close to the men is a more efficient leader, and whether the leader can or should avoid hostile and aggressive attitudes directed toward him by his men.

In general, then, the revisionists recognize clearly that organizational theory must take into account such factors as purpose and goal, status and power differentials, and hierarchy. And, finally, they have come to know that leadership ultimately has to act in ways other than, or in addition to, leading a group discussion.

In this connection, it is particularly illuminating to note that Douglas M. McGregor, an early advocate of human relations and a colleague of Kurt Lewin, began formulating his new theories (which I shall discuss later) after six years of line experience as a college president.

I think McGregor's final note to the alumni and faculty of the college deserves to be printed in full, for its honesty and for its attempt to spell out a significant change in attitude, a change which typifies the prevailing currents in recent organizational theory. Space considerations do not permit this, but the following excerpt captures the main point:

> I believed, for example, that a leader could operate successfully as a kind of adviser to his organization. I thought I could avoid being a "boss." Unconsciously, I suspect, I hoped to duck the unpleasant necessity of making difficult decisions, of taking the responsibility for one course of action, among many uncertain alternatives, of making mistakes and taking the consequences. I thought that maybe I could operate so that everyone would like me, that "good human relations" would eliminate all discord and disagreement.
>
> I couldn't have been more wrong. It took a couple of years, but I finally began to realize that a leader cannot avoid the exercise of authority any more than he can avoid responsibility for what happens to his organization.[10]

The utopian wish to escape conflict, to avoid tough decisions, to create the "happy family," and to stress group and interpersonal factors tinctured the writings of the early human relations students. Yet this was an indispensable antidote, a required emphasis, given the impersonal models of the classical era.

Now the revisionists are concerned with external, economic factors, with productivity, formal status, and so on, but not to the exclusion of the human elements that the traditional theorists neglected. At this point, let us consider the works of some of these revisionists.

PESSIMISTIC RESOLUTION

Robert N. McMurry has presented a cogent case for a Weberian model of organization led at the top by strong and mature personalities. What is needed, he concludes, is "benevolent autocracy."[11] His reasoning is rather interesting. While he believes that "bottom-up" or consultative management (a species of the human relations model) is preferable ideologically, it is not practical, nor is it congruent with what he knows about personality functioning. (He holds a Ph.D. in psychology, and he has had considerable experience as an industrial consultant in this area.)

Managers are hard-driving entrepreneurs, and many of them are stubbornly destructive people. Only about 10 per cent of them *really* believe in the human relations approach. Furthermore, the bureaucratic personality does not want responsibility and independence; it prefers regimentation, routinization, and structure. "It just isn't possible in business," McMurry claims, "to delegate much autonomy below the top echelons of management."[12]

This melancholy view of the "bureaucratic personality" (whatever that truly is) goes on to show that, even if preferred, a human relations viewpoint, which McMurry equates with a radical version of group dynamics, is not really practical.

Benevolent autocracy, on the other hand, gets its results because it rigidly structures and controls the relation of the supervisors to their subordinates. Its major virtue is that it works and makes the best out of the worst. It works because a strong autocrat, who can evoke binding loyalty, respect, and distant worship, dictates, commands, and controls the organization by occupying the only room at the top. "The typical bureaucrat," McMurry says, "is incapable of conceiving or building sound leadership principles on his own initiative."[13]

Let us assume, for the moment, that McMurry's position is valid.

What we see in this approach is a virtuous and popularized psycho-analytic justification for rigid autocracy on the presumptive basis that this is the way people are. McMurry's strong autocrat, whom he does not discuss in any detail (nor does he account for his recruitment or his development), sounds like a nostalgic and romantic image of the old-time entrepreneur: strong, wise, smart, aggressive, the good father, a man utterly independent.

While McMurry's ideas seem to have a close kinship to the classical model of organization, with the resolution of the conflict clearly favoring the organization, he does not hold with the legal and/or scientific rationales of Weber or of Taylor. Rather, he creates the "great man" (the benevolent autocrat).*

When we examine McMurry's thesis more closely, we see that it resolves the conflict between man and the organization by postulating certain human needs which appear to be compatible with a tightly controlled hierarchy: man wants to be dependent, man is incapable of taking responsibility, man needs a strong leader, and so forth. And, most importantly, McMurry appears to assume these needs are fixed and immutable.

Here is where the rub comes. If McMurry's diagnosis of the situation is correct (and I strongly question it, for I have never seen a "typical bureaucrat"), is there no possibility for change, no possibility for producing more mature and able personnel, no possibilty for creating organizational conditions where individuals can take responsibility? McMurry's answers are not very clear.

And if the human relations model has tried to feature man as it would have liked him to be (denying reality), then McMurry appears to be taking man as he is, i.e., denying the possibility of change. Even Freud, known for his tragic view of man and his recognition of the difficulty of human change, once said: "Certainly men are like this, but have you asked yourselves whether they need be so, whether their inmost nature necessitates it?"

UTOPIAN RESOLUTION

Chris Argyris's *Personality and Organization* provides a neat counter-foil to McMurry. For, while they both start with the nature and

---

* For a renewed plea for the great man, see Eugene Jennings, *The Anatomy of Leadership*, Harper & Row, Publishers. Incorporated, New York, 1960.

importance of the human condition within organized settings, they end up with totally opposite diagnoses and conclusions.

Argyris, more than any other recent author, comes directly to grips with the man-organization problem. He feels that the individual's needs and formal organization's demands are basically incompatible. The outcome of this frustration can be inferred and observed through a variety of defense mechanisms and other pathological behaviors on the part of the individual which ultimately lead to the attenuation of the organization's goals and his own mental health.

Let us take a closer look. Argyris postulates a "total personality" signified by a number of dimensions: passivity to activity, dependence to independence, behavioral inflexibility to flexibility, subordinate to superordinate positions, and the like. His model assumes that these dimensions reside on a continuum and that the healthy personality develops along the continuum toward "self-actualization."

In contrast, formal organization is characterized by conditions which stultify this "growth": task specialization, chain of command, unity of direction, span of control, and other repressive and restrictive devices. The picture we get from Argyris, then, is that of an organizational behemoth slowly but surely grinding down the individual's need for growth and actualization.

The contrast between Argyris and McMurry now becomes focused:

For McMurry, most personnel are children (according to Argyris's and his own criteria), and that is the *only way they can and want to be.*

Argyris argues, on the other hand, that that is the way they are, to be sure, but that the organization forces them into this mold and that they can be vastly different.

Argyris does not pretend to solve this dilemma but suggests three possibilities which would enhance work in the industrial organization and thus lead to greater human potentiality: (1) job enlargement, (2) employee-centered leadership, and (3) reality leadership.

These suggestions are not fully developed, nor is their meaning clear. Mason Haire comments, for example, that reality leadership is ". . . flexible leadership tailored to the situation, not too directive, not too non-directive, not too employee-centered, but firm when it should be firm, and like the song in *South Pacific,* broad where it should be broad."[14]

What these proposals lack in clarity, they make up in promise. Through improved "diagnostic skill" on the part of the manager (meaning greater competence in interpersonal relations) and through the use of a staff specialist who will help management and the organization to attain these skills, a fusion process will occur which will help to bring about the optimal actualization of both the organization and the individual.

There are two main difficulties that I have with Argyris's thesis. The first has to do with his notion of "self-actualization," and the second with what he means by "optimal":

1 "Self-actualization" is a term used rather loosely by some psychologists to explain that an individual will "realize his full potential." It is a fuzzy term, drenched in value connotations both of what people are like and of what they can become. I have as much difficulty seeing concretely the self-actualized man as I do seeing the typical bureaucrat.

In order for an abstraction to be meaningful, there must be empirical and experiential validity for it. And when I ask for examples of the self-actualized person, the proponents suggest people like Einstein, Goethe, Spinoza, William James, Schweitzer, Beethoven, and Thoreau.*

The criteria used are not at all obvious, for when they are explored, it is clear that individuals like Lucky Luciano and Adolf Hitler deserve equal consideration as candidates. It is also clear that, for the most part, those public figures who are termed "self-actualizers" rarely fall into the category called "managerial leaders" (or, for that matter, rarely are they alive now!) but fall rather within the area of the arts and sciences.

The heart of the matter is that the assumptions about human behavior made by Argyris and McMurry lead them to construct totally different organizational models. For McMurry, humans are slothful and need leading; for Argyris, humans, if left free, will move naturally toward growth. As for my own belief, I, like Machiavelli, hold that man is both good and evil and that certain conditions in the organization will accentuate the expression of one or the other. Man's goodness and/or badness, this ambivalence, is part of the human condition and, as such, has to be considered in any theory of organization.

* See particularly Abraham Maslow, *Motivation and Personality*, Harper & Row, Publishers, Incorporated, New York, 1954.

2 Related to this point is the idea of "optimizing." This term refers to Argyris's notion that effective leadership can successfully fuse the organization's and the individual's needs in such a way that both will arrive at some peak point.

If this is so, then what becomes of the inevitable conflict between the two? If Argyris is correct, his solution is very similar to the human relations one: greater need-satisfaction on the part of the workers yields higher productivity for the organization. Yet this solution tries to avoid, unsuccessfully, the calculus of values so essential to the problem. For it is clear that simultaneous optimization is not feasible, that there are accommodation and relinquishment of some objectives on both sides, and that the best possible solution will be one wherein neither employer nor employee is at his peak value but where sufficient personnel satisfaction is reached at a viable rate of organizational efficiency.

THE TRAGIC VIEW

Another system of thought, in many ways similar to Argyris's, is now developing; it attempts to deal with the inherent tension between individual needs and organizational demands. It has taken shape in McGregor's recent book, *The Human Side of Enterprise.*

Unlike the quest for optimization, this view seeks no more than a satisfactory resolution. Unlike actualization, it settles for a "commitment toward maturity." Instead of a unidirectional tendency toward growth, it recognizes the basic ambivalence and conflicts within the personality. At its most hopeful, this view asserts that from this basic conflict, new and creative resolutions *may* emerge, but not necessarily. In that sense, this view is tragic.

Taking Peter Drucker's phrase "management by objective," McGregor has recast four principles that outline a new approach to organizational leadership.

1 The starting point is the clear recognition that "if there is a single assumption which pervades conventional organizational theory it is that authority is the central, indispensable means of managerial control."[15] McGregor shows the limitations of various forms of organizational authority based on role or status compared with authority based on task or goal demands, i.e., objectives. Under this concept, management by objective comes about through "target setting," a joint

effort where superior and subordinate attempt to develop the ground rules for work and productivity.*

2 There is the principle of "interdependence," or collaboration between superior and subordinate. This is essential if the two parties are to agree on some mutually satisfactory target.

3 Another principle has to do with the "belief evidenced in practice that subordinates are capable of learning how to exercise effective self-control."[16] Self-control, because it is not governed by external forces, is apparently one of McGregor's indications of maturity.

4 This position asserts the need for "integration," i.e., the bringing together and working through of the differences between individual and organizational needs. This idea was missing in the earlier conclusion of proponents of the human relations approach. According to McGregor: "The central principle which derives from Theory Y is that of integration: the creation of conditions such that members of the organization can achieve their own goals *best* by directing their efforts toward the success of the enterprise."[17]

Self-control, collaboration, and integration—these are the main ingredients of the McGregor approach. Although this approach does not claim theoretical completeness, a number of questions must be raised.

Take the concept of self-control. As I understand it, self-control comes about through the internalization of standards, not through external incentives, and through satisfying tasks, not on the basis of reward-punishment schedules.

But do all or most jobs in industry induce this "instinct of workmanship"? Can we expect assembly-line workers, maintenance personnel, or other workers performing relatively repetitive tasks to be motivated from within? Or is self-control more likely and possible in those jobs where there is a high degree of responsibility and autonomy?

McGregor bases a good deal of his theory on collaboration between subordinate and superior. Like Argyris, he recommends training in human relations to facilitate a process whereby both parties can develop skills and engage in this collaborative activity.

But we have to ask: Can individuals working in organized settings manage to deal and work collaboratively with their superiors?

* For further elaboration, see Douglas M. McGregor, "An Uneasy Look at Performance Appraisal," *Harvard Business Review,* p. 89, May-June, 1957.

Can superiors and subordinates manage to perceive each other as human beings with all their limitations and strengths, as helpers, coordinators, and also as persons with *realistic power?* These questions have to be deferred for empirical investigation, but, right now, we can see no simple solution.

Along these lines, Samuel Goldwyn was reputed to have said to his staff one day: "I want you all to tell me what's wrong with our operation even if it means losing your job!" And this is the point. Authenticity in a relationship which depends on "leveling" and honesty is a prime requisite for collaboration. Authenticity and authority seem almost antithetical to each other. Can they be combined? McGregor feels they can, over a period of time, as long as there is a "commitment to maturity."

But the main strength of McGregor's position is that he, more than other recent students of organizational behavior, has attempted to stress the sticky problem of integration of task requirements with the individual's growth. Role incumbency, personal factors, coercion, external rewards and punishments, and "selling and persuasion" are replaced by objective stress on organizational purpose and attainment. It is the "tragic view" because it comes to grips fully with the calculus of values and because it recognizes the trading, negotiations, and accommodations necessary to realize a true integration.

These brief summaries of the revisionist authors do not do full justice to their ideas; they are far more complex and provisional than I have indicated here. They also provide hope for future research and theory in organizations, work which can illuminate even more clearly the thorny issues which they raise and leave exposed to scientific scrutiny. They are to be praised, moreover, for realizing that leadership is the fulcrum on which the demands of the individual and the demands of the organization are balanced. The classical human relations models minimized this conflict by assuming a similarity between these requirements. At other times, theorists simply dismissed the concept of authority as irrelevant or as nonexistent.

We have a great deal more to learn about leadership. And where the revisionists seem to require particular help is in their theory of the nature of change. Change which facilitates the motivation and skills of managers and their employees and which allows them to develop more authentic human relationships, more true collaboration, and a more reality-centered leadership all within the highly structured organization must always be sought. We must all join the prophet J. H. Leckie, who said: "And whoever would think truly of authority must think reverently of freedom."

NOTES

1. Rousseau, J., *The Social Contract*, tr. by Charles Frankel, Hafner Publishing Company, Inc., New York, 1949, p. I.i.

2. Argyris, C. "The Individual and Organization: Some Problems of Mutual Adjustment," *Administrative Science Quarterly*, p. 24, June, 1957.

3. McGregor, D., *The Human Side of Enterprise*, McGraw-Hill Book Company, New York, 1960, p. vi.

4. Barnard, C. I., *The Functions of the Executive*, Harvard University Press, Cambridge, Mass., 1950.

5. Leavitt, H. J., *Managerial Psychology*, The University of Chicago Press, Chicago, 1958, pp. 257–262.

6. Bendix, R., *Max Weber: An Intellectual Portrait*, Doubleday & Company, Inc., Garden City, N. Y., 1960.

7. Taylor, F. W., *Scientific Management*, Harper & Row, Publishers, Incorporated, New York, 1948.

8. Roethlisberger, F. J., and W. J. Dickson, *Management and the Worker*, Harvard University Press, Cambridge, Mass., 1939.

9. Likert R., "Developing Patterns in Management," *Strengthening Management for the New Technology*, American Management Association, New York, 1955, p. 13.

10. McGregor, D., "On Leadership," *Antioch Notes*, pp. 2–3, May, 1954.

11. McMurry, R. N., "The Case for Benevolent Autocracy," *Harvard Business Review*, p. 82, January-February, 1950.

12. *Ibid.*, p. 12.

13. *Ibid.*, p. 90.

14. Haire, M., "What Price Value?" *Contemporary Psychology*, p. 181, June, 1959.

15. McGregor, *The Human Side of Enterprise*, p. 18.

16. McGregor, D., *Notes on Organizational Theory*, Massachusetts Institute of Technology, Cambridge, Mass., 1957, p. 11. (mimeographed.)

17. McGregor, *The Human Side of Enterprise*, p. 49.

part two

planning and controlling organizational change

What we have all witnessed and participated in in the past two or three decades has been called the "rise of the rational spirit," the belief that science can help better the human condition. The following five chapters describe one indication of this trend, the attempts by behavioral scientists to apply their knowledge (primarily sociological and psychological) toward the improvement of human organizations.

Three assumptions underlie what is to follow: (1) that the proportion of contemporary change that either is planned for, or arises from, deliberate innovation is much higher than in former times; (2) that man's wisdom and mundane behavior are short of perfection insofar as they regulate the fate and selective adaptation of human organization; and (3) that considering the complexity and uncertainty of managing these social systems, behavioral scientists can assist in helping their functioning and effectiveness.*

The following five chapters will deal with the entire range of strategic, methodological, and conceptual issues brought about by this new development in the application of the behavioral sciences.

* I have been aided in this formulation by Wilbert E. Moore's *Social Change*, Prentice-Hall, Inc., Englewood Cliffs, N.J., 1964. Most of the material contained in Chaps. 5 to 7 and in Chap. 9 was included in a keynote address to the International Operational Research Association, Cambridge, England, September 14, 1964.

5

applying behavioral sciences
to planned organizational change

THE NOTATION OF PLANNED CHANGE

Planned change is a method which employs social technology to solve the problems of society. The method encompasses the application of systematic and appropriate knowledge to human affairs for the purpose of creating intelligent action and choices. Planned change aims to relate to the basic disciplines of the behavioral sciences as engineering does to the physical sciences or as medicine does to the biological disciplines.* Thus, planned change can be viewed as a crucial link between theory and practice, between knowledge and action. It plays this role by converting variables from the basic disciplines into strategic instrumentation and programs. In historical perspective, the development of planned change can be viewed as the result of two

* It falls far short of this aim as of today, partly because of the relatively less mature state of the behavioral sciences and even more because of the lack of tradition in the application of the behavioral sciences.

forces: complex problems of modern (organizational) society requiring expert help and the growth and viability of the empirical behavioral sciences. "Behavioral sciences" is a term coined in the period following World War II by the more empirically minded of the profession in order to "safeguard" the social disciplines from the nonquantitative humanists and the depersonalized abstractions of the econometricists. Typically, the field is thought to contain six disciplines: psychology, sociology, anthropology, political science, history, and economics. Planned change, as the term is used here, relies most heavily on the sociological and psychological disciplines.*

The process of planned change involves a *change-agent*, who is typically a behavioral scientist brought in to help a *client-system*, which refers to the target of change.† The change-agent, in *collaboration* with the client-system, attempts to apply *valid knowledge* to the client's problems. These four elements in combination—change-agent, client-system, valid knowledge, and a deliberate and collaborative relationship—circumscribe the class of activities referred to as "planned change." The terms are imprecise and somewhat ambiguous, but it is hoped that their meaning will be clarified through a discussion of concrete illustration.

These four elements also help distinguish planned change from other forms of change. Planned change differs from "technocracy" in that it attempts to implement research results and relies more heavily on the relationship between change-agent and client-system. Planned change differs from most "coercive" change programs in that the change-agent has no formal power over the client-system. Planned change differs from spontaneous and secondary innovations in that it is a conscious and deliberate induction process.

Table 3 presents a typology where eight species of change may be identified. Along the horizontal axis are shown two variables, dichotomized for convenience: mutual goal setting and deliberateness of change. Along the vertical axis, power distribution between the

---

* For a recent inventory of scientific findings of the behavioral sciences, see Berelson and Steiner;[1] for the best single reference on the philosophical foundations of the behavioral sciences, see Kaplan.[2]

† These terms, "change-agent" and "client-system," are awkward, but substitutes which would satisfy aesthetic criteria do not come to mind. And these terms are coming into wider usage. See Lippitt et al.[3] for a fuller account of these terms. See also Bennis et al.[4]

TABLE 3 Typology of change processes

	Collaborative		*Noncollaborative*	
	Mutual goal setting		*Goals set by only one or neither side*	
Power ratio	Deliberate on the part of one or both sides of the relationship	Nondeliberate on the part of both sides	Deliberate on the part of one side of the relation-ship	Nondeliberate on the part of both sides
.5:.5	Planned	Interactional	Technocratic	Natural
1:0	Indoctrina-tional	Socialization	Coercive	Emulative

change-agent and client-system is shown: .5:.5 indicates a fairly equal distribution of power, and 1:0 indicates a tilted or unequal power distribution. (In other words, in a .5:.5 power ratio, each party has the capability of influencing the other; in a 1:0 ratio, only one party is susceptible to influence.) "Valid knowledge" is omitted from the paradigm since it is, for the present, subsumed under "mutual goal setting." In a later section (page 92) we shall return to the question of valid knowledge and its relevance to planned change.

Planned change entails mutual goal setting, an equal power ratio (eventually), and deliberateness on the part of both sides.

Indoctrination involves mutual goal setting and is deliberate, but it involves an imbalanced power ratio. Many schools, prisons, and mental hospitals or other "total institutions"[5] fall into this category.

Coercive change is characterized by nonmutual goal setting, an imbalanced power ratio, and only one-sided deliberateness. Coercive change, as we are using the term, may be exemplified by the thought-control and "brainwashing" practices of the Chinese.[6,*]

* The distinctions between indoctrinational and coercive changes are complex. When all is said and done, hospital administrators and prisoner-of-war commandants may employ similar processes and techniques. There are probably more similarities than would be expected between forms of "acceptable" social influences, such as psychotherapy or teaching, and "unacceptable" forms, such as brainwashing. This paradigm, like all others, creates an ideal and abstract model to which empirical occurrences do not neatly conform. See my typology of change process.[7]

Technocratic change may be distinguished from planned change by the nature of the goal setting. The use of technocratic means to bring about change relies solely on collecting and interpreting data. Technocratic change, then, follows primarily an "engineering" model: the client defines his difficulties as deriving from inadequate knowledge and assumes that this lack of knowledge is accidental or a matter of neglect—not something that is functional to the system itself. The technocrat colludes in this assumption and merely makes and reports his findings.*

Interactional change is characterized by mutual goal setting, a fairly equal power distribution, but no deliberateness on either side of the relationship. (*Unconsciously* either may be committed to changing the other in some direction.) Such changes can be observed among good friends and married couples and in various other nondeliberate transactions among people. Change does occur in such relationships, possibly with beneficial effects, but there is a lack of self-consciousness about it and thus a lack of any definite change-agent–client-system relationship.

Socialization change has a direct kinship with hierarchical controls. Parent-child relationships would be the most obvious example, although the counselor-camper and teacher-pupil relationships would also be instances.

Emulative change takes place for the most part in formal organizations where there is a clear-cut superior-subordinate relationship. Change is brought about through identification with, and emulation of, the "power figures" by the subordinates.

Natural change refers to that class of changes brought about with no apparent deliberateness and no goal setting on the part of those involved in it. Primarily it is a residual category encompassing all accidents, "quirks of fate," unanticipated consequences, spontaneous innovations, etc.

This typology is crude: in nature we can rarely observe these change processes exemplified so neatly. In addition, the distinctions made in it are somewhat arbitrary and certainly not all-inclusive. In order to give the notion of planned change more meaning and substance, it might be useful to compare it with some characteristics of operations research.

* See Gouldner[5] for a full discussion of the technocrat as a change-agent.

PLANNED CHANGE COMPARED WITH
OPERATIONS RESEARCH*

My knowledge of OR stems from three sources: lay articles on OR that one might see in popular periodicals such as *Scientific American* or in Schuchman[9]; more recently, and in preparation for this paper, the basic introductory books recommended by OR professionals; and most of all, the OR "pros" who occasionally sit at the dining table at MIT across from me and talk mysteriously and cheerfully about their work in such a way that I hesitate to ask even the most elementary questions, such as: What do you *really* do? And I ruefully sense a kinship, the mutual incapacity to explain to each other the basic nature of our work. But as I read over some of the literature recently, I was encouraged by certain similarities between OR and what I mean by planned change. It may be useful to discuss these now.

SOME SIMILARITIES BETWEEN
OR AND PLANNED CHANGE

Both are relatively recent *developments*. Both were products of World War II. As I understand it, OR was "founded" just before World War II, developed its status during the war, and flourished thereafter. Planned change, as was true of almost all applied behavioral research, was begun in earnest following World War II and was facilitated and promoted by practitioners who learned during the war that science could be practical.† Later on, I will have more to say about the relationship between science and action, but I should stress at this point that while there have been in the past fruitful liaisons between the behavioral sciences and action in rural sociology, in applied economics, and in clinical psychology—to mention only a few—the quality and quantity of these linkages have taken a significant upturn since World War II. From a pastime, the application of knowledge became a profession.

* This section was written especially for the OR personnel attending the conference for which this paper was written. I have decided to retain it as I think it puts the idea of planned change in better focus.

† Kurt Lewin, one of the leaders of this group, was fond of saying: "There is nothing so practical as a good theory."

Both OR and planned change are problem-centered, as contrasted to the basic disciplines, which emphasize *concept* or *method*. This is a matter of emphasis only, for OR and applied research, in general, have often provided significant inputs to the concepts and methods of their parent basic disciplines. This is not a one-way street.*

Both OR and planned change emphasize improvement and optimization of performance. To that extent, they are *normative* in their approach to problems; that is, they attempt to maximize goals under certain conditions.

Both OR and planned change rely heavily on *empirical science* as their main means of influence. Ellis Johnson points out that the ". . . majority of practitioners of operations research were trained in the basic sciences rather than in engineering or administration."[11] Similarly, practitioners of planned change were mostly trained in psychology, sociology, or anthropology. To both, the old maxim, "Knowledge is power," seems appropriate as a model of action.

Both OR and planned change rely on a relationship with clients based on *confidence* and *valid communication*.

Both OR and planned change emphasize a *systems* approach to problems, meaning essentially an awareness of the interdependencies within the internal parts of the system as well as boundary maintenance with its environment.

Finally, both OR and planned change appear to be most effective when working with *systems which are complex, rapidly changing, and probably science-based*. It will be useful to quote Johnson again on this point:

> In those large and complex organizations for whom once-reliable constants have now become "galloping variables" because of the impact of increasing complexity, trial and error must give way to planning, and acceptance of marginal improvement must give way to an organized search for opportunities to make major shifts in the means of achieving organizational objectives. Today, so many industrial and other organizations are so huge, and major operations are so expensive, that a single major "wrong" decision may be fatal; trial and error becomes "trial and catastrophe."[12]

These characteristics, then—newness, problem orientation, normative approach, basis in science, collaborative relationship with

* See Gouldner[10] for a brilliant exposition on the contributions of applied research to "pure" theory.

clients, systems approach, and effectiveness in rapidly changing environments—show some of the points of common interest and approach of OR and planned change. Let us turn now to some of the differences.

SOME DIFFERENCES BETWEEN OR AND PLANNED CHANGE

Perhaps the most crucial difference between OR and planned change has to do with the *identification of strategic variables,* that is, with those factors which appear to make a difference in the performance of the system under study. The marked difference in the selection of variables must undoubtedly stem from a unique "frame of reference" which leads to divergent problem-definitions. Ackoff and Rivett, for example, classify OR problems in the following way:[13]

Inventory	Routing
Allocation	Replacement
Queuing	Competition
Sequencing	Search

A similar inventory of problems in the planned-change field would probably include the following:

Identification of appropriate mission and values	Utilization of human resources
Human collaboration and conflict	Communication between hierarchical ranks
Control and leadership	Rapid growth
Coping with, and resistance to, change	Management and career development

The divergence of problem-definition leads to the selection of different variables. OR practitioners tend to select economic or engineering variables—most certainly variables which are quantitative and measurable and which appear to be linked directly to the profit and efficiency of the system. Not so of the planned-change practitioners. While there are vigorous attempts to measure rigorously and to conduct evaluation studies, the variables selected tend to be less amenable to statistical treatment and mathematical formulation. Upon even a superficial perusal of some of the literature on planned change and OR, the difference is evident: a significantly lower ratio of tables and mathematical formulas in the former.

An interesting example of the difference in variable identification and selection can be seen if we compare an example of OR with an example of planned change. Ackoff and Rivett, in their introductory chapter, report a case where OR was called on to help a major commercial airline decide how often it should run a class for stewardesses and how large the class should be. This led to a study of the following factors: cost of running the school, forecasts for future requirements, forecasting procedures, expenses and salaries of all personnel, maximum possible average number of flying hours per stewardess that could be obtained, factors in stewardesses' job satisfaction, number of reserve stewardesses required at each air base, number of bases and where they should be located, how flights should be assigned, etc., etc. As Ackoff and Rivett conclude:

> What originally appeared to be a simple and isolated problem turned out to be interconnected with almost all other operating problems of the airline. With extension of the problem the solutions to the parts could be interrelated to assure best overall performance. This avoided a "local" improvement which might result in overall loss of efficiency.[14]

Compare the airline's case with a report of C. Sofer, a sociologist who employs techniques of planned change in his role as a social consultant to a variety of organizations. A small firm called upon him to help in the selection of a senior manager.* This "presenting symptom" led to a series of disclosures and causal mechanisms which Sofer uncovered during a series of talks and meetings with the top management group. The case itself unraveled a complicated cat's cradle of factors including family relationships (among the top management group), fantasies and mistrust among members of the management group, management and career development, selection procedures, etc. Sofer helped the firm overcome these problems through counseling, through devising new organizational structures, through a training program, and through developing improved selection devices. The case was completed in about three years with follow-up consultations from time to time.

When we compare the two cases, what differences appear? First and foremost, as we said before, the problems identified as crucial for the success of the enterprise. In the case of OR, the problems identified appear to be more concrete, more measurable, and more

---

* This example is taken from Sofer's *Organization from Within.*[15] We shall return to this book later on when we take up the strategy and theory of planned organizational change.

obviously related (at least in the short run) to the success of the enterprise, i.e., profits and losses. Sofer identified problems and variables which were less measurable, more subjective in that they were *felt* as problems by the participants, and less obviously linked to the firm's success.

But beyond this, there appear to be some equally marked differences in the two approaches to organizational change. In the example given by Sofer, he concerns himself directly with his relationship to the client, studies this very carefully, and attempts to "use" this relationship both as a diagnostic instrument and as a training device. Even apparently "trivial" decisions, such as whether or not to have lunch with his clients, come under scrutiny:

> My staying to lunch was consistent with what is now a not uncommon Institute [Tavistock] pattern of associating to a certain degree with "clients" outside the professional situation as strictly defined. Not to do so would seem unnatural to them and highly discrepant from the ordinary conventions of business relationships to which they are accustomed. There is also the more positive reason that through such association clients are more likely to remain reality-oriented in their perceptions of the social consultant and to regard him simply as another human being who brings a particular type of expertise to bear on their problems.[16]

So a second major difference between OR and planned organizational change has to do with the *perceived importance* of the *relationship with the client*. The development and maintenance of this relationship are crucial elements in all planned-change programs. And *not solely*, or even most importantly, for "good human relations." Instead, the quality and the nature of the relationship are used as indicators for the measure of progress and as valid sources of data and diagnosis. This is not to say that OR practitioners do not concern themselves with matters of this kind. Undoubtedly they do, and probably the most successful of them operate with great sensitivity toward their clients. But if one looks at what they *say* about their work, there is no question that practitioners of planned change are clearly more *self-conscious* and concerned with the human interactions between client and change-agent.*

---

* It may be that the extent to which science and instrumentation can be used in effecting change is directly and inversely proportional to the use of personal elements of the relationship. We shall return to this speculation later on.

A third major difference can now be identified. In the airline case, the OR practitioner devoted the majority of his time to *research*, to problem solving. In the case Sofer presents, while there was some research effort and data gathering, perhaps slightly more time was spent on *implementation through programs* of one kind or another: counseling, training programs, selection procedures, management development schemes, etc.

A fourth major difference has to do with the degree to which OR and planned-change practitioners take seriously the idea of a *system* in their approaches. Though I said earlier that both were systems-oriented, it seems that this is less stringently upheld in most cases of planned change. Sofer dealt almost exclusively with the top management group, and though the actions taken may have "percolated" down to lower echelons, there is a wide zone of uncertainty regarding the effects of this program on other parts of the system. In a case cited by Argyris[17] which will be discussed later on, we shall see how a particular change program in only one part of the system may create negative disturbances and unanticipated consequences in other parts of the system.*

Two other differences should be mentioned before going on. First, the idea of an interdisciplinary team, so central to OR, does not seem to be a part of most planned-change programs. Usually, only one or two men work on a program. It is true that these change-agents are themselves "generalists" and are capable of bridging disciplines. Yet it is a lack, compared with OR. Many times, for example, an economist or an engineer would add significantly to the change-agent's skills—particularly as they relate to the measurement of effectiveness and performance variables.†

One thing that emerges from a study of these two approaches to organizational change is a realization of the complexity of modern organization. Look through the kaleidoscope one way, and a configur-

---

* See Bavelas and Strauss[18] for a classic case where positive change in one part of a system created such perturbations in adjacent parts of the system that the entire program was scrapped.

† Another factor may be that there is a greater homogeneity of theory among OR practitioners. I do, however, mistrust this observation, no matter how valid it is. My mistrust is based on a fundamental law of social perception; i.e. the "others" always seem more alike to the "outsider" ("Well, they all look alike to me.").

ation of the economic and technological factors appears; tilt it, and nothing appears except the pattern of external environment surrounding the firm. Tilt it again, and what emerges is a pattern of the internal human relations problems confronting the organization. The practitioners of planned organizational change more often than not tend to focus on these last-named human factors and their effects upon the performance of the system.*

A FOCUS OF CONVENIENCE FOR PLANNED ORGANIZATIONAL CHANGE

So far, I have discussed planned change in its broadest context without carefully distinguishing it from applied or developmental research in general. Let us turn to that task now and develop what George Kelley refers to as a "focus of convenience" for planned organizational change. Earlier I defined planned change as a deliberate and collaborative process involving a change-agent and a client-system which are brought together to solve a problem or, more generally, to plan and attain an improved state of functioning in the client-system by utilizing and applying valid knowledge.† This is still a vague and general definition, and I will have to make two aspects of it clearer, particularly the notion of a "collaborative relationship" and that of "valid knowledge."

I have implied in the last section that the outcome of a planned-change effort depends to some extent on the relationship between the client and the change-agent. So let us turn, first, to that. Criteria for evaluating the nature and quality of this relationship can be based on the following questions: (1) How well is the relationship under-

* This is not the place to elaborate on some of the issues involved in the identification of variables *internal* to the system or *external* to the system. This has been one of the pivotal issues dividing economists from social psychologists and other so-called human relationists. It is not unlike the debate Arthur Koestler wrestles with in his distinction between the yogi and the commissar, between those who turn *inward* for insight, for therapy, and for Nirvana and those who turn *outward* to the external environment for the location of variables of promise. This distinction seems to have lost a good deal of its impact recently, almost primarily because of the work of Tavistock groups, particularly Emery and Trist,[19] as well as Wilson,[20] who have brought the *environment* and boundary maintenance back into the mainstream of organizational theory and research.

† For a fuller treatment of some of these ideas, see Bennis.[21]

stood and veridically construed by both parties? (2) To what extent do both parties determine the course and fate of the planned-change program? (3) To what extent is the relationship open to examination and reconstruction by one or both parties? In other words, a deliberate and collaborative relationship can be optimized in a planned-change induction only when the following exist:

1   A joint effort that involves mutual determination of goals
2   A "spirit of inquiry"—a relationship that is governed by data, publicly shared
3   A relationship growing out of the mutual interaction of the client and the change-agent
4   A voluntary relationship between the change-agent and the client, with either free to terminate the relationship after joint consultation
5   A relationship where each party has equal opportunities to influence the other

Now, what is meant by "valid knowledge"? Generally speaking, the criteria for valid knowledge are based on the requirements for a viable applied behavioral science research, that is, an applied behavioral science that

1   Takes into consideration the behavior of persons operating within their specific institutional environments
2   Is capable of accounting for the interrelated levels (person, group, role, and larger organization) within the context of the social change
3   Includes variables that the policy maker and practitioner can understand, manipulate, and evaluate
4   Allows, in specific situations, selection of variables most appropriate to a specific planned change in terms of its own values, ethics, and moralities
5   Accepts the premise that groups and organizations as units are as amenable to empirical and analytical treatment as the individual
6   Takes into account external social processes of change as well as the interpersonal aspects of the collaborative process
7   Includes propositions susceptible to empirical test, focusing on the dynamics of change

The definition and criteria for planned change presented here must be construed as an arbitrary goal and not as an existing reality. To my knowledge, there is no program which fulfills these requirements fully. This realization raises the final consideration in this focus of convenience: the arbitrary selection of those change-agents working on organizational dynamics. This particular class of change-agents was selected not only because of my greater familiarity with their work but for two other factors as well. First, they seem to fulfill the criteria outlined to a greater extent than other change-agents.* Second, equally important in the choice of emphasis is the belief that changes in the sphere of organizations—primarily *industrial*—in patterns of work and relationships, in structure, in technology, and in administration promise to be some of the most significant changes in our society.†

NOTES

1. Berelson, B., and G. A. Steiner, *Human Behavior*, Harcourt, Brace & World, Inc., New York, 1964.

* There are others, from an assortment of fields, who undoubtedly deserve discussion here but who have to be omitted primarily for space reasons. I am referring to the work of rural sociologists such as Loomis, Sower, and Moe (see Rogers[22] for a recent summary of this work); to community and hospital and psychiatric change-agents such as Caplan, Lindemann, S. Levine, L. Howe, B. Paul, D. Klein, the Cummingses, and the Rapoports; to applied anthropologists working on directed culture change such as Holmberg, Goodenough, Kimball, and Barnett; and to those change-oriented economists Hagen, Hoselitz, Rosenstein-Rodan, and Eckaus. Each of these branches implies a research and theoretical tradition which falls beyond the scope of this chapter but which will be touched on briefly in the next section.

† I do not exclude socialist societies from this statement. As Parsons pointed out, the one common feature between so-called capitalist systems and socialist systems is the presence of bureaucracy. In the United States, it is my guess that industrial bureaucracies are the most radical, innovative, and adventurous in adapting new ways of organizing—far ahead, it seems to me, of the government, universities, and labor unions, who appear rigid and stodgy in the face of rapid change. Industrial bureaucracies, at least in the United States, are acting with a verve and imagination regarding rapid change which, I wager, not only will be copied but will be a model for future organizational change programs in other institutions. For an elaboration of this point, see Slater and Bennis.[23]

2. Kaplan, A., *The Conduct of Inquiry*, Chandler, San Francisco, Calif., 1964.

3. Lippitt, R., J. Watson, and B. Westley, *The Dynamics of Planned Change*, Harcourt, Brace & World, Inc., New York, 1958.

4. Bennis, W. G., K. D. Benne, and R. Chin (eds.), *The Planning of Change*, Holt, Rinehart and Winston, Inc., New York, 1961.

5. Goffman, E., *Asylums: Essays on Social Situations of Mental Patients and Other Inmates*, Anchor Books, Doubleday & Company, Inc., Garden City, N.Y., 1961.

6. Schein, E. H., I. Schneier, and C. H. Barker, *Coercive Persuasion: A Socio-psychological Analysis of the "Brainwashing" of American Civilian Prisoners by the Chinese Communists*, W. W. Norton & Company, Inc., New York, 1961.

7. Bennis et al., *op. cit.*, p. 154.

8. Gouldner, A. W., "Engineering and Clinical Approaches to Consulting," in *ibid.*, pp. 643–653.

9. Schuchman, A., *Scientific Decision Making in Business*, Holt, Rinehart and Winston, Inc., New York, 1963.

10. Gouldner, A. W., "Theoretical Requirements of the Applied Social Sciences," in Bennis et al., *op. cit.*, pp. 83–95.

11. Johnson, E. A., "Introduction," in McCloskey and Trefethen (eds.), *Operation Research for Management*, The Johns Hopkins Press, Baltimore, 1954, p. xii.

12. *Ibid.*, p. xix.

13. Ackoff, R. L., and P. Rivett, *A Manager's Guide to Operations Research*, John Wiley & Sons, Inc., New York, 1963, p. 34.

14. *Ibid.*, p. 17.

15. Sofer, C., *The Organization from Within*, Tavistock, London, 1961.

16. *Ibid.*, p. 8.

17. Argyris, C., *Interpersonal Competence and Organizational Effectiveness*, Dorsey Press, Homewood, Ill., 1962.

18. Bavelas, A., and G. Strauss, "Group Dynamics and Intergroup Relations," in Bennis et al., *op. cit.*, pp. 587–591.

19. Emery, F. E., and E. L. Trist, *The Causal Texture of Organizational Environments*, Tavistock Institute, London, 1963. (Mimeographed.)

20. Wilson, A. T. M., "The Manager and His World," paper presented at the Centennial Symposium on Executive Development, Alfred P. Sloan School of Management, Massachusetts Institute of Technology, Cambridge, Mass., April 27, 1961.

21. Bennis, W. G., "A New Role for the Behavioral Sciences: Effecting Organizational Change," *Administrative Science Quarterly*, vol. 8, pp. 125–165, 1963.

22. Rogers, E. M., *Diffusion of Innovations*, The Free Press of Glencoe, New York, 1962.

23. Slater, P. E., and W. G. Bennis, "Democracy Is Inevitable," *Harvard Business Review*, vol. 42, pp. 51–59, 1964.

6

planned organizational
change in perspective

It is important at this juncture to recognize some aspects—theoretical, social, and historical—of planned organizational change which may not be obvious to the general reader and which should be illuminated before going on.

RELATIONSHIP BETWEEN SYSTEMS OF
KNOWLEDGE AND ACTION

It is probably true that the United States has a more practical attitude toward knowledge than any other country.[1] Harrison Salisbury was impressed with the disdain European intellectuals seem to show for practical matters. Even in Russia, he reported, where one would least expect it, there is little interest in the "merely useful."[2] He was struck during his recent travels by the almost total absence of liaison between research and practical application. He saw only one great

95

agricultural experimental station on the American model. In that case, professors were working in the fields. They told Salisbury: "People call us Americans."

There may not be many American professors working in the fields, but they can be found almost everywhere else: in factories,[3] in the government,[4] in underdeveloped countries,[5] in backward areas of the United States,[6] in mental hospitals,[7] in jobs concerned with international matters,[8] in educational systems,[9] and in practically all the institutional crevices that Ph.D. candidates can worm their way into. They are advising, counseling, researching, recruiting, developing, consulting, training, and working for the widest variety of clients imaginable. This is not to say that the deep ambivalence which Americans have toward the intellectual has disappeared—witness the nomination of Goldwater—but it does indicate that the academic intellectual has become *engaged* with spheres of action in greater numbers, with more diligence, and with higher aspirations than at any other time in history.*

The behavioral sciences have been directly implicated in this trend. Recent additions to the vocabulary of the behavioral scientist which can be said to reflect this trend are the following: "clinical sociology," "policy sciences," "action research," "action anthropology," "change-agents," "social catalysts," "human and social engineers," "sociotherapy," "milieu therapy," "knowledge centers," and others. Also, within the past three years, the three primary professional associations of psychology, sociology, and anthropology have been devoting more and more annual meeting time to the problems of application and utilization. The University of Michigan's Institute of Social Research has recently added a third major division under Floyd Mann's direction: a Center for Research on the Utilization of Scientific Knowledge. There has also been a growing literature on planned social change through the uses of the behavioral sciences.[11] Finally, a more subtle trend can be detected: a growing concern with normative planning, with new forms of social architecture, with "realistic" and "vivid" utopias, and with more radical assumptions about social values.[12]

These signs and activities all point in the same direction: toward an emerging *action* role for the behavioral scientist. The *manipulative standpoint,* as Lasswell calls it, is becoming distinguished from the

---

* To the point where other intellectuals have questioned this hyperactivity on behalf of the "establishment." See Baritz[10] for one such statement.

contemplative standpoint and is increasingly ascendant insofar as knowledge utilization is concerned.*

SOME REASONS FOR EMERGENCE OF AN ACTION ROLE

It may be useful to speculate about the reasons for this shift of emphasis, this tendency toward a more direct role of action intervention and manipulation on the part of the behavioral scientist. Most important, but trickiest to identify, are those causative factors bound up in the warp and woof of "our times and age," what is called the *Zeitgeist.* There has been a shift in the intellectual climate of opinion, perhaps aroused by the threat of atomic destruction and reinforced by the exigencies of our time. "The world community of scientists," according to C. P. Snow, "has a final responsibility upon it—a greater responsibility than is pressing on any other body of men. . . . I cannot prove it, but I believe that, simply because scientists cannot escape their own knowledge, they won't be able to avoid showing themselves disposed to good."[15] And from my own vantage point, more and more behavioral scientists are committed to action programs and research projects of significance, pertaining to war and peace, problems of Negro-white relations, problems of economic development, etc. So there seems to be a growing disenchantment with the moral neutrality of the scientists and a willingness to risk scientific method on urgent social problems.

Related to a shift in *Zeitgeist,* and possibly caused by it, may be a general tendency to regard the applied social sciences with less condescension. To be sure, "pure" research still implies that applied research is somehow "impure," but while still not as honorific as pure research, applied or action research does not carry the same opprobrium it once did.

A third reason for this shift of emphasis, perhaps the most crucial, is simply that we know more. Since World War II, when the results

---

* It is beyond the scope of this chapter to discuss some of the *value* implications of the manipulative standpoint. Certainly, science suffers when it becomes the servant of any higher authority. And though it is alive with problems, unless we can discover ways to utilize science to influence policy formulations without losing its soul, science cannot realize its full potential. For excellent discussions of the "value" issues, see Kaplan,[13] whose point of view I follow, and Benne and Swanson.[14]

of applied research could not be brushed aside, and following postwar developments when the impetus for application accelerated, we have obtained large bodies of research and diverse reports on the application of research. Writing in 1951, Merton and Lerner commented on the lack of codified and systematic experience in application.[16] Today, we are in a better position to assess the results and potentialities of applied social sciences precisely because there are more complete reports and analyses available to us.*

Finally, we must mention a fourth factor which has played a key role in the action orientation of the behavioral scientist and which will be of special concern to us throughout this chapter. It has to do with the fate and viability of human organization, particularly as it has been discussed and conceptualized as "bureaucracy." In the past three decades, Weber's vision of organization has been increasingly challenged, not only by practitioners who are facing, firsthand, some problems that current practices and policies of organization cannot cope with, but by the behavioral scientists as well. In the previous section, I presented an inventory of organizational problems as perceived by the managers. A catalog of problems and shortcomings of bureaucracy, as perceived by the behavioral scientists, was presented in Chapter 1. (See footnotes 18 to 27 for examples of these criticisms.) The general meaning of this should be clear: managers and practitioners, on the one hand, and organizational theorists and researchers, on the other, are dissatisfied with the current practices of organizational behavior and are searching for new forms and patterns of organizing work. However wrong their diagnoses may be (and there is no firm evidence for their prognostications), a good deal of activity and many change programs are being generated by this impetus to revise and supplement the idea of bureaucracy in the face of these perceived theoretical and practical exigencies.

---

* While this chapter was being written, for example, the Foundation for Research on Human Behavior sponsored a conference on organizational change and the behavioral sciences. Over a period of five days, about a dozen behavioral scientists and an equal number of industrial practitioners concerned with organizational improvement reported on change programs utilizing the behavioral sciences. These papers are currently being edited for publication by Zand and Buchanan.[17]

THE CONTEMPORARY STATE OF THEORIES OF SOCIAL CHANGE

If there is one truth most social theorists agree on and on which they can arrive at a quick consensus, it is the lack of a viable theory of social change.

Wilbert E. Moore, an intrepid sociologist, says: "The mention of 'theory of social change' will make most social scientists appear defensive, furtive, guilt-ridden, or frightened."[28]

K. D. Naegele, in the introductory essay on social change in the monumental *Theories of Society*, volume II, says: "At the gate of the study of social change stands a host of half-truths."[29]

Finally, Martindale reports an admission made by ". . . leading sociologists that its theory of social change *is the weakest branch of sociological theory*." (Emphasis his.) He goes on to say: "This confession by some of the most highly placed persons in American sociology has usually been accompanied by the assurance that sociology's lack of an adequate theory of change is either of no great importance or merely a temporary state of affairs. One cannot wonder whether this confession and smug reassurance proceed from breathtaking *naiveté* or from an unctuous philistinism."[30]

Sherlock Holmes was reviewing the case. "Then, of course," he reflected, "there is the curious incident of the dog barking in the night."

"But," said Watson, "there was no dog barking in the night."

"Precisely, my dear Watson," said Holmes. "That is what I find so curious."

What Holmes might find so curious about the present state of theories of social change, and what I find so curious, is that they are silent on matters of *directing* and *implementing* change. What I object to—and I include the "newer" theories of neo-conflict,[31] neo-functionalism,[32] and neo-evolutionary theories[33]—is that they tend to identify and explain the dynamic interactions of a system without providing a clue pertaining to the identification of strategic leverages for alteration. They are theories suitable only for *observers* of social change, not theories for *participants* in, or practitioners of, social change. They are theories of *change* and not theories of *changing*.

PREREQUISITES FOR A THEORY OF CHANGING

According to Robert Chin, a theory of changing must do the following:*

1 It must provide levers or handles for influencing the direction, tempo, and quality of change and improvement, i.e., variables that are accessible to control. Variables which "explain" and are casual may be the *least alterable;* hence, a science of "causes" may not be adequate for a theory of changing. For example, we do know that urbanization causes population explosion, but the applied demographer can do little to reduce the birthrate by manipulating the degree of urbanization. Demographers can, however, control contraceptive materials and information. So, most of all, a theory of changing must include manipulable variables.

2 It must take into account the roles of a change-agent and a client-system, each with its own system of values, perceptions, and rights of self-determination; e.g., in the preceding example, it may be that the use of contraceptives in a Catholic country will render this independent variable virtually useless because it conflicts with the client-system's values. In addition to manipulability, then, the variable must not violate the client-system's values.

3 It must take into account the cost of usage. Prohibitive costs may again rule out a highly controllable and value-resonant variable.

4 It must provide a reliable basis of diagnosing the strength and weakness of the conditions facing the client-system.

5 It must account for phases of intervention so that the change-agent can develop estimates for termination of his relationship with the client-system, "self-takeoff" points, etc.

6 It must be able to be communicated with a minimum of distortion to the client-system without destroying its effectiveness.

7 It must be able to assess its own appropriateness for different client-systems.

Such a theory does not now exist, and this probably explains why the change-agents, whom we shall discuss in the next main section (pages 113–119), appear to write like "theoretical orphans." More

* I am deeply indebted to my colleague Robert Chin for many of the ideas presented here. See his articles.[34] See also Gouldner.[35]

important, it also explains why so many change programs based on theories of social change have been inadequate. Let us turn now to some of the most commonly used models of knowledge utilization and assess their effectiveness.

TRADITIONAL CHANGE PROGRAMS BASED ON SOCIAL KNOWLEDGE

The term "traditional" is used here because it describes the thinking of most scholars concerned with adapting knowledge to social-change programs. I would also wager that these so-called traditional ideas are accepted as conventional wisdom and "common sense" in our society. I shall describe eight of the most commonly used programs and then question the assumptions on which they are based.

EIGHT TYPES OF CHANGE PROGRAMS*

It is possible to identify eight types of change programs if we examine their strategic rationales: exposition and propagation, elite corps, human relations training, staff, scholarly consultations, circulation of ideas of the elite, developmental research, and action research.

Exposition and propagation may be the most popular type of change program. It rests almost entirely on the assumption that knowledge is power, that ideas change the world, and that the men who possess "truth" will utimately lead the world. Myrdal presents the case for this method: "My thesis is that, while, there was little participation on the part of social scientists in the actual technical preparation of legislation and still less in administering induced social changes, *their influence was due in the main to their exposition and propagation of certain general thoughts and theories.*"[37] (Emphasis added.)

The *elite-corps* program is based on the idea of "getting the *right man* in the job." Perhaps the best-known contemporary version of this program is the one advocated by C. P. Snow: Get scientists in government.[38] And in a recent issue of *Encounter*, R. H. S. Crossman writes in a manner supporting Snow.[39] The elite-corps idea grows from the justified realization that ideas by themselves (exposition and propagation) do not constitute action and that a strategic *role* (such as that

---

* For a fuller exposition of these ideas, see Bennis.[36]

of a civil servant or a member of Parliament) is a necessity for ideas to be implemented.

A version of the elite-corps idea can be observed in a good deal of the writings in the human relations training field. It is similar to the elite-corps idea in that it depends upon the knowledge and skills of men in power positions; its difference lies in the type of knowledge it requires of the elite. The program of *human relations training* hopes to inculcate key executives with the necessary insight, wisdom, and diagnostic sensitivity. In other words, human relations training attempts to translate concepts from the behavioral sciences so that they take on personal referents for the executives.[*]

The idea of *staff* is to provide a source of intelligence within the client-system such that the appropriate intelligence is available when needed. As Myrdal says, the strategy of the staff idea ". . . is to observe and to analyze actual situations and short and long term developments and, on this basis, to plan rationally the immediate policy reactions to events of a government, an interest organization, or a business firm."[42] Examples of staff are the work of social anthropologists advising military governors after World War II, staff work in large organizations, etc.[†]

By *scholarly consultations*, Zetterberg[44] means a procedure whereby science can be made useful to clients. It includes exploratory inquiry, scholarly understanding, scholarly confrontation, discovery of solutions, and, finally, scientific advice to the client. It is an unusual approach when compared with the others. For rather than taking a research orientation toward the client's problems, the adviser considers the problem in terms of available sociological theory and literature and deduces solutions from combinations of propositions already known.

Circulation of ideas to the elite is a strategy based on a very early idea in American history. The American Revolution, according to historians, was partly triggered by the Council for Correspondence, a remarkable chain letter linking the recipient rebels to a program of action. The idea is simple: "If you want to change things, then get

[*] In addition to human relations training, some advise forms of psychotherapy and psychoanalysis for the translation of theory into practice. See Levinson et al.[40] and Holt.[41]

[†] For a survey of the role of staff in administration, see Barnett.[43]

your ideas to the people in power, or people who influence someone who can influence someone in power."*

The idea of a *developmental research,* as a counterpart to the developmental research of the research and development labs, was advanced recently by Mason Haire:

> The one thing which, more than any other, seems to keep the social sciences from being socially useful is the lack of developmental research. By "developmental research" I mean a kind of work midway between the rarefied aloofness of laboratory tests of theoretical propositions and the somewhat pebble-picking particularity of applied research. It is the research that asks the question, "If this proposition is true in principle, how does it find expression in the operational context of action?" . . . Developmental research would be directed exactly toward the problem of helping people to see, given new theoretical insights, *how* something could be done substantially differently or better.[46]

Like Zetterberg's scholarly-confrontation method, developmental research has to do with seeing whether an idea can be brought to an engineering stage. Unlike the former method, developmental research is directed toward a particular problem, not necessarily a client, and is concerned more with implementation and program. (Incidentally, I would wager that *no* developmental research is being done today in the behavioral sciences.)

Action Research (or applied research) is the last program we shall discuss that aims to apply the behavioral sciences to improve systems performance. The term was coined by Kurt Lewin, and the best statement of its methods and aims can be found in an article by three of his followers.[47] "It is a field," according to them, "which developed to satisfy the needs of the socio-political-individual who recognizes that, in science, he can find the most reliable guide to effective action, and the needs of the scientist who wants his labors to be of maximal social utility as well as of theoretical significance."

In all ways but one, action research is identical to the traditional functions of applied research; that is, it is research undertaken to solve a problem for a client. What distinguishes action research is the nature

* A recent example of this strategy is *The Liberal Papers,* a series of papers inspired by a group of intellectuals who communicated their ideas to a receptive congressional audience.[45]

of the roles of the researchers and subjects in the research endeavor. In the typical applied-research project, the roles are differentiated and static. In action research, the roles may change and reverse. For example, it is not uncommon in action-research programs for the subjects to become researchers and for the researchers to engage in action steps in place of the subjects who they are studying.

CRITIQUE OF THE EIGHT CHANGE PROGRAMS

Although the the eight change programs differ in terms of their objectives, their values, and their means of influence, and although each has its own programmatic implications, they are similar in wanting to use knowledge to gain some socially desirable end. Each seems successful or promising, if current usage is any criterion, and each has its avid supporters and detractors. Intrinsic to the eight programs, I believe, is a bias or flaw which can be questioned and which probably weakens its full impact. Four biases are particularly visible.

Rationalistic Bias: No Implementation or Programs

Present to a greater or lesser degree in all the schemes is the belief that knowledge equals power. Obviously there is some truth in this. But why should the dissimenation of knowledge by itself lead to influence, particularly if the knowledge affects deeply held motives, beliefs, and attitudes, particularly those reinforced by group norms and power blocs? I do not want to minimize the importance of facts and knowledge—certainly, they do play a role in social change; yet in most of the strategies discussed, there is an almost total reliance on rationality. Knowledge *about* something does *not* lead automatically to intelligent action, no matter how "right" the idea. Intelligent action requires *commitment* and *programs* as well as truth.

Technocratic Bias: No Spirit of Collaboration

Related to the rationalistic bias is the assumption that if a program is presented, the client can carry it out with dispatch. We see this most clearly in the strategies related to applied research: scholarly consultation and developmental and applied research. Zetterberg, for example, says: "The client is presented with a translation of the theoretical solutions into the client's language and with references to his specific situation. In short he is told what to do."[48]

But this technocratic approach to planned change rarely works without some form of collaboration between the change-agent and the client. And the degree to which collaboration is required is probably related to the type of change anticipated: the more it involves socio-psychological factors—as opposed to technical—the more collaboration is required. Elliott Jaques is worth quoting in this regard:

> In practice the problem usually boils down to the relationship between the "expert" and the administrator or the executive responsible. We already know how difficult this relationship becomes even in the domain of the physical sciences and engineer; how much farmers, for example, often resent the intrusion of the government agriculture expert with his new and supposedly superior methods. *How much more difficult does the problem of establishing a satisfactory relationship become, however, where not crops but the changing of human behavior itself becomes the target of scientific endeavor?*[49] (Emphasis added.)

F. L. W. Richardson, the action anthropologist, puts it more strongly: "One conclusion, however, is certain; namely, a social scientist's success in an action role, similar to that of a practicing psychiatrist, often depends more on interpersonal than on rational skills."[50]

Why are collaboration and interpersonal skills so necessary in facilitating social change? Because any significant change in human organization involves a rearrangement of patterns of power, association, status, skills, and values. Some individuals and groups may benefit; others may lose. Some may view an anticipated change as "threatening" and reject it, and others may view it as "enhancing" and embrace it.* In any case, change typically involves risk and fear. The trust and support of the change-agent during the period of greatest stress may help to "ready" the client for the change.

Another crucial reason lies at the foundation of this need for collaboration. It has to do with important value differences between change-agents and clients. For the most part, clients are practitioners, managers, men of action. Change-agents tend to be academicians, scholars, researchers, men of contemplation. Inevitably, there are bound to be value conflicts between these two orientations; inevitably there are bound to be ambivalences, false starts, worries, and concerns about the other party to the relationship. Without an opportunity for these fears and worries to be discussed and "worked through," without

* For discussions of "resistance to change," see Mann & Neff.[51]

an opportunity for each party to "test" the competence and confidence of the other, it is doubtful whether the change program can realize its full intent.*

Individualistic Bias: No Organization Strategy

The trouble with those strategies associated with C. P. Snow and G. Myrdal as well as human relations training programs is their assumption that if men in power possess the right ideas they will act in accordance with those ideas. Undoubtedly there is some truth in this, as there is in the rationalistic strategy. But it denies completely the organizational *forces* and *roles* surrounding the individual; in short, this strategy tends to place altogether too much reliance on the individual.

There is a great deal of evidence which questions this assumption. For example, there is simply no guarantee that a wise individual who attains power will act wisely. The noted political scientist Hans Morgenthau (in his review of a book written by an intellectual economic historian who took a highly placed job with the U.S. State Department) writes:

> How could such a mind produce such trash? The answer lies in the corruption of power and the defenselessness of the intellectual in the face of it. The intellectual as a social type is singularly deprived of the enjoyment of power and eminently qualified to understand its importance and what it means not to have it. Thus campuses and literary circles abound with empire builders, petty politicians, and sordid intriguers—all seekers after power, the substance of which eludes them.

* Perhaps the most glaring example in recent history of the failure to develop (or even consider!) the required form of collaboration between client and change-agent can be seen in the early work of F. W. Taylor and his colleagues in "scientific management." To this day, in some government bureaus, stopwatches—the hated emblem of the "time-and-motion boys"—are not allowed to be used by a government industrial engineer. The trouble with Taylor was that he was not *scientific* enough; that is, he did not consider the relationship between the engineer and the client as falling within the domain of scientific management. Another corollary to this can be seen within the Freudian psychoanalytic movement. In the early days, Freud considered it adequate to examine the unconscious of his patients and to tell them what he learned. In some cases, he even analyzed dreams by mail. It turned out that this was not the way to help patients, at least not permanently. Later on, the analysis of relationship and resistance became the hallmark of successful treatment.

When an intellectual finds himself in the seat of power he is tempted to equate the power of his intellect with the power of his office. As he could mould the printed word to suit his ideas so he now expects the real world to respond to his actions.[52]

Perhaps *role corrupts:* both the role of powerlessness and the role of power. For example, Unilever Ltd., if I understand their management development program, aims at early selection of talent, an elite corps of bright young men. But mindful of the fact that bureaucratic norms may corrupt or mistrain this cadre, Unilever attempts to accelerate their progress through the bureaucratic structure and rush them to the top.[53]

The point of all this is that there is no guarantee that placing certain types of people in management—or training them or psychoanalyzing them or making scientists of them—leads to more effective action. Psychoanalytic institutes, according to Clara Thompson, are stricken with the same human predicaments as any other organization;[54] scientists act like administrators—or even more so—when they gain power,* and graduates of human relations training programs tend to act like nonalumni shortly after their return to their organizational base.†

The staff idea, proposed by Myrdal, is limited by the unresolved tensions in the staff-line dilemma noted by students of organizational behavior. This solution ignores, as well, something touched on earlier: the conflicts derived from the role of the intellectual working in bureaucratic structures. Merton catalogs some of these conflicts in his treatment of the problem.[57] He also suggests that the high turnover of expert personnel in public bureaucracies not only is a matter of *client* dissatisfaction but also is the "product of the cumulative frustrations experienced by the intellectual who has been previously conditioned to a sense of personal autonomy and cannot abide the visible constraints imposed by a formal organization."[58]

For all these reasons—organization norms, influence of role pressures, naïveté with respect to power, fade-out effects, value collisions—the idea of getting the right man in the job, the elite

---

* See Jungk[55] for an example of how scientists, such as Oppenheimer, acted more like administrators, forsaking personal and scientific moral imperatives for imperatives of the organization, against their colleagues' expectations.

† This "fade-out" effect has been frequently commented upon and studied. See Fleishman and Argyris.[56]

strategy, has serious drawbacks, primarily because it focuses on the individual and not on the organization.

Insight Bias: No Manipulability

Many of these strategies, but particularly those associated with human relations training programs, reflect a bias held by most clinical psychologists: insight leads to more effective functioning. This is a more sophisticated solution than the purely rationalistic mode, for insight, though usually ill-defined, implies an emotional as well as an intellectual grasp of an issue. My major quarrel is not with the formulation that insight leads to change, though this is presently being challenged by some.[59] What is more serious in the insight approach is the lack of provision of strategic variables, i.e., those accessible to control. How does personal insight get translated into effective programs of change? It is not obvious that insight leads directly to sophistication in rearranging social systems or in making strategic organizational interventions. If anything, planned change depends on the policy maker's controlling the relevant variables. Insight provides these as far as personal manipulation goes, but the question still remains: How can that lead directly to the external manipulation of social factors?

NOTES

1. Lazarsfeld, P. F., in collaboration with S. S. Spivack, *Observations on Organized Social Research in the United States: A Report to the International Social Science Council,* Columbia University Press, New York, 1961. (Mimeographed.)

2. Salisbury, H. E., *To Moscow and Beyond,* Harper & Row, Publishers, Incorporated, New York, 1960, p. 136.

3. Argyris, C., *Interpersonal Competence and Organizational Effectiveness,* Dorsey Press, Homewood, Ill., 1962; Blake, R. R., and J. S. Mouton, *The Managerial Grid,* Gulf Publishing Company, Houston, 1964; Burns, T., and G. M. Stalker, *The Management of Innovation,* Quadrangle, Chicago, 1962; Jaques, E., *The Changing Culture of a Factory,* Tavistock, London, 1951; Lawrence, P., *The Changing of Organizational Behavior Patterns,* Harvard University Press, Cambridge, Mass., 1958; Rice, A. K. *The Enterprise and Its Environment,* Tavistock, London, 1963; Spencer, P., and C. Sofer, "Organizational Change and Its Management," *The Journal of Management Studies,* vol. 1, pp. 26–47, 1964; Walker, C. R., *Modern Technology and Civilization,* McGraw-Hill Book Company, New York, 1962; "Major Issues in Modern Society," in R. J. Smith (ed.), *Human Organization,* 1962, p. 21.

4. Barnett, H. G., *Anthropology in Administration*, Row, Peterson & Company, Evanston, Ill., 1956; Hilsman, R., *Strategic Intelligence and National Decisions*, The Free Press of Glencoe, New York, 1956.

5. Foster, G. M., *Traditional Cultures and the Impact of Technological Change*, Harper & Row, Publishers, Incorporated, New York, 1962; Goodenough, W. H., *Cooperation in Change*, Russell Sage Foundation, New York, 1963; Hagen, E., *On the Theory of Social Change*, Dorsey Press, Homewood, Ill., 1962; McClelland, D. C., *The Achieving Society*, D. Van Nostrand Company, Inc., Princeton, N.J., 1961; Spicer, E. H. (ed.), *Human Problems in Technological Change*, Russell Sage Foundation, New York, 1952; Tax, S., "The Uses of Anthropology," in S. Tax (ed.), *Horizons of Anthropology*, Aldine Publishing Co., London, 1964; Almond, G. A., and S. S. Coleman (eds.), *The Politics of the Developing Areas*, Princeton University Press., Princeton, N.J., 1960.

6. Kimball, S. T., and M. Pearsall, *The Tallageda Story*, University of Alabama Press, University, Ala., 1954.

7. Stanton, A. H., and M. S. Schwartz, *The Mental Hospital*, Basic Books, Inc., Publishers, New York, 1954; Caudill, W., *The Psychiatric Hospital as a Small Society*, Harvard University Press, Cambridge, Mass., 1958.

8. Klineberg, O., *The Human Dimension in International Relations*, Holt, Rinehart and Winston, Inc., New York, 1964.

9. Miles, M. B. (ed.), *Innovation in Education*, Bureau of Publications, Teachers College, Columbia University, New York, 1964.

10. Baritz, L., *Servants of Power*, Wesleyan University Press, Middletown, Conn., 1960.

11. Bennis, W. G., A New Role for the Behavioral Sciences: Effecting Organizational Change," *Administrative Science Quarterly*, vol. 8, pp. 125–165, 1963; Freeman, H. E., "The Strategy of Social Policy Research," *The Social Welfare Forum*, pp. 143–160, 1963; Zetterberg, H., *Social Theory and Social Practice*, Bedminster Press, New York, 1962; Gibb, J.R., and R. Lippitt (eds.), "Consulting with Groups and Organizations," *The Journal of Social Issues*, vol. 15, 1959; Leeds, R., and T. Smith (eds.), *Using Social Science Knowledge in Business and Industry*, Richard D. Irwin, Inc., Homewood, Ill., 1963; Likert, R., and S. P. Hayes, Jr. (eds.), *Some Applications of Behavioral Research*, UNESCO, Paris, 1957; Glock et al., *Case Studies in Bringing Behavioral Science into Use*, Institute of Communication Research, Stanford, Calif., 1960.

12. Friedmann, J., *Issues in Planning Theory*, Massachusetts Institute of Technology, Cambridge, Mass., 1963 (mimeographed); Mead, M., "Toward More Vivid Utopias," *Science*, vol. 126, pp. 957–961, 1957; Mumford, L., *The Transformation of Man*, Harper & Row, Publishers, Incorporated, New York, 1956; Myrdal, G., *Value in Social Theory*, Harper & Row, Publishers, Incorporated, New York, 1958; Perlmutter, H. V., "On Social Architecture," Yale University, New Haven, Conn., 1961.

13. Kaplan, A., *The Conduct of Inquiry*, Chandler, San Francisco, Calif., 1964, chap. 10 (see especially sec. 45).

14. Benne, K. D., and G. Swanson (eds.), "Values and Social Science," *The Journal of Social Issues*, vol. 6, 1950.

15. Snow, C. P., "The Moral Un-neutrality of Science," in P. C. Obler and H. A. Estrin (eds.), *The New Scientist*, Anchor Books, Doubleday & Company, Inc., Garden City, N.Y., 1962.

16. Merton and Lerner, *op. cit.*, p. 56.

17. Zand, D., and P. Buchanan (eds.), *Organization Development: Theory and Practice*, in press.

18. Argyris, C., *Personality and Organization*, Harper & Row, Publishers, Incorporated, New York, 1957; Argyris, C., *Integrating the Individual and the Organization*, John Wiley & Sons, Inc., New York, 1964.

19. Argyris, *Interpersonal Competence and Organizational Effectiveness;* Whyte, W. H., Jr., *The Organization Man*, Simon and Schuster, Inc., New York, 1956.

20. Likert, R., *New Patterns of Management*, McGraw-Hill Book Company, New York, 1961; McGregor, D., *The Human Side of Enterprise*, McGraw-Hill Book Company, New York, 1960.

21. Gouldner, A. W., "Organizational Analysis," in R. K. Merton, L. Broom, and L. S. Cottrell, Jr. (eds.), *Sociology Today: Problems and Prospects*, Basic Books, Inc., Publishers, New York, 1959, pp. 404–412; Roethlisberger, F. J., and W. J. Dickson, *Management and the Worker*, Harvard University Press, Cambridge, Mass., 1941.

22. Shepard, H. A., "Three Management Programs and the Theories behind Them," in *An Action Research Program for Organization Improvement*, Foundation for Research on Human Behavior, Ann Arbor, Mich., 1960; Shepard, H. A., "Changing Interpersonal and Intergroup Relationships in Organizations," in J. March (ed.), *Handbook of Organization*, Rand McNally & Company, Chicago, in press; Slater, P. E., and W. G. Bennis, "Democracy Is Inevitable," *Harvard Business Review*, vol. 42, pp. 51–59, 1964.

23. Evan, W., "Due Process of Law in Military and Industrial Organizations," *Administrative Science Quarterly*, pp. 187–207, 1962.

24. Emery, F. E., and E. L. Trist, *The Causal Texture of Organizational Environments*, Tavistock Institute, London, 1963. (Mimeographed.)

25. Blake, R. R., H. A. Shepard, and J. S. Mouton, *Intergroup Conflict*, Foundation for Research on Human Behavior, Ann Arbor, Mich., 1964.

26. Argyris, *Integrating the Individual and the Organization;* Blake, R. R., and Mouton, J. S., *The Managerial Grid*, Gulf Publishing Company, Houston, 1964; Likert, *op. cit.*

27. Leavitt, H. J., "Unhuman Organizations," in H. J. Leavitt and L. Pondy (eds.), *Readings in Managerial Psychology*, The University of Chicago Press, Chicago, 1964, pp. 542–556; Leavitt, H. J., and T. L. Whisler, "Management in the 1980's," *Harvard Business Review*, pp. 41–48, 1958.

28. Moore, W. E., "A Reconsideration of Theories of Social Change," *American Sociology Review*, vol. 25, pp. 810–818, 1960.

29. Naegele, K. D., "Introduction," in T. Parsons, E. Shils, K. D. Naegele, and J. R. Pitts (eds.), *Theories of Society*, vol. II, The Free Press of Glencoe, New York, 1961, p. 1207.

30. Martindale, D., "Introduction," in G. K. Zollschan and W. Hirsch (eds.), *Explorations in Social Change*, Houghton Mifflin Company, Boston, 1964, p. xii.

31. Coser, L., *The Functions of Social Conflict*, The Free Press of Glencoe, New York, 1956; Dahrendorf, R., "Toward a Theory of Social Conflict," in W. G. Bennis, K. D. Benne, and R. Chin (eds.), *The Planning of Change*, Holt, Rinehart and Winston, Inc., New York, 1961, pp. 445–451.

32. Boskoff, A., "Functional Analysis as a Source of a Theoretical Repertory and Research Tasks in the Study of Social Change," in Zollschan and Hirsch, *op. cit.*, pp. 213–243.

33. Parsons, T., "Evolutionary Universals in Society," *American Sociology Review*, vol. 29, pp. 339–357, 1964.

34. Chin, R., "Models and Ideas about Changing," Paper Given at Symposium on Acceptance of New Ideas, University of Nebraska, November, 1963; Chin, R., "The Utility of System Models and Development Models for Practitioners," in Bennis *et al.*, *op. cit.*, pp. 201–214.

35. Gouldner, *op. cit.*

36. Bennis, *op. cit.*

37. Myrdal, *op. cit.*, p. 26.

38. Snow, C. P., *Science and Government*, Harvard University Press, Cambridge, Mass., 1961.

39. Crossman, R. H. S., "Scientists in Whitehall," *Encounter*, vol. 23, pp. 3–10, 1964.

40. Levinson, H., C. R. Price, K. J. Munden, H. J. Mandl, and C. M. Solley, *Men, Management, and Mental Health*, Harvard University Press, Cambridge, Mass., 1962.

41. Holt, H., "The Psychoanalytic Psychiatrist as a Management Consultant," in G. Fisk (ed.), *The Frontiers of Management Psychology*, Harper & Row, Publishers, Incorporated, New York, 1964, pp. 68–84.

42. Myrdal, *op. cit.*, p. 29.

43. Barnett, *op. cit.*

44. Zetterberg, *op. cit.*

45. Roosevelt, J. (ed.), *The Liberal Papers*, Anchor Books, Doubleday & Company, Inc., Garden City, N.Y., 1962.

46. Haire, M., *Why Have the Social Sciences Contributed So Little to Industrial Relations?* University of California, 1962. (Mimeographed.)

47. Chein, I., S. Cook, and J. Harding, "The Field of Action Research," *The American Psychologist*, vol. 3, pp. 43–50, 1948.

48. Zetterberg, *op. cit.*, p. 136.

49. Jaques, E., "Social Therapy: Technocracy or Collaboration?" in Bennis *et al.*, *op. cit.*, pp. 162–168.

50. Richardson, F. L. W., "Foreword," in Smith, *op. cit.*, p. 61.

51. Mann, F. C., and F. W. Neff, *Managing Major Change in Organizations*, Foundation for Research on Human Behavior, Ann Arbor, Mich., 1961; Zander, A., "Resistance to Change: Its Analysis and Prevention," in Bennis *et al.*, *op. cit.*, pp. 543–548.

52. Morgenthau, H., "The Sweet Smell of Success," *N.Y. Review of Books*, vol. 2, p. 6, 1964.

53. Wilson, A. T. M., *op. cit.*

54. Thompson, C., "A Study of the Emotional Climates of Psychoanalytic Institutes," *Psychiatry*, vol. 21, pp. 42–52, 1958.

55. Jungk, R., *Brighter than a Thousand Suns*, Grove Press, Inc., New York, 1958.

56. Argyris, C., *Interpersonal Competence and Organizational Effectiveness;* Fleishman, E. A., "Leadership Climate, Human Relations Training, and Supervisory Behavior," *Personnel Psychology*, pp. 205–222, 1953.

57. Merton, R. K., *Social Theory and Social Structure*, The Free Press of Glencoe, New York, 1949.

58. *Ibid.*, p. 174.

59. Hobbs, N., "Sources of Gain in Psychotherapy," *The American Psychologist*, vol. 17, pp. 741–747, 1962.

7

change-agents,
change programs, and strategies

The foregoing chapter outlined some of the biases that inhere in traditional models of social change. They will serve as terms of comparison and evaluation in what follows. Now with these preliminary considerations and background factors out of the way, let us turn directly to the main business at hand.

THE CHANGE-AGENTS

In the October 7, 1963, edition of the *New York Times*, a large classified ad was printed announcing a search for "change-agents." It read:

WHAT'S A CHANGE AGENT?
A result oriented individual able to accurately and
quickly resolve complex tangible and intangible
problems. Energy and ambition necessary for
success. . . .

113

Whatever doubts I had had up to this point about Madison Avenue's gifts for simplification and polish were lost. For I realized then and do now that any description of a change-agent I would advance would have to include more factors than "energy and ambition," though these two are probably required.

The change-agents I have in mind are *professionals,* men who, for the most part, have been trained and who hold doctorates in the behavioral sciences. Many of them hold university posts, and others work as full-time consultants, but they owe their professional allegiance to one of the behavioral science disciplines.

While change-agents are not a very homogeneous group, it may be useful to sketch out in broad terms some of their similarities:

1 *Their assumptions* They take for granted the *centrality of work* in our culture, to men and women at work in highly organized, instrumental settings like industries, hospitals, and universities. They are concerned with *organizational effectiveness,* however intangibly defined or measured. So they are concerned with improvement, development, and enhancement. While their prescriptions vary, their diagnosis of organizational health pivots on *interpersonal* or *group relationships* and the implications of these on changes in technology, structure, and tasks. Although they are aware of these three nonpersonal factors and occasionally focus on them, their main preoccupation is with people and the processes of human interaction.* Along these lines, it is important to point out that they are not interested in changing (or transferring) *personnel* but in the relationships, attitudes, perceptions, and values of the existing personnel.

2 *Their roles* They play a variety of roles as change-agents: researchers, trainers, consultants, counselors, teachers, and, in some cases, line managers. Some specialize in one, but for the most part they shift and switch from one to another.

Frequently, the change-agents are not actual members of the client-system; in other cases, they are. There are some who say that significant change depends on the impetus generated by an external agent.[2] They argue that only a skilled outsider-consultant can provide the perspective, detachment, and energy so necessary to effect a true

---

* Contrast this with another approach, of an engineering type, proposed by Chapple and Sayles,[1] where task, structure, and technology are utilized as independent variables.

alteration of existing patterns. Advocates of the internal model take the opposite stand. They argue that the insider possesses the intimate knowledge of the client-system (and the power to legitimize) that the external change-agent lacks. In addition, the internal change-agent does not generate the suspicion and mistrust that the outsider often does. His acceptance and credibility are guaranteed, it is argued, by his organizational status.*

Change-agents tend to be self-conscious about their roles and their role changes vis-à-vis their clients. They go into instructive detail describing their interventions.

3 *Their interventions* Change-agents intervene at different structural points in the organizations (person, group, intergroup, etc.) and at different times. Blake and Mouton[3] list nine major kinds of interventions which facilitate organizational development:

1 Discrepancy: calls attention to a contradiction in action or attitudes
2 Theory: research findings or conceptual understanding which helps the client-system gain perspective
3 Procedural: a critique of existing methods of solving problems
4 Relationships: focuses attention on tensions growing out of group and interpersonal relationships
5 Experimentation: setting up comparisons and testing of several actions *before* a decision is made
6 Dilemma: identifies significant choice points or exigencies in problem solving and attempts to understand assumptions and search for alternatives, if necessary
7 Perspective: an attempt to provide situational and historical understanding of problems through a detached study
8 Organization structure: identifies source of problem as bound in the structure and organizational arrangements
9 Cultural: focuses on an examination of traditions

4 *Their normative goals* These are stated with varying clarity and specificity, but there is unmistakable evidence that their goals

* Thus, General Electric in its change program uses internal change-agents (to gain credibility and to eliminate the typical fear that behavioral scientists are "headshrinkers," "brainwashers," etc.). However, these internal men are not placed within their own company departments.

imply a particular vision of man and organization and a particular set of values which lay the base for this version.

To a large extent, these normative goals are aroused by dissatisfactions with the effectiveness of bureaucratic organizations, set forth on page 6. These objections were probably most cogently articulated and given the greatest force by the writings of McGregor, Likert, and Argyris.[4] These three books are often cited as evidence, and they are used by change-agents as the foundation for various change programs.

Though each change-agent has in mind a set of unique goals, based on his own theoretical position and competencies as well as on the needs of the client-system, roughly speaking there are some general aims which most change-agents would agree to. Argyris provides a graphic model which can serve us as an example. In Fig. 2, he shows (at the far left) the purported value system which dominates modern organizations; i.e., bureaucratic values. These values, basically impersonal and task-oriented and denying humanistic and democratic values, lead to poor, shallow, and mistrustful relationships between members of the organization. Argyris calls these "nonauthentic" relationships and says that they tend to be "phony," unhelpful, and basically incomplete; that is, they do not permit the natural and free expression of feelings which often must accompany task efforts. These nonauthentic relationships lead to a state which Argyris calls "decreased interpersonal competence," a result of the shallow and threatening state of the relationships. Finally, without effective interpersonal competence among the managerial class, the organization is a breeding ground for mistrust, intergroup conflict, rigidity, etc., which in turn leads to a decrease in whatever criteria the organization is using to measure its effectiveness.

This is the paradigm: bureaucratic values tend to stress the rational, task aspects of the work and to ignore the basic human factors which relate to the task and which, if ignored, tend to reduce task competence. Managers brought up under this system of values are badly cast to play the intricate human roles now required of them. Their ineptitude and anxieties lead to systems of discord and defense which interfere with the problem-solving capacity of the organization.

Generally speaking, the normative goals of change-agents derive

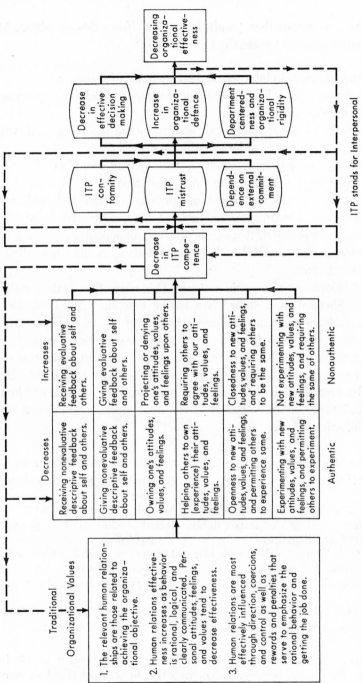

FIG. 2.   Predominant value system in modern organization[4]

117

in one way or another (explicitly or not) from this paradigm. Most commonly strived for are the following:

1 Improvement in interpersonal competence of managers.
2 A change in values so that human factors and feelings come to be considered legitimate.
3 Development of increased understanding between and within working groups in order to reduce tensions.
4 Development of more effective "team management," i.e., the capacity for functional groups to work competently.
5 Development of better methods of "conflict resultion"; rather than the usual bureaucratic methods of conflict resolution, which include suppression, denial, and the use of naked and unprincipled power, more rational and open methods of conflict resolution are sought after.
6 Development of organic systems. This normative goal, as outlined by Shepard and Blake,[6] is a strong reaction against the idea of organizations as mechanisms, which, they claim, has given rise to false conceptions (such as static equilibria, frictional concepts like "resistance to change," etc.) and, worse, to false notions of social engineering and change, e.g., pushing social buttons, thinking of the organization as a machine, etc. Organic systems, as Shepard and Blake conceive them,* differ from mechanical systems in the following ways:

Mechanical systems	*Organic systems*
Individual skills	Relationships between and within groups
Authority-obedience relationships	Mutual confidence and trust
Delegated and divided responsibility rigidly adhered to	Interdependencies and shared responsibility
Strict division of labor and hierarchical supervision	Multigroup membership and responsibility
Centralized decision making	Wide sharing of control and responsibility
Conflict resolution through suppression, arbitration, or warfare	Conflict resolution through bargaining or problem solving

* Burns and Stalker also develop the idea of organic and mechanical systems.[7] They state, however, in contradiction to Shepard that both may be appropriate under differing environmental and organizational conditions.

Change-agents conceptualize and discuss their normative goals in different ways; occasionally they work toward the same goal under different labels and for different goals under similar labels. But allowing for some exceptions, they would probably accept at face value the goals enumerated above. Where the differences among them come into sharper focus is in their choice of instruments or programs for implementing these normative goals.

PROGRAMS FOR IMPLEMENTING PLANNED ORGANIZATIONAL CHANGE

The discussion here will focus on three broad types of change programs that seem to be most widely used; training, consulting and research. Most frequently they are used in some combination depending on the needs of the client-system and the particular skills of the change-agent. For our purposes, we shall consider each of them separately.

Training

"Training" is an inadequate and possibly misleading word to use in this context as its dictionary meaning denotes "drill," "exercise," and the general notion of imparting skills through habit and rote learning. As the term is used here, it has a widely different meaning. It is used here to describe a particular variety of training which has been called "laboratory" training or education or "sensitivity" or "group dynamics" training and in most quarters "T-group training."* The idea of laboratory training originated at Bethel, Maine, in 1947 under the guidance of Bradford, Benne, and Lippitt, all of whom were influenced by Kurt Lewin. This group shared a common concern for the application of the behavioral sciences to practice and policy. The T group emerged as one of the most important components of laboratory training and has evolved over the past eighteen years into one of the main instruments for organizational change. Bradford, as director of the National Training Laboratories, has played a central role in the development of laboratory training; its growth was facili-

* For a popular account of laboratory training as it is used to implement organizational improvement, see Argyris.[8] For other writings on the same subject, see Schein and Bennis,[9] Blake and Mouton,[10] and Argyris.[11] For a theoretical background of laboratory training, see Bradford et al.[12]

tated through the active participation of a number of university-based behavioral scientists and practitioners.* Its main objective at first was *personal change,* or self-insight. Since the late 1950s or so, the emphasis has shifted away from personal growth to *organizational development.*†

As evidence of this shift, more and more laboratory training is conducted for specific organizations, using groups which follow organizational patterns rather than so-called "stranger" labs, where people come together from a variety of organizations and professions.

This is not the place to go deeply into the subject of laboratory training, but it might be useful to say a word or two more about it. It unfolds in an unstructured group setting where the participants examine their interpersonal relationships. The training process relies primarily and almost exclusively on the behavior experienced by the participants; i.e., the *group itself* becomes the focus of inquiry. Conditions are promoted whereby group members by examining data generated by themselves, attempt to understand the dynamics of group behavior, e.g., decision processes, leadership and influence processes, norms, roles, communication distortions, and effects of authority on a number of behavioral patterns, personality and coping mechanisms, etc. In short, the participants learn to analyze and become more sensitive to the processes of human interaction and acquire concepts to order and control these phenomena.

T groups are used in organizations today in the following ways:

Stranger labs Executives from organizations attend labs as "delegates" representing their organizations. The parent organization hopes to improve the organization this way by "seeding" a sufficient number of managers.

Cousin labs Organizations set up labs for individuals with similar organizational ranks but from different functional groups, e.g., all first-line supervisors or all general foremen.

---

* Tavistock Institute has played a similar role in England. Recently a group of European behavioral scientists set up their own counterpart to the National Training Laboratories in the United States.

† I date this more precisely as 1958 because at about this time the employee relations department of the Esso Company, under the leadership of Blake and Shepard, inaugurated a series of laboratory training programs in their refineries throughout the country. Other companies followed suit, but the original Esso programs laid the groundwork for future developments.[13]

Diagonal slices T groups are composed of members from the same company but of different ranks and from different departments. No man is in the same group with anyone from his own work group.

Family or functional groups These groups are identical to the intact group as indicated by the formal organization; e.g., a particular supervisor would be with his work group.

Decisions about type of composition of T group training are based on a variety of factors, e.g., the stage of organizational development of the client-system, particular exigencies facing the client-system, and the competencies of the change-agent. The extent to which laboratory training affects the organizational value system and structure is related to the T-group strategy utilized: the more it approaches the family group, the more the total organizational system is affected.

Consulting

For every type and style of training, there is an equivalent type of consulting. The type we shall be concerned with here is practiced by a number of change-agents and is perhaps best exemplified by the work of the Tavistock Institute.*

The change-agent qua consultant operates very much like the practicing physician or psychoanalyst: "In undertaking my work," writes Sofer, "I entered the same moral order as my respondents, helping them to maintain what was positive in their situation and to alter what was negative."[16] So the consultant starts from the chief "presenting symptom" of the client, articulates it in such a way that the causal and underlying mechanisms of the problem are understood, and then takes remedial action.

He employs an extensive repertory of instrumentation which he uses as flexibly as possible. Using himself, most of all, he aims to detect and get close to the important "data," to exploit every encounter he can in order to help the client-system see "reality." He uses situations, as they develop spontaneously, to work through the tensions and resistances associated with them. Most of all, he uses *himself*

* The work of Jaques, Sofer, and Rice in particular.[14] Sofer has been the most articulate in the sense of adumbrating the principles and assumptions behind this style of social consultancy, so I have used his book *The Organization from Within* most profitably for this paper. Beckhard,[15] in the United States, has also developed a procedure and a unique style with respect to the role of the management consultant.

as a *role model*. More important than the expertise and methodological help they contribute—and it is substantial—is the ". . . *manner* in which my colleagues and I defined and reconceptualized the problems."[17] To the extent that this role model is emulated by the management group, change can occur.

Heavy emphasis is placed on the strategy of role model because the main instrument is the change-agent himself: his skills, insight, and expertise. Sofer reveals this when he suggests that psychotherapy or some form of clinical experience in a mental hospital is necessary preparation for the change-agent.

Argyris provides an interesting example of change-agent qua consultant. He writes about two possible reactions clients have when their attempts to "seduce" him to give the "solutions" fail. One is the expression by the executives of sorrow and dismay. Another reaction is their insistence that, since he is the "expert" consultant, he *should* provide some answers. Argyris writes:

> Moreover, if their expectation of the researcher is that he should give some answers, because in the feedback situation he is the leader, what does this expectation imply concerning what they probably do to their subordinates? Perhaps this indicates that when they (as leaders) make a diagnosis, they feel they must make a prognosis. But if the above analysis is valid, what positive value is a unilateral prognosis? At best it gives their subordinates something to shoot at (just as they are behaving toward the researcher.) But as they just experienced, if the leader (in this case, the researcher) is skilled enough to answer all their objections, he succeeds in making the diagnosis *his* and not theirs. Perhaps, this also occurs when they succeed in answering all the questions of their subordinates when they, as superiors, are "selling" a new policy of practice.[18]

So Argyris, as consultant, confronts the group with their behavior toward him as an analog of their behavior vis-à-vis their own subordinates. He continually searches for experiential referents in the existential ("here-and-now") encounters with his client-system which can be used heuristically for the fuller understanding of the client.

If the description of the role of the consultant makes it sound more ambiguous and vague than the training process, this probably reflects reality, for in the consultant approach, the processes of change and the change-agent's interventions are less systematic and less programmed than in either the training or the applied-research programs. Let us turn to the latter now.

Applied Research: The Utilization of Data as
Feedback Intervention

Almost all planned-change programs utilize research results in one way or another. The particular form of applied or action research I am referring to now is the one in which research results are used systematically as an *intervention*. This type of program was developed primarily by the researchers at the University of Michigan's Institute for Social Research, most particularly by Floyd Mann and his associates.[19] Here is the way it works: Survey data are collected and then reported back to the particular departments (subjects) in "feedback" meetings where the subjects become clients and have a chance to review the findings, test them against their own experiences, and even ask the researchers to test some of their hypotheses. Rather than the traditional uses of research, of a technocratic variety, where the findings are submitted "in triplicate" and probably ignored, this method strives for active participation of the subjects.

In other words, most methods of research application collect information and report it. There the relationship ends. In the survey-feedback approach, the collecting and reporting of results is only the *beginning* of the relationship. On the basis of the research results—and partly because of them—the involvement and participation in the planning, collection, analysis, and interpretation of more data are activated. Objective information, knowledge of results, is the first step in planned change. But more than intellectual committment is usually required. The survey-feedback approach is utilized in order to gain this extra commitment via active participation in the research process.

Richard Beckhard, too, utilizes data as the first step in his work as change-agent, both as a way of diagnosing the initial state of the client-system and as a way of using the data themselves as a springboard for discussions with the executive staff. His procedure is very similar to that of Mann and his associates, except that the data are collected through informal, nonstructured interviews which he then codes by themes about the managerial activities of the client. He then convenes a meeting with the particular subsystem on which the data were collected at an off-site location and uses the research headings as the basis for discussion. The following are examples of these themes:

1   Communications between president and line (or staff)
2   Line-staff communications
3   Location of decision making
4   Role clarification or confusion
5   Communications procedures[20]

I should reiterate that most planned-change inductions involve all three processes: training, consulting, and researching. In most cases, the change-agent himself tries to utilize all their functions. Some change-agents report, however, that they work in collaboration with others and that they divide their functions. For example, Argyris used L. Bradford as a trainer and Roger Harrison as a researcher.[21] Sofer employed his colleagues at Tavistock to augment the services he could perform. It is also true that some change-agents possess distinctive competencies which tend to direct their activities in certain channels.

What should be clear from the foregoing discussion are these three points: (1) Change-agents play a variety of roles; (2) clients play a variety of roles: subject, initiator and planner, client, and participant-researcher; and (3) the final shape of the change-agent's role is not as yet clear, and it is hazardous to describe exactly what they do on the basis of their reports.*

STRATEGIC MODELS EMPLOYED BY CHANGE-AGENTS

In order to gain a deeper understanding of how these change programs are used in practice, it might be useful to sample some of the strategies employed by change-agents. This turns out to be somewhat more difficult than one might think because quite often change-agents

---

* There are other matters with respect to these three functions which space and time limitations make it impossible to more than mention. For example, in *choosing* one particular intervention over another, one would have to consider the following factors: cost, time, degree of collaboration between change-agent and client-system required, ease of measurement of effects, state of target system, whether an internal or an external change-agent is required, the degree to which the program is "instrumented" (for example, Blake's change program is so precisely programmed and "laid out" that first-level line managers within the client-system can conduct their own program based on Blake's ideas without his presence), and the relationship between the type of change sought and the change indication process.

fail to report their strategies or to make them explicit—even to themselves. However, two quite different strategic models are available to us, one developed by R. R. Blake in his "managerial grid" scheme and one through some work I was associated with at an oil refinery.*

Blake has developed a change program based on his analytic framework of managerial styles.[22] On the basis of this twofold analytic framework, it is possible to locate five types of managerial strategies. One dimension is "concern for people"; the other is "concern for production." As Blake points out, the term "concern for" represents the degree of concern for, not the *actual* production of, people's activities. Figure 3 shows the grid and the eight managerial styles. Blake and his colleagues attempt to change the organization in the 9,9 direction.

In their strategic model employed to induce changes in the direction of "team management" (9,9), Blake and his colleagues specify six phases, which represent their most thorough and systematic work so far. Their strategy is based on experience with fifteen different factories, ranging in size from 500 to 5,000 employees.

Phase 1 takes place away from the plant location; factory members are exposed to behavioral science theory (managerial grid, etc.), take part in structural experiments, and participate in face-to-face feedback experiments and sessions of the T-group variety. All members of the managerial organization participate in the laboratory for a one- or two-week session. Groups are composed on a "diagonal-slice" basis. It is believed that this diagonal-slice deployment is the most strategic at first. It allows organizational and interdepartmental issues to be aired more easily than they can be when the usual organizational constraints are present.

Phase 2 is also conducted off site and focuses on *team training*. Training groups are composed of a particular boss and his immediate subordinates, starting with the top team and reaching lower levels later on. Thus, the unit of grouping is the actual "family" group, and actual conditions become the focus of analysis. This phase is based

* It might interest the reader to know that in this case, the strategy—if it can be called that—was strictly a *post hoc recapitulation* of what was done. In fact, it was not developed by the change-agents, themselves, but by Chris Argyris, who was asked to evaluate the program several years after its termination.

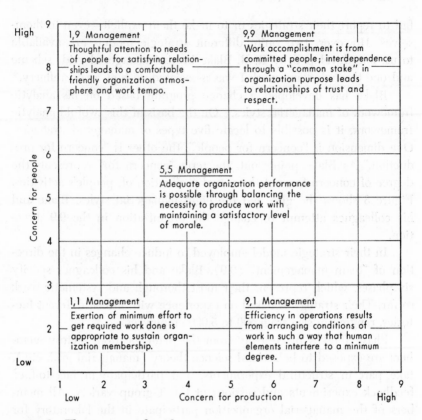

FIG. 3   The managerial grid

on the principle that if organizational change is to take place, it must be supported by the actual organizational groupings and must be exemplified and reinforced by top management.

Phase 3 is designed to achieve better *integration between functional groups* and between various organizational divisions, such as staff and line, technical and practical, sales and production, and so on. The normative goal of this horizontal linking is to create an organizational "culture" which can link relationships and articulate between departments in a more effective way than the bureaucratic model. In this phase, pairs of functional groups work together in order to solve the problems that exist between them. First they work as groups apart from each other, testing their image and stereotypes of their own group vis-à-vis the other and identifying obstacles to better integration. Then they get together and attempt to develop better meth·

ods of joint problem solving. This activity takes place, unlike that of the two previous phases, in the plant location.

Phase 4 gives real meaning to the concept of *planned change*, for it provides the mechanism for ensuring that the changes sought after are planned. In this phase, groups of from ten to twelve managers get together to *set goals for the total organization*. This composition is used at this stage in order to set targets that reflect the variety of forces present in the organization. After the issues, plans, and goal implementations are discussed by the various groups, they are summarized and used as the basis for an intensive organizational change effort.

Blake and his colleagues estimate that the time required for the first four phases, appreciation sessions, team training, horizontal linking, and setting of organizational goals may be two years or longer. Implementing them may require an additional two years or so.

In phase 5, the change-agent attempts to *help the organization realize the goals* established in phase 4. He deals with the organization much as a psychoanalyst would deal with a patient; in fact, the program during this phase resembles the consulting approach discussed earlier.

Phase 6, the final one, is directed toward *stabilizing the changes* brought about during the prior phases. Blake estimates that this period lasts for a year. The role of the change-agent is more passive during this period, and he is called upon for help less and less frequently. Rather than living with the client-system, he is available upon request. The main effort during this phase is to ensure the maintenance of the present state of functioning.

Figure 4 presents another strategy: a recapitulation by Argyris of a change program used by the New York headquarters team of a large oil company to improve the functioning of one of its smaller refineries in New England.[23] For some years, because of certain market changes, the refinery's profits had been declining, and there had been talk of closing it down.

The first change brought about was the recognition by headquarters that a new manager was needed who had the necessary technical skills and administrative experience, *plus* the assurance, for the future operation of the refinery. (See page 128.) This man was sent to two T-group training sessions in order to gain some awareness of the human problem existing in the refinery. Following this, the

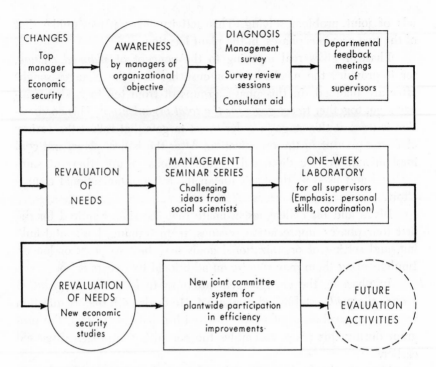

FIG. 4   Elements in one-year program in refinery

New York headquarters organizational development staff came on the scene and conducted a diagnosis through a survey and interviews of the total managerial staff (seventy) and a sample of the hourly employees (40 out of 350). About that time I was asked to consult with and help the New York headquarters staff and the refinery manager. Then, departmental feedback meetings with the supervisors were held and a reevaluation of needs was taken in coordination with the consulting group and top management (which at this point consisted of only the new refinery manager).

It was then decided that a laboratory program of T groups might be effective but possibly premature, and so a series of weekly seminars was held with the top management group (about twenty executives) focusing on new development in human relations. Speakers ranged over a wide variety of subjects, going from the Scanlon Plan to individual psychology. Following this, a one-week laboratory training program was held for all supervisors in diagonal-slice groupings, and then another reevaluation of needs was undertaken.

At this point some structural innovations were suggested and implemented. These included a top management committee consisting of all functional managers and a variety of project groupings working on a number of efficiency programs. During the very last phase of the program (not shown in the figure), the Scanlon Plan was adapted and installed at the refinery (incidentally, this was the first time the Scanlon program was undertaken in a "process" industry and the first time that a union agreed to the Scanlon Plan without a bonus automatically guaranteed).

It is difficult to know how typical or unusual these two planned-change strategies are; insufficient experience and reports dilute any generalizations that I would hazard. If they *are* typical, however, certain features of the strategies can be identified: (1) the length of time—Blake estimates five years, and the refinery program up to the point of the Scanlon Plan took two years; (2) the variety of programs utilized—research, consulting, training, teaching, and planning; (3) the necessity of cooperation with top management and the parent organization; (4) approaching the organization as a system, rather than as a collection of individuals; (5) phasing the program so that it evolves from individual to group to intergroup to overall organization; (6) the intellectual *and* emotional content of the program.

NOTES

1. Chapple, E. D., and L. R. Sayles, *The Measurement of Management*, The Macmillan Company, New York, 1961; Sayles, L., "The Change Process in Organization," in R. J. Smith (ed.), *Human Organization*, 1962, pp. 62–67.

2. Lippitt, R., J. Watson, and B. Westley, *The Dynamics of Planned Change*, Harcourt, Brace & World, Inc., New York, 1958; Seashore, C., and E. Van Egmond, "The Consultant-Trainer Role," in W. G. Bennis, K. D. Benne, and R. Chin (eds.), *The Planning of Change*, Holt, Rinehart and Winston, Inc., New York, 1961, pp. 660–666.

3. Blake, R. R., and J. S. Mouton, "A 9,9 Approach to Organization Development," in D. Zand and P. Buchanan (eds.), *Organization Development: Theory and Practice*, in press.

4. Argyris, C., *Interpersonal Competence and Organizational Effectiveness*, Dorsey Press, Homewood, Ill., 1962; Likert, R., *New Patterns of Management*, McGraw-Hill Book Company, New York, 1961; McGregor, D., *The Human Side of Enterprise*, McGraw-Hill Book Company, New York, 1960.

5. Argyris, *op. cit.*, p. 43.

6. Shepard, H. A., and R. R. Blake, "Changing Behavior through Cognitive Change," in Smith, *op. cit.*, pp. 88–96.

7. Burns, T., and G. M. Stalker, *The Management of Innovation*, Quadrangle, Chicago, 1962.

8. Argyris, C., "T-groups for Organizational Effectiveness," *Harvard Business Review*, vol. 42, pp. 60–74, 1964.

9. Schein, E. H., and W. G. Bennis, *Personal and Organizational Change through Group Methods*, John Wiley & Sons, Inc., New York, 1965.

10. Blake and Mouton, *op. cit.*

11. Argyris, *Interpersonal Competence and Organizational Effectiveness.*

12. Bradford, L. P., J. R. Gibb, and K. D. Benne, *T-group Theory and Laboratory Method*, John Wiley & Sons, Inc., New York, 1964.

13. *An Action Research Program for Organizational Improvement*, Foundation for Research on Human Behavior, Ann Arbor, Mich., 1960.

14. Jaques, E., *The Changing Culture of a Factory*, Tavistock, London, 1951; Rice, A. K., *The Enterprise and Its Environment*, Tavistock, London, 1963. Sofer, C., *The Organization from Within*, Tavistock, London, 1961.

15. Beckhard, R., "An Organization Improvement Program in a Decentralized Organized Organization," in Zand and Buchanan, *op. cit.;* Gibb, J. R., and R. Lippitt (eds.) "Helping a Group with Planned Change," *The Journal of Social Issues,* vol. 15, pp. 13–19, 1959.

16. Sofer, *op. cit.*

17. *Ibid.*

18. Argyris, *Interpersonal Competence and Organizational Effectiveness*, p. 104.

19. Mann, F., "Studying and Creating Change: A means to Understanding Social Organization," *Research in Industrial Relations*, Industrial Relations Research Association Publication 17, 1957; Mann, F., and H. Baumgartel, *The Survey Feedback Experiment: An Evaluation of a Program for the Utilization of Survey Findings*, Foundation for Research on Human Behavior, Ann Arbor, Mich., 1964; Mann, F., and R. Likert, "The Need for Research on the Communication of Research Results," *Human Organization*, vol. 11, pp. 15–19, 1952.

20. Beckhard, *op. cit.*

21. Argyris, *Interpersonal Competence and Organizational Effectiveness.*

22. Blake, R. R., J. S. Mouton, L. B. Barnes, and L. E. Greiner, "A Managerial Grid Approach to Organization Development: The Theory and Some Research Findings," *Harvard Business Review*, vol. 42, 1964.

23. Argyris, C., *Organization Development*, Yale University Press, New Haven, Conn., 1960.

8

principles and strategies
of directing organizational
change via laboratory training*

INTRODUCTION

Two main uses or, put another way, two main target systems or client-systems for the Lab Training can be identified. One is the *individual*: his growth, interpersonal competence, and "self-actualization." The other target system is a *social system,* usually a formal organization or some subsystem or part of it.

In this chapter we shall focus on the *organization* as a change target for Lab Training. We choose this target system primarily because it is with social systems (and their subsystems) that the *strat-*

---

* This is a revision of a chapter in a book written in collaboration with Schein.[1] Although Lab (or T-group) Training is used as the pivotal type of change induction in this essay, please bear in mind that the principles and strategies apply equally to all classes of change programs involving the value and normative systems of the client population. This chapter appears by permission of the coauthor and the publisher.

tegic problems of Lab Training become manifest and where it is so crucial to understand the "fit" between Lab Training values and organizational goals. Where the individual is concerned, the problem of learning or change is ostensibly simpler; he can reject or accept, learn or not, without undue perturbation. When it comes to using Lab Training to change organizational systems, however, the strategic problems become impressive and complex, with seemingly untold unanticipated consequences and risks. So we propose here to examine some of the issues and dilemmas surrounding the use of Lab Training in effecting organizational change with the hope that increased understanding will lead to more effective utilization.

An Issue: Yogis and Commissars

Before going on to outline this chapter, let us take a short detour and discuss a general issue which lies behind the recent impetus to use Lab Training in improving social systems. We stated at the beginning of this chapter that the individual and the social system represent the twin change objectives. In fact, these goals reflect an interesting and ubiquitous tension—rarely stated as such, but always present—concerning the general direction of any change program. Over the years, since the beginning of Lab Training, the conflict has taken a variety of forms, but its capacity to arouse staff debates or arguments over training design or staff strategies has been monumental.

It is hard to state exactly what *the* issue is, but it is very reminiscent of Koestler's distinction between the yogi and the commissar, between those who turn *inward* for insight and Nirvana and those who turn *outward* for social salvation. It is the difference between those who believe in the manipulation of external forces—such as legal, technological, economic, and political factors—for the "good life" and those who look to the personality, to self-actualization, or to the individual for ultimate social improvement.

In the past eighteen years or so of Lab Training's existence, almost all training designs and strategies have—tacitly or explicitly—reflected this conflict. The debate takes different forms: sometimes it appears in the guise of "theoretical preferences," such as Lewin versus Freud or self-actualization versus organizational improvement; sometimes the argument oscillates between "utopianism" and "existential despair." However one finds that, most often, it is argued in terms of: "Who is the client?"—the organization or the individual.

For the most part, the dialogue which the debate has generated has been useful insofar as it has lifted up for analysis certain crucial issues such as (1) the problem of transfer of learning from the lab culture to other cultures and the durability of training effects on the individual *after* the lab, (2) the relationship between self-enhance-ment and organizational improvement—if any, and (3) the ethical-normative-value issues of transporting lab values into the fabric of the organization. We are a long way from resolving any of these is-sues, but one fortunate outcome of the debate is the increase in re-search and the improvement in conceptualization that it has forced.*

The shift in orientation from regarding solely the individual as the ultimate client to regarding the organization, or some other social unit, as the ultimate client is a fairly recent development. Before the late 1950s Lab Training was pretty much confined to a "cultural island" where strangers gathered, underwent an intensive experience, and left in two weeks abruptly—again, as strangers. It was difficult enough to evaluate the effects of the lab on the individual delegate; it was practically impossible to trace the effects on the organization. What data there were implied that the individual could not even maintain his own *self*-changes within the organization, much less modify the organization.

The predicament is real: How do you gain the advantages of a cultural island (particularly "unfreezing") and still transfer com-petencies and values internalized at the lab? Put another way, we can ask: Can you ensure lasting change of the individual without also changing the social fabric (norms, policies, values) of the organiza-tion?

The predicament has been solved over the past several years, as the preceding chapters have indicated, by bringing Lab Training to

---

* The reader is invited to read the excellent summary of research reported by Stock in Bradford et al.[2] See also, in the same book, the chapter by Benne for an excellent history of Lab Training associated with the National Training Laboratories.

the organization rather than the other way around. In other words, instead of sending individuals of a particular organization to a "stranger" lab, the organization has set up, in one form or another, its own Lab Training program.

But introducing Lab Training into the climate of a formal organization (such as a hospital, factory, university, or ship) brings about a set of strategic questions and raises certain issues of social change. In this chapter we would like to discuss and clarify these questions and issues.

OUTLINE OF CHAPTER

I. Background of, and perspectives on, the use of Lab Training for changing social systems
    ◆ A   *Why this recent impetus toward the use of Lab Training for organizational improvement?*
    ◆ B   *What are the conceptual goals of Lab Training with respect to organizational change?*
    ◆ C   *What strategic models for inducing change are used?*
II. Considerations for the successful adoption of Lab Training by social systems
    ◆ A   *State of the target system or subsystem*
        • 1   *Are the learning goals of Lab Training appropriate?*
        • 2   *Is the culutral state of the target system "ready" for Lab Training?*
        • 3   *Are the key people in the target system involved in, or informed of, the Lab Training program?*
        • 4   *Are members of the target system adequately prepared for, and oriented to, Lab Training?*
        • 5   *Is voluntarism (regarding participation) ensured?*
    ◆ B   *Role and competence of the change-agent*
        • 1   *The change-agent's role*
        • 2   *Competence required of the change-agent*
    ◆ C   *Strategies of implementation*
        • 1   *Who is the client?*
        • 2   *What is the point of entry?*
        • 3   *Which systems are involved?*
        • 4   *To what extent can the change-agent involve the target system in planning and executing Lab Training?*

III. Three cases of failure
      ♦ *A   Case 1: a letter from a government training center*
      ♦ *B   Case 2: a letter from medical services*
      ♦ *C   Case 3: the undercover change-agent*
IV. Propositions about the uses of Lab Training in effecting social change

---

I. **Background of, and perspectives on, the use of Lab Training for changing social systems**

    ♦ *A Why this recent impetus toward the use of Lab Training for organizational improvement?*

Obviously, there are many causes to consider in the emergence of any social phenomenon. Similarly, in order to understand the use of Lab Training as an organizational instrument, many social forces must be mentioned. Labor supply, the professionalization of management, automation, the growing complexity of the enterprise, the large-scale and sprawling quality of organizations in conjunction with the need for better communication and decentralization, the improved education of the worker and the changing population characteristics of our work force, the network of boundaries and transactions which clogs up the turbulent environment of the organization, and a host of other factors must be included in even a superficial survey.* For us, the crucial factor is the inadequacy of present-day organizations to cope with the complexity of rapid change and problems of human collaboration. Adaptation and collaboration are two of the main problems confronting contemporary society, and our organizations will fail or succeed depending upon their mastery of these two tasks.

This is only a part of the explanation, however. The inadequacies of bureaucracy have been examined in detail by many organizational theorists for a number of years. These theorists have produced countless thoughtful suggestions and ideas about a new vision of social architecture which would be more in keeping with what is known about human motivation. *The point is that Lab Training provides the instrument whereby the normative goals and improvements set forth by theorists and practitioners of organizations can be achieved.*

Let us take some examples to clarify our meaning. Take the prob-

---

* See Bennis⁴ for a more detailed discussion.

lem of *intergroup conflict.* There is an urgent need to understand the network of interdependencies which stem from the myriad of specialties and complexity of technologies. Managers of large-scale operations frequently mention intergroup conflict and collaboration as one of their main problems. From a theoretical viewpoint, Likert[5] arrives at the same conclusion and suggests the importance of a "linking pin," a mechanism for integrating groups that are work-related. *But how is the mechanism developed?*

Or take the problem of *authority and leadership* in organizations. McGregor,[6] in particular, has focused in his writings on the archaic workings of authority systems in bureaucratic structures. What is now needed, asserts McGregor, are systems of collaboration, of colleagueship between superiors and subordinates, not the blind use of controls and coercions. What we now need is increased autonomy, not dependencies and counterdependencies. *But how are systems created and people "changed" so that bosses trust their subordinates enough to give them more autonomy, and how can subordinates learn to trust so that they can rely on self-control and collaboration?*

Lewin,[7] Allport,[8] and others have, for some time, produced evidence and arguments which show that as individuals participate directly in the decisions that are relevant to their work and life, they develop a higher state of morale and implement the decisions more effectively. *But how do organizations develop better and more responsive mechanisms for participative management?*

One final example: Argyris[9] and others have insisted that *interpersonal competence* is necessary to a manager. He must be able to size up a situation, be aware of human factors impinging on a situation, and develop a diagnostic sensitivity as well as behavioral flexibility in dealing with human problems. *But how do managers and other practitioners develop this interpersonal competence?*

The point of these examples is this. Ever since the historic studies of Mayo and Roethlisberger at Western Electric, there have been many profitable revisions and suggestions developed to improve the operations of the human organization. We have mentioned some of these in the examples above: better systems of collaboration, of adaptation, of authority; greater interpersonal competence; etc. There is no shortage of criticism or prescription. The problem is that there has been no organizational mechanism capable of implementing these suggestions. Lab Training appeared on the scene at the time when formal organizations were most pressed for revision, for change. *Lab Training provided an instrument whereby these normative goals and revisions could be translated into practice.*

♦ **B What are the conceptual goals of Lab Training with respect to organizational change?**

We have just been discussing the growth of Lab Training in terms of the needs and problems of the managers and practitioners, as they saw them. Now we want to shift our emphasis to the *change-agents* who have collaborated with these target systems. What do they have in mind as change goals?

Before answering this question, it might be useful to say a few words about the idea of a "change-agent." It is a rather new term and is used in many different ways.* (See Chapter 7, pages 113–119 for a detailed discussion of change-agents. For a general description of the change-agent's normative goals see p. 116.) We are using the term "change-agent" to refer to a person or group, practitioners or social scientists, who are using the theory which underlies Lab Training in order to improve the functioning and effectiveness of organizations. What do they have in mind as change goals?

The basic paradigm is: bureaucratic values tend to stress the rational, task aspects of the work and to ignore the basic human factors which relate to the task. Managers brought up in this system of values are badly cast to play the intricate human roles now required

---

* I stress their uniformities here, though there is a wide divergence of orientation, outlook, training, and experience. Some change-agents grew out of the tradition of Lewin and academic psychology, others were disciples of psychoanalytic practice; still others came from applied disciplines such as rural sociology or social work or education. Whatever their differences, they seem to receive their impetus as much from the urge to improve society as from simple curiosity about its working. They seem to be as intimately involved in affecting change as they are in studying it. They have developed a self-consciousness about the strategies of social change as well as about its goals. They are driven by a radical rather than conservative ethic, which means simply that their attitude toward social change springs from locating the ills of society in its institutions, where something can be done about them, rather than in human nature, where very little can be done about them. In short, the change-agents are not only *interpreting* the world in different ways; some intend to *change* it.

of them. Their ineptitude and anxieties lead to systems of discord and defense which interfere with the problem-solving capacity of the organization. The aims of change-agents, then, are (1) to effect a change in values so that *human factors and feelings come to be considered as legitimate* and (2) to assist in *developing skills among managers in order to increase interpersonal competence.*

There are variations to this paradigm, to be sure; for example, "changed attitudes toward our own role, role of others, and organizational relationships," or increased adaptibility of the organization to external stress, etc. But basically, the variations show up more sharply in the *strategic models* employed to induce the change than they do in the conceptual goals. Let us turn to that now.

◆ *C   What strategic models for inducing change are used?*

This question has to do with the problem of *how:* How are change agents selected? How do they achieve their goals? How do they gain their influence and power? In order to get a foothold on these issues, let us pose two central questions: (1) Are the change-agents internal or external to the target system; i.e., are they regular employees of the target system or not? (2) What is the basis of the change-agent's power or ability to exert influence on the target system?

1. Change-agents: internal or external? Whether or not the change agents are actual members of the target system or not is a crucial question to practitioners and students of organizational change. There are some who say that a significant change cannot occur without the impetus generated by the external agent.[11,12] They argue that only a skilled outsider-consultant can provide the perspective, detachment, and energy so necessary to effect a true alteration of existing patterns. There are advocates of the internal model, though, who take the opposite stand. They argue that the insider possesses the intimate knowledge of the target system that the external change-agent lacks. In addition, the internal change-agent does not generate the suspicion and mistrust that the outsider often does. His acceptance and credibility are guaranteed, it is argued, by his organizational status.

2. What is the source of the change-agent's power? Generally speaking, he derives his power and influence from a combination of two sources: *expert* power and *legitimate* power. As these terms sug-

gest, the change-agent is seen as possessing certain skills and competencies (expert power), or he is seen as occupying a certain office or holding status in an organization which legitimizes his influence (legitimate power.)*

Now we are in a better position to return to our main question concerning the various strategic models of change. In our experience, the most common model used is the *external* change-agent employing *expert* power. We call this the "Consultant" model because outside change-agents are employed as consultants to the organization (usually, but not always, to the personnel division), and they attempt to help the target system build adequate Lab Training programs. In some cases, the consultants actually conduct Lab Training; in other cases, they coordinate Lab Training activities along with other consulting functions.

Perhaps an example of the consultant model would help clarify its nature. The work of Shepard and other consultants at the Space Technology Laboratories may be one of the best models of this approach. In this case, Shepard acts as consultant to the director of industrial relations. In the course of their work together it was decided that "career development" (preparing managers for the future) was one of the most important problems facing the organization. Following this, Shepard worked most intensively with the manager in charge of career development. A sequence of activities followed, all worked out with Shepard collaborating with this man and the director of industrial relations, finally leading to team training.†

At the other extreme from the consultant model is the line model, a strategy by which the change-agent is internal to the target system and possesses legitimate power. A company president or any line leader who utilizes Lab Training would be an example of this. Alfred J. Marrow, president of the Harwood Manufacturing Company, repre-

---

* We have ignored some of the more personal and intangible elements which enter into questions of strategy, such as the change-agent's personality, charisma, etc. These personal factors are rarely written about explicitly and only infrequently are recognized as such. For these reasons, we do not feel at all confident in stressing anything but their *presence*. See Chap. 9 for a fuller discussion of the change-agent's power.

† See Argyris[13] for a step-by-step analysis of the consultant model. It is the most clearly written account of this model.

sents this approach to Lab Training. Marrow works directly with the external consultants—being a psychologist as well as an entrepreneur—conducts his own T groups, participates in labs, and generally takes an active role in conducting and coordinating Lab Training in his own organization. The president of Non-Linear Systems, Andrew Kaye, and the president of Minnesota Mining, Hugh Harrison, are both, to some extent, examples of the line model. *

A more popular model than the line model, but less so than the consultant model, is the staff model, as exemplified by Shepard while he was at Esso and, more recently, by Buchanan at Esso International. In this model, change-agents are drawn directly from the headquarters staff of the organization; for example, Shepard and his colleagues (some of whom were outside consultants) went to the Baton Rouge refinery in 1959 and 1960 to conduct two-week residential labs for the entire managerial staff of the refinery. The staff model, then, is similar to the consultant model in that it emphasizes expert power, but it is similar to the line model in that its change-agents are drawn from inside the target system.

A purer case of the internal change-agent model was developed by the General Electric Company and is now used by that company in their Business Effectiveness Program. In this case, change-agents (called "catalysts") are trained by headquarters staff and outside consultants to go to a target system (a General Electric location) and "live in" as internal change-agents for as long as it takes to effect a change along the lines specified by the program. Some catalysts have been on location for as long as two years; others terminate after several months. What should be stressed here, for our analysis, is that the change-agents are *paid* and are considered regular employees of the target system itself.

Let us summarize now. Models implementing Lab Training for improving organizations can be viewed along two dimensions, internal versus external and legitimate power versus expert power. If the choice of change strategy is *internal*, then legitimate or expert power can be utilized. The General Electric catalyst program is an example

---

* The extent to which these men actually conduct Lab Training varies. What is most characteristic of the line model is that the top line management—rather than staff—takes the leadership in instituting and sustaining Lab Training.

of the internal-expert model; the work of Alfred J. Marrow at Harwood is an example of the internal-line model. If the choice of the change strategy is *external*, then only one power alternative is open, that of expert, for legitimate power, by definition, must be drawn from sources internal to the target system. There are many examples of the external-expert model. We have already mentioned the work of Argyris, Blake, Shepard, McGregor, and others. It is probably the most widely used of the approaches we have singled out.

The classification we have developed for the uses of change strategies is crude, to be sure, and it ignores some of the more ingenious variations, but we would wager that over 90 per cent of the change efforts utilizing Lab Training can be grouped in it. At the same time, however, new models are now being developed which may make this classification obsolete.

It seems increasingly clear to us that *combinations* and appropriate *sequencing* of these approaches may prove to be most useful. There are more and more signs, for example, that internal and external change-agents, *in concert*, are more effective than either internal or external change-agents working alone. Moreover, a combination of legitimate and expert power cannot help but be more effective, other things being equal, than either working independently of the other. The evidence is far from conclusive at this point, but from certain trends we now see developing, new models for implementing organizational change will be used which rely on external *and* internal change-agents in combination and using legitimate *and* expert power. What this implies is a *team effort* involving a diverse set of skills, status, and roles in order to induce the organizational change. We believe this will prove to be the most useful strategy in the future.

II. Considerations for the successful adoption of Lab Training by social systems

In this section we shall examine the conditions that facilitate the adoption of Lab Training by target systems. We shall consider first the state of the target system or subsystem and, second, the role and competence of the change-agent. Then we shall discuss the interaction between the change-agent and the target system in the strategy of implementation.

♦ A   State of the target system or subsystem*

In considering the state of the target system, a number of questions must be asked:

1 Are the learning goals of Lab Training appropriate?
2 Is the cultural state of the target system "ready" for Lab Training?
3 Are the key people in the target system involved in, or informed of, the Lab Training program?
4 Are members of the target system adequately prepared for, and oriented to, Lab Training?
5 Is voluntarism (regarding participation) ensured?

• 1   Are the learning goals of Lab Training appropriate?

To what extent do the goals relate to the effectiveness of the target system? We can think of many target systems where the answer to these questions may be negative because of market, technological, and competitive conditions. Serious attention must be given, particularly in the early stages, to the appropriateness of Lab Training change goals for the particular target system. A great deal of effort, at first, must be directed to diagnosing the target system's needs in relation to the anticipated outcomes of Lab Training. Are the outcomes relevant to the effectiveness of the target system? Is Lab Training timely, economical, congruent with the anticipated target-system trends, etc.? Later on, after discussing the cases where Lab Training failed, this question of appropriateness will again be raised.

• 2   Is the cultural state of the target system "ready" for Lab Training?

Let us be as clear as we can about what we mean by "cultural readiness." Each target system transmits and maintains a system of values which permeates the organizational climate and which is used as a basis for action and commitments. This does not mean that values are always adhered to, but it usually means that those who exemplify the values are rewarded and that those who violate them are

---

* The boundaries of the target system which Lab Training affects may be a part (or subsystem) of the larger target system. For example, a target system like ALCAN has been directing the bulk of its Lab Training change program at one of its three main divisions. And in the Esso change program, the refinery, a subsystem, became the chief target system. We shall come back to this point later in our discussion of the strategy of implementation.

punished. Lab Training also has a set of values which we specified as authenticity, choice, collaboration, and the expression of feelings among others. There is always bound to be *some* conflict between these values of Lab Training and the values of the target system, but situations should be avoided where the two sets of value systems clash extraordinarily.

The degree and range of value conflicts provide some of the best clues for diagnosing the cultural state of the target system. That is, if the discrepancy between Lab Training values and the target system's values can be realistically assessed, a fairly good idea about the target system's readiness can be obtained. Let us sample some of the most important dimensions of the cultural state.

The *legitimacy of interpersonal relationships,* in terms of both their effects on the work and the degree to which members of the target system view them as susceptible to change, is an important aspect of the target system's culture. In many target systems, interpersonal phenomena are not considered appropriate to discuss, germane to the task, or legitimate as a focus of inquiry. As Henry Ford once said about his own philosophy of management: "You just set the work before the men and have them do it." While this view is becoming slowly outdated by modern techniques of management, there are still many situations where interpersonal influence is regarded as invalid, not legitimate, or an invasion of privacy.

Another cultural variable which must be taken into account is the *control and authority system presently employed by the target system.* If it is too rigid and authoritarian, it may be too much at variance with the values of Lab Training for easy adoption.

The presence and intensity of conflict within the target system represent still another cultural factor which must be considered. It is difficult to generalize about conflict in terms of its relationship to the adoption of Lab Training. The impression we gain, however, is that it is best not to introduce Lab Training under conditions of intense conflict. In this case, the organization is under stress and may be *too* "plastic"; Lab Training may be only a temporary dodge or a tool in a power play by one of the protagonists, or it may be used later on as a convenient scapegoat. This is not to say that Lab Training may not be strategic to employ during periods of conflict but only that the type, causes, and intensity of conflict must be examined in relationship to the Lab Training program.

The internal boundary system of the target system must be carefully examined in order to avoid situations where Lab Training values are internalized in one subpart of the system, only to be rejected by, and cause disruptions in, an adjacent system.* In other words, the interdependence of the parts within the target system must be carefully scrutinized so that unanticipated changes in some parts of the system do not "backfire" and create negative repercussions in another part of the target system.

The last item to consider in assessing the cultural readiness of the target system is the most difficult to render in objective terms, and yet it is possibly the single most important factor in estimating the probability of success. *It has to do with the change-agent's relationship with the target system,* in particular the quality and potentiality of the relationship.

If the change-agent believes that it is possible to establish a relationship with the target system based on a healthy, realistic understanding of his role and with realistic expectations regarding the change, then a change program may be indicated. But if the relationship is based on fantasy, unrealistic hopes, fear, worship, or intimidation, then the change-agent and/or the target system must seriously reexamine the basis for their joint work.†

We are suggesting that one of the best ways of diagnosing cultural readiness has to do with the way the target system reacts to, and establishes a relationship with, the change-agent. The quality and

* Bavelas and Strauss[14] report an interesting example of this. A subunit of girls on an assembly line developed an ingenious and new method which increased their job satisfaction and improved their performance significantly. The only trouble was that it had repercussions on interdependent parts of the organization. The program eventually had to be scuttled. Though we know of no such case, it will be interesting to identify sources of strain that Lab Training might create with the target system's *external* boundary system: suppliers, customers, government, employee sources, etc. It is doubtful that it would generate the same degree of strain as internal interdependencies, but it still bears examination.

† Let us be clear about this. We mean that if the change-agent cannot *foresee* a healthy relationship in the future, he might well reconsider the Lab Training program. We do not think it is possible for the relationship to be totally trusting and realistic during the beginning phases of work. In any case, the main point we want to stress is the diagnostic validity of the relationship; the problems that inhere in that are probably symptomatic of the problems to be encountered.

vicissitudes of this encounter—insofar as it is a replica of the intended change program—provide an important clue regarding the fate of the Lab Training change program.

What we mean by "readiness," then, is the degree of value conflict between Lab Training values and the target system's values in terms of (1) the legitimacy of interpersonal phenomena; (2) the range, depth, and intensity of conflicts and modes of conflict resolution; (3) concepts of control and authority; (4) interdependence of parts of the target system; and (5) the relationship between change-agent and target system. Though they are difficult to measure precisely, they must be given thorough attention, and an assessment must be made before Lab Training can be introduced.

Assuming that the cultural readiness of the target system has been carefully assessed and found to be appropriate, then we must ask:

> • 3 *Are the key people in the target system involved in, or informed of, the Lab Training program?*

It can be disastrous if the people most affected by Lab Training are not involved in, informed of, or even advised of, the Lab Training program. To guarantee this commitment, a great deal of energy and time must be devoted to assessing the extent to which the Lab Training is supported by the key people and the attitudes individuals generally hold regarding Lab Training.

> • 4 *Are members of the target system adequately prepared for, and oriented to, Lab Training?*

The usual forms of *preparation* and *orientation* do not seem too effective for Lab Training, primarily because the written (or spoken) word rarely conveys the sense of the experience. Lab Training, if anything, is experience-based, and words, without an experiential referent, often tend to confuse and, in some cases, cause more apprehension than necessary.

Some introductory *experiences* often prepare and orient future participants adequately. We have tried a "miniature" lab (waggishly called by one of the participants an "instant" lab) to simulate as accurately as we could the lab environment. In this case, an entire lab was compressed into one full day of training. In other situations we have executed a specific training exercise with some prospective delegates in order to give them a feel for the learning environment of

Lab Training. In any case, we are advocating some experience-based orientation in order to provide a reasonable facsimile of lab life.

In our consideration of the state of the target system, we must consider one last factor:

• 5   *Is voluntarism (regarding participation) ensured?*

We feel this is an important, perhaps crucial, factor for the successful adoption of Lab Training by target systems. We think it is crucial not only for the obvious ethical reasons but also for realistic learning considerations. In order for a participant to profit the most from Lab Training, he must not feel coerced or pushed into experiencing it.* Involuntary attendence is particlarly hard to avoid in those cases where the entire organization undergoes Lab Training and where there is a tacit rejection of those who refuse to attend. Still it is important for target systems to provide as much choice and voluntarism regarding Lab Training as possible. And this is done by (1) providing the individuals with as much orientation as possible so that choice is meaningful (simply to ask a person whether he wants to attend Lab Training when he has no understanding of it is ridiculous!) and (2) keeping organizational pressure to attend at a minimum.

In this section, on the state of the target system, we have presented a series of factors to be taken into account in order to increase the probability of the successful adoption of Lab Training. In order to summarize this section as well as to make explicit the sequence of choices, we have constructed a five-step model shown in Table 4.

♦ B   Role and competence of the change-agent

We mentioned earlier that the idea of "change-agentry," as we are using the term here, is very new. And because of its novelty, its fundamental outline is still emerging. Thus the role of the change-agent is protean, changing, difficult to grasp, and practically impossible to generalize about. However, it may be useful to make some tentative remarks about it in this section.

---

* This often creates the dilemma of the people most in need of the Lab Training experience resisting it and those who least need it volunteering for it. However unsatisfactory the resolution of this dilemma is, nothing would be gained, and a lot possibly lost, if people were captive to the experience.

TABLE 4　**Five-step model for diagnosing state of target system**

1　Are Lab Training change goals appropriate to target system?	If *not, stop* and reconsider appropriateness of Lab Training.
If *yes*, then: 2　Is the "cultural state" of target system prepared for Lab Training? 　　Degree and type of value conflict? 　　Legitimacy of interpersonal phenomena? 　　Degree, range, intensity, and resolution of conflict? 　　Concepts of control and authority used? 　　Interdependence of target system? 　　Relationship of trust and confidence between change-agent and target system?	If *not, stop* and examine areas where more preparation is needed or where value conflicts should be reduced.
If *yes*, then: 3　Are key people involved and committed?	If *not, stop* and examine ways to develop more commitment to program.
If *yes*, then: 4　Are members of the target system adequately prepared for, and oriented, to Lab Training?	If *not, stop* and examine ways to develop more commitment to program.
If *yes*, then: 5　Is voluntarism (regarding participation) ensured?	If *not, stop* and examine attitudes toward Lab Training, or *why* people do or do not want to go to labs. After diagnosis, attempt to indicate the place of Lab Training in career development accurately.

• 1　*The change-agent's role*

There are a number of things we would like to call attention to about the role of the change-agent and then go on to discuss each of them in more detail. The change-agent's role must be construed as being professional, marginal, ambiguous, insecure, and risky.

First, the role of the change-agent is *professional;* that is, he counts heavily on a body of certified knowledge in order to realize his aims, under guidance of certain ethical principles, and with the client's interest—not his own—in mind. This last point should be emphasized; the change-agent must defer his own personal gratification in his dealings with the target system, his client. Particularly in dealing with something as important as a large and complex organization —where the change-agent's actions may affect thousands of individuals—he must continually check his own needs, motives, and wishes against the reality of the client's needs.*

Second, the role of the change-agent is *marginal;* that is, he does not have formal membership in the target system or a band of colleagues working close by. Typically he works alone, and his marginality can work to his advantage and to his discomfort. On the positive side, the marginality can enhance his detachment and perception; it can also create insecurity and an absence of mechanisms (like colleagues) for reality-testing. In any case, both the target system and the change-agent have to come to terms with the idea of marginality.†

Third, the role of the change-agent is *ambiguous.* Essentially this means that the basic concept of the change-agent is not widely understood and evokes a wide range of meaning. If one responds to the question "What do you do?" with the answer "I am a psychologist," it does not evoke the same bewilderment as the response "I am a change-agent." (In fact, the responder might be well advised not to answer in that vein.) The ambiguity of the role betrays its lack of legitimacy as well as credibility. It also involves certain risks like drawing suspicion and hostility *because* of its ambiguity. On the other

---

* The change-agent must be made painfully aware of some of the unconscious gratifications of his role too, so that these can be brought under control. We have in mind fantasies of high-powered manipulation or of satisfying an uncontrollable urge for power and omnipotence.

† In a recent case we heard about, a change-agent reported to work for his first day on the job, and the plant manager requested him to do some work which seemed to be inappropriate for a change-agent; that is, it was work which one of the managers should have been doing. The change-agent refused to carry out functions which properly belonged to management. In this case the manager could not come to terms with the marginal role of the change-agent.

side, it can also be helpful in providing the necessary latitude and breadth which more precisely defined roles do not allow.

Fourth, the role of the change-agent is *insecure*. This stems from a variety of causes: the precarious employment basis of the change-agent (the fact that he may be the most expendable person under certain conditions); inadequate knowledge and the lack of guidelines for many of his actions; the profound resistances which develop when one attempts to change an organization—all these factors tend to make the role insecure.

Fifth, and related to the insecure elements in the change-agent's role, is the *risky* quality inherent in it, the risk not only to the target system but also to the agent's professional status. As we shall see in the next section, the complexity of organizational change and some of its unanticipated consequences can lead to totally undesirable outcomes.

In sum, we view the change-agent's role as professional, marginal, ambiguous, insecure, and risky. Let us continue this discussion by identifying some of the competencies required for achieving success in the role.

• 2 Competence required of the change-agent

This must encompass a wide range of knowledge, including conceptual-diagnostic knowledge cutting across the entire sector of the behavioral sciences, theories and methods of organizational change, knowledge of sources of help, and orientation to the ethical and evaluative functions of the change-agent's role.

In addition to this intellectual grasp, the change-agent must also possess operational and relational skills. He must be able to listen, observe, identify, and report; he must have the ability to form relationships and inspire trust; and he must have a high degree of behavioral flexibility.

The change-agent must also be able to "use himself," to be in constant communication with himself, and to recognize and come to terms with (as much as is humanly possible) his own motivations. Particularly in the diagnostic stages of the work, the change-agent must observe how the target system deals with him. Quite often, as we mentioned earlier, the interaction between the change-agent and the target system is crucial for understanding and reaching a conclusion with respect to the state and readiness of the target system. In short, the change-agent should be sensitive and mature.

Finally, the change-agent should act congruently ("authentically"), that is, in accordance with the values he is attempting to superimpose upon the target system's value system. It will not do for the change-agent to impose democratic or humanistic values in an authoritarian or inhuman manner. If the change-agent is concerned with creating more authenticity and collaboration, he must behave in ways that are in accord with these values. We say this not only for the obvious ethical reasons but for deeper reasons as well. The fact of the matter is that so much of the change-agent's influence grows out of his relationship with the target system and the extent to which he is emulated as a role model that any significant discrepancies between his actions and his stated values cannot help but create resistance.

These are the requirements for the effective achievement of the change-agent's role, and they sound almost saintly. We would not expect to find many such supermen among us, but we would expect this job description to be used as something to aim for.

◆ C Strategies of implementation

We have examined the state of the target system and the role and competence of the change-agent. Let us close this section by taking a look at some of the strategy questions which arise in connection with the interaction between the two. These can be stated as choice points, questions which ultimately have to be considered in any change endeavor and which can be decided only after a thorough examination of the target system.

1 Who is the client?
2 What is the point of entry?
3 Which systems are involved?
4 To what extent can the change-agent involve the target system in planning and executing Lab Training?

• 1 Who is the client?

This is the first and perhaps the most important strategic question. Is it the organization? A particular T group? The group or person who appointed and pays the change-agent? An individual in stress?

This is a hard question to answer, and we would guess that the *salient* client changes often throughout the course of a Lab Training program. But the question itself should never be too far from the change-agent's mind.

• 2   *What is the point of entry?*

That is, at what level of the organization should Lab Training be directed first? The top management group? Middle levels? Lower levels? Or where? There are some change-agents, like Argyris[15] and Blansfield,[16] who believe that change can succeed only if it starts at the top and percolates down, that in order for a real change to take place, the highest command must be the primary initiating force.

Others disagree with this strategy. They claim that change programs utilizing Lab Training can start at lower levels of the target system and still be successful. Furthermore, they argue, it is sometimes *preferable* to start the change at lower levels because in some situations—because of a variety of organizational conditions—starting at the top may be too risky.

To some extent, the problem of point of entry can be decided on the basis of the kind of model of change employed. If it is a *line* model, then the consequences of starting at the lower levels may be different from what they would be in a *consultant* or *staff* model.

The kind of model used also pertains to our third question.

• 3   *Which systems are involved?*

Obviously everyone cannot be trained at once, which raises the question of priorities and choice. Can training be isolated in certain components of the organization, leaving other components without it, or should attempts be made to include segments of all subsystems of the target system in the initial stages of the program? In any case, a careful diagnosis needs to be undertaken in order to trace the most strategic circulation of Lab Training effects throughout the total target system. In our experience, some of the most critical unanticipated consequences arose when a diagnosis of the interdependencies of the subsystems within the target system was not carefully worked out.

How to choose the point of entry and which systems to involve are important *and* related strategic questions. There is no simple guideline to use in making these choices—except an intimate knowledge and diagnosis of the target system, which we outlined above in Table 4, and a consideration of the model of change used.

One final question must be raised now:

> • 4   *To what extent can the change-agent involve the target system in planning and executing Lab Training?*

In order to act in accordance with the values of Lab Training, the change-agent should attempt to involve the target system in planning and goal setting for the change program. Sometimes, though, this is easier said than done because the target system may not have the experience or expertise to collaborate realistically with the change-agent. In any case, the change-agent must attempt to make an adequate diagnosis of the extent to which the target system should be involved in the planning, goal setting, and execution of Lab Training.*

These are some of the main questions which come up and perplex change-agents in initiating Lab Training change programs. They do not, by a long shot, exhaust the endless possibilities of problems. And until we have achieved perfect strategic comprehension of the target system in relation to the change-agent, we will be beset by these and still other unanticipated problems.

III.   Three cases of failure

In medical training, students and physicians are exposed quite regularly to an intriguing ordeal called the "clinical pathology conference," in which a pathologist presents the autopsy of a patient and an expert is called in (in full view of all seated in the amphitheater) to diagnose the precise cause of the fatality. No equivalent teaching device exists in the behavioral sciences, unfortunately, mainly because we are in a relatively early stage of developing a practice.† Yet we

---

* There is a dilemma here often commented upon by change-agents and practitioners. How can systems of collaboration be established if one party to the encounter cannot adequately *choose* because of inexperience or lack of knowledge? Does coercion or faith have to be used during the very first phase of change? Can one start a democratic change program, for example, by ordering people to attend? Can a change-agent insist that his client attend a lab so that collaboration, of a deep and enduring kind, can be achieved?

† There are other reasons as well, for example, the understandable desire for secrecy regarding failures or mixed successes and the difficulty of ascertaining precise causes in these complex social-change ventures.

PREFACE

Although I have had some connection with the preparation of this book, it has been as impartial observer and calmly fearless noncombatant. It is therefore easy for me to express my admiration for the combined enthusiasm and good judgment which Mr. Gordon has brought to his self-imposed task. As he remarks in his final chapter, Henry Miller fits none of the recognized patterns of contemporary American fiction, and the very large appreciation of him that has undoubtedly existed for many years has been in the main too spontaneous and inarticulate to be stable. On the other hand, those noteworthy artist-critics who have spoken out for Miller have, rightly or wrongly, been so bounteous in their praises that the ordinary well-disposed reader would have difficulty in accepting them or even in comprehending them. As part of the problem of Miller, also, one should in candor mention those of us, readers and critics too, who have vanquished him with a half-envious grin.

Mr. Gordon's very substantial achievement consists most simply of doing justice to Miller's essential seriousness. To state this problem in elementary terms, and as an outsider: it is easy to be put off by Miller's extravagance and violence, by his fantastic humor and apparent irresponsibility. Not that his tone and tenor are unfamiliar to us in the American novel; they are there, and one may at the same time reflect that he put them there himself through other writers before his own books were available to the general public. But they are associated with experimentalism sans fruition, self-expression with no interesting self to express; the ghastly green-sickness of ambitious immaturity; or, at the other extreme, elaboration of technique without substance. Gordon's thoughtful and sympathetic analysis should be of the greatest assistance to us in keeping our eye on the object when we have in Miller the real thing. In *Tropic of Capricorn,* as a representative instance, the telegraph office may well in its fantastic individuality distract us from the steady progression of the book as a whole. One may put it, too, that Miller has written the "auto-novel" without permitting himself to fall into the "anti-novel," the last pitiable denial of art by wearied former artists. And Gordon, correspondingly, has described Miller's characteristic form with great acuteness.

He has treated the thorny and complex problem of sex and pornography with great skill and honesty. In this matter it is not nearly enough simply to decry popular puritanism and hypocrisy from the vantage point of superior honesty and sophistication. Mr. Gordon has himself had much experience as an expert witness for literature in cases of official censorship, and he is unusually well qualified to speak on the issues involved. Here one must utter a few great immutable truisms. Since sex is life itself, and since it constitutes the fullest relationship—attraction and repulsion alike—between individuals, and since its relation to self-surrender and love is intimate and insoluble, one obviously does not achieve much by dismissing it or explaining it as natural impulse and act, in a limited truth. Literary pornography is the irresponsible treatment of sex in isolation, as a phenomenon without consequences or significant relationships to the individual. Miller's treatment of sex may occasionally lead us to suspect that the percentage both of availability and alacrity he protrays is high even for Brooklyn and to reflect that no one could follow certain acts in his works except acrobats. Yet he is fundamentally both honest and profound; his sexual encounters do have consequences, if sometimes only to the self or protagonist, and he deceives neither himself nor us about their relative importance. In one of his many cogent comments on sex in Miller, Gordon remarks:

The sexual passages in Miller's works must be understood in the light of the development of the hero-narrator toward an integration of all the possibilities of life within an overall unity. To understand and accept this point of view we must make certain assumptions about our culture, which are the basic assumptions characteristic of Miller's general philosophic position. Our culture, in this view, maintains its position through repression, projection, and denial. The lines of the body, man's full existence, have been lost by dividing man against himself. During the process of development the true self, meaning not only what one is, but what one wants, begins to emerge. In order for this process to continue, however, all pressures from fear, loneliness, or social disapproval must be resisted. Otherwise the growth will be choked off and some of the areas of self will not come to light.

Gordon is inclined to view Miller as the greatest romantic of them all, and his connection of Miller with the great nineteenth-century Romantics through the autobiographical tradition is persuasively, even impressively, argued: "Even among the English Romantics the search for individual identity took the form of a descent into the lower levels of psychic life, a passing out of the self in order to discover the relation of the individual to the cosmos and the interaction of art with life. The form is most apparent, however, in those writers who chose autobiography as their typical mode of expression, Wordsworth in England, Thoreau, Emerson, and Whitman in America." The resemblance of William Wordsworth to Henry Miller is a startling notion, and I rather think it would have startled Wordsworth. Yet, as Gordon demonstrates, in their themes of growth, continuity of development, and "progressive self-creation" they are indeed akin. Whitman is a more obvious predecessor, in his Americanism, in his imaginative use of sensuous experience, and in his uncompromising adherence to the doctrines of growth and motion. As for Emerson, he had a strong enough mind and stomach to welcome Whitman as the fulfillment of his dream of the American genius; he could have encompassed Miller with perfect serenity. Thoreau would probably have said something cutting and unexpected, but would gradually have been won over to the new cosmic sincerity. The occasion has stirred Gordon into a very fine discussion of the nature of romanticism, a fitting culmination to his work. Owing something to Morse Peckham, it is nevertheless essentially original, as well as consistent and vital.

As sheer speculation, one might also point to some telling likenesses between Miller and William Blake, who has meant more to twentieth-century writers—at least in the last twenty years—than the more orthodox romantics. Mr. Gordon quite rightly leaves Blake out of account, since he is concerned with the autobiographical strain, and Blake is not overtly autobiographical. Yet, to note two outstanding instances: Blake has been the Bible for Joyce Cary's Gully Jimson, the Blakeian, brawling artist of *The Horse's Mouth,* and to Lawrence Durrell's novelist Pursewarden in *The Alexandria Quartet.* Blake's violence, his extremism, his uncompromising subjectivity, his unflagging sense of his own rightness in a wrongheaded society, his headlong revolt, his anarchism, his absolute alienation, his cosmic myth and vision—all these speak to our time, and all of them may well remind us of Henry Miller.

Blake's vision of the metropolitan city as hell is like Miller's description of his Brooklyn, and the latter's telegraph office is surely one of Blake's dark Satanic mills. Miller's constant sense of revelation, his various discoveries and epiphanies, however, remind us more of Wordsworth and the theme of growth and self-development. His conviction that almost all men except himself are on the wrong track is not only Blakeian but romantic in general. Miller, however, found sympathy abroad, and many kindred spirits; his reprehension, like Mencken's, has been reserved chiefly for his own countrymen, and for North Europeans. To his own imagination, at least, he is a Mediterranean man.

Gordon's book is unquestionably the first serious full-length study of this challenging and controversial figure as an artist. One praises it again for its enthusiasm, its steady insight, its objectivity, its tact, and its thorough independence.

RICHARD HARTER FOGLE

CONTENTS

INTRODUCTION

In 1946 Henry Miller, then living in Big Sur, California, received a letter from his French publisher informing him that he had royalties accumulated in the equivalent of $40,000. Since francs in those immediately postwar years could not be exchanged into dollars and since the publisher was about to run into financial difficulties, Miller's royalties never got to him nor he to them. In the years following, he had a steady if not large market among Americans traveling in Europe. Enough copies of his banned books filtered back into the States to make *Tropic of Cancer* and *Tropic of Capricorn* possibly the best-known illicit books in the world.[1]

By 1946 Henry Miller had projected the course of his life work and had completed several important portions of it. He remained poor, but he kept on writing. A group of devoted Miller fans slowly grew, enthusiasts who wrote stimulating

1 Miller's European reputation which also continued to grow must be the subject of a separate study. He had been translated into many languages and accepted in Europe before being accepted in America. For example, in France rather than in America we find an entire issue of a periodical devoted to Miller. *La Tour de Feu* (Autumn, 1955).

but highly subjective essays about the master. The *Henry Miller Newsletter,* composed by a commercial printer and a machinist from the Honeywell Corporation, was begun in Minneapolis. In New England, *New Directions* continued to release Miller's American books; but, though he had achieved a kind of fame, neither fortune nor critical attention came to him.[2]

In 1960 the great silence about Henry Miller seemed about to come to an end. Grove Press brought out *Tropic of Cancer* and followed it a year later with *Tropic of Capricorn.* In 1965 the three books of *The Rosy Crucifixion* were published, the last of Miller's major works. What happened during those five years was predictable in some ways, surprising in others. As was to be expected, a great cry of outrage went up from the many American communities who had heard of Miller and wanted him excluded from their hospitality. Not unexpectedly some periodicals "noticed" the publication of his works and wrote brief reviews which generally found some simplified label for handling the problem. Those who are against censorship for any reason were for Miller automatically and said so. Few attempted to place him in the American literary tradition or to explain the enthusiastic support from those who admire him. Unexpectedly, the professional critics, especially those associated with universities, ignored his presence. Critical and scholarly journals have spawned a mere handful of articles which could be called, even remotely, serious criticism.

From my personal contact with scholars and critics who knew I was working on Miller, I can hazard a guess why they at least have ignored him. Miller lacks form, they say, and

2 While at Harvard, Laughlin published Miller's essay "Glittering Pie" in the *Harvard Advocate.* The issue was suppressed and burned, "except for a few dozen copies that one less conscientious guardian of the law peddled around town for two dollars and up." Bern Porter (ed.), *The Happy Rock* (Berkeley: Packard Press, 1947), 115.

besides he is a bore. The first of these criticisms any thorough study can disprove. The second is beyond objection. But much still needs to be understood about a writer who can appeal so dynamically to some and leave others not only cold, but repelled. Until now only two book-length critical studies of Miller have been attempted. The first of these, *Henry Miller Expatriate,* is restricted to one aspect of Miller.[3] The second study, which purports to be a more global view, is on the whole too unsympathetic to look beyond its central generalization that Miller is a "rebel-buffoon." [4] No attempt has been made even in the most superficial way to relate Miller to the tradition which he openly and often claims he belongs to, the romantic tradition—American, German, and French.

The appearance of Miller's major works seems to have been untimely as far as critical appreciation goes. During the years after World War I the universities which were not immersed in historical criticism, and therefore uninterested in contemporary writers, were turning to those writers who best exemplified formal organization. The growth of formalism in criticism from World War II until the present has insured that a writer whose works dealt mainly with the ideas and institutions of his times would be ignored. Miller came along during the last flurry of interest in naturalistic writing, and the ideas which influenced him had not yet attracted the attention of American literary critics.[5]

3 Annette Kar Baxter, *Henry Miller Expatriate* (Pittsburgh: University of Pittsburgh Press, 1961).
4 Kingsley Widmer, *Henry Miller* (New York: Twayne Publishers, 1963).
5 The recent collection of essays with commentaries by Richard Ellman and Charles Feidelson, *The Modern Tradition: Backgrounds of Modern Literature* (New York: Oxford University Press, 1965), is the first that seems to encounter directly the relevance of post-evolutionary European philosophy to the study of literature. We have had in America, for example, much Freudian criticism, but few critics who have linked Freud to Nietzsche as this study has done.

One must recognize the objection, of course, that Miller's subject matter is obscene or dull. The sophisticated readers who turned from Miller did so because they were bored by obscenity. They felt that his language was the equivalent of an adolescent writing on the men's room wall. This is perhaps the accusation which is most difficult to counter. I feel that an explanation which places the sexual material in the context of the total structure of the work will go farthest in rescuing Miller from this fate. Many who have reread Miller in some reasonable kind of order have changed their minds.

The greatest problem, however, is that his communication is on a level which makes critical study difficult. Confronting Miller is an affair of the intestines, radiating out toward the intellect, but staying, on the whole, close to the omphalic center. Miller is a realist, but not a literary naturalist. He is a romantic, but not an idealist—not at least in the sense that he believes that life can be beautiful. Like Whitman he searches the deepest springs and motivating impulses of human action; and since these motivating impulses are intimately tied up with the physical organism, the levels of reality in Miller are rooted in the complexities of biological as well as psychological existence.

It has not been uncommon for critics to treat him as a realist in the traditional sense. The chief difference critics find between Miller and other twentieth-century realists is his willingness to describe events with a freedom of language until very recently unexplored outside the hard-shell pornography market. As a superrealist Miller has been praised by anti-Puritans and condemned by moralists, though he is writing for neither group. He is, in fact, not a realist in the historical sense of the word. He is rather a highly symbolic writer, discovering and illuminating the very deepest levels of conscious and unconscious life. To this end Miller's realism—the experiences he recounts, the language he uses—

is the form in which "felt life" is made concrete. Miller's themes are vital ones, vital to the growth and development of the individual. But they are created out of material which has been for the American reader unavailable for consideration.

Henry Miller's principal theme is that the individual must grow in freedom and independence. His voyage of discovery is toward a full acceptance of the possibilities and limitations of the human individual. He is, in the best romantic tradition, a nonconformist. But he is a nonconformist in ways and concerning elements of experience which few people have realized sufficiently to be nonconformist about.

Although Miller has been treated by critics, on the rare occasions when he has been discussed at all, as a late survival of the depression school,[6] I have chosen, in this work, to link him directly to the Romantic tradition to which, I feel, he is most closely allied. Almost any general description of Romanticism in England or in America could easily be applied to Miller. For Miller, as for Keats, the world is "a school in which the human heart must suffer in a thousand diverse ways, to bring forth a soul with individual identity." [7] For Miller, as for Wordsworth and Coleridge, "The mind with its experience in time is an indivisible whole, in which no one event is really separable from the rest; the roots of the conscious lie deep in the unconscious; the child is father of the man beyond the capacity of memory to recall." [8] With

6 See Edmund Wilson, *The Shores of Light* (London: Allen, 1952), 705–10, and Philip Rahv, *Image and Idea* (New York: New Directions, 1949). Both emphasize the "bohemian" element in Miller to the exclusion of other themes and values.

7 J. Middleton Murry, "Keats' Thought: A Discovery of Truth," in Clarence DeWitt Thorpe (ed.), *The Major English Romantics* (Carbondale: University of Illinois Press, 1957), 255–56.

8 Richard Harter Fogle, "A Note on Romantic Oppositions and Reconciliations," in Thorpe (ed.), *The Major English Romantics,* 21.

Wordsworth, Miller succeeds "in making intelligible the growth of the poet's mind, while also preserving the sense of its living unity and continuity. . . ." [9] And Miller, like all romantics, rejects "That finitude which is inherent in all pattern. The universe must always be in process of creation, but it must never be created. . . ." [10] Miller affirms his private vision and assumes its universal validity, transcends himself in order to become more fully himself, must die in order to live, finds a multiplicity of men and things and fragments of the self which he continually reconciles into a greater whole, searches deep within the self to discover the universe. Henry Miller affirms, in short, a romantic view of reality.

Any just evaluation of Henry Miller as a writer is handicapped partly by the order in which his books have appeared before the American public. What we in America have seen until recently have been the commentaries on American life written since his return from Europe, which have sometimes combined in the reader's mind with a faint and usually unfavorable recollection of one or another of the *Tropics*. In the collected essays, such as *The Air-Conditioned Nightmare* or *Remember to Remember,* we seem to be hearing a self-styled prophet who issues sweeping pronouncements on his life and times; in the *Tropics,* a bohemian writing of the "low-life" in Paris and New York. Unfortunately a proper estimate of Miller as a writer depends primarily upon knowing the works which until the present time were almost unavailable, that is, the three books of *The Rosy Crucifixion.* There are four works upon which Miller's reputation must ultimately be based: *Tropic of*

9 *Ibid.,* 22.
10 Hoxie N. Fairchild, "Romanticism: Devil's Advocate," in Thorpe (ed.) , *The Major English Romantics,* 25.

Capricorn, and *Sexus, Plexus,* and *Nexus* (the three books of *The Rosy Crucifixion*). These works taken together develop the theme of the growth of the writer. Each contributes to the overall effect of the growth of the personality toward freedom and identity. The later works show the result of that growth, the joyous acceptance of life by a man who has suffered deeply, who has worked slowly and painfully toward the truth which he possesses.

Since little has yet been done to place Henry Miller in his own historical period and to show the development of his thought, I have devoted my first two chapters to his early life and to his reading. Miller read many authors who, in different ways, were mining the same vein of post-evolutionary speculation, which has made it difficult to avoid repetition. Yet these writers and thinkers are different, and I have tried to concentrate on what is essential in each case. These chapters are an important preliminary to the central task of this book, which is to show the structure and themes of Miller's major works. This task falls principally to Chapters 3, 4, and 5, which take up in turn *Tropic of Cancer, Tropic of Capricorn,* and *The Rosy Crucifixion.* Chapter 6 shows the development of Miller's thinking after Paris, for the most part in *The Colossus of Maroussi.* In Chapter 7 an attempt is made to show the link which exists between Henry Miller and the romantic tradition. Before taking up the main body of the work, I feel it necessary to set down some of the events in the life of Miller, not only because they are as yet little known, but also because they are the main events in his fictionalized biography and some knowledge of their sequence is helpful in understanding what follows.

Henry Valentine Miller was born on December 26, 1891, in New York City, but his family moved to Brooklyn in his first year.[11] It was in the Williamsburg section of Brooklyn, where he grew up, that he acquired the particular savor of life which remains throughout his life and work. As "just a Brooklyn boy" he has faced the world in the United States and Europe, and his early vision, though becoming richer and deeper, has changed little in scope. His life falls into periods separated by significant events which generally show a change of direction, or a step toward or sometimes away from his life goal.

The first period of Miller's life, the Brooklyn period, forms a background against which he was able to view the whole of his later experience. Life in Brooklyn, as Miller presents it, was happy in its allegiances with other boys, but tinged faintly as the years went by with sadness and then despair as he saw what must inevitably happen to his friends and himself as they got caught up in the drudgery and monotony of everyday American life. This period is likewise marked by the first struggles to escape, to rise above the culture into which he was born, that have characterized Miller ever since.

In 1909, at the age of eighteen, Miller took up with his first mistress, a woman "old enough to be his mother," and he was able to break the relationship only with great difficulty. This was a period of growing estrangement from his family, occasioned especially by his expressed desire to marry this woman. It would appear from autobiographical com-

11 See Porter (ed.), *The Happy Rock*, 152–54. The biographical information in this summary is based in part on this chronology and its continuation in Lawrence Durrell (ed.), *The Henry Miller Reader* (New York: New Directions, 1959). Other facts or events are drawn from the novels and essays. Inevitably facts and fiction become confounded during this process, but since Miller himself makes little effort to separate them, it is more suitable to my purpose to provide an outline to aid in understanding the events of the novels than to speculate about what is biographical and what is not.

ments as well as from outside sources that this was a period in which Miller's relationships with his mother and father became highly conscious and critical. An examination of these relationships and their effect on Miller must wait until we consider his works in greater detail. Suffice it to say that he felt from his mother little more than opposition and total lack of understanding, and from his father the same detachment and neglect which was the lot of the rest of the family. It was not until 1939, upon his return from Europe, that he achieved any communication with his father, and this a short two years before his father died. His mother remained a hostile force until her death, and nowhere does he speak well of her. To her he was a failure, not like other mothers' sons. She could understand only what sold; she was unsympathetic to his writing from the beginning. It is obvious from the manner in which Miller draws her character that any possibility of reconciliation was destroyed by the growing bitterness of her own view of life.

Of great importance for his later works was his marriage to Beatrice Sylvas Wickens, a piano teacher. From his life with her he created the character of Maude in *Tropic of Capricorn* and *Sexus*. Here, as with all of Miller's characters, there is a question of how much is fiction and how much is fact. Miller insists that like Proust he used these people in actual life only as a base for his fictional characters. In any event, in the auto-novels we have only Miller's side of the story. As he describes the situation in his works, it is clear that she and Miller were not suited. She was extremely inhibited and, with good reason, jealous. On the basis of the material provided by Miller it is difficult to make out a strong case against her, but it is clear that he considered the relationship repressive, at a time when he was trying hard to find himself. The marriage broke up after seven years. Miller left his wife and four-year-old daughter to live with and eventually marry June Edith Smith, a dance hall hostess whom he had met a year earlier.

The relationship with June Smith provided him with the character of Mona (Mara) of *The Rosy Crucifixion*. Eventually it allowed Miller to quit the job he held as employment manager of Western Union. Miller describes the chaos of the world of messengers in *Tropic of Capricorn*; it was a job in which he evidently proved to have great capabilities of administration and organization, though he hated it passionately. With Mona he was free for the first time to take up a career which had increasingly attracted him, that of writer. This period with Mona was at once his liberation and his enslavement. As a character Mona is one of the greatest mysteries in Miller's works. What she literally was is virtually impossible to say. Her existence in his books has acquired such highly mysterious, symbolic dimensions as to lose the sense of a real human person, or at the very least to make the reality unrecoverable. Mona had evidently mysterious relationships with other men which mysteriously brought quantities of money. What these relationships were the reader may easily guess, but for the fact that Miller wishes no such easy conclusion to be formed. Again, her relationship with her "friend" Stasia, who had come to live with her and Miller, is uncertain, though highly suspicious. The principal characteristic of Mona is her chameleon-like changeability. By Miller she is loved, but not understood.[12]

The period 1924 to 1930, life with Mona, is the time of Miller's greatest suffering, climaxed by an attempt at suicide.

---

12 The recently published volume of the *Diary of Anais Nin* (New York: Harcourt, Brace & World, 1966) confirms the indefinability of June's (Mona's) character. In many passages the relationship between June and Anais is openly erotic, but as Miss Nin relates the episode, the air of mutual embarrassment makes it appear the first time for both.

He explained his situation, the torture of his life with Mona, to a doctor friend and asked for drugs to ease him out of life. He took the drugs and opening the window to the cold, lay down naked on the bed, assuming that if the drugs didn't kill him he would freeze to death. He woke up twelve hours later feeling fine. Yet the first step toward future freedom was undertaken with the help of Mona and at her suggestion. She and Miller toured Europe in 1928 on money donated by her "victim." In 1930 Miller returned to Europe, this time by himself. There he met people, made friends, and began the hand-to-mouth existence which forms the subject matter for his European works, principally *Tropic of Cancer.*

Tropic of Cancer, which he began writing in 1931, was published in 1934. This date marks his entrance into the literary world. At the moment of writing this book Miller was experiencing greater poverty and greater liberation than he had ever before experienced. The book, despite the depressing nature of much of its material, is a song of joy. With this book Miller began the long elaboration of autobiography which has occupied him until the present day. He lived as best he could during these days, sometimes sponging off friends, sometimes finding a job for a short period, sometimes going hungry, but always moving on toward the goal of being a writer. *Tropic of Cancer* was followed by *Black Spring,* in 1936, which recreated the Brooklyn period of his early life, and *Aller Retour New York,* in 1935, a long letter to Alfred Perles, with whom he lived in Paris. *Quiet Days in Clichy,* which was written later, describes life in this Paris suburb chiefly from the standpoint of characters and environment. *Tropic of Capricorn,* published in 1939, and perhaps his greatest work, begins the re-creation of the central experiences surrounding his efforts to become a writer, the period of his employment with Western Union and life with his first wife. The later works, the three books of *The*

Rosy Crucifixion, overlap the period of *Tropic of Capricorn*
and take us up to the flight to Paris.

The years in Paris were evidently the richest of Henry
Miller's life. One gets the impression of unceasing activity
and zest for life. There he met Lawrence Durrell, Blaise
Cendrars, Anais Nin, and Michael Fraenkel. French life was
an environment which brought out all his natural optimism.
With the help of Lawrence Durrell, he and Alfred Perles
took over the publication of a little magazine formerly connected with the American Country Club of France. The story
of the change of this magazine from a country club organ to
a literary periodical is one of the fascinating stories of this
period. Under the enthusiastic direction of Miller and company, the magazine soon outgrew either the needs or the
wishes of the golf club which sponsored it. To sever its last
relations with the respectability of the country club, the
name was changed from *Booster* to *Delta,* and under the new
name the review came out three more times before the war.

The oncoming of the war brought Miller's Paris life to a
close. He headed for Greece at the invitation of the Durrells
who had taken up residence on the isle of Corfu. The short
but important period in Greece is described in *The Colossus
of Maroussi.* It was, as Miller presents it, a period of great
insight and of marked growth toward the freedom which he
had always sought. The books of the Paris period, mostly
concerned with Miller's past life, are grounded historically
in his United States experience. During his short stay in
Greece he evidently sank roots more deeply into the historical
past of Western civilization. The rising crescendo as Miller
finds one by one the great historical sites of Ancient Greece
leads to an almost mystical insight into the mysteries of
Greek life, art, and religion. The rhapsody which follows is
mysterious, mystical, and utterly convincing.

The war threatened, however, and Miller had once more

to move. There was now no place to go except back to the United States. He arrived in March, 1940, visited friends, then in the next year began a one-year tour with a painter friend, Abraham Rattner, around the United States. He published two works based on this trip, *The Air-Conditioned Nightmare* and *Remember to Remember*. His pilgrimage was finally halted by the offer of a home in California, which he accepted in 1942.

Once in California, Miller moved step by step to Big Sur. He moved from Beverly Glen to Monterey and from Monterey to Big Sur, Partington Ridge. Each move was financed by friends since, cut off from his European royalties, Miller was almost penniless. He was married again in 1944, to Martha Lepska. About her little is said except that the period of the marriage was a black one. Lepska left, leaving their two children with Miller; a part of the story of his adventures with them is to be found in *Big Sur and the Oranges of Hieronymus Bosch*. Miller was married again in 1952 to Eve McClure, but that marriage likewise ended in divorce. He now lives alone in Pacific Palisades, California, in order to be near his children. During these years of the war, its aftermath, and two marriages, Miller began and completed many of the works he had outlined for himself while working for the park commissioner in New York in 1927. All that remains to be completed of that ambitious project is the second half of *Nexus,* book three of *The Rosy Crucifixion.* With its publication Miller has said that his responsibility as a writer will cease.

As the central autobiographical work has evolved out of the original plan and as the voluminous essays have been published, we find Miller the man gradually changing. As years go on, the emphasis shifts from art to life. In the last (in time) of his autobiographical works his concern has become almost wholly with the flavor of life itself. True, Miller has always appreciated the quality of experience, but now the contradictions and frustrated ambitions have diminished. Experience is refined, savored in its pure state. Again, as life has gone on he has reached out beyond the immediately physical in experience to the transcendent, the absolute. The evolution is not unlike that of Whitman from the physical basis of "Song of Myself" to the transcendence of "Passage to India." Perhaps it must be the final goal of every romantic writer, the goal indeed which distinguishes Miller from the mere realist.

THE
MIND
AND
ART
OF
HENRY
MILLER

JUST A BROOKLYN BOY

Brooklyn, as a region, as a culture, a way of life, even an attitude to life, is important for Henry Miller in much the same way that the storied Mississippi past was important for Faulkner. For Miller, Brooklyn created the richness and diversity of early life which became both the point of departure and the point of return for his autobiographical romance. He lived in Brooklyn when it was converted from a residential area to an immigrant quarter, from "a city of rubber plants, to a city of contrasts." [1] The kind of life which Miller lived in Brooklyn from the mid-1890's until after World War I is different enough from the lives of other American writers to be taken seriously into account when examining his place in the tradition.

Pausing for a moment to glance at the American literary scene from World War I until the end of the thirties, we

---

1 *Library Journal,* XXXV (February, 1910), 62. This brief commentary on library conditions in Brooklyn in 1910 is effective in recreating the aura which attached to the public library during those years, and the seriousness with which the libraries tried to cope with the enormous difficulties they faced.

recall certain dividing lines which are typical of the American writer's relationship to the American tradition. The postwar writers, for example, tend to act as if nothing had existed before the war. For Ernest Hemingway and the period he dominates, life began anew in the twenties. Nothing from before the war was saved. Not only the memory of the war but the effects of social life, of prohibition, and of the commercial expansion made life after the Armistice seem a wholly different process from what it had been in the dimly remembered pre-1914 period. The writers from before the war who were still living were overshadowed by the writers of the twenties.

Some writers, Theodore Dreiser for example, confronted the problems and forces of the end of the century, but Dreiser turned toward his own dream. He knew the misery of the despised immigrant groups who struggled for a place in American society, but he fled from that knowledge toward success. On the other hand, writers who remained in contact with the proletariat became for the most part politically oriented, and their art did not keep pace with their enthusiasm for justice. *U.S.A.* by John Dos Passos was, for its time, a well-constructed book which attempted to grasp the diversity of life in the United States and the changes it was undergoing from before World War I until 1930. Yet the weight of the book is in its polemics against the existing order, on a social rather than an individual level. Dos Passos remains immersed in the social situation.

Henry Miller published his first significant work in 1934, the middle of the depression. For years he has been taken as the arch example of the American expatriate, late depression period. He has been thought of as the bohemian par excellence, living chiefly on wits and nerve, and as the answer to the failure of the American productive machine, a way out from Puritanism. But, to take Miller as a depression writer, in the historical sense of the term, is not so much to fail to understand him as to ignore what he says. Miller's attitudes are not 1930's vintage, either socialist or bohemian. What he knows about art and literature and philosophy is different from what our writers of the twenties and thirties knew. Miller has read more widely and deeply than most American writers of his time, but more than that, he has read different things. That difference in the kind and quantity of Miller's reading is related both to the Brooklyn in which he grew up and to the century in which he was born; for Miller, though he was born in the same period as Hemingway and Pound and Eliot, did not repudiate his early life. He built upon it.

During the time when he was growing up—let us say from the age of six or seven until the end of high school—Brooklyn rapidly changed its character, especially the Williamsburg section where Miller lived until 1901. Over the years the small country towns which lay against the bank of the East River across from Manhattan had grown into an industrialized urban center. In 1890 Williamsburg was still a quiet town, but its metamorphosis was rapid in the next few years as factories and a growing population took over. Originally the area had been formed of typical yankee towns, but immigrants found it early. A large German population was established by 1850. Many of these Germans were skilled workmen and acquired superior economic positions. Miller's family belonged to this group. His grandfather had arrived in American about 1850, and his father carried on the tradition of merchant tailoring which the family had brought from Europe. The economic level of Miller's early life was subject, however, to the same unfavorable forces from which other merchant tailors were suffering. The ready-made clothing industry was cutting into the market so much as to affect seriously the chances of the master tailor for survival. Miller's recollections of his early life create the impression of a steadily declining prosperity which paralleled the physical decline of his father.[2]

During the 1890's and the early years of the twentieth century, life changed more quickly and more radically in Brooklyn. By this time the immigrant flood had reached its peak. No longer was it the skilled craftsman who flowed into the eastern cities, but the unskilled worker, Irish above all, and German and Pole. Finally came the mass arrival of Jews from Central Europe. Until 1900 these waves of new population swelled New York, especially the East side. Brooklyn got a share, and with the growth of heavy industry the town slowly changed. New buildings were built in which poor people could live more cheaply, though at greater density. Old dignified neighborhoods began to deteriorate. The city was filled with contrasts in appearances and in people. The old population was overwhelmed, though it clung at first to its traditions and neighborhoods. In 1903 the building of the Williamsburg Bridge spelled the end once and for all of the quiet residential community. Across the bridge from Delancey Street on the New York East Side came a steady flow of recent immigrants. The community could not absorb the numbers which arrived and conditions in Brooklyn began to resemble those in the East Side tenements. In Brooklyn, old American families, Americanized Europeans, and new immigrants mingled.[3]

Brooklyn already had its communities with the Old World customs, but now the differences were accentuated. The older immigrants, the Germans for example who came in the forties and fifties, seem to have lost much of their close connection with European literature and philosophy. They

2   Robert Ernst, *Immigrant Life in New York City, 1825–1863* (New York: King's Crown Press, 1949), 77.
3   Ralph Foster Weld, *Our Brooklyn* (Brooklyn: Brooklyn Institute of Arts and Sciences, 1940), 1939.

were the German-Americans with whom Miller grew up, unimaginative men who had nothing to offer. In general Miller
disliked them intensely. On the other hand there were his
father's drinking companions, hearty men who enjoyed life
to the full, men "who could talk humorously and intelligently about all manner of things." Yet if their conversation
was intelligent, it was not necessarily intellectual. For, Miller
tells us, his father never read a book in his life. Although
some of these men could on occasion talk to Miller about
European authors, it seems to have been among the newer
immigrants, the Jews of Eastern Europe, that the real awakening was to come; [4] it was Emma Goldman and the radicals
whose thinking was so passionately alive that carried Miller
to the great writers of Europe. It should be kept in mind
that Henry Miller as a supreme individualist cannot be assimilated into any tradition. Nevertheless, if only unconsciously, the immigrant culture, the anarchist tradition, even
the new kinds of food and the different smells of cooking
must have had some influence, and these things do help us
understand the special flavor of Miller and his philosophy
of the streets.

At the end of the century, Brooklyn, like New York, faced
the enormous task of absorbing the mass of immigrants into
American culture. The mechanism for this process was chiefly
the public school, though libraries and communication me-
dia were important. The growth of libraries kept pace with
the need for education. The number of libraries with over
1,000 volumes increased by 59 per cent. In one New York
library alone the volumes increased from 68,000 to over
450,000. Newspapers published book lists, and open shelves
permitted browsing. At the end of the century the Brooklyn
library reported serving Italians, Jews, Germans, French,

4 *Ibid.*, 242.

Spanish, Syrians, and Irish. Americanization became a national problem and a national preoccupation.[5]

Out of the Americanization process we have evolved a structure for our fiction and autobiography. From "rags to riches," from "shirt-sleeves to silks" has been the process of the American dream. Strangely enough, few writers seem to have undergone the process in reverse, that is, from the American ideal to European ideas. In Greenwich Village during Bodenheim's time an intellectual movement brought European writers into the American scene. Here poetry met socialism, anarchism, and Sigmund Freud. But in general our writers have not been attracted by the European intellectual tradition. The response to America seemed to take

5 See *Library Journal*, XXXV (January, 1910), 243–53. The following statement by Miller (Miller to author, August 20, 1966) throws some interesting light on several of the matters taken up in this chapter: ". . . bookshops were virtually unknown in my Brooklyn days and the neighborhood public library was most inadequate. I also read what the other boys read, such as Sir Walter Scott, Dickens, Dumas, Victor Hugo, and American writers too, especially the poets, practically all of them, up to a certain period. Include Ambrose Bierce, Lafcadio Hearn, Frank Norris, Dreiser, Anderson, Ben Hecht, many, many others. While in my teens, I believe, I read Petronius, Rabelais, Pierre Louys, Remy de Gourmont, Jules Laforgue, Maeterlinck, Pierre Loti, to mention a few. Nearly all of them were important to me. As were the Greek tragedies, and the Restoration dramatists, and the 19th century dramatists of most European countries. Then there was the Hindu religious literature, Chinese philosophers and poets, fairy tales of all countries and so on and so on. This romantic kick you thrust on me is only partially true; the occult and the metaphysical existed side by side with the romantics; and then also books on sociology, ethnology, economics, the scientific studies of Henri Fabre and Maeterlinck, everything imaginable, a full diet. And with all this, listening to soapbox orators (anarchists, I.W.W.'s, Socialists) from whom I learned a great deal. Big influences were persons like Jim Larkin, labor leader, Elizabeth Gurley Flynn, Hubert Harrison (Negro from the Rank School), Cowper Powys and W. E. Burghardt Du Bois—great figures—men of culture, the first I ever encountered in America." My emphasis on Romantic thought, which Miller partially objects to in this passage, is based on the impression drawn from his works rather than what Miller actually believes himself to have been influenced by.

two forms, positive and negative. On the positive side was the fulfillment of a promise or the dream of success. On the negative, the attack on injustice by socialist, anarchist, and muckraker. In each case, the issue was to be fought out in America, with little impetus toward the flight to Europe until after World War I.

Henry Miller's relationship to this changing Brooklyn can be divided into several periods. The first, which he described in *Black Spring* and *Tropic of Capricorn,* is the life in the old neighborhood, the Williamsburg section. The second period is less well defined. Miller calls it the "street of early sorrows." This was Decatur Street in the Bushwick section to the east of Williamsburg. Although the sorrow he associates with that street is not analyzed explicitly, it is vaguely connected with adolescent love. Possibly it was sorrow for what he missed in the old neighborhood, which he preferred. The third period corresponds roughly with the time after school, about 1909 until his first marriage in 1917. It is a time when among his many other activities in the realm of food, drinking, and sex, he began his reading of the European authors who would help him formulate his adult philosophy.

II

For reasons which should become apparent later in this book, Miller strongly emphasizes the influence on his adult character of his childhood life on the streets. When he set out to construct his autobiographical romance, he attributed to his Brooklyn boyhood the formation of his adult character. Therefore, whether fact or myth the life on the streets is pertinent to the study of his work. For Miller it was the symbol of freedom: "To be born in the street means to wander all your life, to be free. It means accident and incident, drama, movement. It means above all dream. A harmony of the irrelevant which gives to your wandering a metaphysical certitude. In the street you learn what human beings really are; otherwise, or afterwards, you invent them. What is not in the streets is false, derived, that is to say, literature." [6]

Miller was raised in a German atmosphere; he spoke German and English until he was school age.[7] He lived among people of a variety of nationalities, and he thinks of the section of his birth as an immigrant quarter. In re-creating the life of the 14th Ward, Miller emphasizes the lasting memories of the boyhood heroes, "Eddie Carney, Lester Reardon, Johnny Paul." Life as Miller remembers it was rich and varied. Certain ugly facts were there and had to be accepted. "Before the great change no one seemed to notice that the streets were ugly or dirty. If you blew your nose you found snot in your handkerchief and not in your nose. There was more of inward peace and contentment. There was the saloon, the racetrack, bicycles, fast women and trot horses." [8] The 14th Ward that he remembers is not a pretty residential section, "Where others remember of their youth a beautiful garden, a fond mother, a sojourn at the seashore, I remember, with a vividness as if it were etched in acid, the grim, soot-covered walls and chimneys of the tin factory opposite us and the bright circular pieces of tin that were strewn in the streets, some bright and gleaming, others rusted, dull, copperish, leaving a stain on the fingers. I remember the iron works where the red furnace glowed. . . . I remember the black hands of the iron-moulders, the grit that had sunk so deep into the skin that nothing could remove it. . . ." [9]

Life in Brooklyn was certainly not the life which the magazines were presenting as American or proper. A variety of characters, a variety of conduct, extremes of good and evil

6 *Black Spring* (Paris: Obelisk Press, 1958), 11.
7 See *The Cosmological Eye* (New York: New Directions, 1939), 365 ff.
8 *Black Spring*, 12.
9 *Ibid.,* 13.

filled every day. Yet to Miller as he recaptures the scene
these things were not good or evil, they just were. He accepted the easy-going indolent type like Bob Ramsay:

"I remember that everybody liked Bob Ramsay,—he was the
black sheep of the family. They liked him because he was a good-
for-nothing and he made no bones about it. Sundays or Wednes-
days made no difference to him; you could see him coming down
the street under the drooping awnings with his coat over his arm
and the sweat rolling down his face; his legs wobbly. . . the
tobacco juice dribbling from his lips, together with warm, silent
curses and some loud and foul ones too. The utter indolence, the
insouciance of the man, the obscenities, the sacrilege. Not a man
of God, like his father. No! a man who inspired love! His frailties
were human frailties and he wore them jauntily, tauntingly,
flauntingly, like banderillas." [10]

Experience went further than the sight of Ramsay charg-
ing down the street, there were the sights in the saloon
across the street. "Just a stone's throw away from the little
burlesque called The Bum. All around The Bum were the
saloons, and Saturday nights there was a long line outside,
milling and pushing and squirming to get at the ticket window. . . . And a little later that night they'd be sure to
come strolling down the street and turn in at the family
entrance. And soon they'd be standing in the bed-room
over the saloon taking off their tight pants and women yank-
ing off their corsets and scratching themselves like monkeys,
while below they were scuttling their suds and biting each
other's ears off. . . . All this from Bob Ramsay's steps." [11]

Life on the streets had its violent side and its amusing side.
Miller is above all a splendid storyteller, and in his ability to

10 *Ibid.*
11 *Ibid.,* 16.

capture the warmth of neighborhood events he is unsur-
passed. The fried banana party in *Tropic of Capricorn* is an
excellent example of Miller's storytelling ability. The story
starts, improbably enough, with getting rotten bananas from
Louis Pirossa's father. Stanley Borowski, son of the violent,
drunken barber, as Miller calls him, has a birthday party
with fried bananas. Nobody approves of eating fried bananas, so they give them to crazy Willie Maine who could
say nothing but "Bjork." A fight starts when Willie's brother
George disapproves of feeding Willie the bananas. Willie
begins hitting everyone, even the girls. Then Stanley's father
comes up and begins hitting Willie Maine, whose brother
gets Mr. Maine, who begins to beat up the barber. Seeing
Willie on the floor eating the bananas as fast as he can, his
father then starts on him with the strap. Finally everyone
begins to laugh and they all get drunk, including Willie
Maine.[12]

In this childhood life as Miller remembers it there was
more unity, less fragmentation than in the life of the adult.
For him life in the streets was real; the boy and his experience were united. Afterward, to note the difference, life is
lived in the mind. The immediacy is gone out of life, and we
try to recapture it by remembering the past. Later events
have meaning in terms of their repetition of early ones. "If
we are stirred by a fat bust it is the fat bust of the whore who
bent over on a rainy night and showed us for the first time
the wonder of the great milky globes; if we are stirred by
the reflections on a wet pavement it is because at the age of
seven we were suddenly speared by a premonition of the
life to come as we stared unthinkingly into that bright liquid
mirror of the street." [13] Everything he sensed and knew was

12 *Tropic of Capricorn* (New York: Grove Press, 1961), 136–37.
13 *Black Spring*, 19.

direct and immediate, not literary, as Miller is fond of saying. The range of smells was wide and related to clear and
specific causes. There was the smell of baking bread, and of
stale horse urine down by the stables. There was the smell
of the iron and of flesh when the veterinarian castrated the
horses. There was the smell of a woman's hair when she
washed it, "like the marsh smell." The discrimination of
odors, of tastes, of people and events was an awareness which
Miller never lost. All of his major books move freely back
and forth among the sensual phenomena of his world. This
awareness he attributes to his childhood in the 14th Ward.

Throughout his works Miller is intent upon establishing
the distinction between the level of experience and the level
of literature, or in the terms of *Tropic of Cancer,* between
art and life. The deliberate effort to recall the life of the
streets, to recall the past of childhood back to and even
anterior to birth becomes the means for establishing a sense
of identity in the present. For Miller experience must be
made to live on every level. No fact, no feeling may be
excluded. Nothing, however shocking, however raw must be
neglected that savors of real life. We sense that Miller's
struggle is to stay on the plane of the concrete, the real, to
stay by whatever strategems out of the clutches of the abstract, so that even his philosophical flights are surrealistic
dream images which take their place within the symbolic
framework which captures the real.

He describes this sense of life in *Tropic of Capricorn,*
passing from a just completed sexual act in a hallway to
memories of the street in the old neighborhood:

I get a very definite feeling of it every time I see an Italian paint-
ing without perspective; if it is a picture of a funeral procession,
for example, it is exactly the sort of experience which I knew as
a child, one of intense immediacy. If it is a picture of the open

street, the women sitting in the windows are sitting *on* the street
and not above it and away from it. Everything that happens is
known immediately by everybody, just as among primitive people. . . . so in the old neighborhood from which I was uprooted
as a child there were those parallel vertical planes on which everything took place and through which, from layer to layer, everything was communicated as if by osmosis.[14]

Miller lived on the street in an interim period when life was
at a precarious balance. His neighborhood was already an
immigrant quarter, but not yet wholly deteriorated: "It
was the most enchanting street I have ever seen in all my
life. It was the ideal street—for a boy, a lover, a maniac,
a drunkard, a crook, a lecher, a thug, an astronomer, a
musician, a poet, a tailor, a shoemaker, a politician. In fact
this was just the sort of street it was, containing just such
representatives of the human race, each one a world unto
himself and all living together harmoniously and inhar-
moniously, *but together,* a solid corporation, a close knit
human spore which could not disintegrate unless the street
itself disintegrated." [15]

Afterwards that balance was lost, and the street lost its
magical quality: "Soon the street began to smell bad, soon
the real people moved away, soon the houses began to deteriorate and even the stoops fell away, like the paint. Soon
the street looked like a dirty mouth with all the prominent
teeth missing, with ugly charred stumps gaping here and
there, the lips rotting, the palate gone. Soon the garbage was
knee deep in the gutter and the fire escapes filled with
bloated bedding, with cockroaches, with dried blood." [16]

The old neighborhood was buried in the avalanche of

14 *Tropic of Capricorn,* 214.
15 *Ibid.,* 215.
16 *Ibid.,* 216.

humanity which swept over it after the building of the Williamsburg Bridge, and it lived on only in memory. In memory, however, it could serve its function, to symbolize that sense of reality, of order, of unity which was so difficult to establish in adult life. The later periods of life in Brooklyn are important; certain vital phases of Miller's development took place and were used in his work. But his essential *flavor*, his sense of people, of concreteness, of the uniqueness of the individual, of particular odors, sounds, of life as it is in its most basic form, he attributes to his life in the 14th Ward between the ages of five and ten.

III

The recovery of early life which Miller made an important part of his artistic process emphasizes his Williamsburg days almost to the exclusion of early adolescence. When he refers explicitly to the glories of childhood and to the loss of it in growing up, he is almost always referring to the 14th Ward. As far as his actual life is concerned Miller's experience after the age of ten must share the importance in his development—though it lacks the dramatic contrast with adult life provided by his earlier years. Much of what happened to him would certainly have happened in any large urban center, and Miller is above all a city man. He has in fact created romance out of Brooklyn in almost the way that Wordsworth idealized the Lake district.

As an adolescent Miller's interest in food and other aspects of the life of the senses did not evidently diminish. But to this interest, indeed, blending with it in a way that he retained as an adult, he added a growing curiosity about the mysteries of sex. Consistent with his American environment, Miller presents sex and love as being strangely contradictory. Sex is at times a mystery, at times a fact. In his early years, he had one terribly sentimental love affair while at the same time losing none of his great interest in the physical organs and functions of sex. Feeling about Miller's interest in sexual activity has been somewhat divided. Popular reviews and large numbers of the public find his sexual descriptions excessive. Some have found his interest in sex adolescent. Kenneth Rexroth is almost alone in his insistence that Miller's descriptions of sex are rather ordinary and normal to the American male.[17] Miller, himself, insists that his sexual life has been rather ordinary. People who have known Miller at later periods in his life generally are surprised by his mildness and lack of aggression. The apparent contradiction between his actual life and the life in the novels can be resolved by distinguishing between those passages which describe the average level of experience typical of the street life in a densely populated urban neighborhood and those heightened and very elaborate descriptions of sexual encounters in books like *Sexus* and *Tropic of Capricorn*. We can also distinguish between his description of the growing interest in the mystery of sex as a child and his use of sexual materials as an adult.

Miller's portrayal of the sexual life in early years has a purpose which is not unlike his more general purpose—to reconcile the real and ideal, to avoid the abstract, to maintain firm hold on the concreteness of life experience. In America, especially in the America which Miller knew in the late twenties and thirties, sex had become an abstraction. The commercial spirit had invaded the sexual sphere as it had invaded every other. In the Village sex had become a battleground, something to be discussed, drawn and quartered. Miller in a sense stood astride two traditions in America—the European tradition which still lived in the immi-

17 Kenneth Rexroth, *Bird in the Bush* (New York: New Directions, 1959).

grant communities, and the Puritan tradition which dominated America and finally overthrew the richer life of the new settlers who had to give up pleasure and embrace the Puritan ethic of work if they were to rise out of the ghettos. The characters whom Miller portrays in *Capricorn*, in *Cancer*, and in *The Rosy Crucifixion* show the signs of this deterioration of healthy sexuality. The act for them has become a battleground for other forces. At the age of forty-three, after publishing *Tropic of Cancer*, Miller looked back to rediscover that immediate sensation of sex directly confronted which he had found so stimulating when he was a boy.

The passages from Miller's very early life are concerned simply with the attempt to discover more concretely the difference between men and women. The earliest form of sexual interest is purely visual, normal at that stage, abnormal if it continues into maturity. In *The World of Sex* Miller points out something of the significance that the visual interest in sexual organs carries, to solve the "mystery of what lies hidden away inside the organ." [18] If carried to extremes it leads to the kind of character Miller created in Van Norden in *Tropic of Cancer*, a man who spent his life inspecting the world's vaginas. The normal for Miller is a matter of the appropriateness of behavior to its time and place. There are no abstract rules for sex. Freedom is what counts. Therefore, his effort in re-creating the early world is to capture that utter fascination of the fact and the sense of mystery that surrounded it. He captures the spirit of that world in this passage from *The World of Sex*:

Depending on the time of the year, the age of the players, the players, the place, and numerous other factors now almost im-

18 *The World of Sex* (New York, 1940), 17.

possible to conceive of, certain genitalia revealed themselves in manifold shapes and essences quite as variegated and as startling, when I come to think of it, as the beings which people the imaginative minds of the occultist. What grew up under the plastic gaze of a child's eye was a nameless phantasmagoria, a pristine shoot of very concrete images which were real, tangible, thinkable, and yet nameless, for they were still separate from the world of experience where everything had a name and a place and a time. Thus it happened that without effort certain little girls were known and spoken of as possessing hidden away beneath their dresses such queer effects as magnolias, cologne bottles, plush buttons, rubber mice and God only knows what. That every little girl had a crack was of course known to every one.[19]

Miller recaptures not only this sense of the appearances of things, but recalls as well the very simple moral code of the streets, half compounded of values created among the boys themselves, half a distortion of traditional values brought from the home. Some girls, he tells us, even at that early age were considered bad. They were "whores, or just plain sluts." [20] There were girls who would do things or show things for presents, and some who were so "angelic that no one even thought of them as having a crack—they didn't even pee." Consistent with his feelings for the "honest whore," Miller holds that the bad girls frequently turned out to be warm, generous adults while the angels for the most part "became unhappy later in life, married the wrong man, or did not marry, or were stricken with mysterious illnesses, or were martyred by their parents." [21]

The earliest interest was rooted in visual appearances—fact. Later, as adolescence developed, obscurity entered.

19   *Ibid.*, 19.
20   *Ibid.*
21   *Ibid.*

Looking was only a preliminary to talking, and abstraction once more became the danger.

Somehow the mind was already beginning to exact its tribute, to deny the simple facts of nature which the eye could embrace. How the damn thing functioned began to be obscured by the deeper query of *why*. And with the birth of this faculty, sorrow set in. The world hitherto so natural and so marvellous, slipped out of grasp. Nothing was absolutely true any more, nothing could be proved or disproved. The hair which began to fill the empty space once so rich in possibilities looked ugly. Even the angels grew pimples. Some were already beginning to bleed between the legs.[22]

With the entry on the scene of an active interest in sexual life, disorder began. "The girls on the street didn't seem the same. Some had to leave school. . . . There were penitentiaries, reformatories, homes for wayward girls. . . ." At the same time the idea of romance developed. Young love would render the boy speechless and awkward. He could not approach or talk to *the* girl. The party ends; he may never see her again. A new element enters life—sorrow. "That's the beginning of sorrow, joyous sorrow, the bitterest and the sweetest that man can know. That's the initiation, the beginning of hunger and loneliness. The lovely red apple holds a worm hidden away in the core and that worm will slowly, relentlessly eat away the apple until there is nothing left but the worm." [23]

What follows is of less importance in Miller's autobiography. There is the fairly brief episode in *Plexus* in which three boys experiment short of consummation with the country girl. One of the earliest episodes which Miller dates

22 *Ibid.*, 20.
23 *Ibid.*, 22–23.

sufficiently to place is the piano teacher encounter in *Capricorn*. Miller, who says he is fifteen at the time, seems already to be an accomplished seducer, though he portrays his methods as crude and juvenile. His technique in seducing Lola Niessen does not seem less subtle than the technique he describes at a much later period in his life. For when it comes to sex, Miller is anything but subtle.

It is in describing his being in love that Miller's art comes nearest to failing, both in his early life and later. Perhaps his technique is more suitable for adolescent love than for that of an adult. In any case he is not often convincing. Miller talks more about the first period than about "the street of early sorrows." He seemed to feel the life in the former was richer. During the latter period his "great love" occurred, evidently while he was attending Eastern District High School in the old neighborhood.[24] His story in *World of Sex* of being reduced to complete misery and inaction by his love for this girl he met at a party long before lacks the concreteness that he gives his sexual narratives. In fact it is not until *The Rosy Crucifixion* that he attempts to describe at any length the feeling of love. From the point of view of the contribution of Brooklyn to his growth we would conclude that his relation to girls occupied two unrelated parallel planes—the early interest in the physical details of sex, and a very romantic, idealized, adolescent love-at-a-distance of an almost unattainable first love.

The sexual activity in Miller's work which has been the cause of so much adverse criticism takes place mainly just before and for several years after his first marriage, that is during the period covered by *Sexus*. His talent for irritating people in these passages seems to exceed by far his ability to shock them. What is disturbing in the last analysis is not so much the explicitness of sexual description, as that it is told

24 See the chronology section of Bern Porter (ed.), *The Happy Rock*.

in the first person. The flaunted phallicism of the "I" of the *Tropics* and of *The Rosy Crucifixion,* especially *Sexus,* is to many not only irritating but outrageous. Within the tradition of our literature a man may present himself as a victim, as an idiot, as a fool, but not as a hero, especially not a sexual hero. Miller as the character of the *Tropics* and *Sexus* is more than a hero, he is Priapus himself, unendingly virile, unlimited, free, promiscuous, singly or in pairs. Furthermore he has not even the decency to be ironic about it. He appears to take his hero, and his potency, quite seriously.

It is of some importance to examine whether there are symbolic levels to hero-Miller, or whether his sexual pose constitutes merely a failure in sensibility. Brooklyn did, as we have noted, provide a background which was not likely to promote disciplined restraint. Yet neither could that background, whatever the amount of early curiosity and experiment, provide a free atmosphere in the sense of having no censoring tradition. The urban community has made a curious contribution to the sexual mores of American life. On the one hand, density promotes sexual experimentation; on the other, urban groups have been among the strictest in their formal ethical code. In a restrictive era among native Americans, certain immigrant groups have been among the most restrictive. Certainly the Irish, who had large numbers in Brooklyn, and who were numbered most frequently among Miller's friends, were in theory as strict as any group in the United States. Therefore, in these areas where such a wide gap lay between theory and practice, there must have been conflict.

Henry Miller's narrator-hero shows many kinds of conflict. He is in conflict with his family because of their middle class, unimaginative, philistine values. He is in conflict with the vicious and stupid. He is in continuing conflict with the prudes and puritans in his culture. But he does not show himself in conflict over sex. As far as can be determined from listening to the narrator, he alone of all those we meet has grown into adult life with his sex life intact and his sexual instincts fully available. His days are linked each to each if not by natural piety, at least by a steadily expanding use of his sexual powers. As far as the evidence is presented, life on the Brooklyn streets has led to the maximization of Miller's potency, and to an almost unrestricted use of that potency.

Between the ages of eighteen and twenty-five Miller shows himself to be not only ready for sexual activity at any time but ready at the expense of wives, mothers-in-law, sisters, friends, no matter who. For the most part during these years, sex is casual and wholly physical. He copulates in the Western Union office, in a hallway, while swimming, at a dinner party, in a taxicab, in his wife's bedroom with another woman while his wife is lying in the bed, alone with two women on several occasions, in company with two men and two women, with a sleeping woman, in a restroom. His descriptions of the sexual act emphasize his instant readiness, the strength, size, and duration of his erections, his willingness to enter freely into any of the bypaths of loveplay, and the almost entire absence of any regret after the episode. Women are presented in a number of different ways. During the period of his early manhood, however, the sexually aggressive woman is most significant; and she is the opposite of what the society would have approved, or even thought possible.[25] Miller's casual sexual encounters are usually with a woman who meets him as an equal. Sometimes she will need coaxing

25   Miller is not alone in suggesting the possibility of radical changes in what seems to most of us culturally fixed limits for man or woman. Havelock Ellis, for example, has outlined what he calls the "erotic personality." Much of Miller's erotic writing fits Ellis' description of what this type would be. See Ellis, "Love as an Art" in Hermann Keyserling (ed.), *The Book of Marriage* (New York: Harcourt, Brace and Co., 1926), 373–90.

and encouragement, but once aroused she gives free vent to her sexual fury.

What we make of this sexual activity is crucial in judging Miller's art. If, as the book jackets are fond of saying, this is "a monumental venture in self-revelation," then we are entitled to ignore any pretext to art and read only to satisfy our curiosity, if indeed we read him at all. Miller claims of course that he is writing about his life, but he also admits that his writing is the symbolic equivalent of his life, rather than a factual chronicle. As a matter of fact it is doubtful whether the literal content or the manner of narration is true in any acceptable sense of the word. A number of arguments may be brought against any literal acceptance of Miller's sexual episodes, the strongest being that he is always embroidering and expanding everything he writes. But the sexual scenes seem to have a more deliberate purpose; that is, they are developed in certain directions to accomplish certain aims of the writer.

Our purpose at present is not to discover the ultimate purpose of Miller's use of sex (that discussion is reserved for Chapter 5), but simply, in a preliminary way, to suggest reasons for the frequency and explicitness of his sexual passages, especially those which involve his life as a young adult. To accomplish this purpose it is necessary to examine briefly the relation of the narrator-hero to Miller the author, a matter which will receive fuller development later. In a sense Miller the author stands in relation to his hero as Wordsworth does to the narrator of *The Prelude*. Both represent an idealization of past life for the purpose of establishing a sense of identity in the present, an identity which will establish the qualifications of the artist and which may be projected into the future. Needless to say, Miller's idealization differs markedly from that of Wordsworth.[26]

26 This point will be more fully developed in Chapter 7.

Miller's hero had to solve certain problems which Miller had discovered in his culture, problems which perhaps he had suffered under, and which perhaps he had not solved. The problem was that the individual's harmonious growth toward inner freedom, toward the use and development of all his powers was impeded by a culture which refused to recognize and accept the simple facts of biological life. We need first to understand the repressive influence of the culture and then to examine the manner in which Miller hoped to deal with it.

The years from 1911 to 1921 when Miller was reaching manhood were almost a highpoint of prudery. The beginnings of the breakdown of the Victorian ethical system, the rise of realism in Europe, and the growing fear of the vast immigration led to a shoring up of middle class mores. Americanism became identified with financial success, economic conservatism, the gospel of work, and a mid-Victorian attitude toward sex. In literature "the public demand was for the quick action and romantic setting of the historical novel. . . ." Books were in a full swing of romantic revival.[27] The continuing struggle to maintain a tone of decency was carried into the twenties, until the identification of business success with the Victorian virtues brought the rising middle class squarely behind the most intolerant evangelical crusaders. The very existence of the biological level of life was denied expression in every possible way. The second or third generation in Miller's Brooklyn followed the American middle class rather than the European traditions with which they were still in contact.

The effects of such restrictions on the individual American have been studied at length in the publications of psychoanalysts, psychologists, and sociologists. The individual's

27 See Harold Underwood Faulkner, *The Quest for Social Justice,
1898–1914* (New York: Macmillan Co., 1931) , 258–61.

basic fear of sexual stimuli and things or words related to sexual stimuli causes intense inhibition of all life activities. The individual is inhibited not only morally, but mentally and physically by this desire to avoid dangerous feelings. A culture such as Miller grew up in, even though there was a certain amount of youthful promiscuity which might even be carried into manhood, had its inhibitions built in so that the individual, whatever he did, could not enjoy his freedom. He might be obsessed with sex or fearful of it, but he could not be spontaneous about it. He would either give in entirely to his desires for promiscuity, restrain them altogether, or alternate irrationally between the two.[28]

Such a society and the individuals it produced were of course as far from Miller's ideal as they could be. To say yes to life in the Nietzschean sense required internal as well as external freedom. To live fully one had to accept life. To accept life one had to look at it, to face it for what it was. The facing of life and the overcoming of inner restraints against acceptance required a kind of death and rebirth, a catharsis brought about by reliving one's youth in a more permissive atmosphere.[29] This reliving process will naturally accentuate those areas of experience where the greatest problems lie, that is in sexual acts and aggressive acts. Miller provides just such a permissive figure in his narrator-hero.

In the world of hero-Miller any act associated with the free and uninhibited release of sexual feeling is not only permissible, it is admirable. He concentrates on the most uninhibited activities, activities which the ordinary man of

28 See Edrita Fried, *On Love and Sexuality* (New York: Grove Press, 1961), 281.
29 This, of course, is one of the conditions of psychotherapy, in which the permissive figure of the analyst allows the patient to undo some of the chains which bind him. See also the role of the permissive parent figure in pornography as analyzed by Eberhard and Phyllis Kronhausen, *Pornography and the Law* (New York: Ballantine Books, 1959).

middle-class American culture would be likely to find most reprehensible (that is, about which he would be most fearful), activities of a kind or under circumstances which he is most unwilling to admit to himself that he desires. What is most censorable, then, is what is most desirable and vice versa. Miller picks almost unerringly what in the American culture has been least acceptable. If in the Victorian world it had always been considered normal (to the extent that sex was considered at all) to have intercourse in only one position, in a bed with the man on top, Miller is careful to describe every other position and every other location. Most frequently the woman jumps into his lap in a straddling position. Such a position de-emphasizes the traditional active-passive relationship and makes both partners active. He varies the locale for sex, takes it outdoors and indoors, in public and private places. He breaks the rule of privacy by having more than one couple present, or having several women, or several men and one woman. He varies sexual practices widely, and goes far outside the professed norms of his culture, especially lower class culture.[30] Mouth-genital contacts even to emission are quite the rule in any prolonged contact with a woman. Often they are the initiatory gambit. Many complex and even athletic positions are used. In one scene in *Sexus* Miller and two women seem to re-enact most of the basic positions of Hindu mythology.

His language during these descriptive passages violates openly all of the American conventions. He uses all of the ordinary four-letter words quite frequently. He does not, like D. H. Lawrence, use them as literal descriptive terms, as they might presumably have been used originally. Indeed

30 As Kinsey pointed out in his study of the American male, the lower class male, although he may be more promiscuous in the strict sense of the word, carries a much heavier burden of taboos than those with more education.

some words have a long and honorable history and might be restored, if only to get rid of the hundreds of miscarried euphemisms which now clutter the language. Miller seems to be striving for an effect altogether different from that of Lawrence. He is actually putting together combinations of words calculated to be as disturbing as possible to the sensitive reader.

He does more than mention the genitalia, he dwells upon them, inspects them, describes them in detail, their parts, colors, and textures, and compares them with others. He describes his own bodily sensations explicitly, the feel of his own erections, and of the occasional detumescences. The phallus becomes a central fact of experience and a central attraction for every woman. The peculiar American brand of modesty which makes a man keep his hat on in a whorehouse, or go through agonies to avoid public urination, is a prime object of attack. The "in" people of Miller's world void themselves grandly and freely, preferably from a great height. Intercourse, defecation, urination, eating, drinking are all activities of man, and moral censure attaches no more to one than to another. Through it all hero-Miller maintains the same insouciant attitude, a broad and genial permissiveness that many have found hard to resist.

Theoretically Miller's sexual material should lead not to promiscuity, though it seems to justify promiscuity, but to a rethinking, or better, a re-experiencing of basic sexual attitudes and a revision of them in the direction of a less-restrictive personal ethic, a freer and less-inhibited sense of self and feeling.[31] The character whom Miller presents as him-

31 George Leite, "The Autochthon" in Porter (ed.), *The Happy Rock,* 140–46, writes a parable in which he shows that one must understand Miller rather than attempt to relive his experiences. Of the two girls in the parable the one who learned through Miller was saved. The one who tried to follow his example was lost.

self in *Capricorn* and *The Rosy Crucifixion,* where the most offensive passages occur, is not yet mature, and to an extent we are experiencing the transitional phase in which sexuality as a purely biological function passes into maturity and the emotion of love.

IV

In the interest of greater clarity we must pursue a separate study of Miller's early intellectual interests, even though we recognize that for him, perhaps above most writers, intellect and senses must remain undivided. In general Miller's reading can be divided into periods, each of which is dominated by certain themes. The first period, that of childhood, found Miller reading the popular boys' books of his day. In his later reflections on these authors, he emphasized his dependence on them and even elevated them to a level of philosophical importance. Thus for Miller, writers like Marie Corelli, Rider Haggard, Eugene Sue, James Fenimore Cooper, and above all G. A. Henty are more than memories of a boy's experience, they are memories of a great debt. For most people the books of childhood and adolescence are pleasant enough memories. For Miller they are linked thematically and artistically with the life which followed.

The books which Miller preferred, perhaps the ones naturally suited to the young adolescent, are those of impossibly romantic achievement, like the stories of G. A. Henty and Rider Haggard, which create an ultra romantic atmosphere revolving around the penetration of some mystery with supernatural overtones, or the finding of a lost heir.[32] Perhaps

32 Phyllis Greenacre, "The Family Romance of the Artist," *The Psychoanalytic Study of the Child,* XIII (1958), 9–36, shows the importance of idealized parent substitutes in the development of the genius. In a note she specifically mentions the Henty stories as degraded forms of the family romance. This idealization can also take the form

because he continues to have natural inclinations toward one
kind of romantic ideal, he has retained an intense loyalty to
them even as an adult. Yet, however much these books were
a part of every American boy's diet, it must be considered
that certain aspects of Miller's Brooklyn experience are different from what the average American boy may have experienced. The enormous problem of absorption created by the
overwhelming percentage of new immigrants led to a great
community interest in books and libraries. Reading and use
of the library was given a great positive value. Normally after
the usual run of boys' books into early adolescence, the young
adult would turn to the reigning literary form in America,
the magazine and newspaper; *Saturday Evening Post* and
McClure's provided a complete, balanced diet of everything
the educated American needed to know. But Miller's interest
continued in another vein. He followed the romantic trail
he had begun into other writers from Europe and America.[33]

The writers who influenced Miller as a young adult are,
with the notable exception of Whitman and Emerson, almost
entirely European: Balzac, Jean Giono, Dostoievski, Thomas
Mann, and Knut Hamsun, to mention only a few. He has
written a book on Arthur Rimbaud and castigated American

---

of "a temporary personal adult substitute or even to extract from a
cosmic conception some useful personalized god conception on which to
project his necessary ideal for his father and himself to enable him to
develop further." The role that Miller's childhood reading plays in the
re-creation of his life is far more important than casual reminiscence,
and the answer may lie in the direction that Greenacre indicates.

33 Despite the Europeanizing of men like Huneker, the United States
remained oriented to action rather than thought during the years when
Miller was growing up. Except for the immigrants who talked European
authors in obscure East Side or Greenwich Village cafes, there is little
trace of any interest in the European intellectual tradition. See, for
example, Van Wyck Brooks, *The Confident Years* (New York: Dutton,
1952), Chapters 7 and 8.

publishers for their neglect of Blaise Cendrars. Among
American writers Miller is almost alone in the degree to
which he has switched his loyalties to the European tradition.
The question is, did Miller follow any particular historical
trend in going in this direction? If so, does the development
of the themes of Miller's essays and of the autobiographical
romance depend exclusively upon his own individual development, or does he share in another tradition? To a great
extent an answer to these questions will illustrate why Miller's attitudes are foreign to our present ways of thinking,
why in fact he is able so easily to stir *Time* magazine to
paroxysms of anger.

There are two separate trends to Miller's reading which
he has tried to combine in one world view. The earliest
grows out of the boyhood books, especially the romances of
Henty and Haggard. Later in his life Miller links Haggard
with Andre Breton's *Nadja* and the surrealist tradition. For
the child, books provided a magic realm which gave meaning
to life, which saved him from the menacing world of the
adult. "These books were part of our daily instruction, part
of our Spartan and our spiritual training. They were the heritage of anterior orders, inconspicuous groups like ourselves,
who from earliest times fought to keep alive and to prolong,
if possible, the golden age of youth." [34] For the adult, surrealism provides access to feelings almost lost in the commercial world. One succeeds the other; both are necessary.

The pattern of adult life which Miller saw develop as he
grew older was, he thought, a denial of everything good and
human. The world of work was destructive; it stamped out
imagination, the only source of growth and light. The world
that Miller lived in destroyed one by one the children he
grew up with. Those it did not kill in the war, it bent to the

34 *Books in My Life* (Norfolk, Conn.: New Directions, 1952), 83.

dehumanizing process of the sweatshop. Books for Miller kept alive the promise of life. They provided the link connecting past and present.

For Miller the life of the child was not simply pre-adult, something merely incomplete, unprepared as yet for work. The life of the child had a reality that adult life had lost. It had its own laws:

For most of us, neither father nor mother were objects of veneration, much less of idolatry. We opposed their dubious authority as best we could—and at great odds. . . . Our law, and it was the only voice of authority we truly respected, was the law of life. That we understood this law was revealed by the games we played, that is, by the way we played them and the inferences we drew from the way the various players entered into them. We established genuine hierarchies; we passed judgment according to our various levels of understanding, our various levels of being. . . . We had faith, reverence and discipline. We created our own ordeals and tests of power and fitness.[35]

The educational process as it existed in the schools and the home seemed for Miller, as for many writers, terribly misguided. In severing the content of education from the process of living, the schools did not enhance, but destroyed growth. He offers, of course, no remedy. He is mainly concerned with showing that his own growth was in the living tradition which began in the streets and on the open shelves of the library, rather than in the schoolroom. It is not youth itself which interests Miller, but that during youth he felt he was directly in contact with the vital process. Miller is linked firmly to the romantic philosophy of the nineteenth century in his feeling for the underlying power and meaning of the process of nature:

35 *Ibid.*

That there is something beyond, above and anterior to earthly life, every boy instinctively divines. It is only a few years since he himself lived wholly in the Spirit. He has an identity which manifests itself at birth. He struggles to preserve this precious identity. He repeats the ritual of his primitive forbears, he relives the struggles and ordeals of mythical heroes, he organizes his own secret order—to preserve a sacred tradition. Neither parents, teachers nor preachers play any part in this all important domain of youth. Looking back upon myself as a boy, I feel exactly like a member of the lost tribe of Israel.[36]

Rider Haggard was apparently the exemplar par excellence of the life of imagination realized in fiction. As an adult, Miller found the continuation of this vital force in European writers. The meaning of life is in the search for identity, and identity is discovered only by returning to the mysterious source of our life's being: "Identity! This is the word which, on rereading Rider Haggard has come to haunt me. It is the riddle of identity which caused such books as *Louis Lambert, Seraphita, Interlinear to Cabeza de Vaca, Siddhartha* to exercise dominion over me." [37]

From Rider Haggard to Balzac, to Giono, Miller has undergone a natural development based on wide reading given direction exclusively by personal need. His reading, like his writing, has been personal, an extension of his browsing on the open shelves of the Brooklyn public library. The other side of Miller's thinking likewise has its roots in the Brooklyn boyhood, but even more necessarily. Miller's spirit of freedom, his refusal to give loyalty to institutions, and his nihilism grow out of the turn-of-the-century immigrant world. By clinging to this spirit of anarchy Miller may have

36 *Ibid.*, 88.
37 *Ibid.*, 96.

made himself an anachronism, but it is the principal reason for his disturbing tone.

The tradition from which Miller's peculiar spirit of rebellion flows is the European tradition preserved in the ghettos of New York in the nineties, which later infiltrated Brooklyn. It is the spirit of Nietzsche and Max Stirner, of Dostoievski reinforced by the polemics of Emma Goodman. What happened to this spirit in American history is of some importance, for it shows to a degree why Miller is outside the tradition of American letters.

The East Side ghetto in New York which lay just across from Williamsburg was filled with the spirit of Russian revolutionary writers long before the intellectuals of the Village ever heard of them.[38] Names like Nietszche, Stirner, and Proudhon dominated the day. Anarchist circles saw the United States only as a huge sweatshop, feeding on the immigrant. Theoretical anarchism had its greatest period of growth from 1890 until World War I, as injustice grew on every side. After that the Russian Revolution and the Red scare of the twenties stopped the growth of political anarchism and left only the weak Socialist party.[39] The identification of the good of the laboring man with socialist-anarchist thought waned as the labor movement grew independent of political theory. Anarchism became a dead movement in history when radical thinkers were absorbed into socialism and then into communism. Yet socialist and anarchist thinking are not the same. Only the practical exigencies of the American scene made them appear so. Anarchism is in fact the opposite of socialism. It holds the individual, and not the state, supreme. It is against institutions, even socialist insti-

38   Van Wyck Brooks, *The Confident Years*, 126–27.
39   George Woodcock, *Anarchism* (Cleveland, Ohio: Meridian Books, 1961), 470.

tutions. It looks upon the law and custom, the traditions of society at their very roots, as means simply to deny the individual full access to life. The fact that industry was the principal means of exploitation at the end of the nineteenth century is accidental and obscures the radical difference between the two movements. The distinction is important in interpreting Miller because he has maintained the difference. He has allied himself with anarchist theory, but he is entirely apolitical. He has developed his early exposure to the root principles of anarchism into a philosophy for the twentieth century.

What makes Miller an anachronism in this respect is that the American writers after World War I turned away from nineteenth-century intellectual traditions. The few writers who maintained any hope that some good could be attained through social action turned to socialism and communism, as did Dos Passos and James T. Farrell. Furthermore, the intellectual life of the Village where socialism was discussed was foreign to Miller's way of living. Miller's ideas seemed to develop in the same way that they did during his days on the street. He has never been concerned with theoretical goals, nor with abstract discussion. He embraced certain writers because to him they made sense in the situation he was living in.

According to Miller's chronology and the references to his works, the tailor-shop period, from about eighteen to twenty-six years of age, was the time of greatest activity—intellectual, social, physical, and sexual. It was a time when appetites were new and voracious. Miller's background had disposed him to satisfy those appetites in every possible direction. On the physical level it was, in Miller's terms, a period of "athleticism which lasted for about seven years." [40] Bicycling

40 Porter (ed.), *The Happy Rock,* 152.

was a very popular sport, and clubs were formed for taking long cycling trips. Miller's description is of interest because it shows concretely the context of his intellectual activity.

Those were the days, drunk or sober, I always rose at five A.M. sharp to take a spin on my Bohemian racing wheel to Coney Island and back. Sometimes, skeetering over the thin ice of a dark winter morning, the fierce wind carrying me along like an iceboat, I would be shaking with laughter over the events of the nights before. . . . This, the Spartan regime, combined with the feasts and festivities, the one man study course, the pleasure reading, the argument and discussions, the clowning and buffoonery, the fights and wrestling bouts, the hockey games, the six-day races at the Garden, the low dance halls, the piano playing and piano teaching, the disastrous love affairs, the perpetual lack of money, the contempt for work, the goings on in the tailor shop, the solitary promenades to the reservoir, to the cemetery. . . to the duck pond where, if the ice were thick enough, I would try out my racing skates—this unilateral, multilingual, sesquipedalian activity night and day, morning, noon and night, in season and out, drunk or sober, or drunk and sober, always in the crowd, always milling around, always searching, struggling, prying, peeping . . . completely gregarious yet utterly solitary, the good sport and at the same time thoroughly secretive and lonely . . . well there it was, a sort of caricature of Elizabethan times, all gathered up and played out in the shabby purlieus of Brooklyn, Manhattan and the Bronx, the foulest city in the world. . . .[41]

Physical exercise here, like reading, parties, and sex were all activities within the general process of life. The various kinds of activities did not succeed each other at different periods of ages. Above all his intellectual activities took place within this total activity, a fact which kept Miller from

41 *Books in My Life*, 313–14.

becoming an intellectual. Names of authors whom Miller was reading do not occur in relationship to ideas; they occur while something else is going on. For example a discussion of man's attempt through the telescope to see the limitless becomes a part of his discussion of the mysterious world of childhood, the limitless world of origins, which finally leads to Knut Hamsun who is thus seen in terms of other life activities familiar to Miller: "These miniature realms, where all is sunken, muted and transformed emerge often as not in books. A page of Hamsun frequently yielded the same mysterious harmonies of enchantment as a walk by the canal. For a brief moment one experiences the same sort of vertigo as when the motorman deserts his post with the trolley in full flight. After that it is pure *volupté*. Surrender to the spell which has rendered the author superfluous." [42] For Miller, life is an encounter, and literature is merely one phase of the encounter. Thinking of his Polish friend Stanley leads him to Hamsun, as thinking of Maxie Schnadig leads him to Dostoievski, or as thinking of Dostoievski leads him to think of the Jew whom he first heard speak the name. "It was exactly five minutes past seven at the corner of Broadway and Kosciusko Street, when Dostoievski first flashed across my horizon. Two men and a woman were dressing a shop window. . . . That is how Dostoievski's name came in. Unostentatiously. Like an old shoe box. The Jew who pronounced his name for me had thick lips; he could not say Vladivostok, for instance, nor Carpathians— but he could say Dostoievski divinely." [43] Names and circumstances intertwine. But with Maxie Schnadig, Odessa, and Dostoievski grows an association with the European elements in the immigrant quarters from which Miller takes his direction.

Of the many writers whose names he encountered during

42 *Plexus* (Paris: Olympia Press, 1959) , 339.
43 *Black Spring,* 23.

these days of young manhood, Friedrich Nietzsche must have been the most important, for Miller wrote his first essay on the subject of Nietzsche's *Antichrist* while working in his father's tailor shop. Linked with Nietzsche is the name of Emma Goldman, whom Miller heard speak in California on his western trip in 1913 and whose consort gave him his first volume of Nietzsche. The moment of hearing her speak was, he felt, a turning point in his life. It is important that Miller was caught up in anarchist ideas before World War I. His individualism, his desire for freedom, his nihilism have an unfamiliar ring in the twentieth-century world. They are unfamiliar because they have their origins in ways of thinking long dead.

To begin to see Nietzsche with Miller's eyes we need to examine the contemporary attitude. Even though many writers were offended by Nietzsche's iconoclasm and egoism, those on the radical left extolled him; and men like Otto Heller, writing in 1918 when Nietzsche's stock was quite low, saw positive virtues in his thought, as the "great sayer of yes." As Heller says, Nietzsche is "the most stimulating optimist of all ages, to Nietzsche reality is alive as perhaps never to man before. He plunges down to the very heart of things, absorbs their vital qualities and meanings, and having himself learned to draw supreme satisfaction from the most ordinary facts and events, he makes the common marvellous to others." [44]

Heller emphasizes Nietzsche's role in calling man to freedom and joy, which reminds us of Miller's tone. We detect Miller's tone again when Heller discusses Nietzsche's attacks on the mass of men who "lack appetite at the banquet of life." [45] Freedom, in another passage Heller quotes, is the equivalent of anarchism, but anarchism is more than a polit-

44 Otto Heller, *Prophets of Dissent* (New York: Alfred A. Knopf, 1918) , 146.
45 *Ibid.*, 147.

ical movement. For both Miller and Nietzsche freedom is inward. "Anarchism stands for the demolition of the extant social apparatus of restraint. Its battle is for the free determination of personal happiness. Nietzsche's prime concern, contrarily, is with internal self liberation from the obsessive desire for personal happiness in any accepted connotation of the term." [46] Nietzsche became for Miller, as for many others who dreamed of a better world, a prophet of the future direction of salvation for mankind. Salvation was to come through internal liberation. Restraints, institutions would fall, not by external attack, but from their own weight. Nietzsche and the anarchists whom he influenced looked forward to a new man who would be the complete antithesis of Western man as he had been up to then. As Heller recognized, it was a philosophy which was entirely oriented toward selfishness, not for its own sake, as in nineteenth-century economic liberalism, but in order that the ideal of greater love might eventually prevail. All that was false had to disappear; then love would come, and that would be the revolution.

Max Stirner, Nietzsche, and Emma Goldman were the names which stirred the ghettos. In connection with these three and their ideas, Miller links always the Jew. Miller owes a tremendous debt to the Jews, which he acknowledges despite his ambivalent attitude toward them.[47] His greatest

46 *Ibid.*, 154. He is using the term anarchism here in a strictly political sense.
47 In his recent book *Waiting for the End* (New York: Dell Publishing Co., 1964), Leslie Fiedler takes Miller to task, along with others, for anti-Semitism, actually comparing him with the Germans. Miller has much to say about Jews, and he is quick to point out faults and what appear to him national traits, but over all the tone of his treatment of Jews is warm and appreciative. Miller seems more puzzled by his affinity for Jews than against anything the Jews may seem to represent.

debt may be to Emma Goldman and to the Jews of the East
Side who directly or indirectly brought him in contact with
anarchism. There are few signs in Miller's writing that he
underwent any great intellectual awakening before the period 1914–17. Only one French philosopher, Henri Bergson,
is mentioned, although Miller became very fond of French
writers later. He is introduced to Herbert Spencer some ten
years after this, and to Otto Rank, Erich Gutkind, and others
not until he gets to Paris. Therefore whatever theoretical
formation Miller went through, we must assume that his
German background plus exposure to the influence of recent
immigrants were of central importance. Furthermore, it may
help us to understand why Miller's thought has been so
puzzling to many. George Orwell for example, while he extolled Miller's revolutionary fervor, could not understand
Miller and ultimately condemned him for his lack of social
conscience. But Orwell spoke with the voice of the depression. Individualism had long been swallowed up by the need
for political action on a vast social scale. What Orwell failed
to see was that Miller had formed his basic philosophy long
before the depression, not through socialism, but through
anarchism.[48]

Anarchism as a political movement has been associated
with violence, ignorance, and immigration from the countries of Eastern Europe. The anarchist panic of the nineties
was similar to the Red scare of the twenties, though with
more apparent cause. Bombs were exploding in all the countries of Europe and in America. The growing division between rich and poor and the resistance to labor organizations
were more apparently the causes than anarchist theories
about doing away with the institutions of government. In
any case individual anarchists did commit acts of violence,

48 If Orwell had understood Miller he probably wouldn't have
approved of him.

and with these acts they are forever identified in the American mind.[49]

The study of anarchism as a theoretical movement, a quasi-philosophy, almost a substitute religion, has been generally neglected since World War I.[50] Anarchism started with a redefinition of the nature of life and law. It was a philosophy which in 1890 had the purpose of liberating the poor man from the bonds not only of economic penury, but from an inner law, a conscience which served no other purpose than to help enrich his enslavers. The first task of anarchism was to rescue the individual from his position as subject to the law of society, for society was the equivalent of privilege and injustice. Anarchism sought to free the individual so that he could find his own manner of life.

As far as the United States is concerned, no more prominent spokesman for anarchism could be found than Emma Goldman, and her view of anarchism is very close to Miller's central thought. First, she held that man lives in relation to natural law, not to government and institutions, which are man-made. To live in harmony with the natural law requires "no machinery of government, needs not the club, the gun, the handcuff, or the prison." For her natural law and freedom are very closely related; natural law requires the exercise of freedom, of "the demand for nutrition, for sex gratification, for light, air, and exercise. . . ."[51] Anarchism is man-centered:

49 See Grant C. Knight, *The Critical Period in American Literature* (Chapel Hill: University of North Carolina Press, 1951), 75 ff.
50 In the popular mind, admittedly a vague reference, anarchism seems to have become inextricably intermingled with Marxism and communism. The philosophical side of anarchism had little vogue in the United States until after World War II. See Woodcock, *Anarchism*, 21 ff.
51 Emma Goldman, *Anarchism and Other Essays* (New York: Mother Earth Publishing Co., 1910), 64.

Anarchism is the only philosophy which brings to man the consciousness of himself; which maintains that God, the State, and
society are non-existent, that their promises are null and void,
since they can be fulfilled only through man's subordination.
Anarchism is therefore the teacher of the unity of life; not
merely in nature, but in man. There is no conflict between the
individual and the social instincts, any more than there is between the heart and the lungs; . . . The individual is the heart
of society conserving the essence of social life; society is the lungs
which are distributing the element to keep the life essence. . . .[52]

In elaborating the corollaries of this central doctrine, the
anarchists inevitably ran afoul of the most sacred traditions
of American society. In addition to their attacks upon the
institutions of government, which caused the most vigorous
reaction, the anarchists attacked Puritanism broadly, especially its more intolerant aspects. Here Emma Goldman dif-
fered from woman leaders of her day. The feminists, the
suffragettes, were inclined to embrace temperance along with
the vote. Goldman believed in the goodness of the natural
life, from which she believed neither alcohol nor sex should
be excluded:

Every stimulus which quickens the imagination and raises the
spirits, [sic] is as necessary to our life as air. It invigorates the
body and deepens our vision of human fellowship. Without stimuli in one form or another, creative work is impossible, nor indeed the spirit of kindliness and generosity. The fact that some
great geniuses have seen their reflection in the goblet too frequently, does not justify Puritanism in attempting to fetter the
whole gamut of human emotions. A Byron and a Poe have
stirred humanity deeper than all the Puritans can ever hope to
do. The former have given life meaning and color; the latter
are turning red blood into water. . . . Puritanism . . . is a poi-

52 *Ibid.*, 58.

sonous germ. . . . With Hippolyte Taine, every truly free spirit has come to realize that "Puritanism is the death of culture, philosophy, humor, and good fellowship; its characteristics are dullness, monotony and gloom." [53]

On the subject of sex she was even more infuriating, especially since she saw marriage as an institution for the enslavement of women. A human relationship, she felt, must be free, passionate, ecstatic. She insisted that society controls these unions by stigmatizing the child. Marriage is invented by man, state, and church. Love has nothing in common with it. Her attacks on custom were calculated to show that the narrow morality of American society had no other purpose than to maintain slavery, especially by preventing the sexual awakening of woman. Her attacks on marriage extended to the advocacy of birth control, the limitation of families to the number of children who could be suitably educated, clothed, and fed. She spoke freely on whatever came to her mind. She criticized women's corsets, an unmentionable subject. She was popularly believed to be living in a rather continuous devil's yule. But her advocacy of free love went furthest to outrage American sensibilities. Of course she did not mean what the term evidently suggested to the American public. To them free love was the equivalent of promiscuous sexual behavior. To Emma it was the equivalent of actions based on feelings, the search for integrity in human relations, rather than deception.[54]

The underlying individualism of the anarchist movement furnished a base upon which Miller could build. He was later attracted to writers who in one way or another emphasized all of the main tenets of the anarchists. His religion

53 *Ibid.,* 182.
54 Richard Drinnon, *Rebel in Paradise* (Chicago: University of Chicago Press, 1961), 149.

developed as did Nietzsche's and Goldman's into a religion of earth, of Dionysiac freedom. From Nietzsche, Miller could go easily to Balzac, to Giono, to Lawrence, to John Cowper Powys, to all the writers who served his later reading. And in this development Miller seems to be unique. His deep roots in the nineteenth century have been obscured by the period in which he wrote. His dependence upon the European romantic tradition has separated him from the ordinary development of American literature. Above all, his rebellion remained free of social and political movements and allowed him to develop in a way unique to himself.

From the beginning of his writing career Miller seemed to grasp one notion firmly, that revolt is no easy matter. Custom is indeed deep almost as life, and the force necessary to overthrow it is frightening. Like the release of energy from the nucleus of the atom, the breaking up of the constellation of habits which makes the individual is accomplished only with explosive results. The amount of force which must be brought to bear must also be overwhelming. His choosing of the Stirner-Nietzsche tradition was for his time the most destructive possible. The sheer nihilism of individualist anarchism is the inversion of a civilization in force since the Greeks. The appeal of a doctrine like Nietzsche's was, to men who were starved for some sense of the self, something which did not come at the hands of society. Instead of the deadly middle class morality, Nietzsche preached a morality which had as its goal only the fuller life for the individual.[55] Like Thomas Carlyle, Ralph Waldo Emerson, and Henrik Ibsen, Nietzsche placed the individual at the center and made the creation of his own life the major purpose of life, rather than the satisfying of the goals of society.

The influence of Nietzsche and his followers upon Miller

55 M. A. Mugge, *Friedrich Nietzsche: His Life and Work* (New York: Brontane's, 1908.)

goes deeper than a simple enhancement of individualism, a justification for self-assertion. In Nietzsche, as in Goldman and the anarchist movement, there is a strong acceptance of destruction. If on the one hand eros is forever creating new unities, thanatos must forever be destroying. Destruction then becomes the other side of the coin.[56] As one sees in studying Miller's individual works, aggression and destruction are important elements in his total feeling. These destructive urges seem to run highest from the time of his first marriage until his departure from Paris. There is a tone of violence in his American writing after the war, but it does not carry the conviction that the earlier feelings did. Finally, in his view of the natural course of events Miller accepted the destruction of what already exists. In personal as well as social structures, destruction had to pave the way for creation. Since he disapproved of the state of affairs pretty generally, even on the individual level, he had to accept destruction, even encourage it. What Nietzsche attacked was the overvaluation of altruism. The advancement of humanity required cooperation with the destructive force in the universe. As Miller said in "The Alcoholic Veteran with the Washboard Cranium," we should help a man in the direction he seems determined to go. If the direction is down, give him a push. Altruism was firmly rooted as a principle of our society. But it was an altruism in which, as Miller describes it, each uses others for his own good. It took the revolutionary fervor of Nietzsche and Goldman to shake him loose.

Having once accepted the ideal of life enhancement, of personal growth and of the concomitant destruction of existing values, Miller was prepared to carry through this romantic strain of thought in his Paris period. Taking the individual and his personal goals as supreme, Miller was

56 F. A. Lea, *The Tragic Philosopher* (New York: Philosophical Library, 1957), 319.

prepared to take himself, Henry Miller, as his only viable hero. *Tropic of Cancer* communicates the first sense of form arising from the sense of self, what Miller called finding his own voice. *Tropic of Capricorn* found a myth for refining and elaborating the original discovery, a myth which had its roots in the development of Miller's interest in European and American romantic philosophy.

THE MIND OF MILLER

Henry Miller's literary career began with the
publication of *Tropic of Cancer* in 1934; but the
attitudes to life which he expressed in this and
later works, and even the form of the work itself,
began at a much earlier date. As a preliminary to the study
of his writing, it is important to note more closely than has
yet been done the way in which his mind was formed. We
have seen how his early life in Brooklyn provided an atmosphere which predisposed him to certain lines of development.
His early life, before 1920 let us say, was no doubt important
to the final form of Miller's character development, but the
reading which brought him more deeply into the European
tradition was important in forming his art. The writers
whom Miller read during the twenties and thirties belong
to a tradition which is relatively coherent and recognizable.
They are those who, like Nietzsche, faced the dilemma of
man in an evolving universe and proposed some order
through which the individual could survive. Those who particularly interested Miller in the early part of his career
found the answer to evolution in the development of the
individual himself, a movement toward supra-individualism.

Nietzsche's response to the new biology, as we have seen, was to place the individual entirely on his own, to remove God from the cosmos, then to seek life enhancement in the individual himself. As a philosopher of will in the Schopenhauer tradition, he held that man is the maker and therefore the artist. Life culminates in art. Nietzsche provided the seeds for a view of life based on individualism and a nihilistic repudiation of all values. For the writer, that is for Miller, art could be embraced as the way simultaneously to enhance life and to create it. The re-creation of life in the past would become the means of living more fully in the present.

According to his commentators, Nietzsche did not remain for long in a godless world. He turned around and deified the very Dionysiac force which he had at first balanced against the Apollonian. Miller, too, accepted the Dionysian, but he went beyond Nietzsche in attributing to it a divine force. He accepted a cyclical view of history as did Nietzsche, but modified by a sense of Destiny or purpose. Rejecting eternal recurrence, Miller, like Vico and Spengler, accepted some kind of evolutionary progress as a future possibility if not as an historical fact. He looks forward to a new man who will live on a higher level than man has achieved before. Some of the support he needed for his ideas of the new man Miller may have found in Otto Rank, who developed a view of the artist which draws on Nietzsche and differs markedly from Freud. The way in which Miller wrote about the conversion of life into art is very close to Rank's analysis of the creative process.[1]

1 Miller was reading Rank in the early thirties and possibly before. He refers to "the Rank book" in writing to Walter Lowenfels; this was during the earliest stages of *Tropic of Cancer*. Durrell has noted the significance of Rank in Miller's thinking. See Alfred Perles and Lawrence Durrell, *Art and Outrage* (New York: E. P. Dutton, 1961), 16. The *Diary of Anais Nin* documents Miller's personal relationship

Miller seemed to need above all a more workable structure than Nietzsche could give him. Nietzsche started with biology and ended in ecstasy. Miller needed a universe in which the heights and depths could more easily be adjusted to the experience of everyday life. For this universe he went to modern psychology and its theories of the unconscious life, particularly to Rank and Jung and to the Dionysiac spirit of D. H. Lawrence. From Nietzsche Miller got his first notions of the emergence of the individual, but it is with Rank and Jung, I believe, that he made these first intimations concrete and workable. Miller was fond of the writing of Elie Faure, who held that the goal of the historical process is the emergence of the individual from the biological mass. Otto Rank and Carl Gustav Jung elaborated that theory on an individual psychological level. In Erich Gutkind, a rather nontraditional Jewish philosopher, Miller found support for several ideas which extended the range of feeling and thought in his autobiography—a workable idea of God, for example, and an association between the process of sinking deep within the self and attaining mystical union with a divine power. Lawrence helped make precise one of Miller's most important themes—that of the polarity between men and women, which represents symbolically the struggle between biology and culture.

Otto Rank has had only passing notice for the part he played in providing Miller with a structure for his autobiographical romance. As a philosopher of will, Rank differs from the Freudians in a number of respects, but for our purposes especially in his affirmation of a self which is more than the sum total of biological functions. He is one of the

---

with Rank and the great influence of Rank on both Nin and Miller during the early thirties. In recent years Miller has expressed reservation about the "German" deficiencies of Rank, but he has never totally rejected him.

many who, from the time of World War I until now, has
tended to look upon the individual human being as the
culminating point of an historical trend. The cyclical process of history, in this view, has worked toward freeing the
individual from the unconscious biological state. The new
conflict is between death, symbolically seen as the desire to
return to the unconscious state, and life, which seeks to be
more individual, more aware. This view of evolution is not
new or unusual, but in Rank it is connected with the artistic
process, which is naturally appealing to the writer. Art provides the means by which the individual may discover his
real self; grasping this self as an ideal, the artist projects it
into a work, which then becomes the world of the artist in
which he finds his life purpose.

Miller goes only a short distance with Rank before he
parts company, but that distance is important. A brief examination of some of Rank's theories will show Miller's
indebtedness. First, Rank differs from Freud and the Freudians in finding that the art process itself is a perfection of the
individual, rather than a product of his illness. In Rank not
even sexuality can be taken as the source of art; for in his
system sexuality belongs to the biological common life, and
art is the product of the individual will. "The will conscious
or unconscious will always be the expression of the individual, the indivisible single being, while sexuality represents
something shared, something generic that is harmonious with
the individually-willed only in the love experience and is
otherwise in perpetual conflict with it." [2] This art work represents the successful culmination of universal forces in the
individual and in a sense deifies the artist. The artist now
becomes a "super-natural, super-real, or super-individual,"

2 Otto Rank, *Art and Artist* (New York: Tudor Publishing Co.,
1932) , 86.

isolated except for the drag of procreation, which pulls him back to the biological level.

For Miller, "being an artist" was a role which gave him the form for his autobiographical narratives. As he has pointed out in *Art and Outrage,* he asked to be an artist and was granted only the power to write about the process of becoming a writer. He set writing as his goal quite early, writing his first novel during his Western Union days.[3] But in all this early work he was unsuccessful, he says. The only way he could break out of mental fetters was to reconstruct his own life history toward the goal of becoming a writer.

Rank was especially important to Miller because he emphasized the self-constructive aspects of personality. For Freud and the social psychologists, ego ideals came principally from the influence of early environment. For Rank, they could be self-constructed. Construction of personality can become, in this view, a conscious process like creating the work of art.[4] The artist type rises out of the social context which threatened to destroy him (which does in fact destroy the neurotic) by creating in his art the world in which he can live. According to Rank, even art will one day pass away, when the man of genius will make of the personality itself the labor of his genius. Foreseeing this goal, the modern artist ends in a struggle between art and life over the conflicting claims of art and personality.

When we add Rank's theory of the birth trauma and its ramifications to the theory of the artist, we have the main outlines of Miller's principal themes. Rank does not empha-

3 Miller wrote two novels before *Tropic of Cancer—Crazy Cock* and *This Gentile World.* His own judgment is that he had not yet found his own voice in these early works. Miller to author, September 3, 1966.
4 Albert William Levi, *Philosophy and the Modern World* (Bloomington: Indiana University Press, 1959), 190.

size, as Freud does, knowledge of the past, but growth out of
the past. Once the individual has been born, the way back to
the womb is blocked by the birth trauma. Yet because of
the attractions of the unconscious life of the womb, the individual must strive constantly toward independence. The goal
of life is self-dependence which means progressive separation
from the mother. The ideas of mother and womb then become symbols of man's dependence; the real mother need
not have any role at all. It is the struggle between the freedom of the individual and his slavery to the biological
process. Rank expresses this idea quite clearly in a somewhat
later work, *Truth and Reality:*

In the creative individual this conflict is manifest only at times
and we can best describe it thus, that nature becomes even more
conscious of herself in a man who at the same time with the
increasing knowledge of himself which we designate as individ-
ualisation, tries always to free himself further from the primitive. It has therefore to do with a conflictual separation of the
individual from the mass, undertaken and continued at every
step of development into the new and this I should like to designate as the never completed birth of individuality. For the
whole consequence of evolution from blind impulse through conscious will to selfconscious knowledge, seems still somehow to
correspond to a continued result of births, rebirths and new
births, which reach from the birth of the child from the mother,
beyond the birth of the individual from the mass, to the birth
of the creative work from the individual and finally to the birth
of knowledge from the work.[5]

In different artists, as Rank sees it, this process can take
different forms. Some fragment the self into characters; some
remain relatively objective and social. The romantic, of

5 Otto Rank, *Will Therapy and Truth and Reality* (New York:
Alfred A. Knopf, 1950), 219.

which Miller is an example, creates art out of the dramatization of his own personality.

The artist who dramatizes the self does more than reconstruct his past. The re-examination of life history is itself
creative in that it chooses, modifies, colors, and even changes
outright the actual relationships of the events and people in
order to create the person whom the author wills himself to
be in the present. The creation of the self accomplished by
the autobiographical narrative enables the individual artist
to form new ethical ideals independent of the social context
in which he lives:

Here then begins the ethical ideal-formation in the self although
the individual may turn to external models, ideal figures from
life or history. But these ideals he chooses in terms of his own
individuality which, as we know, has nothing to do with infantile authorities, least of all the parents. It does not matter
whether the individual succeeds wholly in freeing himself from
the traditional moral concepts; probably he never does, especially not as long as he must live with other individuals who
more or less depend on this traditional morality. It is important,
however, that for everything creative, regardless of how it manifests itself, even in the neurosis, we can thank this striving of
the individual, of his individual will to free himself from the
traditional moral code and to build his own ethical ideals from
himself. . . .[6]

Questioning the prevailing moral sentiments has always been
associated with the writer, especially the romantic. In those
writers who believe in the "decline of the West," it has become a passion. Expatriate writers in general, and Miller
more than most, have attempted not to revise but to replace
entirely the traditional morality. The new morality would

6 *Ibid.*, 263.

have as its primary purpose the encouragement of individual growth. From now on the whole structure of civilized morality would be suspect.

The dramatization of personality, which was Miller's approach to writing, creates the effect of a deeper force operating in life and reality than is provided for in the works of Rank or Nietzsche. The force which for Bergson was the *élan vital*, Miller called destiny. The idea of self-creation is well enough as far as it goes, but there is in Miller's theory an acceptance of reality reminiscent of Whitman. Sometimes our ends are accomplished by letting go, by not struggling, by allowing greater forces to operate through the self. We shall take up that aspect of Miller somewhat later in this chapter. For now we must examine further the work of Rank.

Rank's theory of duality, common in the time in which he wrote, has other implications for the study of Miller; for it led Miller in the direction of D. H. Lawrence, toward the paradox which associates sexuality with both life and death. The general influence of the repudiation of Victorianism in the twenties, along with the influence of Freud, led the most "advanced" people toward an equating of sexual freedom with an enhanced individuality. In a repressed society, sexual freedom became the equivalent of individual freedom. Neither Miller, nor Lawrence, nor Rank would have seen the matter quite so simply. For Rank, sexuality belonged to the collectivity; it was the hold of biology, and thus of the primitive, on man. Therefore with Rank, as with Lawrence and Miller, sexuality might under certain circumstances be equated with individual good, but it also represents, or can represent, the death of the individual. Through love man is rescued from slavery to the instincts, represented by sexual promiscuity; but at the same time, he sacrifices all or a good part of his ego to the loved one. In terms of life enhancement the individual finds himself once more at an impasse.

For the artist who finds himself in the work, a different relationship is possible with a woman, according to Rank. The loved one can become the audience for the work, the equivalent of the muse, to whom the work is addressed and for whom it exists. This relationship with the muse represents a natural contradiction to the extent that she is a real woman; for if she satisfies his artist's ego, she helps take him away from life, which awakens fear. If she draws him toward life, she creates obstacles in him for his work. And when his art ideology changes, the muse-mistress must be cast off. This pattern is in part at least the structure of Miller's relationship with Mona, his most important relationship.

Miller's use of Rank is complex, as Rank himself is complex. If we take as central the works which Miller intended to be central, the *Tropic of Capricorn* and *The Rosy Crucifixion,* we find a fairly clear expression of Rank's general theory of the artist. Miller created the plan for *Capricorn* in 1927, several years before he read Rank. The basic material, therefore, is from Miller's life, but the organization of the subject matter into themes is strongly suggestive of Rank. The "birth of the artist" theme is central in *Capricorn;* and in *Nexus,* the third book of *The Rosy Crucifixion,* we find that the culmination of the growth process comes at a moment when the narrator-hero realizes that his life with Mona exists only for the use of his art. At that moment he dies to life in order to become the artist. The development of this theme is expressed in terms of liberation from the womb, just as his life with Mona was expressed in terms of a descent into the biological matrix of life. The structure of *Capricorn* can be expressed almost entirely in Rankian images: The recovery of the life of the child who lived in the 14th Ward, Brooklyn, emphasizes the deadliness of a modern urban society, which destroys the promise of youth. The job at Western Union is a further intensification of the deadly mechanical and destructive power of society. Mona is the muse-mistress who rescues Miller. Through her he is able to begin the struggle toward art. As the work progresses, Miller, as hero, moves toward realization of himself as a free person; and, paradoxically, that movement is the unfolding of the narrative which is his principal work.

Whether Rank accurately foresaw what the result would be of taking the self as subject of artistic activity, or whether Miller used Rank's theory as the general framework for the story of his development as an artist, Miller seems to arrive at the state of fully realized artist only to find himself in conflict with life, just as Rank predicted. From the end of the Paris period until the present, Miller's favorite theme has shifted from the desire to be an artist to the desire to live. From beginning to end of Miller's major work, from his earliest days in Brooklyn until his coming to rest on the California coast, Miller has followed the pattern described by Rank, that of the development of the artist in the modern world.

During the Paris period and the years immediately pre-ceding it, from the late twenties to the mid-thirties, Henry Miller was taking voluminous notes on most of the great controversial thinkers of his time. He attributes influence freely but in a kind of scattershot fashion. We could go from Rank to any one of a dozen writers and make a case for the importance of his influence on Miller. That is to say, Miller lived in a web of intersecting ideas which provided the con-text for his own thought and the development of his art. From this point, the most profitable direction for tracing the development of Miller's themes seems to be toward D. H. Lawrence. The general feeling for duality which character-ized Nietzsche and Rank became in Lawrence's theory of polarity the working principle of his own novels. Miller was engaged in the early thirties in writing a book to be called

The World of Lawrence. The world of Henry Miller contains a good bit of that world of Lawrence.

For Lawrence, man's final destiny is outward toward culture. Without a passionate purpose in life man will become a slave of the woman, and that would be the destruction of his masculinity. However, before man can act fully, he must recover his lost individuality by a descent to the true self. For Lawrence the greatest danger to man is idealism, that is, the finding of reality in mental states rather than in existence itself. "Idealism is the final peril of human consciousness. It is the death of all spontaneous, creative life, and the substituting of the mechanical principle." [7] The way out of the false idealism of the modern world is not to push the idealism to greater lengths, but to go back to our unconscious: "The pushing of the ideal to any further lengths will not avail us anything. We have actually to go back to our own unconscious. But not to the unconscious which is the inverted reflection of our ideal consciousness. We must discover if we can the true unconscious, where our life bubbles up in us, prior to any mentality. The first bubbling life in us, which is innocent of any mental alteration, this is the unconscious." [8]

This unconscious means for Lawrence "the essential unique nature of every creature, which is by its very nature, unanalysable, undefinable, inconceivable. It cannot be conceived, it can only be experienced in every single instance." [9] To this unique individuality Lawrence gives the name of soul. Although Lawrence leans heavily upon Freud, this mystical self which is the substratum of experience more closely resembles the theories of Jung. On this lower level, of course, man finds more than the self; he finds passion and

7 D. H. Lawrence, *Psychoanalysis and the Unconscious* (New York: Viking Press, 1962), 11.
8 *Ibid.*, 13.
9 *Ibid.*, 15.

that brings him back to the woman. For Lawrence as for Nietzsche the good lay in the inner life, but danger resided there too. Life actually had to be lived in polarity, between the satisfaction of erotic demands which required love and the giving of the self and the cultural demands which were man's mission in the world.

Several fragments of Miller's abortive book on Lawrence have been published in collections of his essays. His attitude to Lawrence reflects his preoccupation with certain themes which were important to him and which appeared in his own work. These themes center upon awareness of life, but an awareness which is inclusive, which embraces the polarity of experience. Miller grows eloquent when he talks about Lawrence:

for the artist there is nothing but the present, the eternal here and now, the expanding infinite moment which is flame and song. And when he succeeds in establishing this criterion of passionate experience (which is what Lawrence meant by obeying the Holy Ghost) then, and only then, is he asserting his humanness. Then only does he live out his pattern as Man. Obedient to every urge—without distinction of morality, ethics, law, customs, etc. He opens himself to all influences—everything is gravy to him, including what he does not understand—*particularly* what he does not understand.[10]

The dream of the artist, the temptation which he must face and conquer is the one which leads him to look for easy answers, to a life free of struggle. This symbolic realm Miller calls "China," and it resembles the prenatal security of the womb. "China" is discovered by the mature artist, and he must learn to surrender it. The need for the realm of

10   Henry Miller, "Creative Death," in his *The Wisdom of the Heart* (New York: New Directions, 1941), 3.

"China" arises in the artist because of his desire to escape from the realm of becoming. It resembles the desire for the womb in its wish for security and immortality, for what is changing and impermanent. It is the artist's dream of the miraculous, that he can "break the wheel of life and death, avoid the struggle and the drama, the pain and the suffering of life." The other realm invented by the artist, the "Land of Fuck" in *Capricorn,* seems to be almost the opposite; it is pure biological being, fecundity. Everything is coming to be. The womb of the realm of "China" instead of being fraught with conflict and suffering is an escape into permanence:

China is a projection into the spiritual domain of his biologic condition of non-being. To be is to have mortal shape, mortal conditions, to struggle, to evolve. Paradise is, like the dream of the Buddhists, a Nirvana where there is no more personality and hence no conflict. It is the expression of man's wish to triumph over reality, over becoming. The artist's dream of the impossible, the miraculous, is simply the resultant of his inability to adapt himself to reality. He creates, therefore, a reality of his own—in the poem—a reality which is suitable to him, a reality in which he can live out his unconscious desires, wishes, dreams. The poem is the dream made flesh.[11]

This reality which the artist creates is the means by which he lives many lives. The artist seeks to reconcile life's opposites, but on the level of experience rather than thought. All of man's life has been a struggle to form and maintain a culture, to keep from sinking back into the unconscious unity of life represented by the primitive unconscious. It is the artist who has been the chief instrument in creating culture and therefore in saving man, because only the artist accepts reality and embraces the whole of it. By embracing

11 *Ibid.,* 4.

unconscious life the artist prevents the progressive idealization of life which would lead to one kind of death, the death
of feeling and love. By embracing life and reality in a living
relationship through his own creativity, he keeps man from
sinking back into the unconscious unity of the womb, even
though the new reality of the artist is in a sense a re-creation
of that womb.

The maturity of the artist ends in independence. The
struggle to become free of the mother and father is completed when the artist accepts his own fatherhood: "Just as
the individual, when he arrives at maturity, evinces his maturity by the acceptance of responsibility, so the artist, when
he recognizes his real nature, his destined role, is obliged to
accept the responsibility of leadership." [12] The poles of life
are the life and death instincts, and life must be lived between them. The creative powers of the artist which drive
him toward expression "through his world of form and
symbol, cause him at last to overlook the purely human,
relative, fundamental aspects of his being—his animal nature,
his very human body. Man rushes up the tree of livingness
to expand in a spiritual flowering. From an insignificant
microcosm, but recently separated from the animal world,
he eventually spreads himself over the heavens in the form
of the great anthropos, the mythical man of the zodiac." [13]
Man finally discovers the limits of form and with those limits,
his own limitations. That is to say he discovers death. The
"endless urge to creation" reaches its limits, and man now
discovers his deep roots in the earth. "The supremacy and
the glory and the magnificence of the body finally asserts itself in full vigor. Only now does the body assume its sacred
character, its true role. The trinal division of body, mind,
and soul becomes a unity, a holy trinity. And with it the re-

12 *Ibid.*, 7.
13 *Ibid.*, 8–9.

alization that one aspect of our nature cannot be exalted above another, except at the expense of one or the other." [14]

This spirit of polarity with its acceptance of the limits of life from the highest level of soul to the lowest level of organic life, is a distinguishing characteristic of Miller. His free-flowing prose, with its uninhibited spilling out of impulse, takes him from art to life and from obscenity to spirituality, not confusing one with the other but unifying them within his overall feeling for existence. The goal of life, as Miller understands it, is unity, a comprehensive unity in which nothing is excluded, in which everything is holy because it is:

Once again it is perceived that the trunk of the tree, the very column of life itself, is religious faith, the acceptance of one's tree-like nature—not a yearning for some other form of being. It is this acceptance of the laws of one's own being which preserves the vital instincts of life, even in death. In the rush upward the "individual aspect of one's being was the imperative, the only obsession. But at the summit, when the limits have been felt and perceived, there unfolds the grand perspective and one recognizes the similitude of surrounding beings, the inter-relationship of all forms and laws of being—the *organic* relatedness, the wholeness, the oneness of life.[15]

For Miller a lofty peak of European civilization is the career of Goethe, who united the extremes of the Dionysian and Apollonian man in a full unfolding of individuality and a probing of the deep roots of the race and its traditions. It is too late now for a Goethe, Miller holds, and we must repudiate the spiritual values of this civilization. It is the end of the era, time for the new man, for the transvaluation of all

14   *Ibid.*, 13.
15   *Ibid.*, 10.

values. Creative death, however, is a more fertilizing process than the other kind of death, which is the return to the womb. For Nietzsche, Rank, Lawrence, and Miller the death of culture will bring the new man who will bring a new flowering. Lawrence failed, according to Miller, because he never succeeded in being fully born. Had he lived he would have arrived at the "mystic way." Because of his short life "only a part of the man's nature succeeded in blossoming— the rest of him was imprisoned and strangled in the dry walls of the womb." [16]

In accepting the duality of Nietzsche and the polarity of Lawrence, Miller has created the dramatic structure which will enable him to move within the dimensions of experience from the biological matrix to the god-feeling. Miller has developed a technique for representing these extremes of experience; and while he does not always use it to the same degree, it tends to appear in all the auto-novels. The middle ground is dominated by straight narrative either of the present or of memory. This straight narrative is more pronounced in *The Rosy Crucifixion,* and much less so in *Tropic of Capricorn.* The passages of narrative tend to set up associations which lead either to fantasy or a kind of ecstasy. The fantasy, which is to a greater or lesser extent surrealistic, is usually associated with the biological level of life; the imagery tends to be archaic and very sensual, archetypal in the Jungian sense. The ecstatic passages are characterized by exuberance of language and the adoption of a prophetic pose. According to Miller the level of fantasy flows straight from the unconscious—almost automatic writing. Possibly his familiarity with Jung and the surrealists provided many of Miller's key images and symbols.

There is no doubt that Miller created most of the symbols

16 *The Cosmological Eye,* 108.

he used in his surrealistic passages out of his own fertile imagination, although certain images like water, snakes, eating, drinking, or various phallic symbols are common to most psychology books. Jung's theories of individuation have been artistically more useful than the theories of Freud, and Jung's theories throw more light on Miller's images. Jung's unconscious is more generalized and primitive than that of Freud, and libido instead of being simply sexual energy is a kind of cosmic energy active in man. Jung's idea of the unconscious, which preserves traces of the primitive roots of man, is more easily converted into flights of fantasy, especially with changed images of space and time. Thus fantasy episodes in Miller frequently take him out of ordinary life to an unrecognizable place where relationships are altered and familiar objects strangely unstable.

In Jung's psychology, the elaboration of literary symbols by the artist leads to an animation of the collective unconscious, a passing beyond individuality to race. Archetypal motifs become the principal level of artistic meaning. In the archetypal pattern of the good and bad mother, for example, the libido is caught between its strivings forward toward continual renewal and its strivings backward to the womb. The reactions to these strivings within the psyche are far from neutral; they are of great intensity, even violent. Jung describes images of eating as a destructive act, consumption by fire, emasculation, and drowning.

Miller occasionally writes a kind of free and spontaneous surrealistic prose which he describes as coming right out of the unconscious. Yet I think we should treat it as imaginative and poetic in origin, rather than archetypal in the Jungian sense, even though the images are generally Jungian in spirit. In this passage from *Black Spring* he is describing the view from Brooklyn Bridge, a kind of archetypal cityscape:

A warm sultry haze lying over the city like a cup of fat, the sweat trickling down between the bare legs, around the slim ankles. A mucous mass of arms and legs, of half moons and weather vanes, of cock-robins and round-robins, of shuttle-cocks and bright bananas with the light lemon pulp lying in the bell of the peel. Five o'clock strikes through the grime and sweat of the afternoon, a strip of bright shadow left by the iron girders. The trolleys wheel round with iron mandibles, crunching the papier-mache of the crowd, spooling it down like punched transfers.[17]

The image of "fat" which is so liquid in consistency suggests a less differentiated version of the body in which individuality is lost in a general liquidity which varies here and there in density. This general image acquires sexual characteristics by its content of "cock" images and the banana. The iron trolleys also pick up sexual overtones and become castrating monsters, although on a primary level they suggest the consuming power of the modern city which devours the papier-mache people.

Miller's acceptance of the "phantoms of long past worlds" allowed him to deal symbolically even with realistic situations. By maintaining in his choice of language a continuous awareness of the primordial level of life he is able to modulate from the level of realistic narrative to pure fantasy without losing a sense of overall realistic narrative. He employed this technique as early as *Tropic of Cancer*, though less successfully than in later works.[18] He is especially apt at con-

17 *Black Spring*, 169–70.
18 In an early obscenity trial involving *Tropic of Cancer*, the judge noted in declaring the book obscene that the so-called obscene portions were not similar in style to other parts of the book, therefore, not integral. He may have reacted to the imperfect blending of realistic and surrealistic passages.

verting the ordinary activities of life—eating, drinking, talking, or going to the toilet—into another level of less-differentiated biological activity simply by extending the imagery slightly beyond the realistic level he has been writing on. In this passage for example he recalls a nightclub sector:

There toward the cool of the evening, you will find the crooked little streets humming with activity, the women, clad in bathing suits or chemise, lounging on the doorsteps, cigarette in mouth, calling to the passers-by. As night falls the walls seem to grow together and from all the little lanes that trickle into the gulch there spills a crowd of curious hungry men who choke the narrow streets, who mill around, dart aimlessly here and there like tailed sperm seeking the ovum, and finally are sucked in by the open maw of the brothels.[19]

His imagery manages to suggest cosmic energy which fulfills itself in man. There is frequently this restless seeking, as if some destiny had to be fulfilled. The more passive sense of a goal to be reached by evolving individuality is super-added to Rank's sense of the "willful" unfolding of individual life. Jung calls the direction which the individual takes his "life-line." These "life-lines" are not principles or ideals, they are directions taken by the life-force, and they must be felt rather than known. "A decline in vital intensity, a noticeable loss of libido or a feeling of constraint indicate the moment when one has quitted one line and entered upon another, or rather ought to have entered upon it." [20] The finding of one's life-line requires an awareness of unconscious desires and a certain amount of letting things go, of letting things happen.

19 *Black Spring*, 61.
20 C. G. Jung, *Two Essays in Analytical Psychology* (New York: Meridian Books, 1961), 301.

To the ideas of Jung, Miller added his own ideas on individual development which are sharpened somewhat in an essay he first published in 1938. The ideas expressed probably go back to the early thirties. As Miller sees it, the man who accepts his own individuality as the main task of life must learn that he is alone: "When at last each man realizes that nothing is to be expected from God, society, or friends, or benevolent tyrants, or democratic governments, or saints, or saviours, or even from the holiest of holies, education, when each man realizes that he must work with his own hands to save himself, and that he need expect no mercy perhaps then . . . *Perhaps!*" [21] When each man takes the responsibility for his own development and for his own individuality the world will be in a fair way to being healed of its ills and not before. Even Freud and the psychoanalysts do not seek followers or disciples; they point the way for each man to "regard himself with awe and wonder, with mystery and reverence; let each one work his own influence, his own havoc, his own miracles. Let each one as an individual, assume the roles of artist, healer, prophet, priest, king, warrior, saint." [22]

Living out one's life, which is the basic theory stated here, is also the theme of Miller's auto-novels. There is a paradox at the heart of this theme, since the way to peace is the opposite of that which our culture usually recommends. Instead of repressing instinct, wishes, desires, and urges, we must live them out. Only thus can man find peace within himself, and peace within the self is the way to peace in the world: "Every time we fail to strike or to kill the person who threatens to humiliate or degrade or enchain us we pay the penalty for it in collective suicide, which is war, or in fratricidal slaughter

21 *Big Sur and the Oranges of Hieronymus Bosch* (New York: New Directions, 1957), 155.
22 *The Cosmological Eye,* 175.

which is revolution. Every day that we fail to live out the maximum of our potentialities we kill the Shakespeare, Dante, Homer, Christ which is in us. Every day that we live in harness with the woman whom we no longer love we destroy our power to love and to have the woman whom we merit." [23] The paradox is that only by living out these underlying currents do we ultimately benefit man. "I am fatuous enough to believe that in living out my own life in my own way I am more apt to give life to others (even though that is not my chief concern) than I would if I simply followed somebody else's idea of how to live my life and thus become a man among men." [24]

Miller has uncovered in these passages one of the basic dilemmas of psychoanalysis. It is all very well if the patient is able to find out what is disturbing him and then make a better adjustment to "reality," which often means the collective will. Suppose, however, that the individual uncovers his true wishes and desires and they go contrary to the collective will. What then? Suppose he cannot stand the life he is leading, that it is not childhood trauma from which he suffers but the idiotic present. Should he, in order to achieve more perfectly the process of development, destroy the culture around him? In these passages Miller emphasizes the necessity of following instinct. Theoretically, of course, if all men were to follow this urging, unprecedented violence would break out. In practice, as it is expressed in Miller's work, the individual passes beyond violence. Through fear man represses his violent emotions. He considers himself a nice guy who wouldn't harm a flea, but in reality he is a murderer and doesn't know it. On the other hand, if he will recognize and experience what he feels, what indeed he is—a murderer,

23 *Ibid.*, 154.
24 *Ibid.*, 157.

rapist, arsonist—then paradoxically he moves through the
wall to another dimension.

Miller discusses a world without law or morality in *World
of Sex;* it is the realization of the world of the dream:

It is the potential, indestructible man who comes to life in the
dream. For his being there is no longer a censorship; taboos,
laws, conventions, customs are annihilated. In the realm of sex
it is the only true freedom he ever knows. He moved toward
the object of his desire unimpeded by time, space, physical obstacles or moral considerations. He may sleep with his mother
as naturally and easily as with another woman. He may take
an animal in the field and satisfy his desires without the slightest revolt. He may fuck his own daughter and find it extremely
pleasurable. In the waking world, crippled and shackled by all
kinds of fetters, everything is wrong or evil except that which
has been prescribed by fear. The real inner being knows that
these things are not wrong, not evil; when he closes his eyes he
gives himself up to all these practices and pursuits which are
prohibited.[25]

The restrictions which society thinks are necessary, Miller says
are a part of the great lie by which society keeps the individual in chains. The point is that man must eventually be
free. "Until the spirit of man can run freely like a river
there will be irruption and upheavals." [26]

Miller is saying that man refrains from following out his
instincts from the fear that they will carry him to the kinds
of actions which he knows emotionally his dreams represent.
There is no way to convince a man otherwise. The fear is real
and so are the dreams. You must then get him to accept
the dreams and the desirability of acting upon his instinct,
to act out every desire. Paradoxically, Miller insists, though

25 *The World of Sex,* 78.
26 *Ibid.,* 79.

there may be a troublesome transition period, the man will be delivered from the violence of his feelings, not led into criminal activity. That is, violence comes from a repressive civilization, from the bottled-up instincts, not from man's nature. Similarly, when civilization as a whole throws over the repression, the same result follows; the human being is capable of more than he is given credit for:

To imagine that men if they were not restricted and hedged in by law and moralities, would immediately set about killing and plundering, or buggering and raping ad lib., is to slander and insult the human being. The human being will live up to the best in him, if he is given half a chance. A certain amount of killing, plundering, raping, and so on, inevitably occurs whenever there is a burst of freedom. Some kind of crude justice has to be dealt out when the scales are tipped and seek to return to balance. Some specimens of the human race ought, out of decency, kindness, and reverence for those to come, be wiped out. These things will happen again and again as long as there is suppression and oppression. The great in spirit do not advocate these things. But the poor in spirit have their say also, whether it be right or wrong.[27]

The existentialist has written about the "courage to be." Miller is writing about the "courage to let things be." In the degree of his willingness "to let things be" he has parted company with many who retain, however faintly, the desire to make the world conform to their own ideal image. He has consistently refused to meddle, and although it is egotism, it is a philosophical egotism through which he seeks ultimately to lead himself to a fuller realization of selfhood. Miller's basic creed is that men get what they want. If they are downtrodden, miserable, craven creatures doomed to failure, it is because they want it that way. His sense of the power of

27 *Ibid.*

the internal forces in man is so great that he feels it is useless to tamper with the direction men have chosen. They will
get what they want despite your best efforts. It is obviously
better, given Miller's basic philosophy, to help men to want
something different, or to help them uncover their true
wants which are buried under the layers of fear and disgust
which civilization has placed there.

Miller does not, therefore, occupy himself with the salvation of men. His works are filled with character studies of
many people; he is always interested in people. Indeed it is
hard to escape the feeling that he loves people deeply. But
he will not interfere with them. Each character whom we
see is charting his own route to his own destiny, either
toward failure or toward success. Miller, the hero-narrator
of the novels, moves from the chaos of unrealized life toward
a philosophy of acceptance. The unfolding of the autobiography is toward growth and the increase of awareness:
"Beauty, truth, power, God, all these come without effort.
The struggle is not for these; the struggle is deeper than
that. The struggle is to synchronize the potential being with
the actual being, to make a fruitful liaison between the man
of yesterday and the man of tomorrow. It is the process of
growth which is painful, but unavoidable." [28]

In this struggle to realize the self Miller shows us that he
does not in fact point us simply toward a return to instinctual
life. Expansion of consciousness requires recovery of instinct,
but instinct alone is not enough. "Guilt, sin, conscience . . .
there is no eradicating these factors of human consciousness.
They are part and parcel of consciousness itself. The stress
on the Unconscious forces of the man does not necessarily
imply the elimination of consciousness. On the contrary, it
implies the expansion of consciousness. There can be no

28 *Ibid.*, 189.

return to an instinctive life, and in fact, even among primitive men I see no evidence of a purely instinctive life." [29]

The goal of expanding consciousness combines with the philosophy of acceptance, a letting things be and a letting things happen. The acceptance of the self and the world as one of the goals of man's development brings Miller into another philosophical key. For this he reaches beyond psychoanalysis to religion and philosophy, to Erich Gutkind, to Taoism, and Zen Buddhism, to Whitman and Emerson, and to the romantic novels of Balzac and Hesse.

Erich Gutkind's *The Absolute Collective* is clearly a theology. It is concerned with the nature of God, and the manner of man's encounter with Him; but it is not Christian, and it does not even suppose an afterlife. According to Gutkind man today has broken the relationship with God, but this bond cannot be re-established by thought, for thought leads only to thought. The bond with God can be regained only by starting in the depths of the body and by uniting body and soul. Immortality is not something which takes place later, after life; it happens now or not at all. The goal of life is holiness through the holiness of God, which is an unlocking of the creature through God.[30]

Gutkind embraces the heights and depths, the same or a similar dualism which Miller found in Nietzsche and Lawrence. Gutkind, however, like Jung, feels that Nietzsche

29 *Ibid.*
30 Erich Gutkind, *The Absolute Collective* (London: C. W. Daniel Co., 1937). Widmer refers to Gutkind as "a minor Jewish mystic," and in a note expands his comment to include a resemblance to Martin Buber. Generally Widmer passes over Miller's "influences" as either irrelevant or superficial. He has atomized the elements of Miller's works to the extent that nothing connects with anything else. But the emphasis in Gutkind, as Widmer expresses it, on the "religious communion with immediate, concrete and fully physical life" is precisely what Miller is trying to express in his own life and art.

failed when he tried to overcome the futility of modern life by a return to biological values. Like Lawrence, Gutkind reaches to the other extreme as well:

Nietzsche saw that the deeper springs of human life were running dry and that the end threatened to be nothing but meanness, futility and artificiality. . . . He tried to evade the doom he saw by a return to biological values. But in the world of reality there is no turning back. . . . To descend is not to go back. . . . Nor can we ascend through mere insight or intention. Our ascent must take its start in the depths of the body. Our action must have its root in the mysterious centre of our dumb, unconscious being, not only in the apparatus of our conscious life, not even in the apparatus of the body. . . . The truly vital stream is an electric current that runs between the upper and nether root. God speaks to both; His voice can be heard in the fatherly sunlit heights and in the dark motherly night.[31]

To go back momentarily to Lawrence and Jung, the dark motherly night, which attracts men by its mystery, is, if embraced exclusively, the death of consciousness and therefore of man. The other extreme, the sunlit heights, is identified with the father, who represents the evolution of consciousness and man's destiny in culture. To embrace this way alone, which is what the modern world has done, leads to another kind of death, the death of the body, without which there is no immortality. Gutkind, as Miller sees him, looks forward to the new man, the unitary man:

Man must open up, prepared to live the life of the world in all its worldliness, if he is to survive. For, as Gutkind cogently points out, even worse than the wholesale slaughter in which we indulge is what he calls "sublimated murder," or the refusal

31 Gutkind, *The Absolute Collective,* 30–31.

to overflow. I stress this aspect of the book particularily, because it has always seemed to me incontrovertible that war is just and necessary, so long as men insist on repressing their murderous instincts. War is not an economic affair, nor a curse of the gods, nor an inevitability; it is the reflection of an inner split, the projection of our continuous repressed lusts and hatreds.[32]

The absolute in which man is realized is for Miller the "hidden axis of our vertical life without which the 'dreary round of predictable events' would make the world appear like a rat trap." To face reality is not the dreary business that the "realists" have made it. ". . . the men who are thoroughly wide-awake and completely alive are in reality, and for these reality has always been close to ecstasy, partaking of a life of fulfillment which knows no bounds. Of them only may it be said that they live in the present. Through them it is permitted us to grasp the meaning of timelessness, of eternity which is victory." [33]

This sense of a life within life which Miller finds in Gutkind marks the final stage of man's progress, and of the progress of Miller's own thinking. It is important, because it sets up a philosophy for the second half of life, a less active state, when things begin to unfold within the one who has opened himself. On the whole, men have not accepted the possibilities which lie all around them because they do not accept the unity of life. To succeed one need only open himself to life. Most men never learn to live: "In a real sense life is something which has not yet begun. . . . Life can only be seized by the whole organism, as something felt, something which demands neither proof nor justification. Nobody can point the way. *Life is,* and in this sense a man is or he is not.

32 Henry Miller, "A Salute Collective" in *The Wisdom of the Heart,* 86.
33 *Ibid.,* 89.

Life is not an 'it' to be grasped by the mind. 'Whoever has not been fully alive in this life,' says Gutkind, 'will not become so through death.' " [34] Miller leaves behind all religious ideas, or any notion of life in the beyond. He chooses, finally, life here and now. We come back to Otto Rank: "We shall have no need for art or religion because we shall be in ourselves a work of art." [35]

From Gutkind there is really no place to go as far as Western philosophy is concerned. After the struggle to be born, which is an active tearing of oneself from the womb, there is the need of culmination, a coming to rest. An attitude of peaceful acceptance becomes predominant in Miller's autobiographical writing only after he left France, but it is anticipated in his essays during the time he was writing the *Tropics*. Miller's key metaphor for the philosophy of acceptance is developed in his essay "The Enormous Womb." The images for this essay are obviously drawn from Rank, but his development of the idea leads him toward a more Eastern expression. He mentions from time to time various oriental philosophies, especially the ideas of the Tao and of Zen Buddhism. For our purposes two books for which Miller expressed admiration will show sufficiently his use of oriental philosophy. *The Spirit of Zen* by Alan Watts and *Siddhartha* by Hermann Hesse.

The image of the womb, either of escape from the womb or return to the womb, is central in Miller's writing. It is not, I think, a superficial metaphor, for it is vitally related to such things as identity, the feeling for growth and development, the struggle within society, and the isolation of the rebel. All these matters are of concern in the process of human growth to maturity and fulfillment. "The Enormous Womb" for this

34 *Ibid.*, 91.
35 *Ibid.*, 92.

reason is a key essay. Miller distinguishes three kinds of womb—the mother's womb, the womb of nature, and the womb "which we call the world." [36] The womb of the world is essentially what we call life, which he distinguishes from the uterine life and the life hereafter. Ordinarily in our culture men identify these latter states with bliss or immortality. But Miller holds that there are men who live a life of bliss here and now. "They have accepted the world as womb, and not as tomb. For they seem neither to regret what has passed nor to fear what is to come. They live in an intense state of awareness and yet are apparently without fear." [37] What brings Miller close to Eastern ways of thinking (of feeling, properly) is his emphasis upon fulfillment here and now. Like the state of satori it does not have to wait until death. In Western culture the man who conquers life is the hero because "he is on the side of life." The hero experiences the world as womb, as a "place where things are engendered, brought to life." The hero is a Nietzschean hero, or his refinement, the Rankian hero.[38] For him life is revealed "as art not as an ordeal." The hero differs from the rest of us, according to Miller, because he lives out his life here and now rather than always in some anticipated future.

The only legitimate form of death is fulfillment. The ones who live closest to this idea of fulfillment are the artists

36 Henry Miller, "The Enormous Womb," in *The Wisdom of the Heart*, 94. The concept of "womb" for Miller goes further than the birth trauma theories of Rank. The sense of being one with all things and sensing all things as one with the self imparts what in psychology has been called the "oceanic feeling." In this state the individual seems to undergo a widening of the ego boundaries to include the universe. The result is a state of great peace.
37 *Ibid.*, 95.
38 See Otto Rank, *The Myth of the Birth of the Hero* (New York: Vintage Books, 1959).

who are the only ones who "have been in favor of living it out." [39] Once again it is the balance of opposites which is the key to success. Yet it is not struggle for its own sake which is the answer. Miller attacks the ordinary concept of Paradise with its implications of the struggle necessary for salvation. In Miller's paradise there is no struggle. In fact, paradise can only be attained when we have ceased to struggle. The chief struggle then is "the struggle not to struggle." [40] The art of becoming aware is like the equilibrist's art, "walking the slack wire above the opposites . . . the consciousness expands to embrace the apparently conflicting opposites. To be supremely aware, which means accepting life for what it is, eliminates the terrors of life and kills false hopes. I should say rather, kills hope, for seen from a beyond hope appears as an evil rather than a good." [41]

The philosophy of acceptance to which the embracing of opposites leads is fascinating as a paper concept, but as a practical philosophy it leads to obvious difficulties over which the individual almost immediately stumbles; for the individual lives by choosing, and he cannot stop choosing at will. Therefore, the process by which one arrives at acceptance is of greatest importance, and it is that process which Miller's auto-novels are concerned with. His "philosophical writing" presents us with the artist of life who has in a sense arrived, who already accepts. The novels portray the painful process of birth which it took to get there. The two are in this sense complementary. Still, when Miller goes on one of his flights he is not easy to believe. The "willing suspension of disbelief" for many has been impossible. For them, I suspect, the man Miller is always grinning through the mask, even the tragic mask; and they become uncomfortably aware of what they

39 Miller, "The Enormous Womb," 98.
40 *Ibid.,* 99.
41 *Ibid.*

feel is a pose. Those who have been his fans and followers
are predisposed, perhaps because of their life circumstances,
to suspend criticism until Miller has woven his spell. Miller's
own feelings of acceptance he expresses in passages such as
this:

I believe more than ever. I believe everything, good and bad. I
believe more and less than what is true. I believe beyond the
whole corpus of man's thinking. *I believe everything.* I believe
in a collective life and in the individual life also. I believe in
the life of the world, the uterus which it is. I believe in the contradictions of the uterine life of this world. I believe in having
money and in not having money too. And whether I believe or
don't believe I always act. I act first and inquire afterwards. . . .
Those who act create reactions, as we say. In the throes of giving
birth the mother is only reacting; it is the foetus which acts. And
whether the mother lives or dies is one and the same to the foetus.
For a foetus the important thing is birth.[42]

The final state of ecstasy to which the philosophy of acceptance leads is the "god-feeling." [43] It is the final stage of
a cycle which takes man from unconscious unity to extreme
separateness and back to unity, but this time to a unity which
has become extremely aware. In this state, which is more like
the satori of Zen Buddhism than like our ordinary notions
of nirvana, the individual passes beyond time and place to
become one with the universe:

When the individual is wholly creative, one with destiny, there
is neither time nor space, nor birth and death. The god-feeling
becomes so intense that everything, organic and inorganic, beats
with a divine rhythm. At the moment of supreme individua-

42 *Ibid.,* 100.
43 Henry Miller, "Uterine Hunger," in *The Wisdom of the Heart,*
191.

tion when the identity of all things is sensed and one is at the same time utterly and blissfully alone, the umbilical cord is at last cut. There is neither a longing for the womb nor a longing for the beyond. The sure feeling of eternality. Beyond this there is no evolution, only a perpetual movement from creation to creation. The personality itself becomes a creation. From symbolizing himself in his works man symbolizes himself in his being.[44]

The auto-novels are about the struggle to become free, that is to learn not to struggle. The later works show a man slowly coming to rest, turning from art to life, the rewards of the struggle being the fuller personality.

One man whom Miller discusses at length, who has apparently reached a very full development, is a psychiatrist, E. Graham Howe. Howe's book on peace and war, which is Miller's main point of discussion, attributes the cause of war to man's determination to choose between good and evil. Once life is organized on the basis of choosing among alternatives, war is the inevitable result. War is in fact no more than the externalization of the inward states of men. Howe is familiar with Eastern philosophies. In fact, he says, since the time of those who discovered the Tao, which recognized the system of polarities as the basis of life, civilization has gone downhill. The fatal mistake according to Howe was to "eliminate that opposite our adversary, calling him Satan the Evil one, thereby reducing everything to a seeming single unity." [45]

Howe, like Miller, accepts a root bisexuality in man.[46] He suggests that acceptance of the law of life is a slow process of germination, letting something grow in us:

44 *Ibid.*
45 E. Graham Howe, *War Dance* (London: Faber & Faber, 1937), 132.
46 See note 58, Chapter 5.

Life is the law for our acceptance, but who can stand the strain
of life and love it? This acceptance of the reality of things as
they are, actively passive, co-operative and reciprocating, as a
seed planted in darkness, operating in the unseen, uncondition-
ally accepting the full measure of experience, is the privilege of
the female role. Seeking only to be a servant of that creation of
which it is the living image, acting as the reflecting mirror of a
deeper light, our single task is faithfully to tend that light
within the intellects which, through its illumination, is prepared
to see all things and live among them.[47]

The acceptance of bisexuality, which is used by both Jung
and Rank, enables the writer to suggest a deeper level in
man, in which he can achieve fulfillment in passive acqui-
escence rather than aggressive action. It is especially important in the second half of life, after the age of forty, when a
man changes from aggressive action which is the means for
carving himself a place in the world, to a facing of the self
and of death. "There is a rhythm in the curve of life which
finds at about the age of forty a deeper need to change
towards this inward path. It is as if the earlier half of life
must learn first how to live, before it can learn the larger
truth of how to die. . . . Now is the time for successful aggressiveness to learn the deeper truth, as the other half of
life comes forward for completeness, changing material
progress to spiritual depth, instinct to intuition, male to
female way of living, and death to rebirth." [48]

Though little now is heard of Howe outside of Miller's
acknowledgment of him, he is fascinating to read. Perhaps
the greatest praise of the man, and for our purpose the best
revelation of what Miller values in him, is Miller's own description of Howe:

47 Howe, *War Dance,* 147.
48 *Ibid.,* 287.

He is not interested in *healing*, but in *being*. He does not seek to cure, but to enjoy a life more abundant. He is not struggling to eliminate disease, but to accept it, and by devouring it, incorporate it in the body of life and health which is man's true heritage. He is not overburdened, because his philosophy of health would not permit him to assume tasks beyond his powers. He takes everything in his stride with measure and balance, consuming only what he can digest and assimilate of experience. If he is a very capable analyst . . . it is not because of what he knows, but because of what he is. He is constantly unloading himself of excess baggage, be it in the form of patients, friends, admirers or possessions. His mind is, as the Chinese well say 'alive and empty.' He is anchored in the flux, neither drowned in it nor vainly trying to dam it. He is a very wise man who is at peace with himself and the world. One knows that instantly merely by shaking hands with him.[49]

Miller's further contact with the Eastern strain in Howe comes from a number of general sources. One book he did mention specifically is Alan Watts's *The Spirit of Zen*. Since Watts's little book came out in 1936, it fits nicely into the period we are discussing. *The Spirit of Zen* has the advantage over many similar books in that it is clear and logical. That may lead to disadvantages, such as a falsification of Zen Buddhism, which is irrational in principle; but it does make it possible to predict the impression it will make on the reader.

According to Watts, Zen is a philosophy without words, a direct pointing to the self and to experience. The "Way" of Zen is the way of ordinary life. Its function historically was to break down the rigid and abstract rituals which had accumulated in Buddhism. But it did not aim to replace one philosophy with another; its whole discipline was aimed at

49 Henry Miller, "Wisdom of the Heart," in *The Wisdom of the Heart,* 40.

keeping in touch with the concrete. For Zen nothing in life remains; everything is always passing away. As soon as we try to grasp something, we lose it. "We cannot take hold of the present moment and make it stay with us; we cannot call back past time or keep for ever a passing sensation. Once we try to do this all we have is a dead memory." [50]

As Watts concludes, Zen is not something which is to be "understood"; it is something to be lived. ". . . Zen is an immediate contact with life, a joining of 'self' and 'life' into so close a unity and rhythm that the distinction between the two is forgotten, that the desire to possess is abandoned because there is nothing that can possess and nothing that can be possessed. The isolated 'self' no longer wishes to grasp at the things which flow by in the stream of events, for it goes forward with the stream and becomes one with it, realizing that all things are but waves in this stream and that to try to clutch hold of them is to make them disappear." [51]

Miller's feeling for the unity of life which is so oriental and so close to Eastern ideas, is combined with the Western sense of the fulfillment of self which would possibly be somewhat strange in the more anonymous East. The combination of the two can be seen quite clearly in another book which Miller admired greatly, *Siddhartha* by Hermann Hesse. Hesse manages remarkably well to create the spirit of the search and to suggest the full effect of the immediacy of experience. Each state of life which Siddhartha enters has something good in itself, but none is complete in itself. Direction for the search comes entirely from the inward voice which leads the searcher at each stage to begin the quest anew.

There are roughly five separate states which Siddhartha enters. Each of them gives a kind of freedom, while creating

50 Alan W. Watts, *The Spirit of Zen* (London: John Murray, 1936), 40.
51 *Ibid.*, 51.

a new kind of slavery. Only in the last, the state of illumination, is he entirely without possessions. He begins as the son
of an aristocrat, a Brahmin. He practices meditation, which
creates awareness so that he can respond to the deeper
promptings of his nature. The next step takes him to the
Samanas, ascetics, who live in the woods and practice fast-
ing and self-denial. He and his friend Govinda soon become
adept at these practices, but Siddhartha soon realizes that
he can never arrive at illumination this way. He leaves with
Govinda to find Gautama, the Holy One. When Govinda
decides to stay with Gautama, Siddhartha continues his
search. While on the road to find Gautama, however, Siddhartha expresses to Govinda the idea of being without
possessions which he is just beginning to understand. When
Govinda expresses some desire to get where he is going, Siddhartha says: "Let us enjoy this fruit and await further ones,
Govinda. This fruit, for which we are already indebted to
the Gautama, consists in the fact that he has enticed us away
from the Samanas. Whether there are still other and better
fruits, let us patiently await and see."[52] It is this progressive
discovery of what it is to be without possessions that is the
central theme of the book, and it is the theme which is most
relevant to Miller and his use of Eastern philosophy.

A slavery to possessions would be totally destructive of the
way to illumination. A desire to have anything without fear
of loss is self-defeating, especially when applied to inward
states. As no person can possess anything in life, no idea can
define what life is.[53] Since truth is life, and life is ungrasp-
able, then the truth of life cannot be grasped. It can only be
experienced. Therefore, "spiritual freedom is just that capacity to be as spontaneous and unfettered as life itself, . . .

52 Hermann Hesse, *Siddhartha* (New York: New Directions, 1951), 25.
53 Watts, *The Spirit of Zen* 59.

But non-attachment does not mean running away from things to some peaceful hermitage, for we can never escape from our own illusions about life; we carry them with us, and if we are afraid of them and wish to escape it means that we are doubly enslaved. . . . hence the non-attachment of Buddhism and Taoism means not running away from life but running with it, for freedom comes through complete acceptance of reality." [54]

The culmination of the way of Zen is satori, a state of sudden illumination in which all the problems and contradictions of life are resolved. "Satori is release from one's habitual state of tenseness, of clinging to false ideas of possession. The whole rigid structure which is man's usual interpretation of life suddenly drops to pieces, resulting in a sense of boundless freedom. . . ." [55] Similarly, Watts stresses the fact that the practitioner of Zen may not even strain after possession of satori, for to seek it is to lose it. Miller has never presented ecstasy in quite these terms. He has claimed a gradual awakening, the quality of which is drawn from or coincidentally resembles the description of satori. Such sudden illuminations, perhaps, being less Western in feeling would have seemed inappropriate for Miller's own use.

The course through life of Siddhartha, when we think of him in the context of Miller's writing, dispels any illusions we may have that the way of acceptance should be a way of unending joy. Siddhartha often suffers. But he is never in the double bind of suffering from the suffering, or because the suffering will not go away. Siddhartha is most exposed to suffering in the transition stages, when one state has ended and a new one has not yet begun. He is able to remain in a state of desire, without wishing either that the desire should be fulfilled or that it should remain. When he sees the courtesan

54 *Ibid.,* 60.
55 *Ibid.,* 69.

and is drawn to her, he acts as simply as he did with the Samanas. He goes to her and tells her he wants to remain and learn the ways of love. She tells him he must be perfumed and bring presents. Again quite simply he goes to the merchant to seek employment. He is extraordinarily successful as a merchant, though he obviously does not care about being a merchant. He does it all as samsara, illusion. For being a merchant is not anything real.

What is perhaps most impressive about *Siddhartha,* and what no doubt attracted Miller, is the tremendous impression of spiritual energy which Hesse is able to create. Siddhartha does all things well, because he is undivided. Whatever he does he does with full devotion. I am reminded somewhat here of the work of Kubie; in *Neurotic Distortions of the Creative Process,* he claims that learning and other intellectual accomplishments would be easy if it were not for neurotic impediments.[56] Perhaps in this, psychiatrist and novelist come together, for Siddhartha is a very efficient human being. At the end of his stay with the courtesan, he finds he has seen through two illusions about reality—first of the intellectual life with the Samanas, secondly of the physical life with the courtesan. Once again he is attracted by some goal but dimly perceived. When he starts again it is as if all the ordinary categories of experience have been exhausted. He feels like a child starting over. It is after all not the world but the self with which he has wrestled. Everything in him has died, the rich man's son, the prince, the man of property, drinker, dice player, priest, Samana, all have died. All that is left is Siddhartha.

Only one more transition stage remains in the life of Siddhartha, that is the love he bears for the son which the courtesan brought to him. When the time comes when he

56 Lawrence Kubie, *Neurotic Distortions of the Creative Process* (New York: Noonday Press, 1961) .

must choose, to give up the son or keep him, he realizes, with the help of the old ferryboat man whose assistant he had become, that even here he cannot exercise his desire for possession. It is not Siddhartha who must decide, but the nature of the boy. As the son of a prince, he must be allowed to have his privileges. He gives up the boy. Now he is prepared for the final state; and listening to the river, the thousand-fold form, he learns to love life and everything in it. The final state of illumination brings all things into the unity of love. Govinda, who reappears at the end, asks the final question: "What if these things are illusion?" Siddhartha's answer once again unifies contradiction. "If they are illusion, then I also am illusion, and so they are always of the same nature as myself. It is that which makes them lovable and venerable."[57]

Nietzsche and Hesse are closely related in spirit, yet there are great differences between them. Nietzsche's is the first trumpet blast calling for the rescue of the self from the surrounding mob. Hesse shows the goal of that journey which ends in a transport of love. Nietzsche said that egoism led to love, but not by the way of humility and weakness. To the extent that Siddhartha is an egotist, perhaps Hesse shows Nietzsche to be right, at least imaginatively. These limits also define the limits of Miller's pilgrimage and the central theme of his art, which moves from the awakening self and its struggles, to union in a spirit of forbearance. Our next task is to see how Miller develops this theme in his autobiographical romance.

57 Hesse, *Siddhartha,* 148.

THE VOLCANO'S ERUPTION

Tropic of Cancer, which came out in 1934, was
Miller's first published full length work.[1] He had
written several "novels" before this, but those
who have read them, including Miller, agree
that they lack his essential quality, that they are derived and
imitative. Although *Tropic of Cancer* is not part of the central work which Miller had planned in 1927, it is a kind of
spontaneous bursting forth of feeling which had been
bottled up for years. It is significant for several reasons, not
the least being that it is still one of his most readable books.
In *Cancer* Miller found and developed the role of hero-
narrator which he has maintained throughout his writing
career. This narrator, even when he is describing his own
personal experiences and feelings, remains detached and
relatively free of his environment. He is what Miller has always said of himself even as a child, at once a part of and
totally independent of the life around him. He is gregarious
and totally alone. He is Dostoievski's "underground man"
who is filled with violence, but he lacks the self-doubts and
tortured inner struggle that mark Dostoievski's heroes. He is

1   *Tropic of Cancer* (New York: Grove Press 1961), 1–2.

presented to us as a man who has finally, once and for all, burst out of the confines of his culture, who has himself become the arbiter of values, who is the herald of a new world to come after this present world shall finally have been destroyed. *Tropic of Cancer* accepts that destruction and celebrates the affirmation of individual life. Its various sections explore the undiscovered life which belongs to the self but has been covered over in the effort to come to terms with a corrupt civilization.

He is the Nietzschean man who wakes one day to exclaim rapturously with Rabelais, "Fay ce que vouldras!" Having discarded the values which he inherited from his culture, hero Miller faces life in Paris in an effort to establish new values. In the process he regresses to almost infantile levels of demand. He is consumed with the desire for food. Everything in life that he wants becomes the object not of will or desire, but of voracious appetite. The first rule of life is survival, and he takes all the means he can find to this end. He sets up a list of friends who will share the responsibility for feeding him, and he calls once a week at the house of each, until he outstays his welcome. He begs and scrounges and yet all the while seems to enjoy life to the full. Everyone worries; he is serene.

Besides developing the character of the hero, *Tropic of Cancer* establishes the style which will be characteristic of Miller from then on. There are generally three elements which he combines in different proportions. The first element is the life of the hero-narrator in the present, which includes his sense of body and mind, the continual rendering of the feeling of living here and now. Secondly there are the anecdotal elements which make Miller's novels one of the great collecting places of strange and unusual characters. Sometimes these anecdotes seem to be told for their own sakes, like the story of Max, the destitute refugee. But usually they function as a foil for the narrator to show his own view of life or to compare the developing values of the hero with the obsessive concerns of the unredeemed. In *Cancer* this role is reserved mainly for Van Norden, who occupies one long chapter besides lengthy passages later in the book.

On the third level and woven into the other material are the free-flowing fantasy-like associations by which the hero-narrator interprets the world in which he lives. These passages are not as fully developed as in later works, but they are still a significant part. They generally arise either out of the narrator's present experience of felt life or out of his anecdotes about others. The fantasy of Miller's shorter works like "Into the Night Life" is pure surrealism, but fantasy as a technique in the major novels is highly integrative. Symbols enable the narrator to reach beyond the present moment to the past and future, and beyond the present limited geographical location to the universe. The fantasy passages allow the narrator to integrate his own past life and the episodes and characters of the present with his major themes —the birth of independence, the discovery of the lines of the body. *Tropic of Cancer* seems to be a less-unified book than *Tropic of Capricorn* because the fantasy passages do not unite and integrate the material into themes as completely as they do in *Capricorn*. Despite this fault, however, *Cancer* has an excitement about it of something new; it is crude but fresh.

Miller tells us something of his own view of *Tropic of Cancer* in *The World of Sex:* "The *Tropic of Cancer* is a sort of human document, written in blood, recording the struggle in the womb of death. The strong sexual odor is, if anything, the aroma of birth, disagreeable, repulsive even, when disassociated from its significance." [2] Miller calls

2 *The World of Sex,* 10–11.

Tropic of Cancer a work of the moment, "the volcano's eruption." [3] Yet it is important because it emphasizes more than other works one aspect of Miller's development, that is, the purposeful treatment of what is ugly, repulsive, and distasteful in life. Miller's struggle in the womb of death is well worth recording, but easily misunderstood.[4] His attitude in *Tropic of Cancer* is not peaceful acceptance as it will become later. It is rather the first assertion of the self against all that seeks to enslave that self, against disgust for the forms that life may take, against conventional easy adjustments to reality, against sentimentalism, self-deception, and obsessions of every sort. It proposes to face frankly the biological facts of existence and especially to treat these facts in the most immediate concrete terms available. It is against art, as Miller saw it practiced in his own day, because it refuses to gloss over anything; it is against all sentimental conceptions of God or religion, against all conventional notions of man, destiny, time, or eternity. It is *for* very little except the complete honesty and integrity of the individual.

As Miller has emphasized in his study of D. H. Lawrence,[5] the refusal to face animal life leads to that idealization which is yet another form of death, because it denies the fundamental nature of man and cuts him off from his source of vital energy. The law of life is growth, and for man that means freeing himself from the womb, achieving independence. Life is a process in which man is constantly being born. The refusal to be born is the acceptance of death.

In the light of what we have already seen of Miller's early life the rebellious sexuality of *Tropic of Cancer* is something

3   Perles and Durrell, *Art and Outrage,* 31.
4   As, for example, George Orwell. Orwell, basing his opinion on early Miller works, overemphasized the passivity in Miller. See also Chapter 2.
5   See Chapter 2.

of a paradox. We can easily imagine a highly repressed individual breaking loose as Miller does in this book, but there
is no evidence that Miller had ever been particularly
repressed. Passages in other books about his early life show
a freedom of approach to sexual experience and an ability
to tolerate sexual images which would seem to indicate an
almost total lack of repression. Yet we must assume on the
basis of the imagery of *Tropic of Cancer* that a great release
of instinctual energy is taking place, and that enabled Miller
to move on to another level of experience.[6]

We can better understand the nature of Miller's rebellion
if we examine his situation at the time of writing *Tropic of
Cancer*. Early in *Tropic of Capricorn,* that is while the narrator was working at Western Union, we find a discussion
of the bottled up rebellion directed against all the forces of
society which hero Miller felt was keeping him from achieving his full potentiality as an individual. There was at this
time a tremendous upsurge of aggression which as yet had not
been channeled in any constructive direction. A second great
emotional upheaval takes place in *Sexus* when he breaks
loose from the depressing relationship with his first wife to
enter a new kind of relation with Mona. The relationship
with Mona, however, does not free Miller; it enslaves him.
He finds himself with time to write, but he is dependent upon
a woman who so dominates his life that he is unable to use
the time constructively. The "Land of Fuck" Interlude of
Tropic of Capricorn shows us a descent to the level of instinct, but does not show us the emergence from that state.
At the end of *Nexus,* just before Miller left for Paris, his aggressive feelings are still largely unchanneled and violent,
and his sexual energies are tied up in a frustrating relationship which has progressively deteriorated. It is clear that

6 This concept will be explored more fully in Chapter 7.

Miller has not yet arrived at a state of free and spontaneous awareness of life which can operate effectively in achieving his full potentiality as a person.

As the great explosion in which both sexual and aggressive energy are released into the work of art, *Tropic of Cancer* is a disturbing book. Its violence has become heavily charged with sexual feeling, and for this reason it is a cathartic of the most violent kind. It has been attacked fanatically and defended in the same way. It is only right that it should be. A rebellion of the nature of Miller's does not usually evoke a lukewarm reaction. Some readers, caught up in Miller's mood to the extent that they feel the same release, love the book; others, disturbed by the raw state of its emotion, dislike it intensely. Such in fact, has been the history of critical reactions to *Tropic of Cancer*.[7]

The hero-narrator of *Tropic of Cancer* is in many ways the Nietzschean hero par excellence, but his rebellion has other elements which we have touched upon. In a symbolic sense the rebellion of the hero is an effort to escape from the womb of the mother. There are many sources, as we have seen, for Miller's womb imagery; but his attitude in *Cancer* seems closest to that which he expressed much later in *The Time of the Assassins*, his study of Rimbaud, and in his comments on James Joyce.[8] In the Rimbaud study Miller draws a character sketch of the man who is striving to break free of the mother, and he associates that effort with violence.

Failure of the individual to free himself from the mother, Miller says, means that the dark side of his nature had not

7   Very few unemotional critical treatments of Miller appear anywhere. Critics in popular magazines who have reviewed his books see him as a public menace. Others, such as Herbert Read, Kenneth Rexroth, and Lawrence Durrell, have treated him as one of the great writers of the age. (Kingsley Widmer's booklength study is, in the main, unfavorable.) Guardians of the public morality in the many litigations over *Tropic of Cancer* have been outraged by Miller's content.
8   *The Time of the Assassins* (New York: New Directions, 1946) .

been faced early in life. He explains how man rejects the dark side of life out of fear that he will lose his individuality, unique identity, and freedom. Man thus becomes a rebel striving for the "freedom to assert his ego unrestrained." [9] The search for freedom then takes the form of a rebellion against life itself, which conceals the bondage to the mother:

All this has one meaning for me—that one is still bound to the mother. All one's rebellion was but dust in the eye, the frantic attempt to conceal this bondage. Men of this stamp are always against their native land—impossible to be otherwise. Enslavement is the great bugaboo, whether it be to country, church or society. Their lives are spent in breaking fetters, but the secret bondage gnaws at their vitals and gives them no rest. They must come to terms with the mother before they can rid themselves of the obsession of fetters. "Outside! Forever outside! Sitting on the doorstep of the mother's womb." . . . No wonder one is alienated from the mother. One does not notice her, except as an obstacle. One wants the comfort and security of the womb, that darkness and ease which for the unborn is the equivalent of illumination and acceptance for the truly born.[10]

Fulfillment of man's destiny, that is, the achievement of man's potentialities for freedom, means that one must leave the security of the mother's womb and accept the world as the true matrix of his development. The world then becomes a womb and man repeats in a different way the process of growth from conception to birth. Miller points out the dangers of remaining linked to the mother in his discussion of James Joyce. Of man's two choices, to accept the world as womb and be born again, or return to the womb of the mother and lose the world forever, Miller has elected the first and recorded his struggle to be born. Joyce, Miller claims, has elected the second; he has returned to the womb of the

9 *Ibid.*, 48–49.
10 *Ibid.*, 49–50.

mother, symbolized in the person of Molly Bloom. His fight is with the mother, symbolized for him in family, country, and church. In his revolt he rejects the world once and for all and returns to this mother, who has become for him "the veridic whore of creation." [11] In the person of Molly Bloom the mother becomes "the quintessence of the great whore which is woman of Babylon, the vessel of abominations. Floating, unresisting, eternal, all-contained, she is like the sea itself. Like the sea she is receptive, fecund, voracious, insatiable. She begets and she destroys; she nourishes and she devastates. With Molly Bloom, *con anonyme,* woman is restored to prime significance—as womb and matrix of life." [12] Joyce's hero is unable to free himself from this woman-matrix. The hero returns to the womb at last:

And so, with final, triumphant vengeance, with suicidal glee, all the threads which were dropped throughout the book are re-capitulated; the pale, diminutive hero, reduced to an intestinal worm and carried like a tickling phallus in the great body of the female, returns to the womb of nature, shorn of everything but the last symbol. In the long retrospective arc which is drawn we have the whole trajectory of man's flight from unknown to unknown, the rainbow of history fades out. The great dissolution is accomplished. After that closing picture of Molly Bloom a-dreaming on her dirty bed we can say, as in Revelation—And there shall be no more curse! Henceforth no sin, no quiet, no fear, no repression, no longing, no pain of separation. The end is accomplished—man returns to the womb.[13]

What Miller was trying to avoid at the time he arrived in Paris was the fate which he has assigned to James Joyce, the

11   Henry Miller, "The Universe of Death," in *The Cosmological Eye,* p. 116.
12   *Ibid.,* 133.
13   *Ibid.,* 133–34.

return to the womb, the flight from life to security. Growth, he was beginning to discover, must be to greater differentiation, to freedom, to independence, and it is precisely that image of woman which he attacks in the person of Molly Bloom that he is attacking in *Tropic of Cancer*. His violence and his sexualizing of experience are a part of his attempt to control his own destiny, which also accounts for his prevailing womb imagery and for his attacks on sexual obsession of all kinds.

Miller's first task in *Tropic of Cancer* is to establish a sense of the self and a sense of the world. He must cling resolutely to the sense of self, a self which is free and independent of external events as the source of his well-being and happiness. The world is a chaos, but the self lives:

It is now the fall of my second year in Paris. I was sent here for a reason I have not yet been able to fathom.

I have no money, no resources, no hopes. I am the happiest man alive. A year ago, six months ago, I thought I was an artist. I no longer think about it. I *am*. Everything that was literature has fallen from me. There are no more books to be written, thank God.[14]

Miller is here in Paris, abandoned by Mona to find himself as best he can. The first year in Paris was a year of suffering; now comes the violent birth. "I had two beginnings really, one here in America, which was abortive, and the other in Europe. How was I able to begin again, one may well ask? I should answer truthfully—by dying. In that first year or so in Paris I literally died, was literally annihilated— and resurrected as a new man." [15]

14 *Tropic of Cancer,* 1.
15 *The World of Sex,* 10.

It would be premature at this point to go much further into the implicit significance of Miller's rebirth in *Tropic of Cancer*. He has said himself that he was not aware of the significance of these events at the time.[16] In fact development in reflective power and insight provides the principal thematic unity in Miller's work. The very imperfection of his knowledge and his growth to greater awareness creates the essential autobiographical form.

To understand Miller's situation in *Tropic of Cancer* we need not go outside of the book itself. Miller has been in Paris for a year, and he has been estranged from Mona during most of that time, though she has not been absent continuously. During that year, we presume, Miller was still very much attached to her and felt her absence very keenly.

For seven years I went about, day and night, with only one thing on my mind—her. Were there a Christian so faithful to his God as I was to her we would all be Jesus Christs today. Day and night I thought of her even when I was deceiving her. And now sometimes, in the very midst of things, sometimes when I feel that I am absolutely free of it all, suddenly, in rounding a corner perhaps, there will bob up a little square, a few trees and a bench, a deserted spot where we stood and had it out, where we drove each other crazy with bitter, jealous scenes. . . . When I realize that she is gone, perhaps gone forever, a great void opens up and I feel that I am falling, falling into deep black space. And this is worse than tears, deeper than regret or pain or sorrow; it is the abyss into which Satan was plunged.[17]

But reflection upon Mona, though it leads to misery, brings about a salutary awareness, and the conversion of life into art. Life with Mona had been a descent into hell, the hell depicted by Strindberg, "in that wild carnival of maggots he

16 *Ibid.*
17 *Tropic of Cancer,* 160–61.

reveled in, in that eternal duel of the sexes, that spiderish ferocity which endeared him to the sodden oafs of the north-land. . . ." [18] It was that duel between the sexes which brought them together. "We came together in a dance of death and so quickly was I sucked down into the vortex that when I came to the surface again I could not recognize the world. When I found myself loose the carnival was over and I had been picked clean. . . ." [19] Now it is time to convert life into art, and even this brief recollection of Mona leads to a reflection on art:

. . . I began to reflect on the meaning of that inferno which Strindberg had so mercilessly depicted. And, as I ruminated, it began to grow clear to me, the mystery of his pilgrimage, the flight which the poet makes over the face of the earth and then, as if he had been ordained to re-enact a lost drama, the heroic descent to the very bowels of the earth, the dark and fearsome sojourn in the belly of the whale, the bloody struggle to liberate himself, to emerge clean of the past, a bright, fiery sun god cast up on an alien shore.[20]

The drama of rebirth, re-enacted over and over in world history, must continue to be enacted in every man's life, and this is the stuff out of which poetry is made. Miller, we assume, has already sojourned in "the belly of the whale"; now the experience must be converted into art. His first book begins with the explosion, the emerging being, ravenously hungry. His first thoughts are aggressive, hostile, primitive, sexual. He dedicates the book to Tania:

It is to you Tania that I am singing. I wish that I could sing better, more melodiously, but then perhaps you would never

18   *Ibid.,* 163.
19   *Ibid.*
20   *Ibid.,* 163–64.

have consented to listen to me. You have heard the others sing
and they have left you cold. . . . The world around me is dissolving, leaving here and there spots of time. The world is a
cancer eating itself away. . . . I am thinking that when the great
silence descends upon all and everywhere music will at last triumph. When into the womb of time everything is again with-
drawn chaos will be restored and chaos is the score upon which
reality is written. You Tania are my chaos. It is why I sing. It is
not even I. It is the world dying, shedding the skin of time. I am
still alive, kicking in your womb, a reality to write upon.[21]

Hunger dominates the mood of *Tropic of Cancer,* hunger
for life, for food, for sex. And all of Miller's hunger has sexual
overtones. He associates with Tania his desire for food, and
his preoccupation is transformed into sexual imagery which
itself is expressed in images of eating:

At night when I look at Boris' goatee lying on the pillow I get
hysterical. Oh Tania, where now is that warm cunt of yours,
those fat, heavy garters, those soft, bulging thighs. There is a
bone in my prick six inches long. I will ream out every wrinkle
in your cunt, Tania, big with seed. I will send you home to your
Sylvester with an ache in your belly and your womb turned inside
out. . . . I am fucking you, Tania, so that you'll stay fucked.
And if you are afraid of being fucked publicly I will fuck you
privately. I will tear off a few hairs from your cunt and paste
them on Boris' chin. I will bite into your clitoris and spit out two
franc pieces.[22]

From Tania and sex his voracious appetite moves to hunger
for food, and never a meal, "Coffee without milk or sugar.
Bread without butter. Meat without gravy, or no meat at all.
Without this and without that!" [23] In one of the most sensual

21   *Ibid.,* 2.
22   *Ibid.,* 4–5.
23   *Ibid.,* 11.

passages in any of Miller's writing, the opening of a wine
bottle becomes the equivalent of a sexual experience: "Boris
is rubbing his hands again. Mr. Wren is still stuttering and
spluttering. I have a bottle between my legs and I'm shoving
the corkscrew in. Mrs. Wren has her mouth parted expec-
tantly. The wine is splashing between my legs, the sun is
splashing through the bay window, and inside my veins there
is a bubble and splash of a thousand crazy things that com-
mence to gush out of me now pell mell. I'm telling them
everything that comes to mind, everything that was bottled
up inside me and which Mrs. Wren's loose laugh has somehow released." [24]

The sequence of imagery is easily converted into sexual
symbolism, the bottle between the legs, shoving the corkscrew, the liquid feeling of the splashing wine, the liquid
feeling of Mrs. Wren's laugh, her parted mouth. Food, wine,
sex, Europe, the sun splashing are all the subject of voracious
appetite and convertible, one into the other.

The association between birth and hunger, sex and appetite, is natural. In the world of dreams and fantasy they are
easily enough converted into each other. Miller has recognized this and dealt with it specifically in "Uterine Hunger."
The world, he says, has seemed as if it were "An artificial
womb, a prison, it seems as though everybody and everything were conspiring to pull me back into the womb from
which I broke loose too soon." [25]

And always I am hungry, voraciously hungry. I am insatiable.
It is a hunger on all fronts: alimentary, sexual, spiritual. I don't
eat—I attach myself, like the amoeba, to whatever morsel of food
presents itself. Once I have ingested it I split—double, triple,
multiple selves floating off in search of fresh morsels of food. It

24 *Ibid.*, 13.
25 "Uterine Hunger," in *The Wisdom of the Heart*, 188.

goes on like that *ad nauseam*. Women—they too seem like morsels
of food. After I attach myself to them I devour them. I fuck my
way through body, brain and soul, and then I split up again.[26]

With hunger, with this voracious appetite for experience,
Miller associates passion. What is missing in the world is
passion; there is nothing but ideas, and ideas are bloodless;
they do not support life:

Nobody as far as I can see is making use of those elements on the
air which give direction and motivation to our lives. Only the
killers seem to be extracting from life some satisfactory measure
of what they are putting into it. The age demands violence, but
we are getting only abortive explosions. Revolutions are nipped
in the bud, or else succeed too quickly. Passion is quickly exhausted. Men fall back on ideas *comme d'habitude*. Nothing is
proposed that can last more than twenty-four hours. We are
living a million lives in the space of a generation.[27]

Miller's later work will become more transcendental, in the
manner of Whitman. In *Tropic of Cancer* he is principally
concerned with restoring the acceptance of bodily function
to the realm of human experience. Man must restore the
unity of experience; love and excrement must be felt on the
same plane of existence, equally acceptable. *Tropic of Cancer*, however, has little to say about love, though it has a
great deal to say about excrement and the failure of life.
Aside from Miller's own reflections on life, the principal subject matter of the book concerns the failure of others to live
fully and freely, that is, with the failure in passion. The
characters in *Tropic of Cancer* indulge freely in sexual experience, but that experience does not flow freely from a
unified life; therefore it is obsessive. The most obsessed of all

26   *Ibid.*
27   *Tropic of Cancer*, 10.

the characters is Van Norden. We are given a succinct summary of his character early in the book: "I like Van Norden but I do not share his opinion of himself. do not agree, for instance, that he is a philosopher, or a thinker. He is cuntstruck, that's all." [28]

At first glance it might appear that there is little difference between Miller and Van Norden. They are both irresponsible, both in search of a good time. Miller is as avid for a woman as Van Norden, as eager for an orgy. But Miller takes it as it comes. He has a great sex drive, but he is not obsessed. His sexual drives can be mobilized in an instant, even his passion, his desire for love. But when he is not actively engaged sexually, he is free to do other things, to eat, to walk, to work. Van Norden is never free. Sex haunts him like another self. Yet fundamentally he is passionless. There are two major episodes which show Van Norden's deficiencies. The first is when he is trying to have intercourse with a woman and is unable, evidently, to penetrate. Miller says:

"for God's sake Joe, give it up! You'll kill the poor girl." "Leave me alone," he grunts. "I almost got it in that time." The posture and the determined way in which he blurts this out suddenly brings to my mind, for the second time the remembrance of my dream. . . . He's like a hero come back from the war, a poor maimed bastard living out the reality of his dreams. Wherever he sits himself the chair collapses; whatever door he enters the room is empty; whatever he puts into his mouth leaves a bad taste. Everything is just the same as it was before; the elements are unchanged, the dream is no different than the reality. Only between the time he went to sleep and the time he woke up, his body was stolen. He's like a machine throwing out newspapers . . . the front page is loaded with catastrophes . . . but he doesn't feel anything. If somebody doesn't turn the switch off he'll never know what it means to die. You can't die if your own

28 *Ibid.*, 4.

proper body has been stolen. You can get over a cunt and work away like a billy goat until eternity; you can go to the trenches and be blown to bits; nothing will create that spark of passion if there isn't the intervention of a human hand.[29]

What is wrong with Van Norden's performance is that passion is missing, and therefore it is meaningless and, more than that, it is uninteresting:

My interest in Van Norden and the girl is nil; if I could sit like this and watch every performance going on at this minute all over the world my interest would be even less than nil. I wouldn't be able to differentiate between this phenomenon and the rain falling or a volcano erupting. As long as that spark of passion is missing there is no human significance in the performance. The machine is better to watch. And these two are like a machine which has slipped its cogs. It needs a touch of a human hand to set it right. It needs a mechanic.[30]

Van Norden's disintegration is completed in the last episode, which might be called the descent into meaninglessness. Like most of Miller's handling of the tragic, there is a spirit of clowning which makes the episode farcical. He has just met Van Norden again after several months' absence from Paris:

Van Norden still bellyaching about his cunts and about washing the dirt out of his belly. Only now he's found a new diversion. He's found that it's less annoying to masturbate. I was amazed when he broke the news to me. I didn't think it possible for a guy like that to find any pleasure in jerking himself off. I was still more amazed when he explained to me how he goes about it. He had "invented" a new stunt, so he put it. "You take an apple," he says, and you bore out the core. Then you rub some

29 *Ibid.*, 131.
30 *Ibid.*, 130.

cold cream on the inside so it doesn't melt too fast. Try it some time! It'll drive you crazy at first. Anyway, it's cheap and you don't have to waste much time." [31]

This is life viewed in the crazy mirror of an amusement park. The meaning is that there is no meaning in a world inhabited by such as Van Norden because they are not rooted in reality.

Miller's own feelings about life jar sharply with those of his friends. For him the chaos of modern life is no less, but he has a source of inner strength. In a sense Miller has been brought to the absolute bottom of life at this point, but still finds he can live and be happy. The secret of life is that it must be lived on all levels, not excluding the physical. It is the wedding of ideas to action: "Still I can't get it out of my mind what a discrepancy there is between ideas and living. A permanent dislocation, though we try to cover the two with a bright awning. And it won't go. Ideas have to be wedded to action; if there is no sex, no vitality in them, there is no action. Ideas cannot exist alone in the vacuum of the mind. Ideas are related to living: liver ideas, kidney ideas, interstitial ideas, etc." [32]

This wedding of thought and action is the basis not only of Miller's subject matter, but of his technique. In *Tropic of Cancer* he first explores the technique which he will perfect in later books. In general Miller's approach to the union of thought and action is to juxtapose concrete experience and fantasy life.

There are three levels of awareness which are interwoven in Miller's works: present actual experiences, present fantasy, and past experience, both fantasy and actual. Shifts in time are far more rare in *Tropic of Cancer* than in later

31 *Ibid.,* 263.
32 *Ibid.,* 219.

works, and for this reason the work has a cruder structure than, say, *Tropic of Capricorn*. In *Cancer* the shift is from external to internal, in which the external taken up into fantasy acquires some universal quality. What makes Miller different is principally the kind of material he chooses to universalize. Emerson, no doubt, would have had misgivings about Miller's material, but the choice is not unlike what he advocated: "The meaner the type by which a law is expressed, the more pungent it is, and the more lasting in the memories of men."

This conversion of the base into the universal is exemplified in Miller's episode with a Hindu, a friend of the Hindu with whom he was leading his usual submarginal existence. The Hindu wishes Miller to accompany him to a house of prostitution, and Miller does. While there the Hindu expresses the need for a toilet. Miller tells him that it is usual to use the bidet for such purposes, assuming the Hindu wished to urinate. Miller next hears a tremendous racket coming from the Hindu's room. Everybody in the house is jabbering away in French, obviously outraged. Miller hurries into the Hindu's room. There in the bidet are "two enormous turds floating in the water." This is a clear violation even of whorehouse etiquette. The episode is converted into a dream sequence a few pages later, a fantasy about the illusion of absolute truth and justice. "And so I think what a miracle it would be if this miracle which man attends eternally should turn out to be nothing more than these two enormous turds which the faithful disciple dropped in the *bidet*. What if at the last moment, when the banquet table is set and the cymbals clash, there should appear suddenly, and wholly without warning, a silver platter on which even the blind could see that there is nothing more and nothing less than two enormous lumps of shit." [33]

33 *Tropic of Cancer*, 89.

It might well be objected that Miller could find other, more acceptable terms in which to express his disillusionment, but that would be to mistake the point and the style. The fact is that the crude and realistic terms which Miller uses, the material out of which he creates his fantasies, are the terms in which fantasy life often works. This is not the social level upon which Miller is communicating, but the most private level of the most private thoughts of all men, the level on which the obscene and the sacred meet. These crude Anglo-Saxon terms are precise because they are the most concrete words in the language, and fantasy is always concrete.

A similar aspect of Miller's writing which has been widely attacked is his bald and often elaborate discussions of sexual organs. *Cancer* has few descriptions of actual sexual activity, what might be called detailed accounts of sexual play. But he does use explicit descriptions in other ways and they are worth a comment. Since Miller's general object is to record those aspects of experience which have been left out of books, then the fascination and significance of the organs of sex are bound to be a part of his material. Our culture lives mainly by denial, and descriptions or pictures of sexual organs usually arouse the righteous to full-scale attack. Children, however, are endlessly fascinated by their own and others' bodies, and it is doubtful that adults have lost much of this fundamental voyeurism. Miller's descriptions are of both the female and male genitalia throughout his work, but in *Cancer* it is mainly the female who comes under consideration.

It is a well-known psychological fact that the female genitals have a significance for the male far beyond their simple biological function. They are of course stimulating to the man's sexual desires, but they can be on occasion the object of fear or of obsessive curiosity. They harbor mysteries which the man seeks to solve but to which he can never find the answer, or they may symbolize fecundity in a very primitive way. Miller shows us in *Cancer* two different attitudes to sexual organs, one self-defeating, the other supposedly successful.

Van Norden represents the inadequate development. For him a woman does not exist as a person, simply as a set of genitals, his "Georgia cunt" or his "Danish cunt." For Van Norden the genitals are "the empty crack of the prematurely disillusioned man." [34] For Miller the female genitals are the occasion for one of the longest fantasy passages in *Tropic of Cancer,* one in which he explores all of the fecundating energy of the cosmos.

The scene occurs when Miller and Fillmore are entertaining two whores, who are acrobats. Miller finds himself suddenly with two legs around his neck and gazing into "a dark hairy crack . . . set in a bright, polished billiard ball." [35] The sight suddenly opens up a corresponding fissure in his brain out of which pours an elaborate flood of images. The mother becomes the great whore of creation, the obscene horror. Sex and obscenity and the destruction of the world become intermingled. It is the underlying reality that he discovers in these moments of revery; once again the sacred and the obscene are united, reconciling the most basic contradiction of our culture. Thus Miller has always insisted that he is for obscenity and against pornography. The obscene we ignore at our peril, the pornographic he seems to feel is worse than useless.

When obscenity has been used in modern literature, it has usually been in a Manichean revulsion from sexuality, as in Baldwin's *Another Country.* Miller tries something which seems to me different; he attempts to make the obscene a

34 *Ibid.,* 223.
35 *Ibid.,* 222.

part of life, accepted, but without losing any of the raw shock of the primitive origins. It is the same with sex and love. We read a great deal nowadays about the need for preserving love and tenderness in sexuality, and of the many disastrous ways in which they may become separated. Miller, like Rank, points out the dangers inherent in identifying love and sexuality. For Miller sexuality must first exist fully for itself before it can take part in a love relationship. Tying sexual activity exclusively to a love relationship seems to bring the danger of diminished potency. In fact the internal split in modern man which creates the problem of psychic impotence appears, from Miller's point of view, to come more from an overemphasis on love and virtue, the sacredness of marriage and the purity of mothers and sisters, than from the full appreciation of sexuality for its own sake. For him, the modern world is dried up like the whore, but the reawakening must be sexual. The writer puts "the live wire of sex right between the legs. . . . if there is nothing but a gaping wound left then it must gush forth though it produce nothing but toads and bats and homunculi."[36]

Tropic of Cancer, like *Quiet Days in Clichy,* is concerned with Miller's present activities at the time of writing. The point of view is that of the man in the street, the man to whom these things are happening. Virtually nothing of the past appears in either book. Similarly there is little exploration of the creative process as such. The creative process is associated in Miller's mind with gestation, birth, fertilization, in general the whole sexual process and its overflow into all the areas of life. For the most part in *Tropic of Cancer* the emphasis is on Miller's immediate relationship with people. The urge to write, when it does appear, is an alienating rather than a unifying element. "Tania is in a hostile mood—

36 *Ibid.,* 225.

I can feel it. She resents me being filled with anything but herself. She knows by the very caliber of my excitement that her value is reduced to zero. She knows that I did not come this evening to fertilize her. She knows there is something germinating inside me which will destroy her." [37] The work to be created remains a minor theme in *Tropic of Cancer*. Miller has not settled yet on the major theme of his later work, the birth of the artist.

On two other occasions Miller touches on this creation theme. The first is in the form of a revery, confronting the works of Henri Matisse. Matisse becomes a symbol of life created in color and light, a change from "the habitual gray of the world." Miller has the impression of being immersed in the very "plexus of life." It is Matisse, "if any man today possesses the gift, who knows when to dissolve the human figure, who has the courage to sacrifice an harmonious line in order to detect the rhythm and murmur of blood. . . . Behind the minutiae, the chaos, the mockery of life, he detects the invisible pattern. . . . No searching for formulation, no crucifixion of ideas, no compulsion other than to create." [38] For Miller creation is inevitably associated with biological processes: "Even as the world falls apart the Paris that belongs to Matisse shudders with bright, gasping orgasms, the air itself is steady with a stagnant sperm, the trees tangled like hair." [39]

With the desire for creation comes the fear of being born. As life is taken up into art, so art is being converted into life. And the birth through creation is analogous to the birth of the self. To create is to become whole and separate, independent, but this independence is also our chief fear.

37 *Ibid.*, 25.
38 *Ibid.*, 147–48.
39 *Ibid.*, 149–50.

Going back in a flash over the women I've know. It's like a chain which I've forged out of my own misery. Each one bound to the other. A fear of living separate, of staying born. The door of the womb always on the latch. Dread and longing. Deep in the blood the pull of paradise. The beyond. Always the beyond. It must have all started with the navel. They cut the umbilical cord, give you a slap on the ass, and presto! you're out in the world, adrift, a ship without a rudder. You look at the stars and then you look at your navel. . . . What is distant becomes near, what is near becomes distant. Inner-outer, a constant flux, a shedding of skins, a turning inside out. You drift around like that for years and years, until you find yourself in the dead center, and there you slowly rot, slowly crumble to pieces, get dispersed again. Only your name remains.[40]

The struggle, the misery, is still there. Mona is absent, but he is not yet self-sufficient. His awareness has increased; he can deal with a self—a real not a false self.

For a fraction of a second, perhaps, I experienced that utter clarity which the epileptic, it is said, is given to know. In that moment I lost completely the illusion of time and space; the world unfurled its drama simultaneously along a meridian which had no axis. In this sort of hair-trigger eternity I felt that everything was justified, supremely justified; I felt the wars inside me that had left behind this pulp and wrack; I felt the crimes that were seething here to emerge tomorrow in blatant screamers; I felt the misery that was grinding itself out with pestle and mortar, the long dull misery that dribbles away in dirty handkerchiefs.[41]

This is the self which senses on the deepest level that it is capable of love, of crime, of any monstrosity, of unlimited

40 *Ibid.*, 258–59.
41 *Ibid.*, 88.

generosity, in short the true self. Man begins to live when he ceases to depend upon external events for his happiness, secure in the knowledge and awareness of the self.

Somehow the realization that nothing was to be hoped for had a salutary effect upon me. For weeks and months, for years, in fact, all my life I had been looking forward to something happening, some extrinsic event that would alter my life, and now suddenly, inspired by the absolute hopelessness of everything, I felt relieved, felt as though a great burden had been lifted from my shoulders.
. . . Walking toward Montparnasse I decided to let myself drift with the tide, to make not the least resistance to fate, no matter in what form it presented itself. Nothing that had happened to me thus far had been sufficient to destroy me; nothing had been destroyed except my illusions. I myself was intact. The world was intact. . . . . Had one single element of man's nature been altered, vitally, fundamentally altered, by the incessant march of history? By what he calls the better part of his nature, man has been betrayed, that is all. At the extreme limits of his spiritual being man finds himself again naked as a savage. When he finds God, as it were, he has been picked clean; he is a skeleton. One must burrow into life again in order to put on flesh. The word must become flesh; the soul thirsts. On whatever crumb my eye fastens, I will pounce and devour. If to live is the paramount thing, then I will live, even if I must become a cannibal.[42]

Miller has returned from the complexity of the life presented to him by his environment, particularly of his early life, to the simple natural fact. At this point he says, "I have found God, but he is insufficient. I am only spiritually dead. Physically I am alive. Morally I am free." [43]

To be secure in that inner happiness we must first be con-

42 Ibid., 89–90.
43 Ibid., 90.

vinced that there is nothing to be hoped for from the world; it has nothing to offer but misery and pain. To accept the world as chaos is to stand on the threshold of total acceptance, of deliverance from the womb. Miller's reasoning in this argument is not hard to follow. Dependence on the mother, that is, refusal to leave the womb, is characterized by a desire to be taken care of, to be fed, to be nursed, to receive good things. As long as one looks to the world to provide those things which are in essence infantile, there is no deliverance. Deliverance comes when we look at the world for what it is and see that it gives nothing; it destroys. If we can face this fact and still be happy, then we seek nothing; we are secure in ourselves; we become fathers, capable of fathering ideas, or children, of accepting responsibility. In *Tropic of Cancer* Miller looks hard at the world and sees nothing but chaos. At the end, as he sits by the banks of the Seine and feels the flow of history, a serene mood of peace comes over him. He accepts life.

After everything had quietly sifted through my head a great peace came over me. Here, where the river gently winds through the girdle of hills, lies a soil so saturated with the past that however far back the mind roams one can never detach it from its human background. Christ, before my eyes there shimmered such a golden peace that only a neurotic could dream of turning his head away. So quietly flows the Seine that one hardly notices its presence. It is always there, quiet and unobtrusive, like a great artery running through the human body. In the wonderful peace that fell over me it seemed as if I had climbed to the top of a high mountain; for a little while I would be able to look around me, to take in the meaning of the landscape.[44]

44 *Ibid.*, 286–87.

ON THE OVARIAN TROLLEY

Tropic of Capricorn is principally concerned
with the first stage in the growth of the man and
the artist, the descent through the biological
levels of life to the womb, to the undifferentiated narcissistic state. Miller finds his primary symbol in a
quite accidental occurrence, the problems of a fellow
worker at the telegraph company whose wife's ovaries are
diseased. "On the Ovarian Trolley" is the subtitle of the
book. It is a theme important to Miller and his work, because
at the time he wrote *Tropic of Capricorn* he was vitally
concerned with the process of unification through which man
experiences body and spirit as one. An examination of the
letters and essays of this time shows a continued use of
womb imagery as a symbol of new ways of thinking about
life. Influenced by Otto Rank, whose birth trauma theory
and studies of the artist supported his view, and by Erich
Gutkind and D. H. Lawrence, Miller felt that human individual life had to find its origins in the dark chaos of biological processes, and that the logical place to begin in the search
for the unifying forces of life was in that process itself. This
was the meaning of the material he was publishing during

these years. Therefore, *Tropic of Capricorn* had to be concerned with a primeval world, a world before form, before birth. The chaos of this book is the chaos of pure nonbeing. The central images of *Capricorn* are centered upon sex, a force which is basic, which underlies every form of human energy. The movement of the book is toward birth; the point of origin is in the fertilized seed which must come to fruition. The beginnings are in sex and passion; the fruition is in creative activity. Sex is not the ultimate purpose of life, but a necessary pre-condition.

The events of the story are simple enough. Henry Miller is married, has one child, and is working for the Cosmodemonic Telegraph Company. This is the lowest point of his existence, though the job is, in the commercial sense, his greatest success. His situation he feels is intolerable, not because of the job, though he hates it, not because of his wife, though he hates her, but because he is unable to fulfill himself as a person and because he fears that slide into anonymity which has been the fate of all his boyhood friends. Mona, whom he meets in a dance hall, is to be the means of escape, but with her he finds himself in yet another trap, of dependency upon a woman in the primordial world of sex and death. Thus for Miller the most promising direction of escape, the only direction perhaps, is itself fraught with dangers of the loss of self. The intensity of the relationship with Mona brought life and new hope, but the sexual world they shared prevented his development as artist. In order to complete his development, he had to convert experience into art. His freedom had its beginnings, as he presents it, at the moment that he began to plan the autobiographical romance.

The first stop on the ovarian trolley is the womb. Why should he leave? What could he want outside? "Why come out of a nice cozy place, a cozy retreat in which everything is offered you gratis?" His forebears offer no hope. They are

Nordics, lovers of cleanliness, "but inwardly they stank. Never once had they opened the door which leads to the soul; never once did they take a blind leap into the dark." [1] These were not adventurers, but cowards, for they refused the one great adventure, "inward toward the self." [2] The voyage, or trolley ride, is one of discovery, the search for the true self. *Tropic of Capricorn* is a plunge into the depths, the first stirrings of self-discovery. Yet there is no final experience of freedom, for the process in this work is not complete. First must come the "Rosy Crucifixion," the exploration of life with Mona.

At the beginning of his pilgrimage Miller knew more about his own situation than most people do about theirs; he knew that he was "unhappy, unwealthy, out of whack and out of step." He is rebellious, but it is all locked up inside. "It would have been better for my peace of mind, for my soul, if I had expressed my rebellion openly, if I had gone to jail for it, if I had rotted there and died." [3] Because of this suppressed rebellion, there is murder in his heart: "I wanted to see America razed from top to bottom. I wanted to see this happen purely out of vengeance, as atonement for the crimes that were committed against me and against others like me who have never been able to lift their voices and express their hatred, their rebellion, their legitimate blood lust." [4] Such is the setting for his story. ". . .but even if everything I say is wrong, is prejudiced, spiteful, malevolent, even if I am a liar and a poisoner, it is nevertheless the truth and it will have to be swallowed." [5]

Miller begins his lifelong trek with the discovery that what he wants most is to express himself. The quartet of books,

1 *Tropic of Capricorn* (New York: Grove Press, 1961), 11.
2 *Ibid.*, 12.
3 *Ibid.*
4 *Ibid.*, 12–13.
5 *Ibid.*, 13.

Tropic of Capricorn, Sexus, Plexus, and *Nexus,* is the story
of his fulfillment as artist, and, as it turns out, the simultaneous discovery that in fulfilling himself as an artist he has
discovered himself as a man. The self which Miller wishes to
express is not the superficial bundle of hypocrisies and lies
that make up the ordinary ego; it is the essential self, and to
find that he must dig deep, return to his origins, retreat to
the primeval chaos where all life has its beginnings. All of his
efforts are concentrated on one end, to say what he thinks
and feels. To Miller, as he expresses it, everything in life
which does not have to do with this essential act is a lie, and
that has been most of his life. Therefore he is concerned not
only with the steps in the right direction, becoming a writer,
but the false directions which take him away from his goal.

Miller got to "the heart of the confusion" in his job with
the Cosmodemonic Telegraph Company of North America.
After he had run through a series of jobs, none of which he
wanted, the day finally came when he needed work. Miller
went into the telegraph company and asked for "the lowest
employment on earth, that of messenger boy." He was turned
down. "The fact that I had a wife and child to support didn't
bother me so much; people didn't offer you jobs because
you had a family to support, that much I understood only too
well. No, what rankled was that they had rejected me, Henry
V. Miller, a competent, superior individual who had asked
for the lowest job in the world. That burned me up." Miller
went to see the president, expecting a run-around. When the
conference was over, Miller was the new employment manager.[6]

Life with the telegraph company became a symbol for
Miller of the entire economic structure of the United States.
He interviewed during those years more than a hundred

6 *Ibid.*

thousand men, men of the very lowest status in society.[7] The whole objective was to keep the ranks of the messengers full. That meant constant shifting, manipulating, hiring every day, trying to keep the huge floating force up to quota.

An hour before my arrival—I was always late—the place was already jammed with applicants. I had to elbow my way up the stairs and literally force my way in to get to my desk. Before I could take my hat off I had to answer a dozen telephone calls. There were three telephones on my desk and they all rang at once. They were bawling the piss out of me before I had even sat down to work. There wasn't even time to take a crap—until five or six in the afternoon. . . . Not one of the hundred and one offices ever had a full staff; Hymie had to play chess with the waybills while I worked like a madman to plug the gaps. If by a miracle I succeeded of a day in filling all the vacancies, the next morning would find the situation exactly the same—or worse. Perhaps twenty per cent of the force was steady; the rest was driftwood.[8]

Miller's experience with the telegraph company was not different from what he expected; it merely capped all the other experiences, reinforced all his other attitudes to American life. He was struggling to keep himself alive in a universe of death.

There was one man in me which had died and all that was left were his remembrances. There was another man who was alive, and that man was supposed to be me, myself, but he was alive only as a tree is alive, or a rock, or a beast of the field. Just as the city itself had become a huge tomb in which men struggled to

7 Sydney Omarr, *Henry Miller: His World of Urania* (London: Villurs Publications, 1960) , 62. This is Miller's claim. It means that in four years, counting 250 working days a year, he had to interview an average of 100 men a day.
8 *Tropic of Capricorn,* 21.

earn a decent death so my own life came to resemble a tomb which I was constructing out of my own death. I was walking around in a stone forest the center of which was chaos; sometimes in the dead center, in the very heart of chaos, I danced or drank myself silly, or I made love, or I befriended some one or I planned a new life, but it was all chaos, all stone, and all hopeless and bewildering. Until the time when I would encounter a force strong enough to whirl me out of this mad stone forest no life would be possible for me nor could one page be written which would have meaning.[9]

The force strong enough to take him out of this chaos would be his love for Mona, but the full story of that was to be reserved for *The Rosy Crucifixion*. *Tropic of Capricorn* centers on the chaos itself, and on the roots of life which Miller is always testing, affirming, exploring—trying to preserve his own sense of life in this universe of death.

The full story of Miller's relations with his first wife, as full at least as Miller is willing to tell it, does not occur in *Tropic of Capricorn*; that story is reserved for *Sexus*, the first volume of *The Rosy Crucifixion*. In *Capricorn* we have only implied criticisms of his wife, and these under conditions which do not create much sympathy for Miller's part in the affair. Critics seem to ignore Miller's statement that he is presenting himself as a "bastard" during these years, that he does not speak well of himself out of "pudeur," that Miller the man was a somewhat better person than he appears in his work.[10] The point is that Miller as hero-narrator is presenting that side of himself which is undeveloped, violent, and treacherous. He used others in order to become more fully himself.

One fact is clear; the narrator hates Maude as he has hated

9 *Ibid.*, 69.
10 Perles and Durrell, *Art and Outrage*, 14.

no other person. She is, from his point of view, "1 mean bitch." She gets angry when he comes home at three o'clock in the morning—he has been drinking with two other women. She is irate when he tries to bring a penniless woman in to live with them. The story of his life with Maude is a story of constant infidelity. We are told in *Sexus* that they already hated each other by the time they were married.[11] Yet Miller, that is, the central figure of the romance, is not really interested in justifying himself, nor in explaining his reasons for leaving his wife. He clings to one set of values in the midst of the threats to personality with which he is surrounded, to a sense of the essential self, and his desire to be a writer. To live with Maude, to be happy with her, was impossible, for she required, absolutely, as a condition of peace, that he conform to her own internal image of the ideal husband, and that image required first and foremost the abandoning of his vigorous sexual nature. Because Miller could not do this, life with Maude was unsupportable.[12]

The theme of birth and growth is worked into this background of life with Maude and life with the Cosmodemonic Telegraph Company. The images of death and the tomb change into images from the ovarian world, and all experience is felt in terms of this biological analogy. The ovarian theme is introduced, as most of Miller's themes are introduced, through an actual event—a conversation with Hymie, a fellow employee of the telegraph company, about the condition of his wife's ovaries. From the word, "ovaries," Miller takes off on a recurring exploration of the basic biological image:

Suddenly looking at Hymie and thinking of that strange word "ovaries" . . . this feeling of icy isolation came over me. . . . I

11 *The World of Sex*, 33.
12 See Chapter 5 for further discussion of Maude.

was jumping from the bridge head first, down into the primeval ooze, the legs clear and waiting for a bite. . . . In the womb nails formed on every finger, every toe; you could stop right there, at a toenail, the tiniest toenail imaginable, and you could break your head over it, trying to figure it out. On one side of the ledger are the books man has written, containing such a hodge-podge of wisdom and nonsense, of truth and falsehood, that if one lived to be as old as Methuselah one couldn't disentangle the mess; on the other side of the ledger things like toenails, hair, teeth, blood, *ovaries* . . . all incalculable and all written in another kind of ink, in another script, an incomprehensible, undecipherable script.[13]

In this primeval ooze of nature and the self, Miller discovers his primary purpose, the work to be done, his devotion to the word:

It was borne in on me again that I had never done what I wanted and out of not doing what I wanted to do there grew up inside me this creation which was nothing but an obsessional plant, a sort of coral growth, which was expropriating everything, including life itself, until life became this which was denied but which constantly asserted itself, making life and killing life at the same time. . . . Through love this might happen, or sorrow, or being born with a club foot; the cause nothing, the event everything. *In the beginning was the Word.* . . . Whatever this was, *the Word,* disease or creation, it was still running rampant; it would run on and on. . . . Any word contained all words—for him who had become detached through love or sorrow or whatever the cause. In every word the current ran back to the beginning which was lost and which would never be found again since there was neither beginning nor end but only that which expressed itself in beginning and end.[14]

13 *Tropic of Capricorn,* 52.
14 *Ibid.,* 54.

To re-enter the stream of real life required detachment from all that was false, particularly from that which was temporary. Miller finds that he has become separate from the world and the individuals in it. He was able to "amuse, to instruct, to nourish," but he could "never be accepted in a genuine way." People sensed in him something different, something which set him apart, and they could not tolerate that difference. It was not possible, Miller found, to live with the herd without becoming indistinguishable from the herd. Even your dreams must be like those of everyone else. In fact, as he says, "Everything American will disappear one day. . . . This is one of the ideas that pushed me outside the warm, comfortable bloodstream where, buffaloes all, we once grazed in peace. . . . But I am not a buffalo and I have no desire to be one, I am not even a *spiritual* buffalo. I have slipped away to rejoin an older stream of consciousness, a race antecedent to the buffaloes, a race that will survive the buffalo." [15]

This intuition of an earlier more primitive world is embodied in many episodes. In its most basic form the primitive world is expressed directly and symbolically in pure fantasy, fantasy which is full of fertility and fecundity, and highly sexualized body imagery. Miller also embodies this sense of a primordial world in his recall of events. For example, he goes back to his life on the streets to find a freer world in which he and his friends, with the directness characteristic of boys,[16] penetrated to the essential being of each other and formed their attitudes directly and openly on the basis of their original estimate of that character. Miller recalls an episode involving the eating of stolen rye bread. Its being

15 *Ibid.*, 55–57.
16 See Perles and Durrell, *Art and Outrage,* 21, for his adult attitude toward children. His admiration of the directness and simplicity of boys is not unlike that of Emerson in "Self-Reliance."

stolen made the bread more than usually delicious, and while they were walking around eating the bread

something in the nature of a revelation occurred. It was like a state of grace, a state of complete ignorance, of self-abnegation. Whatever was imparted to me at those moments I seem to have retained intact. . . . It was just the fact perhaps that it was not knowledge as we ordinarily think of it. It was almost like receiving a truth, though truth is almost too precise a word for it. The important thing about the sour rye discussions is that they always took place away from home, away from the eyes of our parents whom we feared but never respected. Left to ourselves there were no limits to what we might imagine. Facts had little importance for us; what we demanded of a subject was that it allow us opportunity to expand. . . . The learning we received only tended to obscure our vision.[17]

The essence of the "sour rye world" was that it was alive, thus differing sharply from the adult world of death. Emotions were intact; instincts were free and close to the surface. It was a world in which the participants had a keen sense of freedom and of independence:

With the sour rye the world was what it is essentially, a primitive world ruled by magic, a world in which fear plays the most important role. The boy who could inspire the most fear was the leader and he was respected as long as he could maintain his power. There were other boys who were rebels, and they were admired but they never became the leader. . . . The air was full of tension—nothing could be predicted for the morrow. This loose, primitive nucleus of a society created sharp appetites, sharp curiosity. Nothing was taken for granted; each day demanded a new test of power, a new sense of strength or of failure. And so,

17 *Tropic of Capricorn,* 128.

up until the age of nine or ten we had a real taste of life—we were on our own.[18]

These friends, Miller's boyhood companions of the streets, became the lost adults whom he contemplates with such sorrow in his later works. A great part of the bitterness that Miller evidently feels toward America seems to rest upon the blighted promise of those sterling lads—free, vigorous, lovers of life, who become unimaginative drudges in whom even the memory of these happy days was extinguished.[19]

Maturity meant for Miller only loss of the bright and meaningful world of childhood. With the acceptance of adult responsibility the world expands, but mystery is destroyed. To Miller the child, the adult world was unknown and represented a world of promise: "Until we were pushed out to work the world was very small and we were living on the fringe of it, on the frontier, as it were, of the unknown. A small Greek world which was nevertheless deep enough to provide all manner of variation, all manner of adventure and speculation. . . . I have gained nothing by the enlargement of my world; on the contrary, I have lost." [20] The choice, as it appears to Miller is between the compromise which has destroyed so many and open warfare against everything society stands for. He decides for rebellion:

I want to go exactly contrary to the normal line of development, pass into a superinfantile realm of being which will be absolutely crazy and chaotic but not crazy and chaotic as the world about me. . . . I want to break through this enlarged world and stand

18 *Ibid.*, 129.
19 *Ibid.*, 129–30. "My cousin Gene became an absolute nonentity; Stanley became a first-rate failure. . . . There was another, Joey, who became a letter carrier. I could weep when I think what life has made them."
20 *Ibid.*, 145.

again on the frontier of an unknown world which will throw this pale, unilateral world into shadow. I want to pass beyond the responsibility of fatherhood to the irresponsibility of the anarchic man who cannot be coerced nor wheedled nor cajoled nor bribed nor traduced. . . . Everything which the fathers and mothers created, I disown. I am going back . . . to a world which I can always touch with outstretched arms, the world of what I know and see and recognize from moment to moment.[21]

A brief hint of what Miller is looking for at this point comes in the form of a meeting with Roy Hamilton. This is again an instance of the concreteness with which Miller expresses his feelings about life. It is in personal and intimate contact with others that he forms his ideas and reactions. To Miller the "Big Abstraction" is always a lie.[22] Roy Hamilton is a person who lives his philosophy and becomes thereby a model for imitation. ". . . he had no theory at all, except to penetrate to the very essence of things and, in the light of each fresh revelation to so live his life that there would be a minimum of discord between the truths which were revealed to him and the exemplification of these truths in action." [23] Miller will have much more to say in later works about his notions of truth in action, of a philosophy of life. Before Miller himself can arrive at a like state, he must descend into the heart of chaos. *Tropic of Capricorn* is not the story of this discovery; it is the story of rebellion against the universe of death and the beginnings of the descent into chaos. A part of this descent is conceived as a purely negative process of emptying oneself, or descending to the purely biological level of life, affirming that level first. He writes, for ex-

21 *Ibid.,* 145–46. One of the chief characteristics of Miller's style is its concreteness. His anecdotal method keeps him very close to his actual experience.
22 Perles and Durrell, *Art and Outrage,* 23.
23 *Tropic of Capricorn,* 147.

ample, of his life in California: "I look back rapidly and I see myself again in California. I am alone and I am working like a slave in the orange grove at Chula Vista. Am I coming into my own? I think not. I am a very wretched, forlorn, miserable person. I seem to have lost everything. In fact, I am hardly a person—I am more nearly an animal. . . . I have no thoughts, no dreams, no desires. I am thoroughly healthy and empty. I am a nonentity. I am so thoroughly alive and healthy that I am like the luscious deceptive fruit which hangs on the California trees." [24]

The trip to the West was a disappointment to Miller, and he appeals to his memory of Roy Hamilton to explain why. He had not been ready.

The danger that pushes Miller on is that he too will be destroyed as his father was. "I look back rapidly and I see another man who was left to perish quietly in the bosom of his family—*my father* . . . who was deserted at the moment of his greatest need." The full symbolic significance of Miller's father (and mother) is not developed at this point, only the actual disaster. His father was evidently a convivial man with numerous cronies who shared his tastes for food and drink. As he grew older, he retained his air of *bon vivant,* but business was slipping; debts were increasing, and Miller's mother began the attacks which to Miller's mind finally destroyed his father. His father, in answer, swore off drinking; and that was the beginning of his decline in every way. Such an act required enormous strength of will, and shortly his mother began to mock him for his very persistence, but he stuck to it. The results were predictable: "His drinking pals faded away rather quickly. In short, he soon found himself amost completely isolated. . . . before very many weeks had passed, he became deathly ill. . . . in a couple

24 *Ibid.,* 151.

of months he was almost a skeleton. And old. He looked like Lazarus raised from the grave." In a short while he was a living corpse, removed from contact with life forever, a living death.[25]

Following the excursion into boyhood and the destruction of his father comes the long fantasy on sex which is, perhaps, as close to a purely mythological world as conscious art is able to express. The world of the dream presents sex on a level which is unrelated to persons, to love, to family, to anything except pure biological energy. In summary, the passage is a probing into the roots of biological being, to the spermatozoa, the egg, the ovaries, and the womb. The origin of the dream is in the recall of Hymie's wife and her ovaries, a re-evoking of the "ovarian trolley." For this voyage Miller adopts the mask of Samson Lackawanna:

And now here I am, sailing down the river in my little canoe. Anything you would like to have me do I will do for you—gratis. This is the Land of Fuck, in which there are no animals, no trees, no stars, no problems. Here the spermatozoon reigns supreme. Nothing is determined in advance, the future is absolutely uncertain, the past is non-existent. . . . Life is squeezed into a seed, which is a soul. Everything has souls, including minerals, plants, lakes, mountains, rocks. Everything is sentient, even at the lowest stage of consciousness.[26]

Having discovered that the whole universe is sentient, Miller discovers also that the universe is on the journey toward full consciousness, which is God. Man, then, is God in embryo: "Once this fact is grasped there can be no more despair. At the very bottom of the ladder, *chez* the spermatozoon, there is the same condition of bliss as at the top, *chez* God.

25 *Ibid.*, 152–57.
26 *Ibid.*, 204–205.

God is the summation of all the spermatozoon come to full consciousness. Between the bottom and the top there is no stop, no halfway station. The river starts somewhere in the mountains and flows on into the sea. On this river that leads to God the canoe is as serviceable as the dreadnought. From the very start the journey is homeward.[27] Life, then, is a journey, and the flow is relentless. Each man must pilot his own canoe. Again, the beginnings of life are conceived as a muck, a chaos, or in the image of Miller's special hatred, the department store. But out of the muck arises the happy rock, the substantial self. "Just as the slightest breeze can set a vast forest in motion, so, by some unfathomable impulse from within, the rocklike self can begin to grow, and in this growth nothing can prevail against it." [28]

The self which Miller speaks of is not "the self about which books are written," it is a self more ultimate, anterior to all forms ordinarily presented to consciousness. It is, further, a self which grows, and that growth is the work of a lifetime. The growth of the self takes place in an "eternity which has nothing to do with time or space." The struggle is between identity and dissolution. If the "wanderer" opens the door which leads "out onto the world," he is faced with "annihilation." If he opens the door which leads inward, he finds infinite doors and a timeless world without guides of any kind. But in this world one is unable to take root. "Just at the moment when one begins to feel 'established' the whole terrain founders, the soil underfoot is afloat, the constellations are shaken loose from their moorings, the whole known universe, including the imperishable self, starts moving . . . toward an unknown, unseen destination." [29]

Self-discovery, as Miller sees it, consists in two movements,

27   *Ibid.*, 204.
28   *Ibid.*, 206–207.
29   *Ibid.*, 207.

the loss of self, a retreat to the dead center "from which time itself is reckoned," and the rebirth of the new self, free and independent. Miller climaxes this revery with a brief reference to the event which he claims was central to his own experience of rebirth, the discovery of Mona. The key moment was when he passed through the door of the Amarillo Dance Hall "twelve or fourteen years ago." That moment began the interlude which he thinks of as "the Land of Fuck." At that moment "all that I had previously been, was, and about to be foundered. . . . Just as I had previously been bundled out of the womb, so now I was shunted back to some timeless vector where the process of growth is kept in abeyance. . . . There was no fear, only the feeling of fatality. . . . In the plunge the skeleton blew apart, leaving the immutable ego as helpless as a squashed louse." [30]

The time has not yet come for Miller to begin the development of the story of Mona, the girl he met at the Amarillo Dance Hall. Once again we have a foreshadowing of a story to come. For the present Miller breaks the development abruptly at this point to start off in what appears to be a new direction. It is not, of course, a new direction; it is the return to the early world, the time of the great search.

Miller begins with Maxie Schnadig and his sister, Rita, whom he associates with the time he was reading Dostoievski. The scene is Far Rockaway Beach where Miller and Maxie are loafing, Miller more interested in Maxie's sister than in Maxie. On the level of revery the reading of Dostoievski creeps in and Miller stops to explore his reactions to this author who has given him "the first revelation of a soul." Miller feels his aloneness, but discovers at the same time that in this aloneness the first real word comes to him. The revery continues until the actual meeting with Maxie's sister, with whom he has sexual relations. Thinking shortly after-

30 *Ibid.*, 208.

wards of Maxie and Rita, Miller is carried back into the past of his boyhood, a transition caused by Maxie's talk of Odessa, which reminds Miller of the Jews, and of the change in the old neighborhood, which leads in turn to a new fantasy.[31]

The new fantasy recalls the theme earlier stated of limits and boundaries, bringing back the past to which Miller always returns to find a truly human world. The street formed an organism which bound everyone together, "a solid corporation, a close knit human spore which could not disintegrate unless the street itself disintegrated." When the bridge from Delancey Street opened, and the Old World Jews flooded in, the street did disintegrate; the old world disappeared. In the United States change is destructive, for the old is annihilated. "The new is a moth eating into the fabric of life." [32] Without transition, except for a dream obviously related to creative activity, Miller takes up Bergson's "Creative Evolution." Reflection on this book leads to reflection on truths of life which Miller has learned. These are related to independence. Miller claims he never understood the book. What he learned from the book was that he had no need to depend on others:

This book became my friend because it taught me that I had no need of friends. It gave me the courage to stand alone and it enabled me to appreciate loneliness. . . . Everything which once I thought I had understood crumbled, and I was left with a clean slate. My friends, on the other hand, entrenched themselves more solidly in the little ditch of understanding which they had dug for themselves. They died comfortably in their little bed of understanding, to become useful citizens of the world. I pitied them, and in short order I deserted them one by one, without the slightest regret.[33]

31 *Ibid.*, 209–14.
32 *Ibid.*, 215–17.
33 *Ibid.*, 220.

The process was one of "disorientation and reorientation" like a rite of "initiation." As Miller presents it, it is a matter of motion. If your friends do not move with you, you leave them behind. "You move on to new fields of battle, to new triumphs and defeats." [34] The memory of Bergson leads Miller to recall his reading of that book to the Jewish tailors who worked in his father's shop, and finally to a meeting with a Jewess on the elevated line. The crowded quarters make it easy for Miller to set up a date, and he is on the way to keep it when he thinks about Una, his first love. His entire attitude changes suddenly, and a tremendous desire for love comes over him. He had left Una to go to California, and that was the end of it. It seems at this point as though Miller has lost sight of the thread, but it reappears in the form of the boundary motive; Miller has passed the boundary:

Now I know what's happened—I've crossed the boundary line! This Bible that I've been carrying around with me is to instruct me, initiate me into a new way of life. The world I knew is no more, it is dead, finished, cleaned up. . . . I sob aloud, like a child. Now it dawns on me with full clarity: *you are alone in the world!* . . . I am in the dream again, the painful, delirious, pleasurable maddening dream of beyond the boundary. . . . My home is not in this world, nor in the next. I am a man without a home, without a friend, without a wife. I am a monster who belongs to a reality which does not exist yet.[35]

By this time, Miller has completely forgotten his rendezvous with the Jewess, which disappears from his mind as he becomes aware of the night and the beauty of simple things under the light; a simple cabbage leaf becomes the universe.

34 *Ibid.*
35 *Ibid.*, 225.

His mood changes; now everything belongs; he loves everyone, and somewhere a woman is waiting for him. The boundary itself was an illusion self-created. The world is love. "Everything stands in a certain way in a certain place, as our mind stands in relation to God. The world, in its visible, tangible substance, is a map of love. Not God, but *life* is love. Love, love, love. And in the midmost midst of it walks this young man, myself, who is none other than Gottlieb Leberecht Muller." [36]

In the person of Gottlieb Leberecht Muller, Henry Miller presents us with another role of the self. Muller is the ordinary citizen who has been transformed. Muller is the rootless self. Miller, the ordinary citizen, is performing his ordinary tasks in the world, finding a wife, becoming a father, entertaining friends . . . when suddenly he looks around and understands absolutely nothing. His personality changes. "I know how to fend for myself. I know how to avoid work, how to avoid entangling relationships, how to avoid sympathy, bravery, and all the other pitfalls." [37] Everything comes to him at these times. In tracing the journey of Gottlieb Leberecht Muller to the point which Miller has reached at the time of writing, he sees the cause as "a wound." This "wound," no doubt, refers to life with Mona which "killed me and yet I was alive. But I was alive without a memory, without a name; I was cut off from hope as well as from remorse and regret. I had no past and probably would have no future. I was buried alive in a void which was the wound that had been dealt me. *I was the wound itself.*" [38]

From this void, this wound, Miller is reborn "not just once, but innumerable times." The man who is reborn does not become another, a different self; "he is always the same man,

36 *Ibid.,* 227.
37 *Ibid.,* 228.
38 *Ibid.,* 230.

more and more himself with each rebirth. He is only shedding his skin each time, and with his skin his sins." This process is very much like the shedding of layers of an onion to get closer to the essential being. "To shed the first layer is painful beyond words; the next layer is less painful, the next still less, until finally the pain becomes pleasurable, a delight, an ecstasy. And then there is neither pleasure nor pain, but simply darkness yielding before the light. And as the darkness falls away the wound comes out of its hiding place; the wound which is man, man's love, is bathed in light. The identity which was lost is recovered." [39]

Rebirth, as Miller has already pointed out in so many ways, is to identity, and in identity lies freedom. But again let us note that rebirth as a completed process is never the main subject of *Tropic of Capricorn;* rather Miller's subject is the process of death and self-preservation even in death. If Miller retains his optimism, if he seems complacent about his own development, it is because he is writing from a point of view in which certain real achievements towards a discovery of the self have already been accomplished, and Miller uses his knowledge of his present state to throw light on the process of the past. At the time of writing, he has shed enough layers of the onion so that losing further layers is not painful. The period of his life that he is beginning to write about—life with his first wife, with the telegraph company, and with Mona—is the period of the loss of the first layers of that onion, the most painful of all.

We have seen how Miller got from the thought of Una to the subject of "love" and the "self." Quite naturally at this point he recalls Mona, "the one I loved better than all else, better than the world, better that God, better than my own flesh and blood." [40] There follows a long dreamlike recalling

39 *Ibid.,* 230–31.
40 *Ibid.,* 231.

of his love for Mona, suppressing all the details of that love, and rendering his feelings in almost purely symbolic terms. His love for Mona and Mona's love for him was not in itself a deliverance for either of them. It was more like a burial in which they both languished in some eternal dark night, "the grave and womb of love entombing us, the night filling our bowels and the stars shimmering over the black bottomless lake." [41] What ultimately proved so disturbing to Miller was his discovery that Mona had no substantial reality. She was an entirely protean being consisting of everchanging external forms with absolutely nothing underneath. She was all woman and no woman:

I forgot what she looked like, what she felt like, what she smelt like, what she fucked like, piercing deeper and deeper into the night of the fathomless cavern. I followed her to the deepest hole of her being, to the charnel house of her soul, to the breath which had not yet expired from her lips. I sought relentlessly for her whose name was not written anywhere. I penetrated to the very altar and found—nothing. I wrapped myself around this hollow shell of nothingness like a serpent with fiery coils; I lay still for six centuries without breathing as world events sieved through the bottom forming a slimy bed of mucus. . . . I saw through to the last sign and symbol, *but I could not read her face.*[42]

What Miller discovers in his penetration to the most inward being of Mona is everything but Mona herself. He finds a world anterior to this world, of "evanescent forms," "of all relations." He "heard her dreams mumbled in lost tongues." He was bound to her in love which could not be separated until death. And they lived together "in a black hole of our life," looking out into the "black hole of the world." [43] But

41 *Ibid.*
42 *Ibid.*, 232.
43 *Ibid.*, 233.

chiefly she was the embodiment of sexual fury. "And with it all, in the fixed, close intimacy of a night without end she was radiant, jubilant, an ultra-black jubilation streaming from her like a steady flow of sperm from the Mithraic bull with an acetylene torch in her womb. In heat she focused on the grand cosmocrator, her eyes rolled back to the whites, her lips a-slaver. . . . She had the insatiable lust of a unicorn, the itch that laid the Egyptians low. Even the hole in the sky through which the lackluster star shone down was swallowed up in her fury." [44] Miller likens himself to a puppet in the lap of a ventriloquist. He watches Mona go through her endless transformations, into panther and jaguar, the wild ibis, the "swan in rut." Sometimes she was a bird of prey, swooping down on a choice carcass, or a "deep black rose with velvety petals." When she fed him meals, he listened to the "rhythmic predatory wheeze of the succubus devouring her young." [45] But through it all he could see the hole in the ceiling, which led to the other world, which could not be forgotten; it disturbed the womblike peace.

From a description of the fantastic metamorphosis of Mona's psychic being, Miller passes to a description of the changes in physical being. "Even her body went through a radical change, not once but several times. At first she was big and velvety, like the jaguar . . . then she grew emaciated, fragile, delicate . . . and with each change she went through the sublest modulations—of skin, muscle, color, posture, odor, gait, gesture. . . . She changed like a chameleon. Nobody could say what she was really like because with each one she was a different person. After a time she didn't even know herself what she was like." [46] In *Tropic of Capricorn*, Miller deals briefly with Mona from the standpoint of com-

44 *Ibid.*, 233–34.
45 *Ibid.*, 236.
46 *Ibid.*, 237.

pleted experience; her lack of identity is a fact he came to the knowledge of much later. It is in *Sexus* that we find the experience "going on." *Capricorn* is the fruit of suffering completed; *The Rosy Crucifixion,* of suffering going on. What is born in Miller in his relationship with Mona is the consciousness of sex as a new terrain, almost a new form of being, "a being growing into our own being and gradually displacing it. . . ." In this relationship too, Miller finds that everything that Mona tells him is a lie, a fact which puts Miller in a "strait jacket of doubt, jealousy, fear, loneliness." [47]

What is worse, what we see more fully in the later works, is that Mona is destroying herself in her effort to create a whole new being:

She was the world's lying machine in microcosm, geared to the same unending, devastating fear which enables men to throw all their energies into creation of the death apparatus. To look at her one would think her the personification of courage and she *was,* so long as she was not obliged to turn in her traces. Behind her lay the calm fact of reality, a colossus which dogged her every step. Every day this colossal reality took on new proportions, every day she had to grow swifter wings, sharper jaws, more piercing, hypnotic eyes. . . . At the edge of the vacuum stood Truth, ready in one lightning-like sweep to recover the stolen ground.[48]

Mona's flight was away from her real self, and that flight was doomed to failure. But her flight carried her out of reality, "out of the confines of the universe toward a nebula which no instrument could visualize." [49] In this mad flight she carried Miller with her, in a union which could not last,

47 *Ibid.,* 240.
48 *Ibid.,* 241–42.
49 *Ibid.,* 242.

which must ultimately be destructive of both. But Miller was able to survive. Mona, we presume, was destroyed by it.

Since it is not time yet to deal with Mona, Miller returns to the days before her, to his bachelor days. There is a sense of waiting, of dawdling, and a sense also that Miller is doing more than wasting time; he is waiting for his destiny to take shape:

On the surface it was jolly and happy-go-lucky; time passing like a sticky dream. But underneath it was fatalistic, premonitory, leaving me next day morbid and restless. I knew very well I'd have to make a break some day. . . . I knew also there was nothing I could do about it—yet. Something had to happen, something big, something that would sweep me off my feet. All I needed was a push, but it had to be some force outside my world that could give me the right push, that I was certain of. I couldn't eat my heart out, because it wasn't in my nature. All my life things had worked out all right—*in the end*. It wasn't in the cards for me to exert myself. . . . The external situation was bad, admitted—but what bothered me more was the internal situation. I was really afraid of myself, of my appetite, my curiosity, my flexibility, my permeability, my malleability, my geniality, my powers of adaptation. . . . I was really so damned well off inside that I had to take on the problems of the world. And that was why I was in a mess all the time.[50]

Miller begins to achieve his own destiny when he leaves the macrocosm and begins to focus on the microcosm, the self. It is not that his sense of rage over the mess men have made of the world ever stops; it is only that when he has achieved his sense of identity and freedom, he will know better what is wrong with the world, and his criticism will develop more sting. For the moment he needs to find out how to live.

The drifting that Miller was doing during these days lead

50 *Ibid.,* 279.

him to an attempt to find an anchorage. His first anchorage takes the form of an ancient desk taken from his father's office. There he found a solid base from which to consider the "flotsam and jetsam which was whirling about me." What he had written so far, about a million words or so, was nothing, "because the contact was through the head and the head is a useless appendage unless you're anchored in mid-channel deep in the mud." [51] Now the difficulty is not that he lacks thoughts, but that he has too many; "The bloody machine wouldn't stop, that was the difficulty." He has a moment of vision which predicts the future, a moment in which he feels himself "coagulating, becoming a recognizable, consistent mass of jelly." [52] The event occurred while Miller was waiting for the curtain of the theater to rise when he suddenly experienced the raising of the curtain as something going on inside. He felt that he was standing in his own presence "bathed in a luminous reality." Then he was "behind the scenes, moving amidst the sets." He rushed home to try to record the vision.[53]

This early attempt to write leads us back to the first theme of *Tropic of Capricorn,* the ovarian world. Now, however, the ovarian theme is specifically connected with writing. As Miller puts it, he was the unique Dadaist in America, though he had never heard of Dadaism. He was describing a new world, but nobody understood what he was talking about because that world had not yet been discovered. What Miller found was "the indestructible world which man has always carried within him; it was neither old or new, really, but the eternally true world which changes from moment to mo-

51 The "million words or so," according to Miller, were composed in his head while he was walking to and from his father's office. Miller to author, September 3, 1966.
52 *Tropic of Capricorn,* 284.
53 *Ibid.,* 285–86.

ment." The language he wrote was English, because that was the only language he spoke, but only primitive man could understand. The simple fact that Miller was trying to communicate was "that life is indestructible and that there is no such thing as time, only the present." This message men were unwilling to hear because it would interrupt their plunder, rape, and pillage. A great part of Miller's difficulty, he feels, is that the language itself is suitable only to describe the process of murder and rape. "I was delirious with an energy which could not be unleashed except in the service of death and futility." [54]

What Miller wishes to explore is the world of "life rhythm," which contrasts with the death rhythm. There is a paradox in his reflections on life and death. Too much effort, even the effort to stay alive, sows death in the world. "The keeping oneself alive out of a blind urge to defeat death, is in itself a means of sowing death. Every one who has not fully accepted life, who is not incrementing life, is helping to fill the world with death." From this point of view, even activity itself is a "form of death." American life and its rhythm of the dynamo is yet another form of death. To break clear, to discover his own essential rhythm, is the task of the writer. To find his essential self, the man must go back to the source of life, and for a while he will be useless to society: "If in the realization of his terrible need, he begins to act regressively, to become unsocial, to stammer and stutter, to prove so utterly unadapted as to be incapable of earning a living, know that this man has found his way back to the womb and source of life and that tomorrow, instead of the contemptible object of ridicule which you have made of him, he will stand forth as a *man* in his own right and all the powers of the world will be of no avail against him." Miller abhors death as it manifests itself

54. *Ibid.*, 286–87.

in living men. Death has its place, "but only after life." A man must learn to say "yes" to life to become truly alive. Death, which says no to life, makes men bitter and lonely. The writer must say "yes" in a thousand ways, and keep on saying yes.[55]

The debate goes on to the very end of *Tropic of Capricorn.* Nothing is to be finally decided here. There are intimations of the right path, "intimations of immortality" perhaps, but no answer. The drama is enacted in a series of conflicts, between "yes" and "no." At first contemplation beckons. One should stand still, speak the truth one knows, or stand still and do nothing. Finally, man must act, must act like an artist until he can become one. What is needed before the process can become complete is the sound of one's own voice, one's authentic voice.

Every time you come to the limit of what is demanded of you, you are faced with the same problem—to be yourself! And with the first step you make in this direction you realize that there is neither plus nor minus; you throw away the skates and swim. There is no suffering any more because there is nothing which can threaten your security. And there is no desire to be of help to others even, because why rob them of the privilege which must be earned. Life stretches out from moment to moment in stupendous infinitude. . . . You live in the fruits of your action and your action is the harvest of your thought. Thought and action is the harvest of your thought. Thought and action are one, because swimming you are in it and of it, and *it* is everything you desire it to be, no more, no less. . . . You live like a happy rock in the midst of the ocean.[56]

This was the life which Miller was seeking, but neither struggles nor furious activity brought him near it. *To be,* in the

55 *Ibid.,* 289–90.
56 *Ibid.,* 331.

proper sense, is music, which is "the manifestation of activity without activity. It is the pure act of creation swimming on its own bosom. . . . It is a reward which can be given only by one's self.[57]

---

57 *Ibid.*, 332–33.

THE AUTO-NOVEL

Tropic of Capricorn and *The Rosy Crucifixion* stand to each other in some ways like the first and fourth parts of Faulkner's *The Sound and the Fury*. *Tropic of Capricorn* is intuitive, symbolic, even manic in structure and style. Its order is by association rather than by the logic of narration. Its texture and tone are dreamlike, almost surrealist. It resembles the timeless world of Benjy Compson. *The Rosy Crucifixion* [1] is straightforward narrative in style, though with interpolated fantasy passages. Overall it feels more like narrative. *Tropic of Capricorn* has passages in it which are unequalled by anything in *The Rosy Crucifixion,* but the second book of the trilogy, *Plexus,* is on the whole one of the best things Miller has written, though less startling than *Cancer* or *Capricorn.* Even if Miller planned the entire autobiographical romance in 1927, as he claims, we might question whether he foresaw the relation which would exist between works of his Paris period like *Capricorn* and much later works like *Plexus*

1 *Sexus, Plexus,* and *Nexus* (Paris: Olympia Press, 1962, 1959, 1960). Since this study was begun, an American edition has appeared (Grove Press, 1965). All references in this study, unless otherwise stated, are to the Olympia Press edition.

and *Nexus*. In any case, it seems we must accept the relationship as it stands; the works written years apart strangely complement each other.

The autobiographical romance as Miller first outlined it grew out of the period of his life with Mona, which he felt at the time was important and which proved later to be as important as he sensed. The scope of the narrative, in order to encompass the essential material, had to cover the period from the last year of Miller's first marriage to his arrival in Europe.[2] *The Rosy Crucifixion* tells us in narrative form what happened during that period; *Tropic of Capricorn* expresses in symbolic form the meaning of the events and ties them into the past, the early life of Henry Miller.

The Rosy Crucifixion is the story of Henry Miller's liberation and enslavement; it is paradoxical at the very root. Through Mona, Miller was delivered from an unhappy marriage and a demeaning job. With Mona, Miller found for the first time complete, uninhibited sexual release; but he simultaneously lost the independence of his existence and became dependent upon her. Yet the experience with Mona was necessary to the development of Miller the artist; it was the plunge into the depths from which he would emerge free. *The Rosy Crucifixion* itself does not reveal the full meaning of the events which took place during those seven years. It is the "autobiographical romance," the story of a disastrous love which holds the key to Miller's self-discovery, but the full meaning of that self-discovery must be encountered from vantage points outside the work.

In one sense at least Miller has gone far beyond the mere portrayal of a personal experience. In that sense he is Every-

2 According to Miller, the end of the narrative will be his final departure, the second one, for Europe. The second volume of *Nexus* will be in two parts, the first trip to Europe and the last year in New York. Miller to author, September 3, 1966.

man, or perhaps every artist, and Mona is Woman, the pure
female. Their drama, as Miller sees it, is the drama of
woman who absorbs man into her life, the life of sex which
is, finally, death, the death of creative power.

In one sense the conflict in Miller's works is as old as
Western literature, *i.e.*, the conflict between the ideal and the
real. The liberation of man's creative powers depends upon
his passing beyond the sensual to the ideal, the divine. But if
his search for the ideal is not firmly rooted in biological
reality, which is reducible to passionate sex, then his hold on
reality disappears, and his thought is dry and abstract. In
preserving the balance between ideal and real, man needs
woman; for it is she who remains firmly rooted in the earth.
The creative process is a struggle between the animal and
the divine. "By letting go the struggle between the animal
and divine in us we surrender ourselves to life and dissolution." But, by accepting dissolution, by ceasing to struggle,
we unify the disparate elements, uniting in ourselves man
and woman, father and mother. Therefore, in sex and passion man strikes his own roots deep into the heart of reality.[3]
This world of passionate sex is what I take Miller to be
representing in his *Capricorn* interlude, "The Land of
Fuck." It is the world represented realistically in *The Rosy
Crucifixion*.

In the beginning, before meeting Mona, Miller is ma-
rooned in the heart of chaos and death. With Mona he
enters into the world of passion, and descends to the animal
roots of reality. But this world has its own kind of death,
the defeat of "ideal-purpose" in man, and he must pass
beyond, carrying, if possible, the woman with him. The
ideal-purpose appears in "Miller as artist," his awakened
desire to be a writer. But as long as he is dependent upon the

3 *Sunday after the War* (New York: New Directions, 1944), 268.

woman, Mona, he is not free; he cannot express his true self. Through the relationship with Mona he finds himself. He then frees himself of his dependency upon her, and only then does he become a writer, not before.[4]

We see in *The Rosy Crucifixion* a concentration on this theme and countertheme: first, the full development of the relationship with Mona; second, the collapse of that relationship and the movement toward creative freedom. Our investigation is made difficult by the sheer bulk of the three books of this trilogy, amounting to almost seventeen hundred pages. Further, in contrast to *Tropic of Capricorn* the point of view of *The Rosy Crucifixion* is very close to the events going on and, therefore, does not permit the narrator to reveal the full significance of each event looking back from a later period. This is the novel of growth and process, and it is wholly concerned with maintaining the obscurity of that process to the narrator, reflecting the mystery of growth to creative fulfillment. For that reason every event of Miller's life, past and present, plays its part in the slow growth to self-knowledge. Life must be reinterpreted in the light of each new discovery; and the experience is complex, groping, often painful in the extreme.

Concerning Mona herself there are certain difficulties, pertaining mainly to her character, or lack of it. As we have already seen in *Tropic of Capricorn,* Miller is deeply disturbed by the lack of a central essence in Mona; she is totally self-made in order to conform to what she thinks is Miller's ideal image of her. It is my feeling that there is intentionally a symbolic dimension in this treatment of Mona. She is the monster of pure femaleness, the femme fatale.[5] An important part of the story of *The Rosy Cruci-*

4 *Tropic of Cancer,* 258–59.
5 See also Alfred Perles, *My Friend Henry Miller* (New York: John Day Co., 1956), 55–56.

fixion is Miller's gradual discovery that no adequate relationship is possible. Mona cannot be possessed. By submitting his own essential being to her. Miller is submitting to his own destruction. The events of *The Rosy Crucifixion* can be divided into three important parts: the sexual and personal relationship with Mona in comparison with other such relationships in these volumes, the gradual discovery of Mona's true nature with a consequent collapse of their relationship, and the emergence of Miller the writer as he fights free of his dependency upon her.

Sexus, book one of the trilogy, opens with Miller approaching his thirty-third year, ready for his "rosy crucifixion." Married to Maude, he has just met Mona. A whole new life lies before him, if he has the courage to cut the ties. He has resolved to give up everything, to surrender absolutely to the woman he loves. The first, almost immediate effect of the surrender is the birth of something new within:

Embracing her, trembling with the warmth of her passion, my mind jumped clear of the embrace, electrified by the tiny seed she had planted in me. Something that had been chained down, something that had struggled abortively to assert itself ever since I was a child, and had brought my ego into the street for a glance around, now broke loose and went sky-rocketing into the blue. Some phenomenal new being was sprouting with alarming rapidity from the top of my head, from the double crown which was mine from birth.[6]

What Miller seems to be experiencing here is a new and deep sense of commitment to himself, stimulated by the depth of Mona's belief in him. Whether Mona really believed in Miller to the extent that he felt she did is a moot question. It is possible, as Alfred Perles points out, that her

6 *Sexus,* 21.

greatest value to Miller was her very lack of an essential self, which enabled him to create the being whom he needed. In any event, this commitment to himself as artist must lie in abeyance until the complete working out of his passionate relationship with Mona, their passionate and furious sexual collision.

The first stage of Miller's relationship with Mona is characterized by the great spontaneity of their sexual responses, in marked contrast to Miller's life with Maude. The first sexual contact between them occurs in a taxicab:

We got into a cab and, as it wheeled around, Mara [Mona] impulsively climbed over me and straddled me. We went into a blind fuck, with the cab lurching and careening, our teeth knocking, tongue bitten, and the juice pouring from her like hot soup. As we passed an open plaza on the other side of the river, just at daybreak, I caught the astonished glance of a cop as we sped by. "It's dawn, Mara," I said, trying gently to disengage myself. "Wait, wait," she begged, panting and clutching at me furiously, and with that she went into a prolonged orgasm. . . . Finally she slid off and slumped back into her corner, her dress still up over her knees.[7]

Something new has happened in the way of love and passion, something new in the way of a human relationship, and Miller knows it: "Mara, Mara, where are you leading me? It's fateful, it's ominous, but I belong to you body and soul, and you will take me where you will, deliver me to my keeper, bruised, crushed, broken." [8] Something has been liberated in Miller by this experience, and that is one important aspect of *The Rosy Crucifixion*; but something too has been enslaved, and that is another.

7 *Ibid.*, 19.
8 *Ibid.*, 20.

On the next occasion the same impulsive yielding to passion is apparent. This time, Miller has brought Mara home
late; they are standing outside her house. They begin to
make love against a tree when they are interrupted by a
black cat which drops on them. They move to a vacant lot
and then, on the way once more toward her door, they begin
again the sexual encounter up against the same tree, sliding
finally to the middle of the sidewalk:

The sidewalk wasn't too comfortable—I had to pull out and move
over a few feet where there was a bit of soft earth. There was a
little puddle near her elbow and I was for taking it out again
and moving over another inch or so, but when I tried to draw it
out she got frantic. "Don't ever take it out again," she begged,
"it drives me crazy. Fuck me, fuck me!" I held out on her a long
while. As before she came again and again, squealing and
grunting like a stuck pig. Her mouth seemed to have grown
bigger, wider, utterly lascivious; her eyes were turning over, as
if she were going into an epileptic fit.[9]

This state of abandonment is characteristic of their relationship throughout *Sexus*. They copulate on the top of a bus, in
company, sitting at dinner. One effect of these detailed passages is to give sex its proportionate importance in the
relationship, which it would not have if the sexual experiences were merely alluded to, or described in euphemisms
of one kind or another.[10] To make his point more specific,
Miller introduces further experiences, of his own and others,
which lack this spontaneity, this free release of sexual feeling.

9 *Ibid.*, 74.
10 I am maintaining a distinction between two kinds of sexual
passages in Miller's works. The first, which I discussed in Chapter 1, is
in the nature of a frank and open realism, well within the bounds of
Miller's experience. The second type, which I discuss in this chapter, is
founded on a real experience, but goes far beyond realism in its
heightened account of sexual play. This "phallicism" has a symbolic
purpose.

For example there is MacGregor and his wife, Tess: "Mac-
Gregor had married her for purely practical reasons. They
had never pretended to be in love with one another. There
was scarcely even an animal affection between them since,
as he had readily explained to me shortly after their marriage, sex didn't mean a thing to her. She didn't mind being
diddled now and then, but she got no pleasure from it. 'Are
you through?' she would ask every now and then. If he took
too long over it she would ask him to fetch her a drink or
bring her something to eat." [11]

A different, but no more satisfactory, situation exists with
Woodruff, an old friend. His wife Ida, a whore at heart, is
frigid to Woodruff, who is enslaved by her. Ida makes a fool
of him because he cares too much, far beyond what is reasonable. Miller, with his fundamental sense of detachment,
could not be placed in the same position, even by Mona.
Miller visits the house in Woodruff's absence, and Ida proves
to be passionate, and insatiable. The coolness with which
Miller deceives a close friend is certainly contrary to the
ordinary mores of our society, but in these things Miller is a
ruthless realist. If Woodruff cannot handle his own wife, it is
because he is a "sentimentalist," and that is not Miller's
fault. A man is responsible for mending his own fences, and
he has no right to impose restrictions on his friends: if not
Miller, somebody else would deceive Woodruff, so why worry
about it.[12]

Miller's relationship with Maude is presented as the most
striking contrast to his life with Mona. Maude has a polar
character. She hates sex, finds it disgusting, but when sufficiently aroused she throws herself into it with complete
abandon. The great problem is that with her Miller is
obliged to work up to the subject of sex so gradually that it

11 *Sexus*, 151.
12 *Ibid.*, 226–27.

becomes unspontaneous and unsatisfying. He must examine bruises on her legs, imaginary blemishes; he must massage tender spots, arouse her while talking of every other subject under the sun, until she is having sex without ever having admitted the fact.[13] Once started, she shifts personalities, wanting anything, everything. Her overall attitude is best demonstrated in one of Miller's imaginative flights while he is in the act of intercourse:

Maude, if the author were God and not her husband, sees herself standing prissily on a green lawn, holding a beautiful red parasol. There are beautiful gray doves pecking at her shoes. . . . If she should squint her eye while saying benediction over God's little pigeons she would see a shameless hussy offering a naked man the hind part of her body, just like a cow or a mare in the field. She doesn't want to think of this woman, especially in such a disgraceful posture. She tries to keep the green grass around her and the parasol open. . . . The sun is shining brilliantly and now, oh how good it is warming her cool hinder parts. Like a merciful angel she spreads her legs apart: the dove flutters between her legs, the wings brush lightly against the marble arch. The little dove is fluttering madly; she must squeeze his soft little head between her legs.[14]

In Maude, self and sex are alienated. If she gives in to her sexual desires, she loses the self, the only self she knows. To affirm the waking self is to deny all rights to the body; to give in to the body is to be humiliated. "She expected of me a love which I was unable to give her. She wanted me to fondle her like a child, whisper sweet nothings in her ear, pet her, pamper her, humor her. She wanted me to embrace and caress her in some absurd, incestuous way. She didn't want to admit that she had a cunt and I a prick. She wanted love talk and silent furtive pressures, explorations with the

13 See *The World of Sex*, 40.
14 *Sexus*, 106.

hands. I was too forthright, too brutal for her liking." [15] But what disturbed Maude more than anything else was that once aroused she was unable to control herself. What she objected to precisely was "the abandonment. To think there was something hanging between a man's legs which could make her forget herself completely. . . ." [16]

Miller's sexual passages do not imply that he upholds a purely instinctual basis as the goal of human relationships. This fact is clearly apparent in the further development of his union with Mona. There was never a time, even in Paris just before the final collapse of their marriage, that they felt any decrease in their sexual compatibility.[17] In fact the tremendous sexual magnetism of one for the other continued to generate their epic encounters after all else had disappeared. Miller needed more than sexual compatibility. He wanted a close personal relationship, and to this he had totally dedicated his being. With Mona, however, this kind of relationship was impossible. We see the gradual revelation throughout *The Rosy Crucifixion* of what had been symbolically portrayed in *Capricorn,* her chameleon personality, her lack of an essential self. Although Mona remains throughout *Sexus* a force sufficiently attractive to whirl Miller out of his deadly orbit with Maude and the telegraph company, and although the emphasis is placed on her tremendous sexual energy and complete lack of inhibition which contrasts sharply with Maude's rigid character, we have enough hints and suggestions about Mona's character to make the final disposition of events believable. A great part of the first two books of the trilogy is devoted to Miller's gradual discovery of Mona's undependability.

From the very beginning Miller finds it difficult to pin Mona down on where she has been, what she has been doing.

15 *Ibid.,* 280.
16 *Ibid.*
17 Perles, *My Friend Henry Miller,* 122–23.

When she is late for a date, Miller seeks her out in the dance hall. She was late, she explains, because she had been to a "wild-party—not with Carruthers—he had left shortly after me. No, it was Florrie who had organized the party . . . Yes there had been a lot to drink and somebody had asked her to do the split and she had tried—well, she had hurt herself a bit . . . that was all." [18] Always Mona furnishes enough information to make the circumstances uncertain; always she insists on her innocence. It is the same with her recounting of past sexual experience. Mona tells of an automobile ride which happened, she says, many years ago with three brutal Italians by whom she was raped and beaten. The account is vividly concrete; she is obviously enjoying the retelling. Suddenly Miller has a "horrible suspicion" that the "rape" occurred recently, specifically in the last few weeks, that the beatings never occurred, that Mona was something less than unwilling.[19] But he has nothing beyond suspicion, and Miller at this point wants to believe, must believe Mona's stories about how she lost her virginity, about how rich men "always peeling off hundred dollar bills" want to do things for her, but demand nothing in return.[20] These tales build the character of Mona and finally lead to a situation in which Miller, not working, depending on Mona's support, is tortured by doubts about her life away from him.

Mona's family background is another source of mystery. She claims she has her stepmother, father, three brothers, sister, and sister-in-law living on the money she provides. All, according to her, are unreliable, desiring only to be supported. Mona's father sounds too much like a fabrication to be true. He is gentle, but weak, in ill health, the victim of a ruthless wife. From the beginning of *Sexus* Miller is unable

18   *Sexus,* 70.
19   *Ibid.,* 440–46.
20   *Ibid.,* 448.

to get any solid information about what the family is like. It is not until much later, until *Nexus* in fact, that the truth comes out. By this time Miller had reached a low point in his relationship with Mona. He looks up her brother, tells him Mona's version. The brother's story is almost directly contradictory. The passage shows so well Mona's fundamental character that I shall quote at length:

"She was always on her own, always secretive, always pretending that things were other than they were. Nothing but lies, lies, lies."

"But before she went to college—how was she then?"

"*College?* She never finished High School. She left home when she was sixteen."

"Maybe she couldn't get along with her step-mother," I added.

"Step-mother? Did she say she had a step-mother? The bitch!"

"Yes" I said, "she always insists that she couldn't get along with her step-mother. Her father, on the other hand, she loved dearly. . . ."

"Don't say any more," he said, "Stop! It's the other way round, exactly the opposite. My mother was as kind as a mother can be. She was her real mother, not her step-mother. As for my father, he used to get so furious with her that he would beat her unmercifully. Chiefly because of her lying. . . . We see her once a year, maybe, if that often. She always arrives with an armful of gifts, like a princess. And always a pack of lies about the great things she's doing. But you can never put your finger on what it is she's doing." [21]

Miller visits the mother and finds her typical—that is, quiet, forgiving, but intolerant of differences, un-understanding, wishing for Mona to return on bended knees to ask for forgiveness. He leaves with two seemingly irreconcilable ideas: "I thought of the Mona I had waited for outside the dance

21 *Nexus*, 172–73.

hall. I tried to put the two together. I couldn't. I wandered
through the dismal streets with one on either arm. Neither
of them existed any longer. Nor did I perhaps." [22]
    Mona lies not only to Miller, but to others when Miller
is present and knows she is lying. When Mona comes off the
worse for these exchanges, Miller does not reprimand her; he
tries to heal the wounds, to cover up Mona's weakness, particularly her lies. He loves her more rather than less for
these weaknesses: "I tried never to humiliate her by asking
a direct question. I knew just where the ice was thin and I
skated about these dangerous zones with the adroitness and
agility of a professional. In this way I patiently endeavored
to fill in those gaps which were distressingly blatant in one
who was supposed to have graduated from such a venerable
institution of learning as Wellesley." [23] Miller's reaction to
Mona's duplicity, which she refuses to admit even to him
(she must always strive "to make herself invulnerable"), is
to love, even to cherish the defect. "One is not only eager to
overlook the duplicity of the unfortunate one, one makes a
violent and unnatural effort towards identification. 'Let *me*
carry the burden of your sweet defect! is the cry of the
love-sick heart. Only an ingrained egotist can evade the shack-
les imposed by an unequal match. The one who loves thrills
at the thought of greatest tests; he begs mutely that he be
permitted to put his hand in the flame." [24]
    For Miller, significantly, the answer to a woman like Mona
is not to resist, not to fight her, but to surrender to her:

A man can only begin to understand the depths of woman's
nature when he surrenders his soul unequivocally. It is only
then that he begins to grow and truly to fecundate her. There

22 *Ibid.*, 179.
23 *Sexus*, 433.
24 *Ibid.*, 434.

are then no limits to what he may expect of her, because in surrendering he has delimited his own powers. In this sort of union, which is really a marriage of spirit with spirit, a man comes face to face with the meaning of creation. He participates in an experiment which he realizes will always be beyond his feeble comprehension. He senses the drama of the earthbound and the role which woman plays in it. The very possessivity of woman takes on a new light. It becomes as enchanting and mysterious as the law of gravitation.[25]

Miller's desire to surrender to Mona is an important motivation which gives direction to the three books of *The Rosy Crucifixion*. As we have seen, in the beginning he has an almost entirely physical relationship with her which does not exclude the possibility of relationships with other women, likewise physical. But the fact that he experiences this need to surrender forms a progressive commitment to Mona which is at once a liberation and an enslavement. The enslavement motive is understated. It occurs briefly in *Capricorn*, at the very end. It occurs once more at the end of *Sexus*, but does not reappear until the beginning of *Nexus*. Yet it is combination of liberation and enslavement which gives intensity to the relationship. Miller gives himself to Mona in full awareness of her character. He tries to overcome her deficiencies by the power of his love. The attempt is doomed to fail, but it will be the means of Miller's liberation.

Despite the fact that *Sexus* sets up the growth and development theme which continues through *Plexus* and *Nexus*, there is another side to the book which must be considered, that is, the lurid nature of the sexual material. In Chapter 1 we considered, in a preliminary way, the role of Miller's sexual material. But the baldness of the sexual passages in

25 *Ibid.*, 435.

Sexus are by comparison so much more disturbing (even Durrell protested) that further discussion is necessary. Furthermore, some ramifications of sex as symbol may profitably be introduced which could throw light on other volumes. Miller had had a number of things to say about his use of obscenity. About the *Sexus* passages he was at first alarmed, but felt that he was being "dictated to" right out of the unconscious. Later he defended the book to Durrell, but not in terms specific enough to be of much help.

The principal difference between the passages in *Sexus* and those in *Cancer* and *Capricorn* is that they are more complex and more elaborately described. The most elaborate description of an actual event is that of the encounter between Miller, his first wife Maude, and the girl upstairs, Elsa. Miller had already begun to dally with Maude when she went upstairs to get something to drink. When she re-entered the girl was with her, and the three of them spent the rest of the night in elaborate sexual play. On another occasion Miller, his friend Ulric, Mona, and a Negro girl named Lola amuse themselves with somewhat less elaborate but no less public sexual games. There are numerous others, but these are typical. These passages, at least on first reading, give the impression of going far beyond any structural or thematic necessity. It is likely that they will continue to give difficulty; nor is there to my mind any easy defense for them. Yet something may be said by way of explanation, if not in defense.

When Miller named the book *Sexus* he must have had something in mind, and there are a few passages to give us a clue. He recalls during *Sexus* his adolescent love affairs with Una Gifford and a strange Beatrice-like ideal, Miriam Painter. These girls he loved at a distance. When he did not marry immediately and begin to raise a family, he seemed to lose forever the possibility of settling down in society.[26] With the waning of adolescent love came the awakening of sexuality, and it was not to end until it had run its full course. Miller does not, like many writers in America, treat the in-between stage of sexual freedom as evil or destructive. Sex and love, he tells us in *World of Sex*, should be united, but they are different and separable. At various stages of life they will exist in different relationships to each other. Miller loved Mona, he says, and his relationship with her deepened throughout *Plexus* and *Nexus*. But in *Sexus* his love interest and his sexual interest are not yet integrated. Mona is a force sufficient to separate him from his first wife, but she is not yet enough to satisfy wholly the consuming hunger for life which gnaws him.

We may take as an example of this hunger Miller's own analysis in a conversation he has with Rebecca, the wife of an old friend from whom they have rented a room. He is in the process of telling Rebecca, who is fixing dinner, about his sexual relationship with his ex-wife, Maude. Rebecca says, "Do you like Cauliflower? I haven't any other vegetable." Miller answers: "I like any kind of food. I like everything. I like you, I like Mona, I like my wife, I like horses, cows, chickens, pinochle, tapioca, Bach, benzine, prickly heat. . . ." She answers *"You like!* That's you all over. It's wonderful to hear it. You make me hungry too. You like everything, yes; . . . but you don't love. . . . " Miller's answer is really his principal way of attempting to justify his sexual adventuring: "I do too. I love food, wine, women. Of course I do. What makes you think I don't? If you like, you love. Love is only the superlative degree. I love like God loves—without distinction of time, place, race, color, sex and

26 *Sexus* (New York: Grove Press, 1965), 210–11.

so forth. I love you too—that way. It's not enough, I suppose?" [27]

Miller's reasoning is easy enough, too easy perhaps. Monogamy and the so-called virtues, he feels, have created nothing but misery and war, slavery and violence. The simple yielding to hunger leads to peace and happiness. But even this attitude, in all its Rousseauistic simplicity, does not account for the particular flavor of the sexual passages in *Sexus*. The fact is that they sound like what we are accustomed to regard as pornographic writing. The terms are not merely descriptive, they accentuate functions, feelings, and appearances in such a way as to maximize the erotic effect.

We can find a clue, perhaps, to the role of the most disturbing episodes in the analysis of pornography done by the Kronhausens.[28] Pornography, as they see it, is characterized by certain wish-fulfilling functions by which taboo words and activities are deliberately made as appealing as possible. Exaggeration is the key note. Female genitals are large and open and capable of discharging large quantities of fluid. They have a semi-independent life, can open and close, grip tenuously, etc. The male organ is always very large and extremely durable. Detumescence is brief and is followed by even greater and more durable erections. As with the female, there is an emphasis on quantities of sperm along with the minute descriptive details of texture, shape, and size. Taboos of relationships are broken down; incest is common; parental figures are permissive.

All these are typical of Miller's sexual passages. The Italian is described as an animal with a huge penis. He has four or five orgasms within a short period of time, and the fluid

27   *Ibid.*, 492.
28   Eberhard and Phyllis Kronhausen, *Pornography and the Law* (New York: Ballantine Books, 1959).

which pours from him is like that of a bull. Miller emphasizes
the most exaggerated aspects of the whole story. In the episode with his wife he uses nearly the same technique with
different characters. This time it is Miller who has the
perpetual erection. The women pour forth the large quantities of fluid. The relationship with his former wife, and
her failure to be jealous of the other woman, takes the whole
episode out of the normal context of his previous relationships with her. It is noteworthy that in pornography even
lesbian activities are acceptable because they are not offensive
to men. Such is the case here. The women both engage freely
in homosexual acts. Yet neither Miller nor any other male
character is similarly attracted. The whole atmosphere is one
in which female sexuality is aroused beyond the point of
control. Given our Victorian civilization and the prevalence
of inhibition in women, it is likely that all these passages are
wish fulfilling rather than realistic.

I see only one head under which all these possibilities can
be brought to artistic unity. The clue again is in Kronhausen:
"In all these respects, 'obscene' writings are reminiscent of
the phallic worship which antedates our religious system by
several millenniums and which constituted, in pre-Christian
times, the basic element of earlier religious cults the world
over. In these cults, the male and female genitals, or their
pictorial representations, were objects of worship to a people
who saw in them not the 'instruments of sin,' but the symbols
of the procreative life-giving powers of nature."[29] Miller has
two references which suggest that he is aware of the wish-
fulfilling and of the phallic elements in these passages. Both
occur during the burlesque episode in *Sexus*. In the first he
refers to the comedians who "create the illusion of a world in
which the Unconscious reigns supreme." According to Miller,

29 *Ibid.*, 221.

the comedian slays at every performance "the censor who
stands like a ghost on the threshold of the subliminal self." [30]
This is the wish-fulfilling nature of the sexual material. The
phallus-worship reference appears a few pages further on,
and in it the phallus is not the symbol of slavery to nature;
rather it symbolizes a rising above nature. The sexual dance
is "spirit working through instinct." The worship of the
phallus in ritual is an attempt to rise above "the confusion
of mere reproduction." The phallic dance is "a triumphant
victory for man."

In Africa the dance is impersonal, sacred and obscene. When
the phallus becomes erect and is handled like a banana it is not
a 'personal hard-on' we see but a tribal erection. It is a religious
hard-on, directed not towards *a* woman but towards every female member of the tribe. Group souls staging a group fuck.
Man lifting himself out of the animal world through a ritual of
his own invention. By his mimicry he demonstrates that he has
made himself superior to the mere act of intercourse. [31]

By the same token, Miller's sexual dance does not seem to be
a loss of self within the reproductive matrix, but a ritualizing
through which he rises superior to it. *Sexus* is the high point
of the phallic dance. It is in realistic narrative the equivalent of the symbolic "Interlude" of *Capricorn*, the alimentary world of convertible desire which is never quite lost, but
which slips back into its proper perspective in later works.

The sexual passages in Miller's works must be understood
in the light of the development of the hero-narrator toward
an integration of all the possibilities of life within an overall
unity. To understand and accept this point of view we must
make certain assumptions about our culture, which are the

30 *Sexus*, 592.
31 *Ibid.*, 602.

basic assumptions characteristic of Miller's general philo-sophic position. Our culture, in this view, maintains its position through repression, projection, and denial. The lines of the body, man's full existence, have been lost by dividing man against himself. During the process of development the true self, meaning not only what one is but also what one wants, begins to emerge. In order for this process to con-tinue, however, all pressures from fear, loneliness, or social disapproval must be resisted. Otherwise the growth will be choked off and some of the areas of self will not come to light. Miller's early books, those which treat of his late adolescence and young manhood, are more concerned with the emerg-ence of physical desire, of wants which are basic and very primitive. In the sexual passages he explores, without regard for what is acceptable to society, the possibilities inherent in the uninhibited living out of sexual desires, whatever they may be and however they may emerge. Thus, *Sexus* develops the sexual side of the appetites; *Plexus* and *Nexus* are rela-tively free of extended descriptions of sexual activity.[32]

Mona and Miller reached the most stable period of life together in the beginning of *Plexus*. They have an apart-ment, one far beyond their means, where they are living on each other, hardly needing other companionship. While the idyll lasts, especially while they have no one but themselves, it seems that they will succeed in making a comfortable life in which Miller can write and in which Mona can fulfill herself in taking care of Miller. But the respite is for only a few months: "Soon it will be nothing but trouble, nothing but want, nothing but frustration." [33] Miller is sending out manuscripts, waiting daily for acceptance. Mona wishes to take a job in a cabaret. "Her job at the theater had petered

32 Henry Miller, "Obscenity and the Law of Reflection," in *Re-member to Remember* (New York: New Directions, 1957), 283.
33 *Plexus,* 95.

out. The rent has been long overdue. My visits to Maude have become less and less regular and the alimony is paid only now and then, when we make a haul. Soon Mona's wardrobe gives out, and I, like a dolt, make vain efforts to beg a dress or a suit of my old sweethearts. When it gets bitter cold she wears my overcoat." [34] They are saved momentarily by the contributions of a friend, O'Mara, who moves in with them, but they are reaching the end of the string.

The only real source of money that Miller has is from Mona's solicitation of her "admirers," men like Rothermel, a disabled veteran of World War I who is embittered by the loss of a leg, alienated from everyone, in love with Mona, and wealthy. Mona meets him for one purpose, to extract money from him, and this makes him more bitter; but she is all he has, and he gives. The final disaster, however, does not come from these activities, but from another trait of Mona's, only hinted at in *Plexus,* but which will become fully visible in *Nexus.* The few passages which reveal this tendency in her point toward the final fatal involvement in book 3. Miller imagines Mona walking through the Village, brushing antennae with the antlike creatures who bustle about the twisted streets. In one of the houses "there lives a pale timid creature, usually of dubious sex, who belongs to the world of du Maurier, Chekov, or Alain Fournier. . . . Towards such types Mona is fatally drawn. A secret friendship veils all their intercourse in mystery . . . she may take it into her head to surprise her seraphic friend by buying her an old-fashioned cameo smothered in violets, or a rocking chair from the hills of Dakota, or a snuff-box scented with sandalwood. The gifts first and then a few bills fresh from the mint. . . . Rothermel would be powerless to suspect how quickly and for what ends his money goes. All we know,

34 *Ibid.*

who greet her at the end of a feverish day, is that she has managed to buy a few groceries and can dispense a little cash." [35]

The attractiveness to Mona of these helpless girls finally creates the situation which occupies almost the whole of *Nexus*. Mona has taken a job in the Iron Cauldron, a Village night spot. At home the name of Anastasia comes up repeatedly. The facts about this new friend, what few there are, begin to come out under Miller's prodding: " 'I suppose she's a bit on the mannish side. . . .' Not really, said Mona, her eyes glistening. She prefers to dress in men's clothes because she feels more comfortable that way. She's more than a mere female, you see. If she were a man I'd speak about her in the same way. There's some added quality about her which is beyond sexual distinction. . . . The only way to explain it to you, Val, is to say that she's a very superior being." [36] They drop the subject for a moment, but it comes up almost immediately. When Mona refers to Stasia as her "friend", Miller objects; she had only known the girl a short while, why "friend?" Mona answers "She is my friend—the only friend I've ever had." Miller objects; Mona doesn't need a friend like that; he is her friend. Mona answers that he is her husband, not her friend; she needs a woman friend, someone she can confide in.

On the surface there is certainly nothing unnatural in Mona's wish for a woman friend with whom she can share intimacies. By now, however, Miller is suspicious of the relationship. "My friend Stasia" comes up too often. He objects that Mona's support of this "helpless child' is only making her more incapable. She answers that he is in the same position, but he argues that he is able to support a family; he already has. A rift is developing between them,

35   *Ibid.*, 331.
36   *Ibid.*, 627.

now that their private little world is breaking up. He needs
Mona; she, evidently, does not need him. When Stasia moves
in with them, the riot is complete. It is not that the women
are so fond of each other, not even that they have an unnatural relationship; it is that their lives are so surrounded
in lies that Miller is unable to find out what is going on. In
the beginning of their relationship, Mona lied in order to
become for Miller the kind of person that he wanted her
to be. Now, Mona lies to conceal her actions, her thoughts,
her feelings. She is absent much of the time, and Miller
cannot find out where she is going or what she is doing. To
him both these women are unaccountable mysteries. They
have no pasts; they speak of their childhoods as something
that had happened to someone else.[37]

Finally Miller faces Stasia with his own feelings. He brings
his suspicion and concern into the open:

"Now which do you prefer to believe," I began, "that Mona
loves me so much that she has to lie to me night and day? Or
that she loves *you* so much that she hasn't the courage to tell me?
Or that *you* love *her* so much that you can't stand seeing her
unhappy. . . . Listen, if you had asked me if I were jealous of
you, much as I hate to admit it, I would have said yes. I'm not
ashamed to confess that it humiliates me to think someone like
you can make me jealous. . . . I don't like morphodites. . . . It's
most unfortunate, to put it mildly, that my wife should feel so
keenly drawn to you. . . . It's a god-damned shame, is what I
mean to say that she couldn't have chosen a real man, if she had
to betray me, even if he were someone I despised. But you? . . .
Why *shit!* it leaves me absolutely defenseless." [38]

But Miller loses again as Stasia bursts into tears just as Mona
arrives. Mona immediately begins to console Stasia, and to
berate Miller.

37 *Nexus,* 611–12.
38 *Ibid.,* 19.

Miller tries to bridge the gulf by sheer force of will; he generously forgives the past, and swears to love her forever. Close upon this avowal, however, reality begins to intrude once more. Miller is fighting a losing battle and he knows it:

But if the object of this sublime adoration be not worthy! Seldom is it the man who is afflicted by such doubts. Usually it is the one who inspired this rare and overpowering love who falls victim to doubt. Nor is it her feminine nature which is solely at fault, but rather some spiritual lack which, until subjected to the test, had never been in evidence. With such creatures, particularly when endowed with surpassing beauty, their real powers of attraction remain unknown; they are blind to all but the lure of the flesh. The tragedy, for the hero of love, resides in the awakening, often a brutal one, to the fact that beauty, though an attribute of the soul, may be absent in everything but the lines and lineaments of the loved one.[39]

For the first time Miller begins to sense a disproportion between his love and the object of that love. He had been carried away by Mona's passionate acceptance of him, particularly her acceptance of those things in him which no one else had accepted. He had thought that she responded to him in the same degree that he loved her, but now he finds himself living with one who has become a mystery to him. If it had been a case simply of their falling out of love, of Mona's being unfaithful to him, he could have responded appropriately. But such is not the case. Mona seems to be maintaining the same attitudes to Miller she always had, but parts of her do not belong to him, are free to be committed elsewhere, while he is committed passionately to her. The torture for Miller is that he is committed to her, but cannot control her actions toward others.

It is when Mona and Stasia have left for Paris that Miller's remembrance of Mona reveals the depths of his attachment,

39 *Ibid.,* 85–86.

not merely to her as a person, but to the very qualities that create much of his misery, the mystery about her, her changeability, especially her dynamic body. An event occurs when Miller, tortured by desire, picks up another girl in a dance hall. He wonders why he could not have married an easy-going girl like this:

But the moment I began to make comparison between her body and Mona's I knew it was useless to go into it. Whatever flesh and blood qualities she had, this one, they remained flesh and blood. There was nothing more to her than what you could see and touch, hear and smell. With Mona it was another story entirely. Any portion of her body served to inflame me. Her personality was as much in her left teat, so to speak, as in her little right toe. The flesh spoke from every quarter, every angle. Strangely, hers was not a perfect body either. But it was melodious and provocative. Her body echoes her moods. She had no need to flaunt it or fling it about; she only had to inhabit it, to *be* it. . . . What I craved was the elusive. . . . The elusive and insatiable at the same time. A body like Mona's own, which, the more one possessed it the more one became possessed. A body which could bring with it all the woes of Egypt—and its wonders, its marvels.[40]

An almost indescribable burden of meaning rests upon the conviction with which Miller is able to convey the strength of his attachment to Mona and the misery which follows the disintegration of their relationship. In *Tropic of Capricorn*, as we have seen, he uses a dream fantasy to suggest the total involvement of his personality. In *The Rosy Crucifixion* he spells out the circumstances which forge this crucial experience. It is clear that much more is involved in this crisis than physical attachment, much more, even, than love, as we ordinarily conceive it. It would appear that Mona answers a need so basic to Miller that to be deprived of her constitutes a threat to the very existence of his ego; that is to say, Mona

40 *Ibid.,* 209–10.

answers deep unconscious demands which, unsatisfied, threaten to disrupt his sense of fulfillment.

Miller experiences a turning point in his life shortly before Mona returns from Paris. Lying on the grass in Central Park he has a dream in which he seems to be visited by an angel in the role of Comforter. First he imagines himself covered with wounds from head to foot and faints. On seeming to awake, he finds a hole where his heart had been. At that moment "the door to memory" swings open:

I saw in every phase and moment of his pitiful weakness the utter wretch I had been, the blackguard, nothing less, who had striven so vainly and ignominiously to protect his miserable little heart. I saw that it never had been broken, as I imagined, but that paralyzed by fear, it had shrunk almost to nothingness. I saw that the grievous wounds which had brought me low had all been received in a senseless effort to prevent this shriveled heart from breaking. The heart itself had never been touched; it had dwindled from disuse.[41]

Now, without a heart, Miller is no longer vulnerable. His strength returns, but suddenly he is overwhelmed by the emptiness of existence. "Heartless, I had lost the power to communicate with my Creator." Then an angel reappears with the shrunken heart which she blows upon, restoring its fullness, and replaces in Miller's chest. He now feels a new sense of being:

Rising to my feet, a new being entire. I put forth my arms to embrace the world. Nothing had changed. It was the world I had always known. But I saw it now with other eyes. I no longer sought to escape it, to shun its ills, or alter it in any least way. I was fully of it and one with it. I had come through the valley of the shadow of death; I was no longer ashamed to be human, all-too-human.

41 *Ibid.*, 213.

I had found my place. I belonged. My place was in the world, in the midst of death and corruption. For companions I had the sun, the moon, the stars. My heart cleansed of its iniquities, had lost all fear; it ached now to offer itself to the first comer. Indeed, I had the impression that I was all heart, a heart which could never be broken, nor even wounded, since it was forever inseparable from that which had given it birth.[42]

From the time of this dream until the end of *Nexus,* Miller finds himself headed toward his true destiny. Mona returns, and he loves her still, but she is no longer capable of destroying his new orientation. With the conception of his master-work, laid out during Mona's absence, he is ready to fulfill the promise which he has always felt was his goal in life. His work would enshrine Mona, enshrine the past, and, at the same time, liberate him from enslavement to either.

The "beyond" to which Miller must now pass is his commitment to himself as writer. This commitment is not only the culminating theme of *The Rosy Crucifixion,* but remains Miller's major theme throughout the rest of his life. His entire philosophy of life will henceforth be based upon his sense of liberation based on acceptance. Almost every discussion of every subject, from politics to astrology, stems from this insight into his essential self. As the relationship with Mona gradually disintegrates, threatening to take Miller with it (this is the period in which he attempted suicide),[43] the way is open for discovery of the real Miller, and his own authentic voice. This rebirth takes the form of a total reinterpretation of the past, reconstructing those elements which have been essential in creating the writer.

42 *Ibid.,* 214.
43 Emil Schnellock, "Just a Brooklyn Boy," in Bern Porter (ed.) , *The Happy Rock,* 15.

The first sparks of this recovery of the past occur in *Sexus* when Mona's words "Why don't you write?" start a revery on the act and purpose of writing, a revery which carries him back to childhood, to the Brooklyn days, and to what set him apart even then.

Writing must be "an act devoid of will. The word, like the deep ocean current, has to float to the surface of its own impulse." That is, writing must be the innocent activity of the child, not that of the adult who "writes to throw off the poison which he has accumulated because of his false way of life." Miller is not content to write like the ordinary writer who, in his opinion, writes because he lacks the courage to live, "because the very thought of contact with rude and brutal realities frightens him." The "truly great writer," as Miller sees it, "does not want to write; he wants the world to be a place in which he can live the life of the imagination. The first quivering word he puts to the paper is the word of the wounded angel: pain." As for Miller himself, he wants to "enchant, but not to enslave." "I wanted to free the imagination of all men at once because without the support of the whole world, without the world imaginatively unified, the freedom of the imagination becomes a vice. . . . The only benefit . . . which the act of writing could offer me was to remove the differences which separated me from my fellow-man. I definitely did not want to become the artist, in the sense of becoming something strange, something apart and out of the current of life." Writing is an attempt of the few to make available the heights and depths of reality. In "an intelligently ordered world" there would be no need for the writer, for all men would experience that reality directly.[44]

We discover more about Miller, the writer-to-be, in an episode which occurs near the beginning of *Sexus*. It is short,

44 *Sexus,* 24–26.

but its implications are so great that full discussion is warranted. Miller has met a strange woman, Sylvia, who speaks like the Delphic Oracle, though more plainly. She seems to read Miller to the depths of his character. Not only does she know his actual situation—that he is in love, that he wants to write—but her prophetic tone has an implied truth about it that seems confirmed by what we know of Miller's subsequent history. How true or fictional the event is, it is impossible to say.

After telling Miller that he is protected, that he was meant to lead a dangerous life, she reveals to him his reaction to her:

"You knew that I would throw myself in your arms as soon as he left. I did. But you were paralyzed—a little frightened of me, shall I say? Why? . . . Do you want to tell me the truth?"

I nodded helplessly.

"You were afraid that if I did ask you to do something for me you would not be able to refuse. You were perplexed because, being in love with one woman, you already felt yourself the potential victim of another. It isn't a woman you need—it is an instrument to liberate yourself. You crave a more adventurous life, you want to break your chains. Whoever this woman is you love I pity her. To you she will appear to be the stronger, but that is only because you doubt yourself. *You* are the stronger. You will always be stronger—because you can think only of yourself, of your destiny. If you were just a little stronger I would fear for you. You might make a dangerous fanatic. But that is not your fate. You're too sane, too healthy. You love life even more than your own self. You are confused because whomever you give yourself to is never enough for you—isn't that true? Nobody can hold you for long; you are always looking beyond the object of your love, looking for something you will never find. You will have to look inside yourself if you ever hope to free yourself of torment." [45]

45 *Ibid.,* 51–52.

Occuring early in *Sexus* as the passage does, it provides a fore-shadowing of the end of the affair with Mona, and also points ahead to the events of the future, chiefly in terms of dedication to art. Miller will be a writer; nothing will get in his way.

In a continuation of her revelation, Sylvia points out that Miller is an animal who wants to throw her on the rug, but that he is afraid of this side of himself, at least afraid to reveal it. The animal quality in Miller she expresses again in showing him how he chooses the right path by instinct, how he is wary of traps. Finally, as a culmination of her revelation, she shows Miller that if he thought he could accomplish what he had to accomplish without Mona, he would not return. Then, even more to the point, she says he is incapable of giving love:

A woman wants love and you're incapable of giving love. If you were a lower type of man you would be a monster; but you will convert your frustration into something useful. Yes, by all means go on writing. Art can transform the hideous into the beautiful. Better a monstrous book than a monstrous life. . . . If you don't die in the attempt, your work may transform you into a sociable, charitable human being. . . . Probably when you have lived enough, you will discover that there is something beyond what you now call life. You may yet live to live for others.[46]

Through art the artist discovers life. This is no more than Miller himself concludes in later works, but there follows a more obscure analysis of Miller's character, an analysis which again Miller confirms, but which will have to be discussed in its full implications later in this study, that is, that Miller's strength lies in virtues which are more feminine than masculine: "You have all the feminine virtues, but you are ashamed

46 *Ibid.*, 54.

to acknowledge them to yourself. You think because you are strong sexually that you are a virile man, but you are more of a woman than a man. Your sexual virility is only the sign of a greater power which you haven't begun to use. . . . You will have a harder time than other men because to dominate another doesn't interest you. You will always be trying to dominate yourself; the woman you love will only be an instrument to practice on." [47]

It is what sets Miller apart as a man which will lead to his becoming a writer. First there is the necessity of becoming himself, which means getting rid of entangling alliances in order to dedicate himself to discovery of truth. His own hunger for life attracted others who wove their lives into the pattern of his own,[48] and to shake himself free required great effort. Miller's purpose is becoming more and more clear, to own nothing, to desire nothing, to be interested in nothing except to create; these must be his terms.

The rebirth which occurs at the end of *The Rosy Cruci-fixion,* an event which strikes us almost unawares, has actually been well provided for in the periodic insights that Miller gets into the heart of a deeper reality. These moments are usually the result of an external stimulus, not permanent states of feeling. For example, midway through *Plexus,* Miller recalls the effects of Spring during childhood, effects which carry him to the heart of the cosmos:

In the twinkle of an eye one is divorced from the illusory world of material reality; with every step one places himself anew at the *carrefour* of the concentric radiations which are the true substance of an all-encompassing and all-pervading reality. Death has no meaning. All is change, vibration, creation and re-creation. The song of the world, registered in every particle of

47   *Ibid.,* 55.
48   *Ibid.,* 262.

that spacious substance called matter, issues forth in an ineffable harmony which filters through the angelic being lying dormant in the shell of the physical creature called man. Once the angel assumes dominion, the physical being flowers. Throughout all realms a quiet, persistent blossoming takes place.[49]

Before Miller can find his own voice as a writer, he must make this vision a permanent part of his experience. In the meantime, he must struggle toward the goal, writing when he can and what he can. As *Plexus* goes on, and throughout *Nexus*, Miller's dedication to his vocation increases in intensity; more and more he struggles with themes, organization, grandiose plans for works of all kinds.

The closer Miller gets to a realization of his destiny, the more he reaches back into the past in an effort to recapture the days of his early life. He cannot know during the period in which *The Rosy Crucifixion* takes place that this material from the past will form the nucleus of his greatest work. The return to the past is instinctive, a part of the general search for the self to which Miller is dedicated. When he arrives finally at the nature of his true identity it is largely because he has been able to re-live the past and understand that past in terms of the present. Re-living the past becomes the means of grasping the self in the present. Perhaps the most interesting, the greatest, in a sense, of Miller's writing is that concerned simply with the recounting of boyhood experience. Sometimes the circumstances are tragic, sometimes joyful. In either case the nostalgia is such a warm human thing that we feel absolutely at one with the experiences Miller is creating.

Though Miller was working hard at writing, he had not yet become a writer. In the beginning of *Plexus* he shows us why:

49 *Plexus,* 337.

. . . I had no order, no discipline, no set goal. I was completely at the mercy of my impulses, my whims, my desires. My frenzy to live the life of the writer was so great that I overlooked the vast reservoir of material which had accumulated during the years leading up to this moment. I felt impelled to write about the immediate, about what was happening outside my very door. *Something fresh,* that's what I was after. To do this was compulsive because, whether I was aware of it or not, the material which I had stored up had been chewed to a frazzle during the years of frustration, doubt and despair when everything I had to say was written out in my head. . . . These first efforts . . . these fantasies and fantasias, these prose poems and rambling divagations of all sorts, were like the grand tuning up of the instrument.[50]

This "tuning up of the instrument" is one of the necessary preconditions of Miller's becoming a writer. The other is his rebirth as an individual, a greater insight into himself and the universe. To further the illusion of this rebirth process Miller introduces, near the end of *Plexus,* another prophetic person named Claude, a person not unlike the Sylvia of *Sexus.* Sylvia, however, gave Miller himself, interpreting for him his true nature. Claude hands Miller the universe, as it will appear to him when he gains true vision:

"Imagine, if you can, what it would be like if your heart began to beat with a cosmic rhythm. . . . There will come a time when man will no longer distinguish between man and god. When the human being is raised to his full powers he will be divine—his human consciousness will have fallen away. What is called death will have disappeared. . . . Man will be free. . . . Once he becomes the god which he is, he will have realized his destiny— which is freedom. Freedom includes everything. Freedom converts everything to its basic nature, which is perfection." [51]

50 *Ibid.,* 55–56.
51 *Ibid.,* 608.

To realize this kind of freedom requires, above all, a suspension of fear, a fear experienced as a fall into nothingness. To conquer this fear it is first of all necessary to realize that "there is nothing to fall into." [52] It is not even a question of possessing, it is a question of being.

The two worlds, the world of experience and the world of the writer come closer and closer together as the trilogy draws toward a close. In the beginning of *Nexus*, Miller is working on a play. He has it all mapped out, with the plan tacked to the wall, when he receives a visit from Stanley.[53] When Miller dismisses his play with "I'll probably never write it," Stanley replies, "My thought exactly. You'll never write a play or anything else worth talking about. You'll write and write and never get anywhere." [54] Miller's response is to look at the play more closely. He can see it completed. He can even hear the applause of the audience. What he cannot see is himself writing it. "I could never write it in words. It had to be written in blood." [55] Faced with Stanley's denunciation, Miller, in a moment of deep intuition, probes to the source of creativity to discover that being and writing are one, instead of two separate activities as he had felt:

Reduced to ashes by Stanley's heartless words, I had come face to face with the source, with authorship itself, one might say. And how utterly different this was, this quiet flow from the source, than the strident act of creation which is writing! "Dive deep and never come up!" should be the motto for all who hunger to create in words. For only in the tranquil depths is it granted us to see and hear, to move and be. What a boon to sink to the very bottom of one's being and never stir again! [56]

52 *Ibid.,* 609.
53 *Nexus,* 86–87.
54 *Ibid.,* 87.
55 *Ibid.,* 88.
56 *Ibid.,* 90.

The answer to Miller's question of how to be a writer begins to become more clear. A book is the revelation of a person. Every author has a different way of beginning, and the beginning reveals the man. "The way a book opened was the way an author walked or talked, the way he looked at life, the way he took courage or concealed his fears." This "lifting of the veil" is a terrible ordeal. "No one, not even the greatest could be certain what he might be called upon to present to the profane eye. Once engaged, anything could happen." [57] Miller emphasizes what he will continue to emphasize in all later references to becoming a writer, that is, the necessity of giving scope to the powers within, allowing these powers to work within the self. One "undergoes" creation as much as one creates. The combination of activity and passivity in the successful writer is a combination of masculine and feminine attributes which Miller will express more explicitly later.[58] Now, he is still groping toward the goal.

The grand plan for *Tropic of Capricorn* and *The Rosy Crucifixion* was conceived during the time Mona was in Paris and Miller was working for the park department. As we have seen in our discussion of *Tropic of Capricorn*, the writing of this book would be the means of finally attaining freedom from dependence upon Mona. When he put her in a book, he converted the material of his life into the material of art, and the way to a fuller life was opened up. Bored by his situation in the park department, depressed by his inability to get to Europe, Miller sat down to outline a book he would write someday:

57 *Ibid.*, 158.
58 Miller accepts the early psychoanalytical doctrine that each individual, man or woman, is composed of elements of both sexes. For Jung this was of central importance. Though opposition to this idea has been expressed recently [see Commentary by Mortimer Kaplan, in *Literature and Psychology*, XIV (Spring, Summer, and Fall, 1964) for a summary], the concept is still a useful one on the symbolic level.

I wrote rapidly, in telegraphic style, commencing with the evening I first met her. For some inexplicable reason I found myself recording chronologically *and without effort,* the long chain of events which filled the interval between that fateful evening and the present. Page after page I turned out, and always there was more to put down. . . . As I wrote I laughed and wept. Though I was only making notes it seemed as if I were actually writing the book there and then; I relived the whole tragedy over again step by step, day by day.[59]

Looking over his notes the next day Miller realized that he had planned a work which would require several volumes, and while musing on the "enormity" of the task, he realized that something had changed. "Musing thus, an appalling thought struck me. It was this—our love is ended. That could be the only meaning for planning such a work. I refused, however, to accept this conclusion. I told myself that my true purpose was merely to relate . . . the story of my misfortunes. . . . I would write the book for her—to her—and in reading it she would understand, her eyes would be opened, she would help bury the past, we would begin a new life together." [60] In other words, Miller "squelched these inner voices, these inner promptings which only the devil could inspire." [61] He still needed Mona.

The passage of inspiration in Central Park from which Miller arose to embark on a new life was only one step on the road to liberation, though a most important step. Yet the achieving of independence cannot come all at once; there must be many liberations before he attains his full maturity as an artist. *Nexus* carries us only as far as the plan to leave for Paris. Miller looks forward to Europe with the hope that this journey will carry him closer to his destiny. *Nexus* ends

59 *Nexus,* 200.
60 *Ibid.*
61 *Ibid.*

with the preparations for the first trip to Europe complete, but the story of *The Rosy Crucifixion* is not yet finished. Presumably the uncompleted second half of *Nexus* will end the grand project formed more than thirty years ago, will round out Miller's journey to fulfillment, meeting *Tropic of Cancer,* his first published work.[62]

62 Perles and Durrell, *Art and Outrage,* 29.

PARIS AND AFTER

The remainder of Miller's published work consists of essays, correspondence, his reflections on life in Greece, and some rather loosely organized commentaries on his life in America. The total amount is large and by no means consistent in quality. Furthermore, the essays, letters, and journals are highly repetitive, so that a complete survey is unnecessary. The most important published works are those which carry out the development of his life and art from the point at which he left off in *Tropic of Cancer* to the present.[1]

So far two major themes have been developed in Miller's works: the discovery of himself as man, and the discovery of himself as artist. The two themes have not as yet been

---

1 We have already had occasion to refer to essays written during the Paris period and later collected in book form. Two of these, *The Wisdom of the Heart* and *The Cosmological Eye,* contain some of the most readable and most important of Miller's essays. *The Colossus of Maroussi,* Miller's book on Greece, is, although recognizably Miller's, unique in tone. The other essays of the American years like *Sunday after the War* and *Remember to Remember* are spotty. *Big Sur and the Oranges of Hieronymus Bosch,* a book-length essay, is interesting in parts but lacks dramatic force. *Stand Still Like the Hummingbird* consists of odds and ends from several periods.

clearly unified. Miller himself suggested in *Nexus* that he became free of his bondage to Mona when he incorporated her in his great plan for *The Rosy Crucifixion*. This was the birth of the artist, premature but important. When in *Tropic of Cancer* Miller discovered his authentic voice and felt all that was "artist" dropping away from him, he made another important step. Four years later, in 1940, his essay "Reflections on Art" [2] further clarified the relationship between life and art. For him, Henry Miller, the man and the artist could not be separated. Art was a means to greater life. When he reached his fullest development as a man, the need for art would cease.

Artists have understandably resisted such an interpretation of art because it seems to make art arise out of sickness rather than health. The artist reflecting upon his own intentions finds himself aware mainly of his great passion for expression, and he loses sight of even the possibility that art may also bring about changes in the artist. For many artists the work of art is the end which is sought, the end to which everything in life is ruthlessly subordinated. Artists have, indeed, considered that their views have changed, or matured, that their insights have deepened; but almost never have they looked upon art as a means which would wither once the end had been accomplished. We may, to some extent, attribute Miller's peculiarity in this matter to his awareness of psychoanalytic thought.[3] The discoveries of every age become the means in that age for a modification

2   "Reflections on Art," in *The Wisdom of the Heart*.
3   Miller insists that he got much more from mystics and oriental thinkers than from psychologists and psychoanalysts, that he has actually ridiculed these people for their inadequacies; but the fact remains that his vocabulary, his dialogues, and his attitudes reveal directly the influence of those whom he was enthusiastic about during the thirties, especially Rank and Jung.

of sensibility. As the writers after Darwin could find themselves victims of abstract forces over which they had no control, so writers after Freud became aware of experiences made available to them through the writings of psychoanalysts. The gradual turning from art to life which Miller foreshadowed, and which, in fact, had already begun to happen, is explained in terms of the use of art as means rather than end.

Miller tells us that he does not consider himself a writer in the ordinary sense of the word. He is "a man telling the story of his life, which appears more and more inexhaustible as I go on." In the very process of telling his story, however, he became "more and more indifferent to my fate, as writer, and more and more certain of my destiny as man." The first step in the process was discovering his own voice:

I began assiduously examining the style and technique of those whom I once admired and worshipped: Nietzsche, Dostoievski, Hamsun, even Thomas Mann. . . . I imitated every style in the hope of finding the clue to the gnawing secret of how to write. Finally I came to a dead end, to a despair and desperation which few men have known, because there was no divorce between myself as writer and myself as man: to fail as a writer meant to fail as man. And I failed. I realized that I was nothing—less than nothing—a minus quantity. It was at this point, in the midst of the dead Sargasso Sea, so to speak, that I really began to write. I began from scratch, throwing everything overboard, even those whom I most loved. Immediately I heard my own voice I was enchanted: the fact that it was a separate, distinct, unique voice sustained me. It didn't matter to me if what I wrote should be considered bad. Good and bad dropped out of my vocabulary. . . . My life itself became a work of art. I had found a voice, I was whole again.[4]

4 "Reflections on Art," 20–21.

In the search for his own voice, which would become for Miller the means of his expression, he found a great deal more; he found himself. Having stripped himself of artifice, of false roles, having reduced himself to the one unique element which was truly his own, he found himself speaking in his own person, not through the voice of another. The discovery of his voice became, then, a process analogous to the discovery of the self which he developed through the autobiography. Art and life become analogous processes, one repeating the other and eventually convertible into the other. In discovering himself as writer, Miller discovered his destiny and his place in the cosmos:

The real problem is not one of getting on with one's neighbor or of contributing to the development of one's country, but of discovering one's destiny, of making a life in accord with the deep-centered rhythm of the cosmos. To be able to use the word cosmos boldly, to use the word soul, to deal with things "spiritual"—and to shun definitions, alibis, proofs, duties. Paradise is everywhere and every road, if one continues along it far enough, leads to it. One can only go forward by going backward and then sideways and then up and then down. There is no progress; there is perpetual movement, displacement, which is circular, spiral, endless. Every man has his own destiny: the only imperative is to follow it, to accept it, no matter where it leads him.[5]

As the self moves, so does the writer and so do his words. "I would like my words to flow along in the same way that the world flows along, a serpentine movement through the incalculable dimensions, axes, latitudes, climates, conditions." It goes without saying that art cannot attain its ideal, to mirror life perfectly, that every writer is in that sense a failure. But in that sense too the universe, its own perfection unrealized, is a failure. The essence of life is imperfection:

5 *Ibid.,* 22.

In the ultimate sense, the world itself is pregnant with failure, is the perfect manifestation of imperfection, of the consciousness of failure. In the realization of this, failure itself is eliminated. Like the primal spirit of the universe, like the unshakeable Absolute, the One, the All, the creator, i. e., the artist, expresses himself by and through imperfection. It is the stuff of life, the very sign of livingness. One gets nearer to the heart of truth, which I suppose is the ultimate aim of the writer, in the measure that he ceases to struggle, in the measure that he abandons the will.[6]

Miller's final statement on the relation of art to life is that life must finally pass beyond art. "Art is only a means to life, to the life more abundant. It is not in itself the life more abundant. It merely points the way." For now, Miller implies, art is a necessary means to the achievement of a fuller life, especially, it would appear, for the artist. Finally, however, art will disappear, at least in the form that we know it. "But the artist will remain, and life itself will become not 'an art,' but *art,* i.e., will definitely and for all time usurp the field." [7]

Miller confesses that for him art was the necessary outlet. He had tried other avenues, but in none of them could he find success. He was in everything else he tried a "self-willed failure." He began to write, he tells us, not in order to escape reality, but to plunge more deeply "into the brackish pool." One finally arrives at the state of *artist,* which is like nothing else in the world:

I had to learn to think, feel, and see in a totally new fashion, in an educated way, *in my own way,* which is the hardest thing in the world. I had to throw myself into the current, knowing that I would probably sink. The great majority of artists are throwing

6 *Ibid.,* 23.
7 *Ibid.,* 23–24.

themselves in with life-preservers around their necks, and more often than not it is the life-preserver that sinks them. Nobody can drown in the ocean of reality who voluntarily gives himself up to the experience. Whatever there be of progress in life comes not through adaptation but through daring, through obeying the blind urge. . . . The whole logic of the universe is contained in daring, i.e., in creating from the flimsiest, slenderest support. In the beginning this daring is mistaken for will, but with time the will drops away and the automatic process takes its place, which again has to be broken or dropped and a new certitude established which has nothing to do with knowledge, skill, technique or faith. By daring one arrives at the mysterious X position of the artist, and it is this anchorage which no one can describe in words but yet subsists and exudes from every line that is written.[8]

To live at this mysterious X position is to live beyond art. Possibly at this time Miller had not established himself at this point, whatever it is, except imaginatively. But, as frequently happens, to capture an image in art is to achieve its realization in life. It seems true that Miller has grown both as man and artist since 1940, but it is nonetheless true that he foresaw what goal he was to achieve and gave it form in art many years before its full realization in life. Yet whatever has been Miller's growth as a man in the intervening years, we are dealing here with his art, and the next great step, perhaps even the final great step in the autobiographical romance occurred in the next work to be considered, *The Colossus of Maroussi*.

The Colossus of Maroussi is like no other work Miller has written. In a sense it is the work which is the hardest to discuss. Its expression is in many ways so direct and so perfect as to make any discussion false by the very act of abstraction which enables the critic to organize his viewpoints. *The*

8   *Ibid.*, 29–30.

Colossus of Maroussi is a book about Greece, which Miller visited after he left Paris in 1939. His discussion of the Greek people does not resemble his usual character sketch against a Paris or New York background. The people are not separate from the land, nor seen against the land; they arise out of the land; they are continuous with the soil, the rocks, the dust, the vines and livestock, the olive trees; above all they share and exude the light which bathes the Greek landscape in luminous tones. Miller felt that nothing exists separately in Greece, and he was able to render this feeling. It is the perfection of this rendering which makes any isolation of the elements of the work falsify the tone which unifies the whole.

The mood which dominates *The Colossus of Maroussi* is peace, which Miller felt he had discovered for the first time. Peace seems to flow not only from the people and landscape of modern Greece, which Miller insists he loves greatly, but from the history of Greece, which he experiences as layers of time existing all at one moment. First he affirms that he is not talking about what the world means by peace. For most men peace is only the opposite of war:

Peace is not the opposite of war any more than death is the opposite of life. The poverty of language, which is to say the poverty of man's imagination or the poverty of his inner life, has created an ambivalence which is absoultely false. I am thinking of course of the peace which passeth all understanding. There is no other kind. The peace which most of us know is merely a cessation of hostilities, a truce, an interregnum, a lull, a respite, which is negative. The peace of the heart is positive and invincible, demanding no conditions, requiring no protection. It just is. If it is a victory it is a peculiar one because it is based entirely on surrender, a voluntary surrender to be sure. [9]

9 *The Colossus of Maroussi* (New York: New Directions, 1941), 76.

Miller had previously emphasized the links of man with nature. Now, in Greece, a new element has been added, the experience of man as a link between nature and the divine. What Miller felt in Greece was more than a spirit of nature; it was the presence of divinity. In Greece the divine manifested itself to Miller through the pagan past, but more than that through the present experience of the blinding light, which becomes at last the source of spiritual illumination. It was this light which gave ancient Greece its gods and its mysteries, and the light remains, though overlaid with centuries of Christianity:

Everything here speaks now, as it did centuries ago, of illumination, of blinding joyous illumination. Light acquires a transcendental quality; it is not the light of the Mediterranean alone, it is something more, something unfathomable, something holy. Here the light penetrates directly to the soul, opens the doors and windows of the heart, makes one naked, exposed, isolated in a metaphysical bliss which makes everything clear without being known. No analysis can go on in this light; here the neurotic is either instantly healed or goes mad. . . . One must glide through this gully with extreme caution, naked, alone, and devoid of all the Christian humbug. One must throw off two thousand years of ignorance and superstition, of morbid, sickly subterranean living and lying. At Eleusis one realizes, if never before, that there is no salvation in becoming adapted to a world which is crazy. At Eleusis one becomes adapted to the cosmos.[10]

Miller made the circuit of the principal Greek historical sites, Hydra, Mycenae, Tiryns, Epidaurus. In each location he discovered a new aspect of the cosmos never before revealed to him. At Hydra it was the rocks. "But this rock is a living rock, a divine wave of energy suspended in time and space, creating a pause of long or short duration in the

10 *Ibid.*, 45.

endless melody." At Mycenae he felt the mystery of a lost civilization, of a terrible tragedy. As his journey progressed he felt his bond with the old familiar world breaking. He entered a new phase:

At Epidaurus I felt a stillness so intense that for a fraction of a second I heard the great heart of the world beat and I understood the meaning of pain and sorrow; at Tiryns I stood in the shadow of the Cyclopean man and felt the blaze of that inner eye which has now become a sickly gland; at Argos the whole plain was a fiery mist. . . . In each place I open a new vein of experience, a miner digging deeper into the earth, approaching the heart of a star which is not yet extinguished. The light is no longer solar or lunar; it is the starry light of the planet to which man has given life. The earth is alive to its innermost depths; at the center it is a sun in the form of a man crucified. The sun bleeds on its cross in the hidden depths. The sun is man struggling to emerge toward another light. From light to light, from calvary to calvary. The earth song. . . .[11]

Miller's experience of the cosmos is neither cyclical nor deterministic; it is progressive. Man struggles to emerge toward another light, but the struggle is not that of blind evolution. It is the struggle of man for growth. All is change, but change with direction.

The effect of his Grecian trip on Miller was, in the final analysis, strangely anti-literary. True, he has written a book about that trip, a book which contains some of his best writing. But if we eliminate the purely descriptive elements we find a handful of pages which create the effect of an experience almost mystical in its intensity. Miller had previously speculated about the possibilities of passing from art to life. The trip to Greece seemed to reinforce that tendency

11 *Ibid.,* 56–57.

in him and to show him, as well, the course of his future development:

There are friends that tell me that I will never stop writing, that I can't. But I did stop, for a good interval while in Greece, and I know that I can in the future, any time I wish and for good. I feel under no compulsion to do a particular thing. I feel, on the contrary, a growing liberation, supplemented more and more by a desire to serve the world in the highest possible way. What that way is I have not yet determined, but it seems clear to me that I shall pass from art to life, to exemplify whatever I have mastered through art by my living. I said I felt chastened. It is true that I also felt exalted. But above all I felt a sense of responsibility such as I had never known before. A sense of responsibility to myself, let me hasten to add.[12]

When he wrote *Colossus of Maroussi,* Miller was living in America; a year had passed. Looking back on his Greek experience he was able to say that what he felt then about life had since become frighteningly true. Once the process of self-realization had begun, there was no stopping it. "I am in the delicate position of one who has to be careful not to wish for something he really does not desire. The effect . . . has been to make me desire less and less. The one desire which grows more and more is to give." The kind of giving that Miller is talking about is not philanthropy, and it is not civic activity. It is a way of giving the self in order to respond to the deepest needs of another:

It is not until I look about me and realize that the vast majority of my fellow-men are desperately trying to hold on to what they possess or to increase their possessions that I begin to understand that the wisdom of giving is not so simple as it seems. Giving

12   *Ibid.,* 205–206.

and receiving are at bottom one thing, dependent upon whether one lives open or closed. Living openly one becomes a medium, a transmitter; living thus, as a river, one experiences life to the full, flows along with the current of life, and dies in order to live again as an ocean.[13]

The change from the image of river to that of ocean is important. Up until *The Colossus of Maroussi* Miller's voyage images had centered upon the experience of the river's flow. He ended *Cancer* on the banks of the Seine. Now he envisions a goal of the voyage, reaching the ocean. Whether the ocean is to be reached now or after death is of little moment. There is a goal to be reached, a final peace; that is very important. Having seen the goal of life, which is otherwise conceived as becoming more oneself, what remains to be done? One must record what one has seen, give what one has received, be what one essentially is:

A line of Maeterlinck's concerning truth and action altered my whole conception of life. It took me twenty-five years to fully awaken to the meaning of his phrase. Other men are quicker to coordinate vision and action. But the point is that in Greece I finally achieved that coordination. I became deflated, restored to proper human proportions, ready to accept my lot and prepared to give of all that I have received. Standing in Agamemnon's tomb I went through a veritable rebirth. I don't mind in the least what people think or say when they read such a statement. I have no desire to convert any one to my way of thinking. I know now that any influence I may have upon the world will be a result of the example I set and not because of my words.[14]

In 1941 at the age of fifty-one Miller had evidently put his last rebirth behind him. Having discovered the divinity in

13 *Ibid.,* 207.
14 *Ibid.,* 237.

man, having reached out into the cosmos, he had no place left to go. No further dramatic narratives are possible. From what we can see of Miller's work since that date, he has fulfilled his prediction. As he said in the last lines of *The Colossus of Maroussi:* "From that day forth my life was dedicated to the recovery of the divinity of man. Peace to all men, I say, and life more abundant!" [15]

Miller's return to America during the war provoked a series of essays about what he saw around him in his native country. These attitudes have been studied in some detail by Annette Kar Baxter, and there is no need to cover the same ground. Some aspects of that American experience are relevant, however, to the particular themes I have been discussing, especially that of the development of the artist and his relationship with society. Some of Miller's attacks on American life have the general carping tone which seems indistinguishable from the usual expatriate complaints about the grossness of American materialism, but even these observations are related to the themes which we have already discussed, especially to Miller's particular brand of philosophical nihilism. Miller's recipes are, even more than we often realize, far beyond anything which a social program or a poltical program can bring about. Philosophical anarchism, with which Miller's views are always imbued, holds out uncompromisingly for the rise of the individual and the corresponding disappearance of the state. His dispassionate attitude toward his own country comes from a feeling that things have already gone far beyond the power of politics or social action to change. He is like someone watching the funeral of a man who hasn't yet become aware that he is dead.

Since in a general way Miller feels that all nations are tyrannies, that law enforcement is authorized brutality, that

15 *Ibid.,* 241.

industry is disguised slavery, and that the middle class is mindless, his studies of individual situations can be expected to bear out that general attitude. More than that, however, there is a philosophical skeleton supporting his belief that all will be swept away, which does not always appear on the surface of his remarks. Miller's carping about American Babbitry in his individual essays must be understood, I believe, against the background of his apocalyptic world view. That view can be stated quite simply: whatever enhances individual life is good. That is bad which destroys it. But the generalization in itself is meaningless, unless it can be made to live in the countless situations of life itself. Not a knowledge of generalizations, but insight into the human possibilities of each moment is what makes life better.

Routine examples of the corrupting influence of modern life, Miller finds all around him. When he visits a prison, for example, the "Irish priest" who shows him around laughs about the stained glass windows of the self-taught convict, but likes the "cigar box illustrations" of the convict trained in art. In Miller's view only the stained glass windows are worthy of admiration. But the convict who did them is being taught to copy pictures from magazines. This kind of education is destructive, and all because the guardians could not recognize a true product of the free human spirit.[16]

Miller laments especially the failure of America to solve the problem of old age. After working as robots all their lives men at the age of retirement (shortly after forty-five as Miller describes it) are ready for the scrap heap. The only exceptions to this rule are those whom he calls "artists," men that is who "do as they please." These men are easily recognized: "their countenance registers something far more

16 *The Air-Conditioned Nightmare* (New York: New Directions, 1945), 130.

vital, far more effective, than the lust for power. They do
not seek to dominate, but to realize themselves. They operate from a center which is at rest. They evolve, they grow,
they give nourishment, just by being what they are." [17]

Miller's survey of the United States, summed up in *The
Air-Conditioned Nightmare* and *Remember to Remember*,
is partly devoted to studying some of the individuals who
he feels have successfully lived their lives. One of these is
Dr. Marion Souchon the "painter-surgeon." Dr. Souchon is
a man who began to paint late in life and who, without
sacrificing any of his other duties, has explored with tremendous energy and intensity his own special vision. It is
this intensity that Miller admires, the ability to be ever
renewed by the process of life itself. These men never grow
tired, are never ready for the scrap heap. These artists of life
are not all painters and writers. Some are human people.
They all share an ability to remain free in a slave world.
Pretentious people, the snobs of the world are always on the
outside in Miller's world. He passed up the opportunity to
meet Whitehead, but he remembers with pleasure the boot-
black who wrote novels. A seaman, a college professor, or the
lavatory attendant in a hotel have a claim to Miller's admiration, if they live out the life which is in them.[18]

When Miller turns to matters of national or worldwide
importance, we realize even more fully the degree to which
he has divorced himself from his times. Writing just before

17 *Ibid.*, 117.
18 Albert Maillet, "Henry Miller: Superman and Prophet" in Emil
White (ed.), *Henry Miller: Between Heaven and Hell*, makes this his
main point. It is not that Miller extended his experience to areas
previously taboo, but that he totally escaped the sense of sin and evil
which characterized the literature of the "decadence." He compares him
to Whitman. "They are strong, full of life and at peace with themselves.
They believe in life and they plunge into the intoxication of living
with childlike brutality," 66.

our entry into World War II he expresses sentiments which if openly voiced a few months later would no doubt have been labeled treasonable: "Those who live under democratic rule today have as little freedom of choice, in this matter of acting or not acting, as those living under the Communist or Fascist yoke. . . . The difference between being out of step with a dictator and being out of step with the democratic majority is practically negligible." [19] Miller concludes from the rising flood of war which comes despite men's best efforts that men do not really want peace. His view, stated with his usual deceptive simplicity, is that the way to get peace is to act peaceably, not to go to war. But what draft board would respond to that argument? Miller's solution to the threat of violence in Europe is consistent with his confidence in the strength of life-force. He would, in effect, let Hitler have Europe:

There is one great fallacy in this logic of violence. We forget that the conquerers are always conquered by the defeated. The surest way to defeat Hitler would, in my opinion, be for Europe to surrender willingly. I go farther—I say let him have the whole world. Can you see what would happen to his grandiose ideas if there were no resistance? Hitler, or any one who seeks power, is only a force so long as he is opposed. Let him play God and he would fall apart. Imagine the whole world submitting to the will of this little man; imagine laying the problems of all the world before him and granting him the freedom to solve them! The man would die of brain fever overnight.[20]

On the other hand, Miller holds, if war is thought to be necessary, then stop everything in favor of the war. Turn everything over to war and throw away the rules. No quarter,

19 *Remember to Remember,* 130.
20 *Ibid.,* 135–36.

no Red Cross, no holds barred, and no delays. Because what we have in the modern world is neither all out war nor peace.

The pitting of nation against nation, Miller says elsewhere, is simply a failure to recognize that nations themselves are an outmoded form. Instead of being Englishmen or Americans or Germans, people will occupy themselves simply in being human. The dissolving process will not happen all at once, but it will be inevitable. Miller does not, in this particular context, anticipate the results of the withering away of nations; but in another essay, "Art and the Future," he describes a worldwide chaos which twenty years later has begun to look uncomfortably prophetic. The worldwide collapse will begin with the fall of Germany and Italy. The leaders will lose control, and the "masses" will carry on the slaughter for awhile. Chaos will reign until 1960. "All boundaries will be broken down, class lines obliterated and money become worthless." [21] The next stage will occur when the West must consolidate to face the newly awakened nations of Asia.

After the East and West have met "in a series of death-like embraces," the new world will appear:

After that the barriers between people and races will break down and the melting pot (which America only pretends to be) will become an actuality. Then and only then, will the embryonic man of the new order appear, the man who has no feeling of class, caste, color or country, the man who has no need of possessions, no use for money, no archaic prejudices about the sanctity of the home or of marriage with its accompanying treadmill of divorce. A totally new concept of individuality will be born, one in which the collective life is the dominant note. In short for the first time in history, men will serve one

21 *Ibid.,* 150.

another, first out of an enlightened self-interest, and finally out
of a greater conception of love.[22]

Strangely enough this new era will not be one in which the
great and long-anticipated peace will reign, but an era in
which the forces of conflict will be felt more fully. "Immense horizons will open up, dazzling and frightening ones.
The ensuing conflicts will assume more and more the character of clashes between wizards, making our wars appear
puny and trifling by comparison. The white and the black
forces will come out in the open. Antagonisms will be conscious and deliberate, engaged in joyously and triumphantly,
and to the bitter end." [23] Miller's view of the future course
of history has so closely paralleled actual postwar events that
we are bound to admire his gift of prophecy. But that gift is
based on a fairly clear philosophical position: that the op-
pressed spirit of mankind and the hidden creative powers will
rise and overthrow the forces which have so long enslaved
them. That means that racial differences as well as national
differences must finally disappear. In the new world all will
possess the earth.

The new world will provide the scene for the new man,
and we have anticipated what he would be in our examination of the ideas of Otto Rank. The new man will be one who
will make of himself a work of art; for art as we know it is
only an intermediate step to reality: "To put it quite simply,
art is only a stepping-stone to reality; it is the vestibule in
which we undergo the rites of initiation. Man's task is to
make of himself a work of art. The creations which man
makes manifest have no validity in themselves; they serve to
awaken, that is all." [24] When that time comes a new man will

22 *Ibid.*
23 *Ibid.*, 151.
24 *Ibid.*, 155.

walk the earth, and he will be so unimaginably different from the man that exists now that he will seem to be from another planet. Miller's argument is based on the fact that since superior individuals have existed they will be able to exist in even greater numbers once the present impediments have been banished. Man, too, must recognize the polarity within himself and between man and woman. Woman will come into her own, but not as a feeble imitation of man. She will reveal to man what is now hidden in "the womb of night."

The rest of Miller's work, though interesting in itself,[25] shows no radical change. Since 1941 Miller has finished all but one book of *The Rosy Crucifixion,* but that is a work of the past brought to completion in the present. Two significant works of this later period are *Big Sur and the Oranges* of *Hieronymus Bosch,* published in 1957, and *Stand Still Like the Hummingbird,* published in 1961.

Big Sur and the Oranges of Hieronymus Bosch is a slow, quiet, meditative book about Miller's life in California. Big Sur is a wild and lonely place, but not without neighbors and friends. Miller tells a rambling story of people and events, of upsets and disturbances, of a miserable marriage, of a chaotic attempt to care for his own children; but he tells all in a spirit of such deep peace that we feel the unruffled depths of a man who lives wisely. I do not know whether Miller is indeed the way he presents himself. Some have said he is.[26] At any rate, he is able in his art to create a

25   *Ibid.,* 160.
26   The biography written by his old Paris friend Alfred Perles makes no attempt to distinguish between the Miller of his acquaintance and the Miller of the auto-novels. In *Art and Outrage,* however, Perles and Lawrence Durrell admit that although the Miller of the auto-novels is recognizable, he lacks many positive qualities that they admire in Miller the man. Miller answers that he has presented the worst side of himself, "out of *pudeur.*"

character who is neither free from troubles nor overwhelmed by them, who is able to live joyfully in the midst of suffering. This in its essence is the philosophy of acceptance, to accept one's destiny, to live fully in the real world:

Only when we are truly alone does the fullness and richness of life reveal itself to us. In simplifying our lives, everything acquires a significance hitherto unknown. When we are one with ourselves the most insignificant blade of grass assumes its proper place in the universe. Or a piece of manure, for that matter. Properly attuned, it's all one come Christmas, as we say. One thing becomes just as important as another, one person as good as another. Lowest and highest become interchangeable. The own precious self gets swallowed up in the ocean of being. It is then that the carrion bird no longer seems hideous, nor merely to be tolerated because of his scavenger propensities. Nor do the stones of the field then seem inanimate, or to be regarded with an eye toward future walls and buttresses. Even if it lasts for only a few moments, the privilege of looking at the world as a spectacle of unending life and not as a repository of persons, creatures and objects to be impressed into our service is something never to be forgotten.[27]

Miller's lifelong work as a writer has been a progression toward that felt unity of all existence which enables the individual to live fully in himself and fully in the world. The means for the accomplishment of this goal are the arts in all their forms. Men suffer because "art is not the primary moving force in their lives." Art as a way of life means primarily living out the truth in oneself. Truth is not always pleasant; for the most part, indeed, it may be the opposite. But we must face what we are not, as well as what we are, if we are to establish communication. The writer must begin by eschewing literary standards; his whole attention must be

27 *Big Sur and the Oranges of Hieronymus Bosch,* 34.

directed to delivering himself "naked and vulnerable." The artist does not need to seek great models for his art; "he has only to give us, in his own language, the saga of his woes and tribulations, the saga of his non-existentialism. In this mirror of not-ness everyone will recognize himself for what he is as well as what he is not. . . . He will have to admit that he—not the other fellow—is that terrible person who is contributing, wittingly or unwittingly, to the speedy downfall and disintegration of his own people." [28]

Miller's criticism of the United States reflects his lifelong preoccupation with truth of utterance and truth of life. Our mechanistic age, in his opinion, has neither. There is no truth of utterance because people misrepresent, consciously or unconsciously, what is true about themselves. There is no truth of life because people do not want truth; they want the romantic lie. The result for our culture has been extreme atomization, a loss of unity of experience in the individual, a loss of a common culture. The community thrown together haphazardly at Big Sur, a community in which neighbors may live many miles apart, has more unity of life than Miller has found anywhere else outside of Europe. The unity stems from a common purpose arrived at individually, that is, the desire to make more out of life than the cities will permit. Miller's stories of his neighbors (and *Big Sur* is in essence just that) show men and women who have despaired of the possibility of living in the centers of civilization and have come to this isolated wilderness to find whatever is to be found by living alone in nature. What they found was each other as well as themselves, and the beginnings of a real community.

This "real community" contains a curious paradox which is at the heart of Miller's social writings. It is made up of

28   *Ibid.*, 57–58.

those who live mostly for themselves. The good neighbors are the "lone travelers":

They think for themselves, they know where they stand, they travel light, and they're always available. They are not laboring to "establish peace and tranquility in the minds of others." But neither are they indifferent to the plight of others about them. They do not overlook, do not ignore, those who are less fortunate than themselves. . . . What I wish to stress is that it is easy to get at them, easy to enlist their support, moral or physical. They do not make problems of small issues. Nor do they make lame excuses. They answer Yes or No.[29]

These are the people who, in Miller's opinion, are creating the new fabric of life in the United States. Until this time Miller has had little to say about what he thinks the ideal community would be. He has said much about the need for anarchy, for rebellion, for living for the self. In *Big Sur* he shows us how anarchy and community can coexist. The way of life of these "loners" is one in which only the essentials count. In living their way these people "point up the non-essentials which make *our* way of life so absurd and futile." Furthermore, being preoccupied only with essentials, they are able to give of themselves in helping others to discover and obtain what is essential for themselves.

We always get what we wish for, Miller tells us; and evidently he wanted peace, because he seems to have attained it, at least in the measure that imperfect beings can ever attain perfection. The last paragraph of *Big Sur and the Oranges of Hieronymus Bosch* is a hymn to peace:

And that is why I choose to remain here, on the slope of Santa Lucia, where to give thanks to the Creator comes natural and

29 *Ibid.*, 264–65.

easy. Out yonder they may curse, revile and torture one another, defile all the human instincts, make a shambles of creation . . ., but here, no, here it is unthinkable, here there is abiding peace, the peace of God, and the serene security created by a handful of good neighbors living at one with the creature world, with noble, ancient trees, scrub and sagebrush, wild lilac and lovely lupin, with poppies and buzzards, eagles and humming birds, gophers and rattlesnakes, and sea and sky unending.[30]

When and if he publishes the second half of *Nexus* Henry Miller's planned work will come to an end. In a real sense his work has already come to an end, since out of his art he has created a life. He has gone on speaking to the world, and may go on speaking in the future, but in a different voice, the voice of a man who does not expect too much, who knows the world will not listen, because it does not want to change. He does not plead for reform; he states the facts: reform or die. He has now a cosmic view which refuses to be ruffled by what man has made of man, or of himself. At the same time he firmly believes that the world which we have known is rapidly drawing to a close; men are in revolt everywhere and will someday create a new world in which man can live and be happy. The kind of revolution Miller hopes for and expects is a "cosmological revolution." The new world, when it comes, will be a world of light, the world foretold by the prophets and visionaries, a world ruled by love:

Buddha gave us the eight-fold path. Jesus showed us the perfect life. Lao-tzu rode off on a water buffalo, having condensed his vast and joyous wisdom into a few imperishable words. What they tried to convey to us, these luminaries, was that there is no need for all these laws of ours, these codes and conventions, these

30   *Ibid.*, 404.

books of learning, these armies and navies, these rockets and spaceships, these thousand and one impediments which weigh us down, keep us apart, and bring sickness and death. We need only to behave as brothers and sisters, follow our hearts not our minds, play not work, create and not add invention upon invention.[31]

Before the revolution can come, before the growth can begin, we must lie fallow. Revolutions are bred in silence. The constant activity of the modern world cannot lead to anything but greater chaos. "Travail there must be, but travail of the womb, in darkness and certitude." As yet we are in darkness, and man cannot move toward the light until he plumbs the bottom of the darkness. Yet man will not perish: "At the darkest hour his eyes will be opened. The earth and the fullness thereof are his, but not to destroy. Jehovah made that forever clear in answering Job. . . . In no celestial register is it written how far we must go or how much we must endure. It is we, we ourselves, who must decide. . . . Whoever has experienced the oneness of life and the joy of life knows that to be is the all. 'Ripeness is all,' said Shakespeare. It is the same thing." [32]

31 *Stand Still Like the Hummingbird* (New York: New Directions, 1962), 190–92.
32 *Ibid.,* 20.

THE ART OF MILLER

In outlining the major trends of Miller's thought and the major influences on his development, I have suggested with some seriousness that Miller should not be undervalued in the scope and depth of his grasp of the contemporary crisis. In turning now to the autobiographical form through which he chose to express himself, I am suggesting with equal seriousness that there is more formal coherence and unity in Miller than he has usually been given credit for. Miller is a prolific writer and an expansive one. He does not write tightly controlled prose, and the very looseness of his organization is at times intensely exasperating.[1] Yet for all that, there is an

1 The question of Miller's formlessness comes up repeatedly. He has given his opinion of the matter in an interview published in *Playboy* magazine: "I've never pretended to be a careful inch-by-inch writer like Hemingway was—but neither am I one of those careless sprawling writers who feel that the slag belongs with the ore, that it's all one, part and parcel of the same thing. I must confess there's a great joy, for me, in cutting a thing down, in taking the ax to my words and destroying what I thought was so wonderful in the heat of first writing. . . . But this editing at least for me, is not aimed at achieving flawlessness. I believe that defects in a writer's work, as in a person's character, are no less important than his virtues." *Playboy* (September, 1964), 77–90.

198

order and development which has been little noted because so few have read Miller on the same level on which he writes. He has chosen autobiography no doubt because it was most congenial to him, but he has attempted to make out of autobiography something more than what it was when he found it. He has tried to give it the pulse of life by recording as closely as possible the struggle of the birth process.

Miller had enough to say about writing to allow a book to be collected on that topic, but the most illuminating remarks about autobiographical form are those he makes about the diary of Anais Nin.[2] This diary, which at that time had reached fifty unpublished volumes, is no more, apparently, than the daily chronicle of the living person, with no greater unity than its chronological development. "The fifty volumes are crammed with human figures, incidents, voyages read and commented upon, reveries, metaphysical speculations, the dramas in which she is enveloped, her daily work, her preoccupation with the welfare of others, in short with a thousand and one things which go to make up her life."[3] This catch-all quality, normal in a diary, resembles the content of Miller's own auto-novels, which is no special argument for their formal order. Yet even in the diary Miller finds an underlying form which is not simply chronological. The "seeing" which the catalogues give testimony to is itself an awareness to be developed. "The diarist in particular is obsessed with the notion that everything must be preserved. And this again is born out of a sense of destiny. Not only, as with the ordinary artist, is there the tyrannical desire to immortalize one's self, but there is also the idea of im-

2   See Henry Miller, "Etre Etoilique" in *The Cosmological Eye* (New York: New Directions, 1939). See also Miller, *On Writing* (New York: New Directions, 1964), 20.
3   Miller, "Etre Etoilique," 278. The Nin diary has now reached 150 volumes.

mortalizing the world in which the diarist lives and has his being." [4] It is this sense of destiny which creates the underlying form; for each new insight into self and world leads to new expansion of the autobiography, and it is the sense of destiny which makes us anticipate the development, which creates in us the sense of expectation which is to be satisfied.

The form of the diary is common enough in romantic art, but because the author is not independent of the hero of his work, there is no outside consciousness to retain objectivity. So we descend at first into the maelstrom, losing form, losing boundaries and bearings: "In the previous volumes we had the record of the struggle to penetrate to the very sanctum of the self; it is a description of a shadowy world in which the outline of people, things and events becomes more and more blurred by the involutional inquisition. The further we penetrate into the darkness and confusion below, however, the greater becomes the illumination. The whole personality seems to become a devouring eye turned pitilessly on the self." [5] In this process of descent the normal world is lost to view. Finally, however, the individual sees with such blinding clarity that vision is restored and everything returns to normal. Now the essence of life is control and purpose.

Whereas in the earlier volumes the accent was one of sadness, of disillusionment, of being *de trop,* now the accent becomes one of joy and fulfillment. Fire, audacity, dynamite, laughter—the very choice of words is sufficient to indicate the changed conditions. The world spreads out before her like a banquet table; something to *enjoy.* But the appetite, seemingly insatiable, is controlled. The old obsessional desire to devour everything in sight in order that it be preserved in her own private tomb is gone. She eats now only what nourishes her.[6]

4 *On Writing,* 106–107.
5 *Ibid.,* 284.
6 *Ibid.*

Having returned to life, reborn, the slow development of the mature character goes on, expressed in familiar biological terms of the new creature, which goes on developing new organs: "The once ubiquitous digestive tract, the great whale into which she had made herself, is replaced by other organs with other functions." She loses her exaggerated sympathy for others, and acquires a sense of humor, proof of greater objectivity. "The totality of vision brings about a new kind of sympathy, a free non-compulsive sort." The pace slows down; there are lapses. "The eye too seems to close, content to let the body *feel* the presence of the world about, rather than pierce it with devastating vision. It is no longer a world of black and white, of good and evil, or harmony and dissonance; no, now the world has at last become an orchestra in which there are innumerable instruments capable of rendering every tone and color, an orchestra in which even the most shattering dissonances are resolved into meaningful expression. It is the ultimate poetic world of *As Is*." [7]

A discussion of Miller's writing technique in comparison with the diary of Anais Nin is complicated by the fact that writing as a significant activity of the hero-narrator of the autobiography is also the subject of the work. The descent into the depths, or, in terms of the Nin essay, into the belly of the whale, leads to a discovery of the self, but also to the discovery of a theme. In retelling the story of his life, Miller freely invents in order to communicate the sense of sinking deep within the self and then writes about the effects of writing about his life. This could lead to an infinite regression, but by convention the writer stays at a level which if not simple is at least understandable. The material of his art consists of recollections of his own life, early and late, which led him toward the process of being a writer. The

7 *Ibid.*, 284–85.

metaphor of the "belly of the whale" makes the relationship between art and life somewhat clearer.

To descend into the belly of the whale is to descend into death, but "by voluntarily going down into death," we suddenly find illumination:

> For when this moment is attained we who imagined that we were sitting in the belly of the whale and doomed to nothingness suddenly discover that the whale was a projection of our own insufficiency. The whale remains, but the whale becomes the whole wide world, with stars and seasons, with banquets and festivals, with everything that is wonderful to see and touch, and being that it is no longer a whale but something nameless because something that is inside as well as outside us. We may, if we like, devour the whale too. . . . No matter how much is ingested there will always remain more whale than man; because what man appropriates of the whale returns to the whale again in one form or another. . . . Each man who climbs into the body of the whale and works therein his own resurrection is bringing about the miraculous transfiguration of the world which, because it is human, is none the less limitless.[8]

Life in the belly of the whale describes the paradox of being an artist. It is a form of life in death. The reascent to life is not to ordinary life, but to the creative life. In a sense the artist in his metaphor of the whale never does reascend; he brings life with him into the belly of the whale and makes a new world there. The voice of the artist issuing from this tomb is the voice of the creative spirit which embraces both life and death:

> The voices of the earth mingle in an eternal resonance which issues from the delta of the fecundating river of death. It is the voice of creation which is constantly being drowned in the

8 *Ibid.,* 285–86.

daylight frenzy of a man-made world. It comes like the light breeze which sets the ocean swaying; it comes with a calm, quiet force which is irresistible, like the movement of the great Will gathered up by the instincts and rippling out in long silky flashes of enigmatic dynamism. Then a lull in which the mysterious centralized forces roll back to the matrix, gather up again in a sublime all-sufficiency. Nothing lost, nothing used up, nothing relinquished. The great mystery of conservation in which creation and destruction are but the antipodal symbols of a single constant energy which is inscrutable.[9]

Henry Miller's cycle of autobiographical novels develops on the same principle as the diaries of Anais Nin. In the original plan one large work would incorporate the material from the central period of his life, from his first marriage to his flight to Paris. The original plan expanded to include four works, *Tropic of Capricorn* and the three books of *The Rosy Crucifixion*. Obviously the plan could not have been complete at the time he made it in 1927 because he had not yet become a writer, and that destiny had to be present in order to give direction to the development. By the time he actually wrote *Tropic of Capricorn* in the late thirties, he had already published *Tropic of Cancer* and *Black Spring,* among other shorter pieces, and his career as writer was sufficiently established to make it the goal of his development in the auto-novels.

The key to autobiographical form is the search for individual identity; and in his use of that form, Miller resembles in many ways, so far little noted, the great nineteenth-century Romantics. Even among the English Romantics the search for individual identity took the form of a descent into the lower levels of psychic life, a passing out of the self in order to discover the relation of the individual to the cosmos and

9 *Ibid.,* 290.

the interaction of art with life. The form is most apparent, however, in those writers who chose autobiography as their typical mode of expression—Wordsworth in England and Thoreau, Emerson, and Whitman in America. The autobiographical poem as it appears in Wordsworth and Whitman is radically different from the personal lyric in that it tries to render an experience going on in time; its inner principle is the idea of growth.

Wordsworth seems to have been less conscious of the growth principle in his work than was Whitman, and the past tendencies of critics to concentrate upon "Tintern Abbey," the "Immortality Ode," and a handful of shorter lyrics has tended to obscure the importance of *The Prelude* as the base upon which he was erecting his entire poetic structure. The increase in respect on the part of critics for *The Prelude* has tended to restore the perspective, and makes possible a re-evaluation of Wordworths's total structure. We see in *The Prelude* a study of the growth of the poet from earliest childhood to the moment when the man, fully realizing his destiny, can commit himself to the life of a poet. The movements within *The Prelude* show an idealization of childhood as the background for poetic experience, a gradual increase in a sense of destiny, engagement in the world with near tragic consequences, and finally the restoration to immediate experience, with the help of Dorothy (and at one time Coleridge), which brings the fully realized sense of destiny.

The Prelude, and the autobiographical mode which it represents, can be seen as the progressive self-creation of the poet and the man toward a goal at first dimly, later clearly perceived. The whole poem, then, is a journey toward a personality to be achieved and expressed in art. The various steps along the way are circlings, now away from, now toward the line of true development which willl bring the poet to his destiny. The poet, writing in the present, projects a vision of the future backward on the past, recreating that past so as to establish the desired continuity of development conceived as "destiny."

Wordsworth's great poems until 1805 relate clearly enough to the basic themes established in *The Prelude*. If, as Ferry claims, that vision was impossible of achievement, it is no argument against the principle that in this autobiographical mode the poet works toward a vision of a self to be created and expressed.[10] It means simply that at some point the original vision was exhausted as poetic material, and that lacking new insights which would either continue the growth or change its direction, the poet came to terms with society. Wordsworth's attempt to achieve a final harmony, reconciling all things in unity, came squarely against an irreconcilable contradiction implicit in the goal of his mystical yearning. Man's effort to discover unity can go backward or forward. The pull of his deepest levels of feeling is toward the past, to discover a primordial harmony which is regarded as a basic level of all human experience. Man recovers the past, however, only to break with it. True growth is away from the loss of self implicit in the notion of aboriginal harmony; it is toward greater individuation, a turning to the chaos and mystery of existence, toward a fuller participation in life.

Wordsworth failed in the achievement of his vision. He did

10 Attention has increasingly been turned to the dynamic elements in Romanticism. The "emergence of the self" is conceived as a process never finally completed. See Morse Peckham, "Toward a Theory of Romanticism," *PMLA*, LXVI (March, 1951), 3–23. Peckham has suggested in his later book that the past is created in terms of the present and future. Morse Peckham, *Beyond the Tragic Vision* (New York: George Braziller, Inc., 1962), Chapters 1 and 6. See David Ferry, *The Limits of Mortality* (Middletown, Conn.: Wesleyan University Press, 1959), 165.

not, evidently, perceive that self-creation must rest firmly on the realization that life is growth. Wordsworth's poetic vision shared too much the static world view of the eighteenth century which freezes the world into patterns. Whitman overcame this limitation. Conceiving the self as imperfect, as growing toward that which it wants to be though never arriving, living in a universe which is itself in process, Whitman was able to organize his poetic vision around the push and pull of opposites in an essentially organic world. As a result Whitman's process of self-realization, the source of his poetic creation, did not stop until his death. Like Wordsworth, Whitman sought the experience of unity; unlike Wordsworth, he did not exclude discordant elements. We feel in Whitman, as in Wordsworth, the pull of the past; but the past recovered is for Whitman the means toward reconciliation with the present and future. Unity is a state to be realized progressively, a state in which all experience must be assimilated.

Whitman adds something else to the romantic idea which is lacking in the English Romantics, that is, the assimilation of sensual experience without coming into conflict with the spiritual. Many have felt that Whitman's poetry lacks dramatic force because it fails to accept the tension between the real and the ideal, a tension which had provided the poetic structure for much of the poetry in the entire English tradition. The resolution of that age-old contradiction can never be easy; it may be impossible. In any event Whitman attempted it. In the beginning of *Leaves of Grass,* particularly in "Song of Myself," he embraces the sensual and discovers unity between body and soul. Body and soul are not separate, but dual principles within a living unity. In the following sections, "Calamus" and "Children of Adam," he discovers that these same two principles, now conceived as the active and passive, operate throughout nature. The sexual imagery based on human passion is transferred to nature, creating a bond between man and nature. The next major step in development, typified by "Out of the Cradle Endlessly Rocking," associates love with death and confronts the poet with a need for assimilating death into his cosmos. The assimilation of death and the conviction of immortality are finally achieved in the poems of transcendence, such as "Passage to India." Whitman cuts straight across the contradiction between ideal and real by expanding his consciousness until it contains both. The subject of the poem is the life of the man, and the theme is that of growth from embryo to a maturity which finally accepts all of life.

The idea of self-creation which appears most fully in the poetry of Wordsworth and Whitman presupposes a philosophy of nature which makes ultimate harmony possible. This philosophy has to be antimechanistic because it has to abolish the split between matter and spirit. The romantic philosophy of nature envisioned man as having his roots deep in nature, a nature which was not excluded from man. Thus man on the deepest levels of his being participated in nature, and upon this participation depended his sense of joy. Ultimately the romantic philosophy had to be individualistic because the experience of unity could not be taught; it was a journey which each man had to make for himself. Though the Romantics were attracted by the idea of creating a new philosophy of life, they were necessarily unsuccessful. They could only offer the example, which other men might imitate, of the successful growth of one individual.

Once the idea of self-creation had been grasped, there followed the notion that each man might be an artist with respect to his own life, whether he produced artistic works or not. Such a close relation of art and life led to the paradox that a poem ostensibly about life could be read as a poem about the artist and his art, and that its theme could be understood as having pertinence to the life of every man. The experience of the artist became the prototype for the experience of man creating himself. Thus the artist could use as the material of his art the creative process itself, and the creative process thus rendered would have relevance to the life of every man.

The romantic insight into the close relation of man to nature and the relevance of the creative process to the life of every individual failed to affect the development toward the industrialized collective society which we now see full blown. It may well be that the full significance of the romantic revolt had to wait until the developments in philosophy, psychology, and sociology had borne out the original insights of the great Romantics. Because those insights have now been made explicit, they have furnished the basis for a resurgence of these attitudes. In some ways, of course, romanticism has never died, and the individualism of the modern artist in his opposition to the regimentation of society is an expression of that romanticism. But revolt alone does not make the romantic. It is necessary that there be some destiny toward which the individual is developing, some vision to be expressed in life and art.

The nineteenth-century Romantics did not achieve any real solution to the historic conflicts within the data of consciousness. As awareness expanded, these conflicts could not be reconciled with the system of moral, political, and social absolutes. Wordsworth, who extolled the common life, gave no hint of vulgarity among the vulgar. Even his own erotic adventures were well covered up. Coleridge went furthest, perhaps, in suggesting the extremes of experience, though on a symbolic level only. The cavernous depths of "Kubla Khan," the "demon lover," the ambiguities of Geraldine, suggest Jungian depths long before Jung. Whitman even more explicitly explored the range of his own feeling and, through sympathy, that of other men. The shocked repudiation of Whitman in his own times testifies to the degree of his success.

Wordsworth still hoped that life and art would intersect, but they could not, even for him. Keats more wisely created a poetic solution. For him death was too obviously the end of life to allow him the illusion of a real unification of all experience, of mortality and immortality, of real and ideal. During the later nineteenth and the early twentieth century, however, a postevolutionary romanticism uncovered new problems and new solutions. The world of moral and philosophical absolutes within which the early Romantics worked was attacked first by Darwin, then by Einstein. From the debris of Western thought arose not one but a variety of ways to deal with the new situation. Idealism, pragmatism, scientism, instrumentalism, in addition to what was left over from the previous age provided more of a market place for ideas than a coherent system of thought. With the decline in external guides, we find a growth in subjectivism. Man turns, in the absence of alternatives, to the data of his own consciousness of reality for help and direction.[11] Philosophical, psychological, and artistic developments helped support and advance this new direction. The men who led the scientific and artistic revolt, those we have considered in Chapter 2, are the new romantics. The new vision of life to be achieved by art and by thought were no longer separated by the irreconcilable opposites of traditional Western moral, theological, and philosophical absolutes. With the shift in point of view from self and the world to world in the self—that is to self-awareness as primary—the way was open, theoretically at least, to unify even life and death. If eternity could be

11 This, too, finds support in Peckham's theory that in periods of stress when traditional standards of value are lost, man turns to himself for his sole guide.

conceived as the moment expanded into eternity, then even death was illusory. Eternity ceased to be something which followed life; it existed as an ever-present possibility, here and now. The division of time horizontally into past and present was to be replaced by the vertical line of human awareness. Through increasing awareness the illusion of past and present would finally disappear. To integrate that view into the experience of life was the task of the artist. Henceforth joy was to be unmixed with melancholy.[12]

It has been my purpose to show that Henry Miller belongs to this new romantic tradition, and that his art is characterized by a different concept of the role of the artist than that which formal criticism has elaborated since World War I. Philip Rahv criticized Miller because he could not "afford the continual sacrifice of personality that the act of creation requires . . . ." [13] But in Miller's world nothing is left except personality, and the artist has no choice but to make his life the material of his art. We may hold, if we like, that such an art is better or worse than the objective art which Rahv is talking about, but we must at least perform the critical task of showing how such an art is organized and what the nature of its communication is.

The form of Miller's art we shall call autobiographical, for want of a better name. Miller's own term, "auto-novels," performs several valuable functions. It distinguishes between what is fictional or constructive and what is personal and autobiographical. As in the autobiographical form of Wordsworth and Whitman, the events and thoughts of the central

12 Dostoievski presented this idea through Kirilov in *The Possessed*. Philosophers, artists, and mystics who turn toward consciousness itself as the ultimate reality discount objective time as illusory. Pure duration can conceivably be extended infinitely. Under certain conditions this view is able to admit a God-force in the world, but refuses to put salvation in any world other than this one.
13 Rahv, *Image and Idea*, 163.

character are from experience, for the most part at least; but the structure, which formal critics admit to being an aspect of meaning, is created by the artist. Since the goal of the work is a destiny to be achieved—a point at which art and life intersect and art passes into life—then the structure has a special form which is necessary to attain that end. The best descriptive analogy for that form is taken from music, the art of the fugue. Thus, in structure, the art of the auto-biographical artist will more closely resemble the fugue than the symphony. The same themes and motifs will be repeated many times, leading not so much to a climax as to an accumu-lation of meaning which is sensed as more and more signifi-cant. Each time a familiar fragment appears it acquires a slightly new meaning by reason of the new context.[14] Ro-mantic autobiography has a tendency to appear repetitive unless we become aware that each reappearance of the fa-miliar theme results in a greater realization by the author of his precise destiny. The overall theme is based on the idea of growth toward fulfillment, of the conversion of vital energy into form, which enhances the individual's sense of identity and completion.

Thus we must search for the form of Henry Miller's work in his total development toward his goals in life, not in each individual work, though these too have their own partial forms. Each single work expresses a fragment of insight, an insight which frequently will concern the frustration of the protagonist who finds himself momentarily without sense of direction. Miller has said that his work is the story of his life, which is very true if we assume that a significant part of his experience grew out of his work. Miller's art, as I see it, is devoted to the creation of both his life and his work, in the sense that he brought together those elements of his life

14 Wallace Fowlie has applied the fugal analogy to the works of Gide in Fowlie, *Clowns and Angels* (New York: Sheed and Ward, 1943), 17.

which showed a continuity of development toward the goals he wished to achieve. He emphasizes in his development a growth from the frustrated individual caught in a hostile society to the man who has achieved his life goals, who has become self-sufficient and independent. To that extent his achievement does not differ greatly from that of Wordsworth and Whitman. Yet Miller is different, and he is different precisely to the extent that he is doing consciously what the Romantics did by intuition. Miller, who was as we have seen widely read in romantic literature, had access to the researches of psychology, through which he could more consciously give form to the development in depth of the individual life. At the center of Miller's art is his blending of conscious and apparently unconscious material. Miller has drawn, as any writer must, upon unconscious material, but mainly he has created a myth of the unconscious to carry out his basic journey theme. The conscious creation of a myth is indicated by the importance Miller attached to Freud's statement "Into the night life are relegated the things that belonged to the day." Presumably, as the myth goes, before the growth of consciousness and the appearance of civilization, the primary instincts were closer to the surface, not only available, but continually active in life. These instincts, being to civilized man less necessary, or at least inappropriate, sank from sight into the prehuman animal level which characterizes the unconscious processes. Unhappily, the frustration that follows from the too frequent and too rigid denial of these instincts creates serious problems for civilized man in attaining satisfaction. Thence issue discontent and even neuroses.

Since the days of Freud, psychoanalysts have refined these concepts, but the idea of "the night life" remains. In recovering or appearing to recover repressed material from earlier stages of his own life, and symbolically from the earlier stages of civilized man, Miller effectively expresses unconscious levels of life. This unconscious material appears in Miller's works chiefly in the form of his violent needs and desires. He recognizes the existence of these drives in *Hamlet:* "We are moving about in response to urgent needs, driven by secret inner forces, desires, impulses, hungers, of which we have only the barest inkling from time to time. Men have been moving about this way since time began— space-binders and time-binders. A restless energy, an endless quest, desires unfathomable." [15] These urgent needs have been described by Simon Lesser in his study of fiction and the unconscious as "that almost inaccessible realm in us which our night impulses inhabit like subdued but sullen beasts. . . . In most people certain infantile ideas, interests, and impulses—most particularly those which are frowned upon and later subjected to repression—tenaciously retain their strength." [16]

Miller uses two general levels of technique, the realistic story and the fantasy or dream sequence. Of the two, it is the realistic part which carries the heaviest burden of unconscious content. Since unconscious material is unavailable for direct study, it must appear indirectly, as dream work or in an acting out of unconscious desires. Miller's dream sequences, I believe, are sheer poetic myth, powerfully resembling unconscious dream symbolization. His description of his early life is an imaginative acting out of basic instinctual levels, a bringing into the day what had been restricted to the night.

Miller's use of unconscious material is exemplified in the crucial period of his life, when his frustrations were at their highest point, when he was working for the telegraph com-

15 Henry Miller and Michael Fraenkel, *Hamlet* (New York: Carrefour Press, 1941), 49. See also pp. 374–75.
16 Simon O. Lesser, *Fiction and the Unconscious* (Boston: Beacon Press, 1957), 42.

pany and about to break with his wife. He faced at this time a crisis based on the kinds of demands which external reality was making upon him. He was being asked to renounce his attachment to his childhood vision of life, to accept the view of life and responsibility offered him by the society in which he lived. That meant ambition, work, accepting the limitations of his marital situation, the renunciation of his deeply felt desires for expansion and growth. At this point he refuses to renounce that vision of life, reconciles himself to the loss of his wife and child, and goes to live with Mona. The situation in which Miller acts at this moment is an almost classical one in terms of Freud's description of the growth of the artist. It has been analyzed by Daniel Schneider as follows:

When Freud stated that the artist is a man who cannot accept the renunciation of instinctual gratifications in the way it is first demanded of him, that this refusal to renounce is a constant source of fantasy, and finally that with his special gifts he knows how to find his way back to reality and so to mold his fantasy as to force the world to accord his art the merit of being valid and a source of joy, he described in a few sketchy words a vast subject . . . for each of these factors has as integral a relationship to the content as to the form of art.[17]

What we must note in connection with Miller is that he not only refused to renounce the satisfaction of his needs, but that he used as the material of his art the very needs themselves. The recovery of the past in his autobiographical romance became the means of clarifying for himself the full nature of these needs. This quality of his art has been noted by Lawrence Durrell: ". . . he has retained (as every artist

17   Daniel E. Schneider, *The Psychoanalyst and the Artist* (New York: International Universities Press, 1950), 141.

must) an abnormally large part of his childhood fantasy life intact—with all its wounds and ardours and fantastically *unreasonable* demands upon the world, upon men. He has re-enacted it all as an adult, and then written it all out, unwittingly providing a catharsis for the dammed-up phantasy life of the Anglo-Saxon."[18] The past as Miller relived it was a period of almost untrammeled joy, a time when the world was "forever warm and still to be enjoyed." Not only Miller, but his friends as well were always open to experience. The demands made by the world destroyed his friends. Miller, feeling the same demands upon himself, reacted with the full force of his own destructive energy. The manner of Miller's acting during the period of his young manhood until he met Mona is a revelation of the full scope of man's capacity to unleash his own primitive aggressions against the world. There can be little doubt that the levels of life which Miller is expressing here are highly regressive, associated with infantile demands upon reality.

We have dealt previously with the food-sex imagery in *Tropic of Cancer*. Certainly the interchangeability of food and sex indicates an early level of human desire, while revealing at the same time certain tendencies to destructiveness through incorporation. More important to an understanding of the significant sexual passages in *Tropic of Capricorn* and *The Rosy Crucifixion* is an awareness of the manner in which aggression is expressed through the sexual act itself. Whereas Miller's sexual experience with Mona has a certain primitive violence, he has a less destructive attitude to her. The sexual experiences with those women who mean less to him become almost sadistic encounters in which he uses the sexual organ more like a weapon than an instrument of pleasure. He expresses this attitude indirectly

18   Perles and Durrell, *Art and Outrage,* 54.

in his cultivated detachment from the woman as he brings her to an orgasm and directly, as in this passage with Rita Schnadig, with the words: "I could have held it indefinitely —it was incredible how detached I was and yet thoroughly aware of every quiver and jolt she made. But somebody had to pay for making me walk around in the rain grubbing a dime. Somebody had to pay for the ecstasy produced by the germination of all those unwritten books inside me." [19]

If this destructiveness is indeed to be associated with earlier states of human development, the question arises as to whether the author is writing out of the sickness of permanent regression, or whether he is able, as Freud suggested, to regress deliberately to earlier states in order to use the material for his art. We should assume, I believe, that Miller's reactions are within the scope of normality. Faced with a deadening society which wants him to adopt death as life, he is fighting to preserve his openness to experience and to himself. Most men are open in childhood, but in the course of adjusting themselves to society they lose their flexibility, originality, and self-identity. Therefore, at this juncture Miller turns to the period when openness was the habitual condition, when the energy to keep that openness was fully available, that is, childhood. In reorganizing the experience of childhood, he regains at the same time the full intensity of childhood demands, even to the point of awakening the oral demands of infancy and the narcissistic needs of earlier stages of growth. The artist shows his health in being able to submit this material to the demands of literary form, and for Miller this meant assimilating the material from his past life into his autobiographical romance.

Miller's use of fantasy I take to be an artistic and symbolic rather than a literal reproduction of his own dream life. Not only his familiarity with psychoanalytical material, but also

19 *Tropic of Capricorn,* 213.

his awareness of life and the work of other artists enabled
him to reproduce imitations of dream states as, for example,
Joyce was able to create imitations of the stream of consciousness. In these passages Miller is attempting to capture
an emotion based on insight, an insight too fundamental,
too obscure, too general for direct expression. The areas of
his life which he most frequently expresses in these sequences
are those involved with sexuality in its purest form, the very
essence of sexual feeling which expands into the universe,
until the universe itself becomes a great sexual orgy:

Everything is packed into a second which is either consummated
or not consummated. The earth is not an arid plateau of health
and comfort, but a great sprawling female with velvet torso that
swells and heaves with ocean billows; she squirms beneath the
diadem of sweat and anguish. Naked and sexed she rolls among
the clouds in the violet light of the stars. All of her, from her
generous breasts to her gleaming thighs, blazes with furious
ardor. She moves among the seasons and the years with a grand
whoopla that seizes the torso with paroxysmal fury, that shakes
the cobwebs out of the sky; she subsides on her pivotal orbits
with volcanic tremors.[20]

Here the idea is relatively familiar, that of the fertility of
the universe, but the treatment is peculiarly Miller's. We
feel that we are relatively distanced from direct feeling. In
other passages both the idea and the treatment are further
from usual human experience; the imagery suggests direct
penetration of the unconscious. In this passage Miller is
dancing at a taxi-dance hall:

We taxi from one perfect female to another seeking the
vulnerable defect, but they are flawless and impermeable in their
impeccable lunar consistency. This is the icy white maiden head

20 *Tropic of Cancer,* 225–26.

of love's logic, the web of the ebbed tide, the fringe of absolute vacuity. And on this fringe of the virginal logic of perfection I am dancing the soul dance of white desperation, the last white man pulling the trigger on the last emotion, the gorilla of despair beating his breast with immaculate gloved paws. I am the gorilla who feels his wings growing, a giddy gorilla in the center of a satin-like emptiness; the night too grows like an electrical plant, shooting white hot buds into velvet black space. I am the black space of the night in which the buds break with anguish, a starfish swimming on the frozen dew of the moon. I am the germ of a new insanity, a freak dressed in intelligible language, a sob that is buried like a splinter in the quick of the soul.[21]

The contrast in images here creates the emotion of the occasion, the contrast between the civilized and the primitive— "gorilla in immaculate gloved paws"—between hot and cold —"shooting white hot buds" with "icy white maiden head of love's logic." The situation which is supposed to be warm and passionate, supposed to stimulate erotic feeling, only induces a feverish search for lost emotions, frozen in the mechanistic world of the dance hall.

Since Miller uses fantasy as an important part of his total expression it is important whether it directly illuminates the world of unconscious association or symbolizes that world through the creation of a symbolic form. Although I believe that Miller as a writer has more than usual access to this world of unconscious elaboration, I believe even more strongly in the poetic quality of his imagination, and that his knowledge of dream symbolism led him to his particular style. That is not to say that these symbolic passages do not arise from material deeply perceived, but rather that he chose this form to express his own insights into unconscious states.

21 *Ibid.,* 121.

We have finally to examine Miller's cosmic consciousness as an element of his own experience. The feeling of being at one with the universe has been sought after since men have recorded their struggle with themselves and their environment. It has been called in recent psychological literature the "oceanic feeling." [22] To achieve this feeling is at once the most desired of human experiences and the most dangerous. The reason for the danger was not explicitly stated until the psychoanalytic investigations of this century revealed that the state of unconscious harmony which characterizes the stage before birth could be sought so avidly that men would give up their life in reality. The desire for perfect security remains an aspect of all men's desires, but it remains also a threat, since regaining that security as it once existed would mean loss of self—or loss of consciousness, which is the same thing. Therefore the feeling of being at one with the cosmos must for the mature adult coexist with the fullest attainment of consciousness. It is upon this point that the successful journey into the self depends. When that journey awakens fears of the return to primordial darkness, unconscious life itself is experienced as something dark and threatening, like the dark world of "Christabel," or the caves of Hawthorne. On the other hand when the individual arrives at full acceptance of the self through the inward journey and discovers the world as a place of growth and development, then the stage is set for the experience of unity which is called cosmic consciousness.

Few of the Romantics claimed to have attained this state. Coleridge recognized the unconscious world as both the source of vital energy and as a threat. Hawthorne and Melville tended to fear the dark side. Wordsworth came closer, but his regressive orientation ultimately forced him to surrender

22 Otto Fenichel, *The Psychoanalytic Theory of Neurosis* (New York: W. W. Norton, 1945), 31 ff.

in order to preserve full identity. By embracing the dichotomy of love and death in his transcendental poems, Whitman went further than the other Romantics in evoking the sense of cosmic consciousness. Miller is closest to Whitman in this regard. The movement toward cosmic consciousness must come through a death of the self. The descent to the womb, which awakens the terrors of loss of self, also enables the person to throw off his accumulated prejudices. Coming back, then, to reality, he goes through a series of "births," each of which brings him closer to his true self. To the fully developed person in his new state of awareness there comes too the expanded ability to love, by means of which he is able to break through the ego barriers, to feel at one with the universe. This was the meaning of Whitman's message of love; it is the main theme of Henry Miller. The search for unity never stops, but there are two ways to find it, by regression and progression. One cannot stop. One must be born every minute or give up and die.

Cosmic consciousness, the experience of unity, is the latest gift of the romantic idea to the modern world. More and more writers have adopted the view that the industrial world is a world of death, that men are, in fact, dying of ennui and restlessness. The Romantics foresaw the dangers which the trends of their time held; those dangers were reinterpreted by Whitman for his times. Miller has attempted to give them new form in our century. It is his great power that for many he can make the danger so real and the process of rebirth so compelling.

We are living in times of extreme change, and Henry Miller is a part of what is changing. The end is not yet in sight, but we can begin to anticipate some of the directions that the contemporary revolution is taking. The individual has always been more important in the West than the East, but now he has taken a position which is unprecedented in our society. Until now the development of individuality has always seemed to be relative to the forces which opposed it. The individual was engaged in a struggle with society or family or the forces of evil within himself. Now individualism has been defined as something absolute in itself. Self-development is not a limited goal to be achieved within the demands of a social context, but the goal of evolution itself. It is clear that as the evolutionary idea has begun to dominate Western culture, its implications have become more and more the governing spirit of Western life. By projecting the line of individual development forward from the supposed primitive animal roots of man, a vision is developed of an earthly paradise. In this view all the efforts of man must be devoted to being born, "to be fully born, to become what one potentially is; it means to have the full capacity for joy, and for sadness or . . . to awake from the half slumber the average man lives in, and to be fully awake." [23]

Lancelot Law Whyte has expressed the goal of evolutionary man as "unitary man." Man would no longer be divided within himself; his experience of unity among once warring forces would be so profound that it would seem like paradise.[24] No longer is struggle represented by the hostility of external forces. Now the struggle is within. The apparent conflict with the environment is simply the projection of inner conflict. Success and failure come from the individual, not the world. It is one of the redeeming features of Henry Miller as a writer and as a person that he has managed to be consistent in his point of view about the evils of the modern world. His attacks are seldom caused by what they world has done to him. As a man reborn, he is happy or not

23 Erich Fromm, *Zen Buddhism and Psychoanalysis* (New York: Harper, 1960), 91.
24 Lancelot Law Whyte, *The Next Development in Man* (New York: Mentor Books, 1950).

to the extent that he has maintained his own unity. His attacks on the world are on the behalf of others who, in his opinion, are being ruined by the industrial society. Miller's own joy or lack of it has come from his ability or inability to release his creative powers. Despite his enjoyment of sensual life, he has been as independent as one can be of the things which in our age money can buy.

The future course of Miller's reputation remains uncertain. He has always had a strong following among those for whom he was an important part of a personal liberation. In a real sense Miller has never been appreciated by the public or the academy for what he has accomplished. At a time when Western civilization was at the crossroads, Miller showed us the new world of individual man. At the moment, that old world is in deep crisis; the structure of society itself seems threatened by widespread revolt. That society, in the name of Americanism and the other tribal gods, is striking back hard. If the revolt fails, if a new generation of conservatives reasserts the tribal myth, then Miller will have to wait until a much later time for the fullness of his recognition. If, on the other hand, the revolution succeeds, he must inevitably be looked upon as a prophet and shaper of a new world. For the present we can be sure that the publication of *Tropic of Cancer* in America marks a milestone in our history. In the new freedom which we all enjoy, in the rolling back of the forces of hypocrisy, intolerance, and prudery, Henry Miller has already made an important contribution.

INDEX

Abstraction: as destructive, 140; Miller against, 34

Acceptance: 25, 53, 76, 179; of destiny, 108; and Jung, 64; philosophy of, xxiii, 75; and suffering, 82

Adolescence: 15, 18; love in, 15

Adult: responsibility, 120; world, destructiveness of, 30

Agamemnon: tomb of, 185

Aggression: 25, 44; and hunger, 95; in Miller, 89; through sexual act, 215; and life, 78

Alienation: of self and sex, 146

Alimentary world, 156

Altruism, 44

Amarillo Dance Hall, 125

American Country Club of France, xxx

American: experience, 186 *passim;* life, 135

Americanism, 222

Americanization, 8

Anarchic man, 121

Anarchism: 37, 38, 39 *passim;* and Henry Miller, 34; spirit of, 32; in the United States, 33; philosophical, 186

Anarchists, 8

Anglo-Saxon: fantasy life of, 215; words, concreteness of, 103

Animal: Miller as, 122

Annihilation, 124

Anonymity: effects of in modern world, 111

Anti-Christ, 37

Anti-novel, xii

Apocalyptic world view, 187

Apollonian: and Nietzsche, 47

Archetypes, 62

Art: and experience, 111; and illness, 49; and life, 176, 179

Artist: as creator of culture, 58; Miller as, 93; and self creation, 207 *passim;* as state of life, 179; type, 50; and the womb, 59

Artistic process, 49

Athleticism, 34

Autobiographical romance: 48, 84, 111, 138, 216; origin of, 139; the works in, 203. *See* Auto-novel

Autobiography: 199; as form, 50, 94, 210; as growth, 69; as mode, 204; narrative in, 52; novels as, 203; romantic, 211; and self-expression, 178; tradition of, xiii

Automatic writing, 61

Auto-novel: xiii, 61, 75, 77, 199; the